CORNISH STUDIES

Second Series

THIRTEEN

INSTITUTE OF CORNISH STUDIES

University *of* Exeter
IN CORNWALL

EDITOR'S NOTE

Cornish Studies (second series) exists to reflect current research conducted internationally in the inter-disciplinary field of Cornish Studies. It is edited by Professor Philip Payton, Director of the Institute of Cornish Studies at the University of Exeter in Cornwall, and is published by the University of Exeter Press. The opinions expressed in *Cornish Studies* are those of individual authors and are not necessarily those of the editor or publisher. The support of Cornwall County Council is gratefully acknowledged.

Cover illustration: Virginia Woolf at the age of twenty.
Photograph by G. C. Beresford (reproduced courtesy of the National Portrait Gallery).

CORNISH STUDIES

Second Series

THIRTEEN

Edited by

Philip Payton

UNIVERSITY
of
EXETER
PRESS

First published in 2005 by
University of Exeter Press
Reed Hall, Streatham Drive
Exeter, Devon EX4 4QR
UK
www.exeterpress.co.uk

British Library Cataloguing in Publication Data
A catalogue record for this book is
available from the British Library

ISBN 0 85989 771 0
ISSN 1352-271X

Typeset in 10/12pt Times by Kestrel Data, Exeter

Printed and bound in Great Britain by
Short Run Press Ltd, Exeter

Contents

REVIEW ARTICLE

INTRODUCTION

As this series has been fond of reiterating, a significant feature of the Cornish Studies project has been the encouragement of cross-disciplinary contact, the formation of sub-disciplinary 'schools' or 'communities' among Cornish Studies practitioners, and the stimulation of debate about the nature of our subject area. The extent to which the rhetoric of this intention has been matched by reality is itself a matter of debate. But within this edition of *Cornish Studies* there is evidence that real progress is being made in each of these areas. To begin with, there is engagement by two significant Cornish scholars—Malcolm Williams and Alan M. Kent—with the challenging suggestion by Bernard Deacon in *Cornish Studies: Twelve* that Cornish Studies should embrace 'critical discourse analysis' as a guiding methodology. Here there is evidence of both cross-disciplinary contact —as social science, cultural studies, and language and literature collide —and a willingness to pose searching questions about both the methods and purposes of Cornish Studies. Moreover, there is evidence too of an increasing coherence—partly unwitting but also the result of a determined effort by some scholars to align their work—so that in areas such as language, literature and identity, or the history of the Great Emigration, there is considerable cross-fertilization of ideas and an increasing readiness among scholars to learn from each other and to build upon one another's endeavours.

Malcolm Williams, in his contribution, welcomes Bernard Deacon's advocacy of 'critical discourse analysis' as 'an important milestone in the development of the discipline [Cornish Studies] —[and] its ability to reflect on the ways knowledge of its subject matter is acquired and validated'. However, as a sociologist with a strong interest in quantitative and applied research in dealing with 'real' policy issues such as in-migration and housing, Williams offers his own critique of Deacon's position and argues for a methodological pluralism in Cornish Studies.

Deacon, for example, in explaining his advocacy of critical discourse analysis, offers the contrasting discourses of the early nineteenth-century Cornish as 'dynamic' and the contemporary Cornish as 'lethargic'. But, while allowing for the powerful influence of ethnic stereotyping in constructing such discourses, Williams also points out that the class structure of Cornwall has altered fundamentally over the period in question, a highly-skilled 'labour aristocracy' giving way (not least through emigration) to the situation today where 'there is good evidence of an association . . . between "being Cornish" and coming from an unskilled manual class'. It is not enough to contrast the differing discourses: one has to understand and make plain the historical processes—social, economic and cultural—that underpin them.

Similarly, Williams is concerned about the search for 'truth'—warning that an embrace of critical discourse analysis may presage '[a]n abandonment of the search for truth [which] leads to a dilemma: either the adoption of a normative discourse(s) or a refusal to privilege any discourse'. One either picks one's preferred discourse, or one refuses to choose any of them. Williams prefers to admit the existence of 'partial truths', taking as *his* example the development in nineteenth-century Cornwall of water-cooled rock drills. At the time, there were rival discourses as to the advantages and disadvantages of 'wet' and 'dry' drills, but in environmental health terms we know that that discourse advocating the 'dry' was 'wrong'. Likewise, Williams is concerned that an 'abrogation of truth' may leave us with merely contested discourses which offer differing realities or 'worlds': 'Contrast the gallery owner in "down along" St Ives with the pensioner living on the Penbeagle estate, a few hundred yards away.' For the two individuals involved, their experiences do indeed constitute very different realities. But for the social scientist investigating either or both of them, argues Williams, 'they each fit into an overarching reality, the characteristics of which may even offer an explanation for both'. In such a context, Williams adds, the social scientist will seek a 'methodological pluralism', acknowledging the conceptual value of critical discourse analysis but avoiding its tendency towards relativism by adopting a triangulation of research methods such as 'survey research, analysis of official statistics, ethnographic interviewing, life histories, economic analysis and so on', all 'underwritten by a clearer and more robust methodology'.

Alan M. Kent is similarly invigorated by Deacon's challenge. He insists in his article that while 'Deacon correctly argues for the integration of "critical discourse analysis" within Cornish Studies, there is a need to go one stage further'. 'It seems', Kent argues, 'that to truly develop the field, then there is a need to establish new methodologies which may better fit the Cornish experience than those offered by traditional and often Anglo-centric scholarship'. Here Kent has in mind alternative methodologies in language and literature studies in Cornwall. Irritated by the continuing divide in linguistic studies in Cornwall—with Cornish language scholars dealing with the Cornish language and dialectologists or English literature scholars dealing with English—he goes on to examine two methodologies that may, he argues, have direct relevance to Cornish Studies.

The first of these methodologies is that developed by Salikoko S. Mufwene, whose model breaks new ground in understanding the conditions in which languages and dialects may be maintained and nourished. Mufwene draws to a considerable degree on the work of David Crystal—whose six criteria for 'healthy' language maintenance have uncanny echoes of William Scawen's seventeenth-century reasons for the decline of the Cornish language—but he constructs an alternative view of 'genetic linguistics' in which there are 'internal' and 'external' 'ecologies' which 'play significant roles in determining the evolutionary trajectories of a language'. Mufwene, says Kent, envisages this in terms of a number of co-existent 'biological parasitic species' —which in Cornwall would equate to English, Cornu-English and Cornish. The 'ecologies' of mining and fishing, for example, determined the survival of specific Cornish-language words in those socio-economic/cultural communities long after the language had ceased to be medium of communication in Cornwall as a whole. Today, there is a County Council-sponsored *Strategy for the Cornish Language* but, argues Kent, it fails to consider the ecologies of language in the round in Cornwall—not least the position of Cornu-English. More research, then, needs to be done in understanding the 'ecologies' at work in Cornwall and to develop policies relevant to the language mix in its entirety. As Kent remarks, neither Cornish nor Cornu-English is dead, and an integrated language policy would need to take account of both.

Kent moves on to assert a link between Mufwene's socio-linguistic system and the method of literary scholarship that Kent himself has long espoused—cultural materialism. Here there is also a constant 'ecological' struggle for power, not least in Cornwall, with some writers and their works being accepted readily as part of the 'canon' of Cornish literature (and others not), with the 'official culture' of the 'dominating social institutions' determining who and what will be remembered in the community for the longest time. This corresponds closely to Even-Zohar's model of 'a literary system'—with its constituent concepts of Institution, Producer, Consumer, Market, Product and Repertoire—which Kent contends is highly relevant to Cornwall with its 'unique cultural position' and 'highly distinctive' linguistic and literary 'ecology'. Together with Mufwene, Even-Zohar has much to offer debate in Cornwall, Kent argues, but he admits that this will be difficult 'when so few are aware of the importance of the debate'.

Amongst other things, Kent in his article points to the appearance in an otherwise healthily critical *Cornish Studies* series of a 'liberal humanist' approach to literary and other work that seemingly ignores or even negates the normative project that he otherwise detects within the series' pages. At first glance, Michael Bender's treatment of Virginia Woolf's well-known novel *To the Lighthouse* might well be taken as an example of just such a 'liberal humanist' position. Bender, in his article, picks up on the familiar view that Woolf moved the 'real' setting of her novel—St Ives (the 'lighthouse' in question being Godrevy)—to the 'Isles of Skye'. Today a conventional wisdom, this relocation once eluded even such distinguished literary commentators as David Daiches, who searched in vain for topographical evidence of the 'real' locality in the Inner Hebrides. Bender returns to the issue afresh, arguing that—because of the novel's intense personal and psychological importance to Woolf and her relationships—she needed the emotional 'distance' that the relocation provided.

In this Bender, a psychologist by training, is well-placed to offer his detailed perspectives, illuminating the quasi-autobiographical features of the book and equating the principal fictional characters with real people in Woolf's family and life. But he also notices that the St Ives that Woolf describes (but does not name) is extremely limited topographically and hardly extends to the town's limits let alone the wider hinterland of West Penwith. This—in an intriguing parallel of Malcolm Williams' contrast between the gallery owner in 'down along' and the pensioner on the Penbeagle estate—is because, Bender argues, Woolf was merely concerned with the immediate milieu in which exists the house-party that forms the novel's focus. She was not interested in the people beyond her household.

But if the wider geographical context was so unimportant, why the precise relocation to 'the Isles of Skye'? Here Bender offers an important explanation which moves beyond the 'liberal humanist'. Like the wider 'artists' colony' that had emerged in St Ives, the presence of Woolf's parents' household and their guests was inherently 'colonial', evidence of an 'internal colonization' in which elements of the metropolitan elite co-opted peripheral localities such as St Ives. Likewise, the dealings in the novel, such as they are, between members of the household and the local Cornish/Scots also reveal deep-seated colonial attitudes, Bender argues. To maintain the colonial relationship with the locals and the colonial milieu so central to the book, then,

Woolf, in her desire to create emotional distance and space for herself, had nonetheless to alight upon another 'colonized Celtic periphery'. The 'Isles of Skye' was the obvious choice.

Andrew C. Symons continues the literary theme in his article on Jack Clemo, the clay-country novelist and poet, and the mystical-erotic quest that dominated his life. Like Kent, Symons considers the 'ecological' background of language to be significant in any examination of Clemo's life and work. Commentators have focused generally on Clemo's working-class background and his twin disabilities of encroaching blindness and deafness, but Symons concentrates initially upon the Cornu-English dialect of Clemo's writings. Although Clemo, rejecting the emphases and preoccupations of the Cornish-Celtic Revivalists, dismissed the 'infinite remoteness' of the Cornish language, imagining it located in some dim and distant Arthurian or medieval world hardly relevant to his modern predicament, Symons offers a different interpretation. He argues that the rhythms and stresses of Clemo's poetry do not reflect the normal English-language pattern but reveal instead a 'Celtic' influence inherited from Cornish. Moreover, Symons adds, this was but one strand of a 'tangled web of languages and cultures' that prevailed in clay-country Cornwall and 'needs to be teased out if Clemo is to be properly understood'.

To explain the influence of Cornish-language forms on the Cornu-English that Clemo spoke and thus upon his writings in English, Symons argues that Cornish—in its Late (or 'Modern') form—survived relatively late on the Hensbarrow uplands of mid-Cornwall, with families such as the Clemos and the Polmounters (from which Jack Clemo sprang) being members of that strata of society which retained it the longest. Drawing upon the work of Charles Henderson on Constantine and P.A.S. Pool on West Penwith, Symons charts the fortunes of Cornish on Hensbarrow, finding evidence to suggest its at least fragmented survival there until the late seventeenth century. Thus, as Symons observes, '[i]n proclaiming the "infinite remoteness" of the Celtic past Clemo was obscuring one of his major achievements, the creation of poetic forms capable of conveying the rhythms, intonation and dissociations of Late Cornish and its wrecked culture'. Moreover, '[t]he disturbing power of the clayscape poems, written at a time [the 1940s] when Europe was surveying the wreckage of its own civilization, makes them particularly apposite'.

From the linguistic background, Symons moves into other areas of the 'tangled web', noting (for example) the enduring influence on Clemo of the Bible Christian revivalist tradition in the Polmounter family, which led to both his rejection of conventional Methodism and the evolution of a singular theological vision made plain in his novel *The Clay Kiln*. This, in turn, prompted Clemo's 'vision of a future wife', a 'wife imbued with God's grace', leading eventually to his marriage to Ruth Peaty in 1968. Thereafter, Clemo devoted the rest of his life (he died in 1994) to 'exploring the parameters of the mystical life and of the nature of religious experience, with the relationship of human and divine love . . . as a central theme'.

The sense evident in Symons' study, that the Cornish language was not principally a medieval phenomenon (as even some present-day Revivalists would have us believe) but survived long enough in its Late ('Modern') form to inform contemporary Cornish culture, is echoed in Matthew Spriggs' article on William Scawen (1600–89). As Spriggs notes, there has been a vigorous historiographical debate in recent years about how Cornwall's history should be written and read, with the issue of Cornish 'difference' at the centre of a sometimes heated contest between those who insist that Cornwall is no different from any English county and those who see in its cultural identity and historical experience all the hallmarks of a separate nationality. In its current form, this is very recent debate—part of a much wider debate about 'the new British historiography'—but, as Spriggs remarks, its basic tenets would have been familiar enough to William Scawen over three hundred years ago. And there is no doubt about whose 'side' Scawen was on—in the latter years of his life he embarked on a patriotic project to record and even revive the Cornish language, at the same time championing the Cornish as the descendents of 'Ancient Britons' and (as Spriggs puts it) 'heirs to one of the original pre-Roman kingdoms of Britain'. This project led to the completion of his *Antiquities Cornubrittanic*, four versions of which still exist, the final one still subject to editing by Scawen at the time of his death aged 89.

As Spriggs readily acknowledges, it is Mark Stoyle who—in his *West Britons: Cornish Identities and the Early Modern British State* (Exeter, 2002)—has been largely responsible for bringing William Scawen to the attention of the early twenty-first-century reader. As Stoyle has remarked, it is strange that the final version of Scawen's *Antiquities Cornubrittanic*, deposited now in Cornwall Record Office in Truro, has never been published, for it is a treatise that affords an illuminating insight into a seventeenth-century Cornishman's attitude to the Cornish identity and the Cornish language. Spriggs intends to rectify this deficiency in due course, but in the meantime in his current article he offers a discussion of Scawen's work in support of the Cornish language, especially his influence on the early Celticist Edward Lhuyd and a generation of like-minded Cornish-language enthusiasts in Cornwall, together with a comparative analysis of the four versions of *Antiquities Cornubrittanic.*

An unpaginated epilogue, appended to the fourth version right at the end of his life, serves as a fitting encapsulation of Scawen's sentiment: 'To my worthy Countrymen of Cornwall and all other who doe or may claime Descent from or have the honour for the Brittish Blood, Prosperity and encrease of Renowne is wished.' But Spriggs poses an intriguing question—was Scawen a lone voice in his impassioned assertion of Cornish identity, or was he echoing a more general sense of Cornish 'difference' expressed at the time? The evidence, Spriggs argues, points to the latter, and he cites a telling letter from William Borlase to Thomas Tonkin in November 1730. Commenting on Tonkin's discovery of allegedly Roman remains in Gwendron (Wendron), Borlase warns him that '[o]ne thing I am afraid of, which is you will incur the severe censure of some Antient Britons who value themselves above all things, like their brethren in Wales, upon their never having been overcome by the Romans'.

The belief that Cornwall 'was never conquered yet' runs through Cornish history. It was evident at the end of the Civil War, as Hugh Peters warned his Parliamentarian colleagues, and was a sentiment articulated by the predominantly Cornish trade unions on South Australia's Yorke Peninsula in the 1870s. It was also present to a degree, as several scholars have argued, in the late medieval/early modern Cornish miracle play *Beunans Meriasek* (the 'Life of St Meriasek'), where the theme of tyranny looms large and the virtuous Duke of Cornwall defeats the evil Teudar—a scarcely veiled reference to Henry VII, perhaps. In this volume, Paul Manning returns afresh to the medieval Cornish drama, including *Beunans Meriasek.* He offers a reading that departs from both the overtly 'Cornu-centric' interpretations offered recently and the more conventional analyses that place the Cornish miracle plays within a wider European tradition that asserts the fundamental values of Christendom. His emphasis here is on the violence inherent in all the plays—from the *Ordinalia* to the recently discovered *Beunans Ke* (the 'Life of St Kea')—and made explicit in very detailed staging instructions.

The plays, Manning argues, 'provide material of great interest to historical anthropologists and sociologists who are interested in the way violence is imagined in relation to the emerging notion of a state entity with a monopoly on violence, or a civilizing process in which violence is increasingly displaced from everyday life and "confined to barracks"'. The plays, to that extent, are quite literally 'staging the state', demonstrating the use and management of violence, with the deployment of 'torturers' to represent the 'monopolization of violence upon which states depend'. But there are subtle differences over time, Manning observes, not least in the staging of the torturers. In earlier plays, notably the *Ordinalia*, violence is legitimate if it can be shown to be compatible with the demands of Christian kingship. In later plays the situation is more complex, the tension between tyranny and the legitimate authority of kings reflected in the way torturers are used, the latter now only deployed by tyrannical states whose attempted monopolization of violence is illegitimate.

The medieval Cornish miracle plays were, of course, written in the Cornish language—lending them an impenetrable, even subversive quality in the estimation of monoglot English-speaking observers. Four hundred or so years later, in the late eighteenth and early nineteenth centuries, Cornwall—though now Anglophone and at the forefront of British industrialization—was still a decidedly 'different' place in the eyes of many visitors from across the Tamar. As Cynthia Lane explains in her article, many of these visitors came to Cornwall in anticipation of finding the 'West Barbary' of popular fancy but actually encountered something rather more complex. Some thought they had found their West Barbary—especially if they had had occasion to enter Cornwall across the bleak Bodmin Moor—but many more were surprised to discover an alternative 'industrial civilization' which evidenced a Cornwall at the forefront of industrial innovation. However, as Lane argues, 'this industrial civilization, though indisputably "modern", was often also outlandish in the eyes of external visitors—emphasizing Cornwall and the Cornish as "other". Despite the onset of modernity, Cornwall remained different.'

Visitors were impressed by the intimidating might of the Cornish mining industry. In 1854 one Walter White described a 'hungry landscape' with 'screaming locomotives with hurrying trains; whirling and vibrating, the forest of tall beams, make up an astonishing maze of machinery and motion'. In this fearsome landscape, '[g]iant arms of Steam-engines swing up and down; and the stamping mills appear to try which can thunder the loudest, proclaiming afar the progress made in disemboweling the bountiful old earth'. But, amazed as he was by this modernity, White also wrote that 'frequently did I fancy myself out of England while in Cornwall'. As he put it: [u]nder the influence of . . . strange names, the peculiarities of the people, and unfamiliar landscape features, it seemed to me more than once that I was in a foreign country, and I caught myself saying in conversation—"When I get back to England".'

Echoing Bender's estimation of Virginia Woolf's 'colonial' presence at St Ives, Lane concludes that 'Cornwall might have embraced modernity but it remained a world away from the culture, standards and norms of the English metropolis' as expressed in the opinions of travellers and visitors. As she puts it: 'beneath this veneer of modernity, and sometimes because of it, Cornwall remained "different" . . . with travellers thinking themselves in a land apart from England where the locals exhibited a fierce local patriotism and a non-deferential individualism and independence in the face of outsiders'.

The complex juxtaposition of 'modernity' and 'traditional belief' in nineteenth-century Cornwall also informs the discussion of 'Bridget Cleary and Cornish Studies'. Taking its cue from Angela Bourke's important book *The Burning of Bridget Cleary* (1999), the article argues that—just as in Ireland where traditional beliefs, such as those in fairies and the healing powers of holy wells, existed beneath the modernity imposed by both British rule and the Catholic Church—so in Cornwall there was a similar tension between the 'old' and the 'new'. In the (true) story of Bridget Cleary, her behaviour and ailment had led her husband and his friends to conclude that she was a changeling planted by the fairies, a changeling that needed to be exposed if the real Bridget was to be restored. The exposure was pursued with tragic results, for fire was the last resort in dealing with a changeling and poor Bridget Cleary was burned to death by her husband.

In Cornwall, it is argued, a similar veneer of modernity had descended during the nineteenth century, industrialization bringing in its wake a modernity that transformed Cornish society, with Methodism playing the role of a modernizing religion akin to that of Catholicism in Ireland—not least in its opposition to traditional beliefs. As the folklore collections of M.A. Courtney, William Bottrell and Robert Hunt attest, there was a rich oral tradition still extant in Cornwall in the mid-nineteenth century, and amongst this folklore was a similar concern with changelings—including remedies that also included the use of heat and fire. But there were also documented cases in Cornwall of changeling belief, a belief not restricted to story-telling around the hearthside but exhibited in the behaviour of real people who, for example, ill-treated small children they imagined to be changelings.

However, despite this persistence of traditional belief, there was also—as Alan M. Kent argued in *Cornish Studies: Twelve*—a fundamental shift in story-telling in nineteenth-century Cornwall, itself a function of modernity, with the old 'drolls' such as those recorded by Hunt giving way to the new Cousin Jack narratives of the New World. These narratives, it is argued here, were prevalent enough by the second half of the nineteenth century to influence Bottrell's later work, his collection of 1880 including several stories which acknowledged the significance of the emigrant Cousin Jack within Cornish life and culture. And just as the story of Bridget Cleary continues to resonate in early twenty-first-century County Tipperary, so the grand narrative of Cousin Jack continues to exercise its influence at home and abroad—sometimes with surprising results, as in Aboriginal Queensland.

The grand narrative of Cousin Jack overseas underpins Paul Manning's second contribution to this volume, a fascinating discussion of the 'sprites of capitalism' in Cornish mines at home and abroad: an analysis that also examines the relationship between traditional belief and modernity. As Manning explains, by the sixteenth century Cornish tinners were attributing ancient workings to 'old men' or 'Jews'. By the nineteenth, as mining had moved deep underground, so had these 'Jews'. They had become associated with ghosts or fairies called 'knackers' (or 'knockers'), part of the fairy world that the Cornish imagined to exist all around them. When the Cornish emigrated overseas to the American mining frontier, the 'knackers' went with them and were re-invented as 'Tommyknockers'. They lost their 'Jewish' ethnicity, becoming instead the spirits of deceased miners, and became commonplace in the belief systems of not only the Cousin Jacks but also other ethnic groups at work in the American mines.

This Cousin Jack exodus to the New World had commenced shortly after the end of the Napoleonic wars, as Cornish miners hoped to escape the vacillations of the mining industry at home and follow enterprising British capital to the new opportunities of Latin America. Sharron P. Schwartz has made the study of Cornish emigration to Latin America her own specialist area of expertise, and in this volume she presents a case study of Latin America as an adjunct to a wider Leverhulme-funded project currently being undertaken by her and Bernard Deacon at the Institute of Cornish Studies. Intent on exposing Cornish migration networks and explaining the transnationalization of social capital, she argues that hitherto we have known very little about the micro-level detail of Cornish emigration, Cornwall-wide generalizations all too often obscuring 'startling differences in the timing and direction of migration flows from mining parishes only a few miles apart'.

Schwartz's article rests on a detailed scrutiny of some 2,500 collected records of Cornish migrants to Latin America (defined broadly as South and Central America and the Spanish Caribbean) between the years 1811 and 1930. She identifies the principal destinations of these Cornish emigrants (mainly males) but also unveils some fascinating details as to their geographical origins. Perhaps not surprisingly, the Central Mining District (Camborne, Redruth,

Gwennap)—the principal focus of Cornish mining throughout the period under discussion—accounts for the majority of this emigration, along with neighbouring St Agnes. But there are relatively few emigrants to Latin America from the St Austell, St Ives and Tregonning/Wendron districts, and even fewer from St Just-in-Penwith, the Caradon mines around St Cleer, and the Tamar Valley mines of Gunnislake and Calstock. It is tempting to suggest that this is merely the result of population density—a great many mining families lived in Camborne-Redruth and environs—but Schwartz warns against such an interpretation. She notes that if the emigration figures to Latin America for each sub-registration district are calculated against the total population of that sub-district in the year 1871, only Gwennap, Redruth and Camborne (in that order) are statistically visible. Population density, therefore, was not the only factor at work.

There were also others considerations—as in the 'Hungry Forties' when an increasing reservoir of intending Cornish migrants was enticed to important new destinations such as Wisconsin and Michigan in the United States and Kapunda and Burra Burra in South Australia—and the burgeoning nature of the international mining frontier meant that Latin America as a destination would have to compete with an ever increasing range of alternative places. But even at the micro level there are intriguing variations, so that the migration patterns from Redruth to Latin America are different from those of Camborne, and so on. Patterns of kinship and association were important in building and maintaining these micro emigration flows but in the end the migration networks to Latin America did break down, beginning as early as the 1830s with the sudden unpopularity of Cuba (due to the prevalence of yellow fever) and aggravated over time by events such as the Mexican Revolution of 1910.

Latin America emerged early in the nineteenth century as a destination for emigrant Cornish miners. A later destination, crucial towards the end of the nineteenth century and into the early twentieth, was South Africa—the land of gold and diamonds. In the second case study of Cornish emigration in this volume, Gary Magee and Andrew Thompson alight on an often overlooked dimension of the transnational experience—the remittances of funds earned overseas by emigrants to their dependents back 'home'. They acknowledge that thus far in the corpus of British emigration history it is only in consideration of the Cornish 'diaspora' that serious attention has been afforded these so-called 'migrapounds'. They also emphasize the significance of the Cornish emigration experience in the broader discussion of South African (and wider Imperial and American) remittance patterns, concluding that 'the injection of "migrapounds" into the Cornish economy was substantial and likely to have far-reaching repercussions'. Cornwall—absolutely, relatively and comparatively—was significant in the world of transnational remittances.

Magee and Thompson also contend that remittances, while interesting and significant in their own right, are but part of a larger canvas that social theorists have dubbed the 'transnational public sphere'. Remittances in themselves did not nurture the enduring linkages between the home and host societies, and here there is an important echo of Sharron Schwartz's work, a desire to learn more about the mechanisms that kept alive the conduits of information and population movement between specific places in Cornwall and destinations overseas. Magee and Thompson note 'the increasing inter-dependence between Cornwall and South Africa' at the end of the nineteenth century. Pondering its characteristics, they conclude that '[f]or many Cornish migrants, their departure from Britain was not so much a case of "cut and run" as of run, remit and (eventually) return.'

By the end of the nineteenth century, with Cornwall so clearly dependent on the economic support of South Africa and with Cornish mining and engineering but a shadow of their former selves, the enormity of the socio-economic—and cultural crisis—facing Cornish society and its identity helped to give credence to the aspirations of the Cornish-Celtic Revivalists: those who looked back beyond the now fast decaying industrial Cornwall to an earlier Cornish-speaking, Celtic-Catholic Cornwall. Foremost amongst these visionaries was Henry Jenner, the so-called Father of the Cornish Language Revival, the subject of a recent book edited by Derek R. Williams—*Henry and Katherine Jenner: A Celebration of Cornwall's Culture*—and reviewed here by Amy Hale.

As well as welcoming the attention given to the often over-shadowed literary career of Kitty Lee (Katherine) Jenner, Hale acknowledges 'Jenner's place at the head of the canon of Cornish Revivalist luminaries', a position emphasized in the book in question. However, she also observes that 'what makes Jenner truly fascinating is that while the scope of his work was in some ways intensely localized to Cornwall, his range of influences and interest was in fact international'. She considers that more 'comparative research' on these tangential activities might have provided 'a more complete picture of Jenner and his place in modern Cornish history'.

Indeed it might, and Hale's plea for us to be ever alert to the comparative possibilities of Cornish Studies is—notwithstanding the positive evidence of such comparison evident in this volume—a timely word of both encouragement and caution for those of us who seek to further secure Cornish Studies within the wider world of international scholarly endeavour. That this volume includes contributions from scholars not only in Cornwall and elsewhere in the United Kingdom but from the United States of America, Canada and Australia suggests, perhaps, that we are on the right track.

Professor Philip Payton,
Director, Institute of Cornish Studies,
University of Exeter in Cornwall,
Tremough, Penryn, Cornwall.

DISCOURSE AND SOCIAL SCIENCE IN CORNISH STUDIES—A REPLY TO BERNARD DEACON

Malcolm Williams

INTRODUCTION

Bernard Deacon's article in *Cornish Studies: Twelve* on methodology in Cornish Studies[1] marks an important milestone in the development of the discipline—its ability to reflect on the ways knowledge of its subject matter is acquired and validated. He makes a persuasive case for the use of discourse analysis (and specifically Critical Discourse Analysis CDA) as a method and in this article it is not my intention to challenge this. However, I would like to do three things in this response: first I would like to briefly discuss some of the limits to a discourse approach to method. Second, I would like to make a plea for a methodological pluralism[2] that is grounded in some slightly different ontological assumptions that give rise to my concerns about CDA. Third, I would like to develop the 'realist' element in CDA he refers to towards the end of his article.

DISCOURSE, TRUTH AND REALITY

i) Discourse: Poststructuralism and its emergent discourse analysis have had a seductive appeal for social scientists keen to rid themselves of the constructive and often fallacious empiricist approaches that dominated social science up until recent decades.[3] However, as Deacon points out, the consequences may well be a relativism that privileges equally all of the discourses. There are non-linguistic limits upon discourse and indeed discourse itself can have non linguistic consequences. Often the linguistic and non-linguistic are enmeshed in complex ways.

One of Deacon's examples is the opposite discourses of early nineteenth-century 'Cornish dynamism' and that of the contemporary Cornish as 'lethargic'. Whilst these discourses may take a great deal from ethnic stereotyping, they owe at least something to deeper structural changes in Cornish society. Through much of the nineteenth century Cornwall was materially dynamic in the development of extractive and associated industries. This in turn produced a capitalist class and labour aristocracy that developed both an internal and external reputation for dynamism. However, as result of internal decline of such industries and several waves of migration, the class structure of Cornwall has itself changed. Now there is good evidence to indicate an association, in contemporary Cornwall, between 'being Cornish' and coming from an unskilled manual class.[4] Conversely, in-migrants to Cornwall are much more likely to come from skilled manual, or non-manual, backgrounds. Because their skills were in demand in the nineteenth century, the Cornish constituted a 'migratory elite' with the social capital to migrate, along with a reputation for hard work and innovation. Over a long period of time the migratory elite did indeed migrate, and the class structure in Cornwall changed. Now it seems that it is the sons and daughters of the in-migrants who are more likely to move out of Cornwall—they are the new migratory elite.

Stereotyping discourses may themselves have material consequences. The above data on contemporary class and migration comes from a study by Philipa Aldous. She found that the migration intentions amongst young Cornish residents often shaped anti-Cornish attitudes or encouraged (through resistance) pro-Cornish identities.[5] What is important, however, is that the identities so formed became important to migration decisions. They had non-linguistic consequences.

ii) Truth: I accept that my original plea (in *Cornish Studies: Ten*) for a new Cornish social science 'to describe what contemporary Cornwall is like and to understand what people in Cornwall think' was not without philosophical and methodological implications. In *understanding* I think I had in mind something like a discourse method, but in *description* my goal was for an accurate differentiation and specification of historic and contemporary social actors and structures. Indeed, I could have gone further and called for both description and explanation. Now these entail (at least in a moderate sense) both a search for truth and an attempt to be 'scientific'. I will come back to science presently, but first truth.

One of the constructions of poststructuralism and anti-empiricism/ anti-positivism more generally, was a straw person called 'truth'. Truth is a villain because not only does he (and in much feminist discourse truth is male and hegemonic) claim to exist, but also he claims that we can come to know him. For poststructuralists, this is a wicked conceit. However, this leads to difficulties, for if truth does not exist then discourses really are equal, not just in their moral claim, but also in their ontological status. Bernard Deacon makes it clear that he believes such consequences are unattractive and in adopting CDA he attempts to avoid them. However, CDA inevitably implies a normative privileging of one discourse over another in much same way as does the feminist standpoint position, because 'truth' is seen as too ambitious.[6] An abandonment of the search for truth leads to a dilemma: either the adoption of a normative discourse(s) or a refusal to privilege any discourse.

The straw person of truth is characterized by certainty, the view that the goal of science is truth and that truth may be obtained. The first is certainly the case, but it would be hard to find any scientist or philosopher of science, these days, who would make claim to the latter. A prevailing view in latter circles[7] and an alternative to the relativization of truth is that partial truths, or the elimination of error, may indeed be possible, for if this were not the case technological advancement would not occur. A historic Cornish example of this might be the discovery that water-cooled rock drills would prevent the aerosol effect of quartz particles associated with their dry predecessors and consequently reduce the incidence of respiratory disease. Presumably, at the time, there would have been rival discourses associated with wet and dry drilling. But in health terms one of those discourses would have been 'wrong'.

My call for description was a call for the best possible description and, by implication, the best possible explanation. This does not imply a commitment to context, or theory-free description—in this respect Bernard Deacon is quite correct in his characterization of 'old' Cornish studies as often embodying that belief. However, what is important is that one aims for the most accurate description possible, but at the same time accepting that the explanation that may follow from it may have rivals and that these may well be the function of prior theoretical positions. Where does this leave us, for example, in respect of the peripheral or 'down here' discourse, versus perhaps a Cornish anti-metropolitan one? I submit that the work of description and explanation we have to do as social scientists is first to uncover these discourses and to describe them as faithfully as we can (to their authors' intentions).

This alone is methodologically not necessarily straightforward, because—as Bernard Deacon implies—their description requires a prior conceptual framework. Nevertheless, both the description and the framework are themselves open to challenge, as is any scientific description. The explanatory part of the task lies in locating the discourses in social structures, but I will come back to that below. However, one last point I will make on this is that the social scientist, in describing and explaining rival discourses, is under no obligation to adjudicate upon which discourse itself better describes the world, though when she switches off her computer, leaves the university and becomes a citizen she may choose to do so. Moreover, that choice as citizen may come to inform her role as social scientist, though, as I argued in *Cornish Studies: Ten*, her citizen commitment may be better served by her objectivity as a scientist.[8]

iii) Reality: The abrogation of truth has consequences for what we can say of reality and indeed poststructuralists will often talk of multiple realities. This can be taken to mean that if truth boils down to contested discourses, then these discourses will come to constitute different realities or 'worlds'. Contrast the gallery owner in 'down along' St Ives with the pensioner living on the Penbeagle estate, a few hundred metres away. For each of these such diverse experiences do constitute different realities, but for the social scientist investigating either or both they each fit into an overarching reality, the characteristics of which may even offer an explanation of both. I realize there is a potential logical regress here in which the social scientists overarching explanation of reality might be subsumed into an even bigger one, but this is not problematic as long as the description and explanation is no more than a claim to being potential or partial.

SCIENTIFIC METHOD, EXPLANATION AND DISCOURSE

My concern with discourse method is not with its status as a method, but with privileging it as a methodological framework for doing Cornish (or any other kind) of social science. In this section I will make a plea for a pluralistic scientific methodology and illustrate this with a reference to the study of migration to, from and within Cornwall.

Writing in the early part of the twentieth century, the sociologist Max Weber tried to bridge the gap between two rival ways of studying the social world,[9] the nomothetic associated with the descriptive and explanatory methods of natural science and the idiographic associated with the arts or humanities. The latter sought to understand and interpret social contexts in the way an artist might interpret a land-scape, or a literary critic a novel. Weber did not see these approaches as incompatible in studies of the social world. The nomothetic is necessary to explain the causal properties of social structures, but the idiographic is necessary to show how individuals interpret those structures and act upon them. A science of the social, in Weber's view, required both.

This 'methodological pluralism' has underwritten many of the contemporary studies of migration in Cornwall. The starting point for these studies, conducted since the mid 1980s, was the simple demographic fact of population turnaround in Cornwall since the 1960s. Until that decade each Census had shown a decline in Cornwall's population, but since then Cornwall's population has grown considerably at each Census. This growth has been wholly attributable to in-migration and indeed the net population growth has hidden continuing large-scale out-migration. Net population growth through in-migration is not uncommon in other areas of Britain (and Western countries more generally), but what is so unusual in Cornwall is that population growth has been accompanied not by growing economic prosperity, as has been the case in most other areas, but by economic stagnation and even decline.[10] Geographers and sociologists have sought explanations, some of which can be inferred from economic data, but by no means all. The proffered explanations are complex and have been discussed at length elsewhere,[11] but a consensual position of key features can be summarized thus:

From the late 1950s Cornwall was increasingly the destination for tourists and a substantial tourist industry has existed ever since. Some of the tourists subsequently moved to Cornwall, and this has been established through several surveys of in-migrants since. Additionally, economic policy for much of this period predicted economic growth would be stimulated through in-migration. This policy was operationalized, especially in the 1970s, through initiatives aimed at bringing enterprises to Cornwall. In-migration did not stimulate economic growth, but nevertheless in-migrants continued to arrive, often moving from areas of prosperity such as the South East of England.

Thus far is seems safe to say that the description is uncontested —there are no rival discourses—but once we move beyond this point, this is no longer the case. Let us examine two rival discourses:

Migrants move to Cornwall for economic reasons vs. migrants move to Cornwall to Cornwall for lifestyle reasons. On the face of it the first seems implausible; why would a rational person, of working age, move from an area of greater prosperity to one of less prosperity (most migrant origins are areas of greater prosperity)? Seminal studies of migratory motives by Perry *et al* and Cornwall Council (in the mid-1980s)[12] produced conflicting evidence. However, subsequent research has revealed a complex picture.[13] First, a move to Cornwall can make economic sense for a homeowner in many areas of the country (but especially the South East), because house prices in Cornwall are lower. By selling elsewhere and buying in Cornwall, migrants can make a substantial gain. This much can be inferred from house-price and migration data and can be seen as the 'nomothetic' side of the research. An idiographic approach through qualitative research confirms this to be the case, but at least one study produced evidence to indicate that in-migrants moved to Cornwall on the basis of a belief that it was prosperous and that there were plenty of jobs![14] Perhaps in-migrants do not research GDP, income or employment data, but rather base their decisions on the apparent prosperity on show in the resorts they visited as tourists?

But the situation is more complex still, because virtually every study has also shown that many people move to Cornwall for purely lifestyle reasons, whilst others cite both economic and lifestyle reasons. These may appear to lead to rival explanations or discourses. The theoretical challenge is to seek an overall explanatory framework and the methodological one is to successfully access the reasons for migrants' decisions, when they may have reconstructed them in line with their post-migration interpretation of their situation.

The second discourse is closer to the kind illustrated by Deacon in that it encompasses not just rival explanations of data, but rival ideological positions:

Population led growth stimulates the Cornish economy vs. population led growth has been a key factor in Cornwall's economic decline. The economic evidence would seem to have conclusively refuted the first argument. In practice this is the case and few policy makers would continue to advance it, but for a long while a riposte was that without the business investment of in-migrants, Cornwall's situation would have been even worse. Its opponents, both academic and political, have pointed to data indicating that large numbers of in-migrants become economically inactive either immediately after moving to Cornwall or some time later on. The evidence against the efficacy of population-led growth is probably clinching overall, yet at a local level the picture may be more complex. Current joint research between the University of Plymouth and Cornwall Council uses micro-level data from electoral wards to compare prosperity over time and to look not just at in-migration patterns, but patterns of internal migration. Preliminary results indicate that some wards, mainly in tourist areas, may have benefited from 'population led growth', but a consequence of this has been both out-migration and internal migration to the larger towns, such as Camborne-Redruth and Penzance. At present it is hypothesized that the internal migrants are more likely to be younger, poorer and Cornish.

The 'scientific method' I have advocated (and which, I think, for the most part has been deployed in the research programmes I cite) has both a nomothetic and idiographic element. There is a search for truth, but perhaps only through the elimination of error. Certainly, part of the methodological approach involves the uncovering and analysis of discourses, but this sits within a less modest aim to provide the best description and explanation of migration that is possible.

CDA AND REALISM

As Bernard Deacon notes, CDA embraces a degree of relativism.[15] I would suggest that it is hard to clearly mark it off from the thorough-going relativism of Laclau and Mouffe. Whilst, on the face of it, it seems reasonable to speak of a dialectic between discourse and society, if the tools or the will to establish the ontological status of either of these are absent, then their definition becomes arbitrary or elective. Nevertheless, the recommended method of explanatory critique imported from critical realism[16] seems entirely sensible, but (at least in the first three stages) also seems to imply something like the scientific method of description and explanation I advocate, along with a realist ontology.

A realist ontology would begin from the premise that there are real causal structures that give rise to the 'process of top down regionalization'. This might be seen as a mechanism, albeit a complex and dynamic one that may even have arisen as an unintended consequence of other decisions and policies. For example, the refusal of the Office of the Deputy Prime Minister to recognize a grass-roots desire for devolution in Cornwall may not just be a discourse of 'bloody-mindedness' or prejudice, but instead the inevitable consequence of the long-standing structures and functionings of UK Standard Regions. However, the mechanism may operate within a context, which may include such factors as individual personalities and contemporary political positions. The 'space' of Cornish decision-making is the outcome,[17] but outcomes themselves can produce mechanisms. Within Cornwall we can identify a complex alternative mechanism of pressure groups and politicians who are actively challenging the mechanism of top-down decision-making. This group, in turn, is at least partly composed of those involved in the day-to-day governance of Cornwall.

Mechanisms and their characteristics are hypothesized. Just because a researcher 'identifies' a mechanism (as I have done here) does not mean that it exists, or exists in the form hypothesized. However, mechanisms do exist and it is the job of the researcher to uncover them. Finally, the term 'mechanism' may be a little misleading.

These are not Newtonian 'clockwork' mechanisms, but dynamic, mathematically complex social and material structures.

CONCLUDING REMARKS

One can treat all of these political manifestations as discourses, and at one level this may be helpful in so far as the 'discourses' can be treated as evidence of deeper and broader mechanisms. Bernard Deacon rightly rejects the approach to discourse characterized by the work of Laclau and Mouffe. However, CDA seems to inhabit a 'no persons' land' between relativism and realism. By importing its method of explanatory critique from critical realism it inevitably must tilt away from relativism to toward a moderate realism. Finally then, whilst I would not disagree that discourse analysis has much to offer as a method, it, like other methods such as survey research, analysis of official statistics, ethnographic interviewing, life histories, economic analysis and so on, needs to be underwritten by a clearer and more robust methodology. Like Deacon, I too would want to reject the empiricism associated with 'old' Cornish Studies, but I think in realism we can retain a commitment to social theory alongside rigorous scientific method.

NOTES AND REFERENCES

1. Bernard Deacon, 'From "Cornish Studies" to "Critical Cornish Studies"': Reflections on Methodology', in Philip Payton (ed.), *Cornish Studies: Twelve*, Exeter, 2004.
2. In this article I distinguish between 'methodology', the underlying strategies, approach and justification to research that is informed by particular epistemological principles, and 'methods' the range of investigative techniques available to the researcher.
3. Malcolm Williams, *Science and Social Science*, London, 2000, Chapter 2.
4. Philipa Aldous, 'Young People and Migration Choices in Cornwall', unpublished MPhil thesis, University of Plymouth, 2002.
5. The 'resistance' from these young people may well come to challenge the discourse of the lack of dynamism amongst the contemporary Cornish and this in turn may well have economic and social consequences.
6. Deacon, 2004, p. 24.
7. See, for example, D. C. Philips, *Philosophy, Science and Social Inquiry*, Oxford, 1987, p. 24.
8. I have developed this argument in depth in: Malcolm Williams, 'Situated Objectivity', *Journal for the Theory of Social Behavior* 35.1, 2005, pp. 99–120.
9. Max Weber, *Roscher and Knies*, New York, 1975.
10. Malcolm Williams and Tony Champion, 'Cornwall, Poverty and In-Migration', in Philip Payton (ed.), *Cornish Studies: Eight*, Exeter, 1998.
11. See, for example, Ron Perry, Ken Dean, and B. Brown,

Counterurbanisation: Case Studies in Urban to Rural Movement, Norwich, 1986.

12. Peter Mitchell, 'The Demographic Revolution', in Philip Payton (ed.), *Cornwall Since the War: The Contemporary History of a European Region*, Redruth, 1993.

13. Carol Williams, 'Counterurbanisation and Housing Need in Cornwall', unpublished PhD thesis, University of Plymouth, 1997.

14. Mary Buck, Lyn Bryant and Malcolm Williams, *Housing and Households in Cornwall: A Pilot Study of Cornish Families*, Plymouth, 1992.

15. Deacon, 2004, p. 24.

16. Deacon, 2004, p. 26.

17. In a merging of critical realism with scientific realism Ray Pawson has proposed the schema context, plus mechanism gives rise to outcomes (C+M=O). Pawson's mechanisms are complex (in the mathematical sense), multi-faceted and changing. Ray Pawson, *Measure for Measure*, London, 1989.

SCATTING IT T'LERRUPS: PROVISIONAL NOTES TOWARDS ALTERNATIVE METHODOLOGIES IN LANGUAGE AND LITERARY STUDIES IN CORNWALL

Alan M. Kent

INTRODUCTION: CRITICAL LERRUPS

> Now hear this. You are mountain people. You hear me? Your language is dead. It is forbidden. It is not permitted to speak your mountain language in this place. You cannot speak your language to your men. It is not permitted. Do you understand? You may not speak it. It is outlawed. You may speak only the language of the capital. That is the only language permitted in this place. You will be badly punished if you attempt to speak your mountain language in this place. This is military decree. It is the law. Your language is forbidden. It is dead. No one is allowed to speak your language. Your language no longer exists.[1]

To anyone even remotely interested in the language and literary culture of Cornwall—or indeed any other Celtic or minority language which has experienced language-loss or death—the above speech will resonate. It is from Act One of Harold Pinter's 1988 allegorical play *Mountain Language* in which an officer abruptly addresses a group of women. The action takes place in and outside a prison in a fictional European territory. Pinter is not usually a playwright associated with Celtic Studies, although his plays frequently deal with the nuances of colloquial and non-standard speech, the difficulties of communication and the many layers of meaning in language. In that sense, *Mountain Language*—which is a text concerning the theme of language and oppression—fits his usual concerns as a writer.[2] In several ways, during the course of the play, the audience is forced to re-evaluate their own preconceptions about language, making them—in the Cornu-English expression—'scat t'lerrups' everything they have known before. 'Lerrups' in Cornu-English dialect means 'in shreds' or 'pieces', and in some ways that is what I wish to do here: re-think language and literary studies.

As a parallel, as I have argued elsewhere, received narratives about linguistic and literary culture have been peddled about Cornwall for some decades now, a monolith which only recently has started to be reconfigured.[3] In this article I wish to re-examine some of that narrative in the light of what Bernard Deacon has termed 'Critical Cornish Studies', labelling these narratives as 'foundation myths',[4] and then examine two hitherto unnoticed methodological concepts which scholars operating in the field of Cornish Studies might wish to examine further. Whilst Deacon correctly argues for the integration of 'critical discourse analysis' within Cornish Studies (especially in the social sciences), and for scholars to be more self-critical, there is a need to go one stage further.[5] It seems that to truly develop the field, there is a need to establish new methodologies which may fit better the Cornish experience than those offered by traditional—and often Anglo-centric —scholarship. There is also a need for the academy in Cornwall to develop new methodologies and paradigms which might also fit the experiences of other territories and groups—to be, say, as applicable as the speech in Pinter's play to other minority cultures across the globe. Cornish Studies, no longer on the margins, has the potential to lead the way.

Deacon's wish in 2004 for an appropriate 'critical discourse analysis' for the social sciences finds literary resonance in two small articles I contributed to *An Baner Kernewek/The Cornish Banner* in 1993 and 1994, where I argued for a 'new correlation between Cornish politics, society and literature'[6] and what I then termed a 'new cultural poetics'[7] which could help shape language and literary studies in Cornwall. In the former article I argued a need to progress beyond the normalized 'Liberal Humanist' approach to earlier Cornish Studies, which then seemed to be encapsulated in the criticism of the day, in particular amongst work by respected observers such as Denys Val Baker, F.E. Halliday and A.L. Rowse.[8] Although the overall standard of discourse has been raised by the second series of *Cornish Studies* volumes and the 'New Cornish Studies' project generally, there is still 'Liberal Humanist' seepage into its pages. This seems ironic, given that

Cornish Studies has in effect registered its commitment to a normative project which among other things includes the transformation of a social order which exploits people on the grounds of their identity. In other words, it recognizes that there are people who self-identify as Cornish, that there is a Cornish language, and that there is something called Cornish Studies, and it is attempting to change perceptions of these both within Cornwall and outside.[9]

In the 1994 article, I argued that 'Cornish writers must face the issue of trying to make a nation as well as a literature and deal with a language that through disuse over so many years has become the victim of an inbuilt preterite.'[10] That preterite (iconography, subject-matter, literary form) might be changing in the fact that Cornish is in recovery and ascension, and there is now a sense of community effort to take the language beyond its peripheral usage into something much more dynamic and stable.[11] I reiterate the observation I made in 1994: 'It seems almost impossible that such an extraordinary thing could have happened',[12] a comment echoed in David Crystal's observations on the revival of Cornish in his book *Language Death*,[13] where Cornish is cited as the one language which had the right preconditions for re-emergence despite an appreciable gap since its apparent demise.

In Cornwall—particularly in the light of a millennial review, and, as we shall see, strategy documentation on the Cornish language—it has also been remarkably difficult to make people aware of the delicate and important interaction between Cornish-speaking and English-speaking language groups, not to mention Cornish and English literatures, without even considering the extra complexity of Cornu-English dialect.[14] What M. Wynn Thomas and others have understood —in the Welsh context—is that the two linguistic cultures (three if one considers English dialect in Wales) have long co-existed and have, over time, often corresponded and overlapped.[15] On the face of this, Wales would seem to be more aware of its bicultural past and present, understanding that the territory's history cannot be fully understood unless the coexistence of the two or more cultures is taken in to account. This paradigm is apparently missing in all the thinking on language and literary studies in Cornwall. Because Cornish has had by nature to be defensive to survive, there has been less acknowledgement of co-existence, and indeed, in some cases outright refusal to see influence and change. Cornish language scholars deal with Cornish language and literature; dialectologists, 'English' literary scholars and others deal with the English language. This reluctance to deal with them in tandem needs to change.

I propose here to examine two methodologies which have direct application to this and the development of Deacon's 'Critical Cornish

Studies', and to my own wish for a 'new cultural poetics' of literature within Cornwall. Interestingly, both of the theories considered here were developed in academies and fields far removed from Anglo-centric scholarship (which paradoxically forms the base of much of the work in current Cornish Studies). Indeed, not only are they outside the British academy, but also the mainstream European academy.

TOWARDS A SYSTEM OF 'GREEN' SOCIO-LINGUISTICS

The first system has been developed by Salikoko S. Mufwene the present Professor and Chair of the Department of Linguistics at the University of Chicago. Mufwene has written extensively on the development of creoles and language endangerment, and what he broadly terms 'the ecology of language evolution'.[16] Mufwene's model therefore has many applications in Cornwall, not only to the Cornish language itself, but perhaps more importantly to Cornu-English. Mufwene's theorization of an ecology of language, in particular, makes for useful comparative study with the situation in Cornwall. Put simply, Mufwene's model goes several stages further than the received theories of how minority languages and dialects are to be maintained and nourished. His model is one of genetic linguistics, which discusses the nature and significance of internal and external factors—or what he terms 'ecologies'—that bear on the evolution of a language over time.[17] This has particular resonance not only for language death, but also for language recovery.

Paradoxically, in many senses, Mufwene's work draws on and develops the work of other established authorities on language such as David Crystal.[18] Crystal's book *Language Death* is highly influential, not only in prompting world-wide debate over the decline of languages, academic and popular enquiry into the reasons behind language attrition, but also reasons for the global pre-eminence of English, in relation to factors such as the mass-media and the internet.[19] Crystal primarily deals with what he terms 'languages proper' in his study, to which Cornish fits, although his observations about maintaining them could equally apply to dialects of English as well, including Cornu-English. Crystal's six criteria for healthy language maintenance, effectively 'Green' or 'Environmentally-friendly' socio-linguistics, are followed by my own brief observations in italics: [20]

1. An endangered language will progress if speakers increase their prestige within the dominant community.
Cornish speakers were, at the end of the nineteenth and into the twentieth century, few and far between and even the so-called 'grandfather' of the Cornish Revival, Henry Jenner, was sceptical about the actual revival of

Cornish.[21] *Prestige for the language has been hard to achieve in the postwar period; too often the language was associated with the nationalist fringe in Cornwall, that it was the domain of 'beardy weirdies', that it was hobbyist and that it was made-up. For the dominant community the language remains a curiosity: glad it is there, but not wishing to learn it.*

For Cornu-English the signs here are not good. Prestige is not associated with dialect speakers. In fact, the reverse is true. Dialect speakers feel the need to modulate their 'true' voice to cope in a contemporary United Kingdom that does not value 'West Country', let alone Cornu-English, voices.

2. An endangered language will progress if its speakers increase their wealth relative to the dominant community.
For the bulk of the twentieth century there were few signs that any Cornish speakers increased their wealth by learning the language. This has altered slightly in two areas: the Arts, where Cornish is seen as a useful card to play, allowing some workers, particularly within the realms of theatre and verbal arts, to explore difference, refining a vision of Cornish as 'exotic' other. The second area is business and cultural tourism activities, although these are still relatively underdeveloped.

Cornu-English speakers cannot increase their wealth relative to the dominant community because the dominant community does not recognize those speakers as economically sophisticated. Cornu-English speakers have to adapt to the dominant culture.

3. An endangered language will progress if its speakers increase their legitimate power in the eyes of the dominant community.
Some progress has been made in terms of the respect given to speakers by the dominant community. For example, being 'barded' by the Cornish Gorseth is seen as important. However, it is questionable whether this offers those speakers legitimate power, particularly when the Gorseth itself is middle-class, self-appointed and intrinsically amateur by its nature.

Cornu-English speakers only have legitimate power in the immediate community in which they operate. The dominant community does not value their contribution unless it is for comic or 'yokel' purposes.

4. An endangered language will progress if its speakers have a strong presence in the educational system.
Both Cornish and Cornu-English speakers have negligible presence within the educational system, despite the efforts, say, of the 'Sense of

Place' project.[22] *The National Curriculum or Examination System in the United Kingdom pays little attention to Cornish history or culture. Cornish and Cornu-English speakers are not yet valued in the Combined Universities in Cornwall project. There is no degree in Cornish language.*

5. An endangered language will progress if its speakers can write their language down.
The writing down of Cornish by previous generations of speakers and writers was fortunate. A higher literary standard is now being reached, which is being published outside of Cornwall.[23] *Dictionaries, grammars and anthologies are being compiled.*

Much Cornu-English has also been recorded, but is present writing indicative of the real state, grammar and vocabulary of Cornu-English? Cornu-English is never valued for serious or intellectual debate.

6. An endangered language will progress if its speakers can make use of electronic technology.
Cornish makes good use of electronic technology both in short-run publishing, the internet, CD Rom courses, interactive chat rooms and other resources.

Cornu-English does not use electronic technology—an irony since it was the voice of 'cutting edge' technological Cornwall in the eighteenth and nineteenth centuries.

With the exception of number 6, it is curious to note how many of these success criteria can be turned around as 'death criteria' and matched to the sixteen reasons cited by William Scawen in his influential 1680 essay 'Antiquities Cornubrittanic: The Causes of Cornish Speech's Decay', discussed elsewhere in this volume by Matthew Spriggs.[24]

Obviously Scawen did not note the lack of electronic technology, but there is a sense that he is interested in any new mechanisms which could prevent further loss. It feels as if socio-linguistics have not altered much in three centuries. In the same volume, Crystal cites the work of two other socio-linguistics with theories on the 'well-being' of languages. The first is derived from Akira Yamamoto, who has distinguished nine features 'that can help maintain and promote the small languages':

- the existence of a dominant culture in favour of linguistic diversity;
- a strong sense of ethnic identity within the endangered community;
- the promotion of educational programmes about the endangered language and culture;

- the creation of bilingual/bicultural school programmes;
- the training of native speakers as teachers;
- the involvement of the speech community as a whole;
- the creation of language materials that are easy to use;
- the development of written literature, both traditional and new;
- the creation and strengthening of the environments in which the language must be used.[25]

The second is from Lynn Landweer, who similarly provides eight 'indicators of ethnolinguistic vitality' for an endangered language:

- the extent to which it can resist influence by a dominant urban culture;
- the number of domains in which it is used;
- the frequency and type of code switching;
- the existence of a critical mass of fluent speakers;
- the distribution of speakers across social networks;
- the internal and external recognition of the group as a unique community;
- its relative prestige, compared with surrounding languages;
- its access to a stable economic base.[26]

For Cornish speakers and learners, many of the above 'criteria' have been incorporated into the *Stratejy rag an Tavas Kernewek/ Strategy for the Cornish Language*. The consultation process during 2004 resulted in a series of 'Visions' for Cornish; in effect a 'wish-list' of developmental need:

Vision 1: Where there is opportunity for all who wish to learn Cornish, at all levels of education. The targets here include an accessible education programme from pre-school to higher and adult education; effective partnership between statutory bodies, the formal education sector and the voluntary sector; the development of new ways to access the Cornish language and support systems both for new learners and newly fluent speakers; effective, modern teaching resources; research programmes which inform both the resource base and the process of language planning.

Vision 2: Where the learning of Cornish is valued in the same way as the learning of other languages. The targets here include high standards in the teaching of the Cornish language; training provision for voluntary teachers, effective skills sharing and delivery mechanisms; recognized qualifications in the language for learners and teachers; a change in those perceptions of Cornish which form barriers to teaching and learning leading to a greater take-up of the language by young people.

Vision 3: Where the Cornish language is recognised in public life as a valued and visible part of Cornwall's distinct culture and heritage. The targets here include the wider use of Cornish in public life, particularly through use in signage and promotional materials; effective partnerships between the language sector and public bodies; more prominent use of Cornish at public and cultural events; effective use of media and new technologies in assisting Cornish language activity and greater media exposure.

Vision 4: Where the Cornish language is recognized as contributing positively to the Cornish economy. The targets here are the encouragement of new business activity in the sector and recognize and develop existing activity; the encouragement of the use of Cornish where appropriate to assist Cornish branding; the exploration and encouragement of the use of Cornish to support cultural tourism initiatives.

Vision 5: Where the Cornish language enjoys respect alongside the other regional and minority languages of the UK such that its standing is enhanced. The targets here are strong partnerships between public bodies and voluntary language groups; the achievement of further recognition and support as and when appropriate; the development and maintenance of links with other European language communities.

Vision 6: Where the Cornish language has established ways of working, including a strong support infrastructure appropriate to for its needs which will enable Visions 1–5 to be realized. The targets here are the development of a support infrastructure appropriate to the changing circumstances of the language; the development of centres of activity; the establishment of structures for monitoring progress and ensuring on-going consultation; a single written form of Cornish for use in official documentation and formal education.[27]

These are all laudable and important aims but the success of these will need careful monitoring. The final target would appear the most difficult to achieve, given the well-documented 'internal review' of the language,[28] or put another way, its subdivision into three or more 'distinctive' systems or dialects.[29] There is no equivalent document regarding Cornu-English. Perhaps even more curiously, in the whole of the *Stratejy rag an Tavas Kernewek/Strategy for the Cornish Language*, there is no mention of the very 'corresponding culture' that is necessary for a more authentic development of Cornish culture. Once again, Cornu-English is the poor relation. For cultural commentators on Cornwall, this conclusion should come as no surprise, nor should the series of visions hoped for in the *Strategy* document. However, they do follow conventional methodological ventures in terms of language planning—those in Wales, Scotland and Éire—and most notably the Isle of Man.[30]

Crystal's work and the aims of the *Strategy* above reflect the usual conceptions about the prevention of language death, the reduction of loss and recovery. As Ichiro Yuhara notes, 'despite Crystal's good intention, his analysis is rather superficial, innocently ethnocentric (reflecting particularly Western perspectives) and ultimately deceiving. Though he admits that generalization of various factors surrounding language endangerment is difficult, he attributes language death to speakers' lack of pride in their language (which leads him to say "language suicide") and ultimately in their culture'.[31] I agree with Yuhara's understanding of Crystal since, fundamentally, language (and I include Cornu-English here) becomes endangered not because of the speakers' lack of pride in it, but put simply, because of their adaptive response to changing socio-economic conditions. Lack of pride in their language or dialect has nothing to do with it. Put another way, a language or dialect will decline and die when its speakers no longer find it necessary to speak it while they are being integrated and absorbed into a more influential socio-economic community, which in turn gives them a more vital and hospitable environment for survival.

GENETICS AND PARASITES: AN ALTERNATIVE VISION OF LANGUAGE CHANGE IN CORNWALL

Now let us reconfigure the approach to Cornish and Cornu-English in the light of the methodological practice developed by Mufwene. As a scholar, Mufwene is interested in language evolution and ecology, and from the outset he argues that the kinds of systems outlined by Crystal and, indeed, contained within the *Strategy* document, are much more complex. The structures and pragmatics of real language evolution need to be explained in alternative ways: what he terms 'genetic linguistics'.[32] Therefore, if we are interested in the processes of promoting Cornish or Cornu-English there needs to be more attention not only to the socio-economic and ethnographic environment in which a language has evolved (what Mufwene terms its 'external ecology')[33] —such as the contact setting and power relations between groups of speakers—but also to the nature of the co-existence of the units and principles of a linguistic system before and/or during the change (its 'internal ecology')[34]. In Cornwall the ecological systems are complex because we are dealing with the revival of an initially 'moribund' language, with its own external and internal ecology. Likewise, Cornu-English has its own external and internal ecology. Mufwene then argues that these 'external and internal ecologies play significant roles in determining the evolutionary trajectories of a language', which he analogizes with 'a biological parasitic species'.[35] Crucially, and this is why Mufwene's theories are applicable in Cornwall, he argues for the predominance of populations 'consisting of several coexistent species';[36] in Cornwall there is English, Cornu-English and Cornish.

Mufwene deals specifically with the development of creoles, and there is a need to assert the difference here between a creole and dialect of English, such as Cornu-English. According to Crystal, a creole is 'a pidgin language which has become the mother tongue of a community—a definition which emphasizes that pidgins and creoles are two stages in a single process of development. Pidgins are systems of communication which grow up amongst people who want to talk to each other, usually for reasons of trade.'[37] They are 'contact languages', but when within a multilingual community increasing numbers of people use the pidgin, then this expansion is known as a creole. More research needs to be completed, as to whether early forms of English in Cornwall worked in this way. A Dialect or variety of English (or another base language) remains a Dialect for as long as it shares a common core of features with other dialects or varieties of that base language. Crucially then, dialects of the same language are mutually intelligible. A dialect is different since speakers who have distinctive regional dialect will have a distinctive regional accent. We must note that it is possible to have a regional accent yet speak dialect which conveys nothing about geographical origin.

However, at the same time, at the various points of language transfer in Cornwall from, say, 1549 onwards,[38] it has been ecology which has rolled the dice in terms of the competitions and selections which have determined the way in which not only the competing language (English) prevails, but also which units and principles are selected from Cornish into the prevailing variety.[39] A couple of examples here would be helpful: W.G. Orchard's volume *A Glossary of Mining Terms* (1991)[40] contains many Cornish language terms and vocabulary which were retained in the mining community long after Cornish had disappeared; and though a more self-consciously 'revivalist' endeavour, the same principle might be applied to Robert Morton Nance's *A Glossary of Cornish Sea Words* (1963). These three brief examples of entries show how the 'ecology' of fishing gave rise to the 'natural selection':

pedn-borbas. The three-bearded rockling, *Gaudropsarus mediterraneus* (Linn.), Mousehole. [Other species of fish of this genus are included here, but the three-bearded rocklings of Cornish waters remain to be worked out by naturalists.] C. *pen (pedn) barfus*, 'bearded head'. PEDN-A-BORBAS and PEDNY-BORBAS are variants. Although many Welsh fish-names are formed of pen with some qualifying word, this is almost the only surviving Cornish example. See BARFUS, BORBAS, PLUMZUGEN.

pedn-ha-garen. Fish too lean to be saleable. St Ives. C. *pen ha garen*, head and shank (or stem), W. *garan*, B. *garenn*.

pedn-ha-teen. C. *pen ha tyn*, head and tail, descriptive of the manner of packing pilchards in a barrel, used in the Pilchard Verses. This is reversed in W. *tin ben*, with the same meaning. The fish are packed alternately with heads out and tails all together in the middle in a rosette pattern, and *vice versa*.[41]

The twin ecologies of mining and fishing determined the survival. Presently the ecology of, say, the global media and news, determine the transfer back into Cornish. This selection is actively made in the pages of the Cornish-language magazine *An Gannas*, whose back pages, 'Tros an Bys Bras', consider contemporary politics and philosophy.[42]

Mufwene goes further. Put simply, his theory argues that languages can be compared to 'parasitic species' in biology. These species change according to how their hosts (or speakers) adapt to their own changing living conditions. Therefore, to explain language death or decline, it is imperative to understand the external ecology alluded to above: the environmental factors which surround its speakers, in terms of how it is favourable to them. Necessarily, however, it needs to be considered in terms of costs and benefits, disadvantages and advantaged for the speakers. It is this which Crystal does not consider, and on the whole, what is lacking in the *Strategy* document on Cornish language. We might go further, and argue that the proposals may actually only work for language preservation and not for language revitalization. More work is needed, therefore, in language evolution in Cornwall to take into account a realistic social and historical context; certainly one in which Cornu-English is crucial.

Much of this is, of course, profoundly relevant for anyone promoting, writing or speaking Cornish, although is it doubtful that the contributors to the present *Stratejy rag an Tavas Kernewek/Strategy for the Cornish Language* will have considered Mufwene's theories; the strategy itself can then be criticized, to use Yuhara's term, as being 'innocently ethnocentric'. The notion of green socio-linguistics and the theory of the ecology of language evolution directly relevant to Cornish. It is also profoundly relevant to Cornu-English, which directly fits the application made by Mufwene onto what we may conveniently term the 'creolization' of English in Cornwall, after the transition from Cornish. English in Cornwall has been developing its own inherent traditions, grammar and vocabulary for well over four hundred years, but there are frequent concerns in the letters pages of the local press, in cultural organizations such as the Cornish Gorseth,[43] and by dialect practitioners that Cornu-English (like Cornish in then eighteenth century) is itself dying. In 2003 one of those practitioners, Joy Stevenson, wrote: 'One sign of change in Cornwall has been the decline of our lovely old dialect . . . Over the years I have recorded our dialect I sometimes feel that dialect recorders, speakers and writers are looked on as licensed fools . . . The day we no longer hear the rich sounds of it will be the death knell of a Cornishness which can never be resurrected or put into a museum.'[44]

Yet these concerns and laments have always been expressed in Cornish culture. Eighty years earlier, Robert Morton Nance rendered the following prologue to the manuscript of his *The Cledry Plays: Drolls of Old Cornwall for Village Acting and Home Reading* (eventually published in 1956):

> Old Cornwall, too, is changing,
> As surely if as slowly—
> New words and ways estranging
> With time transform us wholly—
> The tongue of our forebears cherished
> Is lost from living speeches;
> Yet, as of vessels perished
> The board drift up on beaches,
> So here and there, time still may spare
> Some ancientry that lingers—
> Let's, as each goes, its eyelids close
> At least with loving finger.[45]

One hundred years before Nance, an early nineteenth-century imagining of this loss is also to be found in the poetry of Henry Quick (1792–1857) which offers a strikingly familiar image of linguistic and cultural change:

Our Cornish drolls are dead, each one;
The fairies from their haunts have gone;
There's scarce a witch in all the land,
The world has grown so learn'd and grand.[46]

I have argued elsewhere that we should be sceptical about this kind of lament,[47] when we are actually witnessing dynamic language evolution. One further note of caution ought to be added. Traditionally, there has been what we may term a 'regionalization of dialects' within Cornwall,[48] but as the twentieth century unfolded, to an extent this regionalization of dialects was altered, so that there are now fewer identifiable features within, say, the vocabulary or grammar base. Although different elements between Cornu-English in west, mid- and east Cornwall are perhaps identifiable,[49] there is a sense that the fight to retrain Cornu-English has brought about its own internal compromises. I recognize this in my own verse.[50] There are certainly also practitioners in Cornwall who, in order to sustain dialect, have adopted what Crystal usefully terms 'heritage dialects or accents',[51] particularly in literature (especially in historical romantic fiction), on television or in film, or in performance. At its most reductive, this is seen in the following verse about the 2005 Royal Wedding:

I wuz waitin' fer the postman. Ess, I wuz waitin' every day,
Jus' to see that man from the Royal Mail cummin' down our way.
Ess, I wuz waitin' fer the postman, in the sun an' in the rain,
I wuz watchin' out each mornin', but alas, I watched in vain.
See, I'd bin lookin' fer several weeks, wey, ever since we 'eard
That ol' Charlie, Duke ov Cornwall, into action 'ad been stirred.
When I 'eard there, on the telly, the engagement wuz announced,
I wuz dancin' in the 'allway – in the kitchen then I bounced!
'I'm jus' sure to be invited,' to faather then I said.
I'm bound to go to Windsor, to see ol' Charlie wed.[52]

Even though the writer is operating in mid-Cornwall, she uses the term 'faather' [father], which is more associated with speech around Camborne and Redruth. These practitioners may in fact not reflect the real state of dialect usage but rather persist in injecting life into concepts that are in fact moribund or near dead, for cultural revivalist reasons. It is not that far removed from prize-winning entries in the Cornish Gorseth's annual dialect competition. The worrying aspect of such heritage dialects or accents is that they are in fact 'false'—both geographically and culturally, as in the above example. The position of the dialect speaker is also negated: Windsor is cultured, Cornwall is not. Twenty-first-century Cornu-English speakers are still prone to much forelock-tugging. Given this we might at some future point end up with a Cornu-English literature which has no bearing on what is being spoken on the streets of St Dennis, St Ives or St Minver. The alignment of dialect with a particular phase of Cornish history (Cousin Jack and Jenny, mining, bal-maidens and fish jowsters) does nothing to help the situation either, since it falsifies the historical context, projecting a mythic nineteenth-century version of Cornwall forwards in time. Thankfully, other practitioners appear to be aiming to 'keep it real'. A strong example is to be found in the storytelling work of Will Coleman:

> 'Tom Snook!' said Mrs Roscrow, 'Your pig is in my begonia bed, munching its way through the flowers!'
> 'Oh Heng!' said Tom, 'I best come and sort it out!'
> Sure enough piggy was out again destroying Mrs Roscrow's prize flowerbeds.
> Once again, it took half the men, boys and girls of Churchtown to round piggy up and get it back into Tom's sty and, once more, Tom had to pay for the damage.
> 'Right, we'll keep you in, boy!' said Tom.
> He put chicken wire around the sty. But the pig still got out.[53]

Although a different genre, there is subtlety and dialectical sophistication in the voice here: 'Heng!', 'I best . . .' and '. . . boy!' mediate patterns of real speech of present day Cornwall. Put in Mufwene's terms—writers like Coleman, and a limited number of other practitioners aside—the ecological conditions for the survival or even evolution of Cornu-English are not right. The general moribund nature of this situation has not been helped by the fact that, as both Philip Payton and I have argued,[54] the Cornish Revival has tended to eschew Cornu-English or lead it only in the direction of the pithy, self-depreciating comic narrative, prioritizing instead Cornish, which has been deemed the appropriate language for a 'would-be' nation like Cornwall. Interestingly, although it is not much commented upon (perhaps because it is now so long established), policy statements and manifestos from Cornwall's main 'devolutionist' party Mebyon Kernow always set out their plans for the Cornish language,[55] but never feature any awareness of Cornu-English: bizarrely since this is the *lingua franca* of the very voters they wish to capture. This may even go some way to explaining Mebyon Kernow's limited success at both local council and parliamentary elections.[56] From this we may infer that the party's name itself is not right 'ecologically': it is an imposed species, in effect. There are other 'environmentally unfriendly' acts of imposed language onto Cornwall from a variety of sources; some, like Mebyon Kernow, pro-Cornish (the Gorseth ceremony in Cornish with its Anglican undertones,[57] the alternate labelling of pagan space in Penwith);[58] others remarkably hostile and ignorant of cultural politics: the *South West of England Regional Development Agency* and the well-documented concerns over *English Heritage*.[59]

DECONSTRUCTING IDIOLECTS, DIALECTS AND THE CELTIC SUBSTRATUM

The implications of this are crucial in our understanding and future development of Deacon's 'Critical Cornish Studies'. In Robert Penhallurick's influential collection of essays on the philosophy of Dialect Study,[60] contributors grapple with some of the issues which tend to have been taken for granted in those branches of linguistics concerned with regional variation in language, providing a thorough re-examination of the principal constructs and object of the study of dialectology. One of the most important essays within this volume is 'Dialectology and Deconstruction' in which Nicholas Royle provides the foundations for twenty-first century dialectology, removing the antiquarian, not to mention the modernist, project of the dialectician.[61] The unexpected parallels of dialectology and deconstruction relates well to Jacques Derrida's original intentions: writers and dialecticians attempt to impose ordering strategies on language, but these usually prove to be inadequate.[62] A deconstructive reading is a 'double-reading' since it acknowledges the way in which the writer attempts to order things, but then points to the contradictions and problems in the text, the complications that the writers cannot pull into his system. This should be considered in the light of several Cornish dialecticians who have tried to order 'Cornu-English' but have continued to note exceptions to the rule.[63]

The observer's own response can also be deconstructed, because he or she is trying to create order where none exists. Derrida's method is to look at individual texts, searching for the contradictions, and particularly in his studies of philosophical writing, to examine the gaps in what appears to be a logical argument. Royle applies this method to dialect study, aware of the fact that his own readings can be deconstructed, for all readings are misreadings in that they attempt to impose ordering strategies. He argues four crucial points which have much relevance to language and literary studies in Cornwall. First of all, 'the dialectologist works with language, across and between languages, in a language which is neither one thing nor the other';[64] secondly, 'far from seeing dialectology as an outmoded or dying discipline, one might see it on the eve of another beginning, a quite different articulation and elaboration';[65] thirdly, '[Deconstruction] is not "anti-voice", nor is it primarily concerned simply with a reversal (if such a thing were possible) of the perceived hierarchies of speech/ writing and a consequent privileging of "writing" over "speech". Rather it can increasingly be seen that the most intimate concern is with speech and with the experience of voice . . . the overflowing of dialogue form, a polyphonic tracery';[66] fourthly, 'dialectology shares with deconstruction a love or memory and archive, a respect for the strangeness of remains, margins and the idiomatic; it has also from the beginning, been a discipline attentive to the voices of the dead, a responsiveness to the ghostly character of the present and of itself'.[67]

Royle's consideration of this respect for 'the strangeness of remains, margins and the idiomatic' shared by deconstruction and dialectology, applies well not only of course to Cornu-English, but Cornish, and the neglected field of different dialects within historical and contemporary Cornish. Mufwene's response to the deconstructive process of dialectology is his exploration of linguistic systems. Language transmission, be it Cornu-English or Cornish, is modelled on the idea of the gene in biology.[68] He qualifies this by observing that none of his theories need to be analogous to biology, but that it is a convenient concept for him. Mufwene draws on Chomsky's established idea of a distinction between internalized language (I-language) and externalized language (E-language).[69] An I-language is basically an idiolect, an individual's system of a language, whereas an E-language is the set of sentences produced by a population speaking a particular language. All kinds of questions arise from this—to what extent does the Cornish of an I-language transcend and pass into the E-language? What proportion of E-language vocabulary and grammar (derived from Cornish) enter the I-language of individuals in the past? These debates are interesting but fail to address the crucial question of dialectology: what roles do individual speakers and communities play in language change?

Mufwene suggests the answer may lie in what he terms 'feature pools', which are the results of the blending of languages and/or dialects. Three models of language development might be applied in the Cornish context. The first has as inputs varieties and regional variations of traditional Cornish which are fed into the 'feature pool'.[70] The 'feature pool' works as an arena where grammatical functions, need and what is known as 'blending inheritance'[71] compete with other new inputs—in Cornwall's case, English. Because of the nature of the 'feature pool', the original coded features of Cornish are modified or 'exapted' to fit the new system. The ethnographic and symbiotic output is both an altered and blended Cornish, and an English with Cornish features: what some observers—such as Filppula, Klemola and Pitkänen—would call a 'Celtic substratum'.[72]

A second model might be seen in Cornu-English and its geographical variations being accorded input into the 'feature pool'—in this arena biologically competing with English Englishes, global Englishes and American Englishes. The blending might see a mixture of Cornu-English with contemporary urban slang, surfing lingo, or web and texting grammars; it could also see it wiped out completely if, paradoxically, demarginalization of Cornu-English speakers occurs. Complexity is added to this by the various Cornu-Englishes spoken and written in the territories to which the Cornish travelled: North America, Australasia and Southern Africa, not to mention the variations between speakers in those territories; for example, in North America, there are clear differences between Cornu-American-English in Grass Valley, California and that used in south-western Wisconsin.

A third model is seen in the complex 'feature pool' of Revived Cornish, where the inputs of one language (Unified, Kemmyn, Modern, Unified Cornish Revised) are very varied. The final output and perhaps over-riding 'vision' desired by the *Strategy* document is 'a single written form of Cornish for use in official documentation and formal education'.[73] Deconstruction and dialectology tell us that such complications cannot always be resolved. When I debated this issue (which has consumed so much passionate scholarship inside and outside of Cornwall) regarding Cornish with Salikoko S. Mufwene, he was not at all surprised that so small a language had so much 'ecological' variation.[74] Many African languages, such as Voltaic, Kwa, Ubangian and Mande, have what he terms 'compromise varieties from among diverse dialects of the same language' and this is not to be seen as 'negative' but an indicator of health, of evolution.

The above examples might seem quite doom-laden if one considers the nineteenth-century, moribund nature of Cornish. It is a model which seems to fit all that Crystal and other socio-linguists and dialectologists have noted about language change. Crucially, however, Mufwene notes that, 'there is no particular input-to-output ratio of number of varieties. There may be fewer outputs than input varieties and vice-versa, just as the number of outputs may be equal. What matters is that the structures of the output and input varieties are not identical.'[75] Cornish and Cornu-English are not dead. Mufwene concludes that ecological systems do not always work in logical ways, and languages are the same.

BEYOND CULTURAL MATERIALISM: 'THE LITERARY SYSTEM'

Having outlined new models for dealing with language and socio-linguistics in Cornwall, I would now like to progress to a new model for literary studies, which is closely related to the ecological system proposed by Mufwene and Royle's re-assessment of dialectology explored above. To present a context for the second model I wish to discuss, I need to re-assert the principal method of literary scholarship I have long espoused as being appropriate to the needs of literary scholarship in Cornwall.[76] This is Cultural Materialism, and I, in common with many, was introduced to this theory through reading *Political Shakespeare: New Essays in Cultural Materialism* edited by Jonathan Dollimore and Alan Sinfield, first published in 1985.[77] Dollimore and Sinfield initially define cultural materialism against 'traditional approaches' to literary texts, which, at the time of writing, they suggested were fragmenting. In direct contrast to the standard values and goals of literary criticism, cultural materialism offers

> a combination of historical context, theoretical method, political commitment and textual analysis. Historical context undermines the transcendent significance traditionally accorded to the literary text and allows us to recover its histories; theoretical method detaches the text from immanent criticism which seeks only to reproduce it in its own terms; socialist and feminist commitment confronts conservative categories in which most criticism has hitherto been con-ducted; textual analysis locates the critique of traditional approaches where it cannot be ignored. We call this 'cultural materialism'.[78]

Whilst applications of this theory—or derivations or varieties of it (such as 'New Historicism' in the United States of America)—have been made by a number of scholars operating on Cornish literary studies, the methodology is not entirely satisfactory.[79] Of particular difficulty has been the political commitment, which for Dollimore and Sinfield was socialist, but never 'devolutionist'. The operation of 'cultural materialism', ironically, seemed to best fit 'traditional' literary situations and only rarely quite got to grips with Wynn Thomas' 'corresponding cultures'. While cultural materialism seemed to fit with reading against the grain, and in particular responses to say, feminist or queer readings of literary texts, the model was too inflexible to always be applied with complete satisfaction on minority literatures, where to use Dollimore and Sinfield's term 'recovering histories' was more of a challenge, particularly in the light of larger, often imperialist literatures located nearby and those literatures which crossed 'borders' of cultural activity. [80]

Like the work of Salikoko S. Mufwene on African dialects and language evolution, the other methodological thread is derived from the academy in Israel. Although operating separately from 'cultural materialist' scholarship in Europe or 'New Historicism' in the United States of America, the University of Tel Aviv and in particular the work of Itamar Even-Zohar (Professor of Poetics and Comparative Literature) offers an enhancement to the general theories of 'cultural materialism' which are apt for Cornwall, but refines the struggle for power within literary activity. Much of his scholarship has been shaped by work on Hebrew and Russian literature. Even-Zohar defines this struggle as 'The Literary System'. This is 'the network of relations that is hypothesized to obtain between a number of activities called "literary", and consequently these activities themselves observed via that network' or 'the complex of activities, or any section thereof, for which systemic relations can be hypothesized to support the option of considering them literary'.[81] This might usefully be considered an 'ecological' perspective as well.

He further adds that the literary system is part of the hierarchy within the polysystem, where the polysystem is the term used to describe the whole network of systems, literary or extraliterary, in society. Therefore, like cultural materialism, it includes all kinds of writing, from canonical texts (in Cornwall, this might include in the Cornish continuum: *Ordinalia, Beunans Meriasek* and *John of Chyanhor*,[82] and in the English continuum Daphne du Maurier's *Jamaica Inn*, Charles Causley's *Figgie Hobbin* and A. L. Rowse's *A Cornish Childhood*),[83] those which have been accepted as superior within the hierarchy in the literary system, to those that are non-canonical (say an anonymous comic pamphlet distributed at Keskerdh Kernow celebrations in 1997, *Puskes, Sten ha Emmets: Satirical Humour for the Cornish*, or the Cornish-language literary magazine *Delyow Derow/Oak Leaves*).[84]

Even-Zohar argues in *Polysystem Theory* that 'as a rule, the center or the whole polysystem is identical with the most prestigious canonised repertoire'.[85] Thus, the literary system is a complex entity, in which each item is understood in relationship to all other items in the system. There is a permanent struggle taking place (perhaps emphasized in new books on Cornwall for sale in *Ottakars* bookshop in Truro, where external publishers compete against local ones,[86] or external authors on Cornwall compete against indigenous ones),[87] not only within the literary system but between it and other systems in the polysystem, a struggle for power and for centrality. However, it is this struggle that is the cause of the dynamism at the heart of each literary system. It is not a static thing, but on the contrary, in constant change, development and movement.

Literature is, thus, always in a dynamic relationship with Cornish society. Although there is a constant struggle for power and centrality, there is actually a great amount of flexibility and openness in these terms, which are applicable not only to Cornwall but to other literary systems as well. Correspondingly, since the literary system is in a dynamic network of relations with other systems, so the Cornish literary system is involved with other literary systems—for example, medieval links with Brittany and Wales (*Beunans Meriasek* and *Beunans Ke*), links to Germany and Italy (especially with the mobilisation of the Tristan narrative),[88] links to Plymouth and Devon, links to centres of publication: Exeter, Tiverton, Bristol, Oxford and London. Likewise, with the period from 1850 to the present, when a new literary system was being developed—that of writing in Revived Cornish, it would be impossible to understand this new movement in isolation.[89] It was a movement with some precedents in earlier periods in Cornwall,[90] yet in other ways completely different. It could be read as a response to a feared 'Celtic twilight'. On the other hand, it is characteristic of other nations or 'would-be' nations in development.[91]

The literary system also emphasizes the dynamic and changeable character of literature and the fact that a constant 'ecological' struggle for power (the survival of the fittest) is taking place within the literary system itself as between it and other literatures. This is witnessed in the competing paradigms of, for instance, the Daphne du Maurier Festival of Arts and Literature, where external and internal writers share the same forum.[92] The term also helps to emphasize the changeable and dynamic aspects of new literatures, embodied in, say, contributors to texts such as *Poetry Cornwall* and *Scryfa*.[93] The criteria on which those writers become either accepted or rejected by the hierarchy are dependant on the poetics of the time. The Cornish language poet, Tim Saunders, is a case in point, since for a very long time his work was rejected by those active in the Cornish Revival, yet his importance in the continuum is now established.[94] Given all of this it would then be possible to understand micro-literary systems, such as the proliferation of Anglo-Cornish literature during the second half of the twentieth century which emerged from around St Austell and the china-clay mining region.

All aspects of the literary system are in a complementary relationship: the writer depends not only on his or her readers but on other factors within the literary system and within society, and some of these factors are, for example, supply and demand. Even-Zohar, like Dollimore and Sinfield, sees literature as ecologically inseparable from society. As in commerce, there is a relationship between the consumer and the producer, an interdependence, so in this system, there is the ideas that the writer needs society and society needs the writer to produce a certain text in line within the demands of the market. He or she is not the solitary figure that the Romantic Movement had postulated, but someone who partakes in the dynamic struggle for power which is so much a part of humanity. Two figures who demonstrate this notion within the Cornish context are the poets John Harris and Robert Stephen Hawker, even though they are often held up as the examples of the Romantic Movement in Cornwall.[95] Yet writing is much more complex than this and, in order to explain the complexities of the literary system, Even-Zohar uses a schematic:

INSTITUTION [context]
REPERTOIRE [code]

PRODUCER [addresser]————————[addressee] CONSUMER

['writer']   ['reader']

MARKET [contact/channel]
PRODUCT [message][96]

We can now examine these terms in detail and make application of them in a 'Critical Cornish Studies'. Even-Zohar defines the Institution as the aggregate of factors involved with the maintenance of literature as a socio-cultural activity. The institution therefore governs the norms of this activity, sanctioning some and rejecting others. Being empowered by the dominating social institutions also remunerates and reprimands those who work as producers and agents. Official culture also determines who, and which products, will be remembered by a community for a longer period of time.[97] In Cornwall examples of these literary products might range from the iconoclastic figure of Robert Morton Nance as Cornish Language Revivalist, the corpus of folktales recorded by Robert Hunt, or Winston Graham's *Poldark* series of novels. Specifically, the institution would be comprised of some of the producers (Cornish writers), critics (in newspapers, such as the *Guardian*, the *Observer*, the *Western Morning News*, the *West Briton*), publishing houses (University of Exeter Press, Dyllansow Truran, Tor

Mark, Halsgrove, Cornish Hillside Publications, Patten Press, Francis Boutle, Cornwall Editions, Alison Hodge, the Cornish Language Board, Teere ha Tavaz), periodicals (*Cornish World/Bys Kernowyon, An Baner Kernewek/The Cornish Banner, Poetry Cornwall/ Bardhonyeth Kernow*), clubs (Lanner Writers, Truro Library writers), groups of writers (D. M. Thomas' 'Stray Dogs'), government bodies (English Heritage), schools (A Sense of Place project), universities (Combined Universities in Cornwall, University of Exeter, University of Plymouth, the Open University in the South West) and mass media (Carlton Westcountry and the BBC).

The Producer can be defined as the writer, although in Even-Zohar's view, there ought to be an emphasis on what he defines as the active role of the writer in the society. Thus the writer plays an important political role apart from generating texts.[98] The political nature of the writer therefore carries much importance in a culture with as complex an 'ecology' as that to be found in twenty-first century Cornwall. The political role of that writer then plays much importance posthumously: witness the interest in the two mid-Cornwall writers Daphne du Maurier and A. L. Rowse.[99] Jack Clemo continues to have a politic attached to his writing some ten years after his death.[100] Just as the Producer's role is complex, so is that of the Consumer, since he or she is more than simply the reader. He or she is the consumer of texts. As a member of this ecological community a consumer can be exposed directly and indirectly to different texts. Indirect consumers are those members of the Cornish community who are exposed to literary fragments, idioms and interviews. Direct consumers are more involved in literary activity. There are not only single consumers in the literary system but groups of consumers whom we may term the public.[101] Thus literature in Cornwall is actually read in a communal way, and not just by one sector.

It is also important to consider the Market. Even-Zohar defines this as 'the aggregate of factors involved with the selling and buying of literary products and with the promotion of types of consumption'.[102] This is standard cultural materialism, and while this may work else-where in these islands, in Cornwall it is sometimes the very absence of a market that is interesting, since this may directly influence a writer's decision to stay within his or her own community, and also the type of literature he or she produces. We only need look at publication in the Cornish-language community to understand this phenomenon. Even-Zohar clarifies this by commenting on how the writer is affected by the exigencies of the public: 'In the absence of a market, there is no socio-cultural space where any aspect of literary activities can gain any ground. Moreover, a restricted market naturally restricts the possibilities of literature to evolve as a socio-cultural activity. So proliferating the market lies in the very interest of the literary system.'[103] In short, what is needed is some kind of Cornish feeling of 'nationhood', which is something that has ebbed and flowed over the centuries, and clearly it would be too easy to say that this is something felt now rather than in previous ages.

The Product is 'any performed (or performable) set of signs . . . Thus, any outcome of any activity whatsoever can be considered "a product", whatever its ontological manifestation may be'.[104] Clearly Even-Zohar gives cultural significance to varieties of text in all its manifestations. Different levels of texts are important entities for consumption; one only needs to look at children's literature to see the relevance of this.[105] The Repertoire is closely related to the Product. This is the part of the literary system that 'designates the aggregate of rules and materials which govern both the making and use of any given product'.[106] To Even-Zohar, this may be likened to the combination of the 'grammar' and 'lexicon' of any given 'language'.[107] Importantly, the Repertoire is 'the shared knowledge necessary for producing and (understanding) a text'[108] with and against other products of the system. Another issue is the fact that when a literary system is young 'its repertoire may be limited, which renders it more disposed to using other available systems (for example, other languages, cultures, literatures)',[109] and this may be the case with Revived Cornish; or even any re-energised Cornu-English. Repertoire may sound like a 'literary tradition' but it is not that. Neither is it the 'continuum' of writing within a culture. Even-Zohar's model is more ecological: it is rather more the 'network of positions into which the various elements are inserted'.[110]

Even-Zohar's model of a literary system is not perfect, but it offers a much better critical framework for understanding literary activity within Cornwall, not just with texts emerging in the twenty-first century, but also throughout history. The concepts of Institution, Producer, Consumer, Market, Product and Repertoire give better academic treatment to our reading of texts. Combined with Mufwene's ecological model of language evolution, we have two very sophisticated critical tools which may go some way to shaping a more 'Critical Cornish Studies'.

CONCLUSION: BUILDING OV UT UP 'GAIN

My hope is that these provisional notes go some way in responding to Deacon's wish for a 'Critical Cornish Studies'. Cornwall's unique cultural position means that its linguistic and literary 'ecology' is highly distinctive. If theories such as those of Mufwene and Even-Zohar can help mould a more self-reflective forum, making the academy here more 'critical practitioners', then that is for the common good. It is difficult, however, to develop this kind of critical practice when so few are aware of the importance of the debate. Language and literary studies is but one area that needs reconfiguring.

There are still conceptual debates which, sadly, are absent within Cornish Studies. Philosophy, the History of Cornish Ideas, anthropology, architecture, visual history (beyond the St Ives, Newlyn and Lamorna Schools) and folk art are gaping holes in the critical forums already established in Cornwall, yet they are where the best 'critical' scholarship is emerging in similar territories.[111] Scholars operating in the field of Cornish Studies need to expand and follow new horizons. Can Cornish Studies move beyond the realms of the 'trad' Cornish subject matter of mining, Methodism and emigration? In addition, with a bewildering plethora of historical studies—mainly of a chronological nature—being published, maybe it is time to re-evaluate the kind of history being written. The layeredness and continuum of the Cornish mind need 'Critical Cornish Studies' too, just in the way that Ackroyd, Giles and Middleton, and Weight have treated English-ness,[112] so too, must we treat Cornishness. Here, the ethos of Pinter's *Mountain Language* is a long way away. The good thing is that this 'critical lerrups' is not going to go away; indeed, it is a healthy and ecologically sound position for a culture to be in.

ACKNOWLEDGEMENTS

In the preparation of this chapter, I am indebted to Salikoko S. Mufwene, Joan C. Beal, Piotr Stalmaszczyk, Graham Shorrocks, Andrew C. Symons, John C. C. Probert, Antonio Raúl de Toro Santos and Anne MacCarthy for their illuminating discussions with me regarding Cornish and Cornu-English.

NOTES AND REFERENCES

1. Harold Pinter, *Mountain Language*, London, 1988, p. 23. The play was first performed at the National Theatre, London on 20 October 1988.
2. See Harold Pinter, *Plays: One*, London, 1985; *Plays: Two*, London, 1985; *Plays Three*, London, 1985.
3. See, for example, Matthew Spriggs, 'Where Cornish was Spoken and When: A Provisional Synthesis', in Philip Payton (ed.), *Cornish Studies: Eleven*, Exeter, 2003, pp. 228–69; Sharon Lowena, '"*Noscitur*" A *Sociis*': Jenner, Duncombe-Jewell and their Milieu', in Philip Payton (ed.) *Cornish Studies: Twelve*, Exeter, 2004, pp. 61–87.
4. Bernard Deacon, 'From "Cornish Studies" to "Critical Cornish Studies": Reflections on Methodology', in Philip Payton (ed.), 2004, pp. 13–29.
5. Ibid.

6. Alan M. Kent, 'Cornish Politics, Society and Literature: A Plea for Correlation', in *An Banner Kernewek/The Cornish Banner*, No. 72, 1993.

7. Alan M. Kent, 'A New Cultural Poetics', in *An Banner Kernewek/The Cornish Banner*, No. 78, 1994.

8. See, for example, Denys Val Baker, *The Timeless Land: The Creative Spirit in Cornwall*, Bath, 1973; *A View from Land's End: Writers Against a Cornish Background*, London, 1982; F. E. Halliday, *A History of Cornwall*, London, 1959; *A Cornish Chronicle: The Carews of Antony from Armada to Civil War*, Newton Abbot, 1967; A. L. Rowse, *Quiller Couch: A Portrait of 'Q'*, London, 1988; *A. L. Rowse's Cornwall*, London, 1988.

9. See the contributions to Philip Payton (ed.), *Cornish Studies: Ten*, Exeter, 2002, which celebrated ten years of academic progress.

10. Kent, 1994.

11. See Cornwall County Council, *Strategy for the Cornish Language: Consultation Draft*, Truro 2004a. Three Cornish language versions of this document were produced reflecting the three 'micro-dialects' of Cornish: *Strategy rag an tavas Kernewek: Kens Scryf rag Cusulyans*, *Strateji rag an Tavas Kernuack: Screef rag cossyllians* and *Strateji rag an Yeth Kernewek: Kyns Skriv rag Keskusulyans*. See also Cornwall County Council, *Stratejy rag an Tavas Kernewek/Strategy for the Cornish Language*, Truro, 2004b.

12. Kent, 1994.

13. David Crystal, *Language Death*, Cambridge, 2000, p. 162.

14. See Alan M. Kent, 'Bringin' the Dunkey down from the Carn: Cornu-English in Context', in Hildegard L. C. Tristram (ed.), *The Celtic Englishes IV*, Heidelberg, forthcoming.

15. M. Wynn Thomas, *Corresponding Cultures: The Two Literatures of Wales*, Cardiff, 1999.

16. Salikoko S. Mufwene, 'Analogs Anywhere: The flow of highway traffic and language evolution', in *Contemporary Linguistics: Perspectives on Language Evolution*, 3, 2002, pp. 39–58.

17. Salikoko S. Mufwene, *The Ecology of Language Evolution*, Cambridge, 2001.

18. David Crystal, *The Cambridge Encyclopedia of the English Language*, Cambridge, 1995.

19. Daniel Nettle and Suzanne Romaine, *Vanishing Voices: The Extinction of the World's Languages*, Oxford, 2000; Mark Ably, *Spoken Here: Travels among Threatened Languages*, London, 2003.

20. Crystal, 2000, pp. 130–43.

21. See Derek Williams (ed.), *Henry and Katharine Jenner: A Celebration of Cornwall's Culture, Language and Identity*, London, 2004; Lowena, 2004.

22. www.sense-of-place.cornwall.gov.uk. The projects has three main aims: to foster creativity leading to fun in the classroom and experiential learning, to forge links between subject areas and generate innovative teaching and learning opportunities, and to place learning within a personal, social and cultural framework. Current units include 'Lost Your Tongue' (an

introduction to the Cornish language), 'Land of Saints', 'Voyage of the Mystery', 'Wrecks and Rescue', 'An Gof 1497' and 'Cornish Seashore'.

23. See Tim Saunders (ed.), *The Wheel: An Anthology of Modern Poetry in Cornish 1850–1980*, London, 1999. See the observations on literary standards in Brian Murdoch, *Cornish Literature*, Cambridge, 1993, pp. 144–50.

24. The full essay is found in Alan M. Kent and Tim Saunders (eds), *Looking at the Mermaid: A Reader in Cornish Literature 900–1900*, London, 2000, pp. 281–93; see also Craig Weatherhill, *Cornish Place Names and Language*, Wilmslow, 1995, p. 109.

25. Akira Yamamoto, 'Respect and prospect on new emerging language communities', in Nicholas Ostler (ed.), *Endangered Languages: What role for the Specialist? (Proceedings of the Second FEL Conference, University of Edinburgh, 25–7 September 1998)*, Bath, 1998.

26. Lynn Landweer, 'Indicators of Ethnolinguistic Vitality: Case Study of two languages—Labu and Vanimo', in Ostler (ed.), ibid.

27. Cornwall County Council, 2004b, pp. 10–18 (Kernewek and English).

28. Alan M. Kent, *The Literature of Cornwall: Continuity, Identity, Difference 1000–2000*, Bristol, 2000, p. 262.

29. Bernard Deacon, 'Language Revival and Language Debate: Modernity and Postmodernity' in Philip Payton (ed.), *Cornish Studies: Four*, Exeter, 1996, pp. 88–108.

30. The Strategy document thanks the Government of the Isle of Man. Kenneth Mackinnon completed an excellent independent Study of Cornish, which informed some of the document. See Kenneth Mackinnon, 'Cornish at its Millennium: An Independent Study of the Language Undertaken in 2000', in Payton (ed.), 2002, pp. 266–82, '"As Cornish As Possible"—"Not an Outcast Anymore": Speakers' and Learners' Opinions on Cornish', in Payton (ed.), 2004, pp. 268–87.

31. Ichiro Yuhara, 'An Ecological Perspective of Language Change: The Ainu Language and the two types of Colonization', in *Contemporary Linguistics: Perspectives on Language Evolution*, 3, 2002, pp. 81–91.

32. Mufwene, 2001, p. xi.

33. Mufwene, 2001, p. xii.

34. Mufwene, 2001, p. xii.

35. Mufwene, 2001, p. xii.

36. Mufwene, 2001, p. xii.

37. Crystal, 1995, p. 346. For insight on processes of creolisation involving Celtic-Englishes, see contributors to Raymond Hickey (ed.), *Legacies of Colonial English: Studies in Transported Dialects*, Cambridge, 2005.

38. See, for example, P. A. S. Pool, *The Death of Cornish*, Cornwall, 1982; Rod Trevelyan Lyon, *Cornish: The Struggle for Survival*, Cornwall, 2001; idem, *Notes on the Penwith Dialect of Cornish*, Cornwall, 2001. All these publications present linguistic activity in Cornwall as a decline from a fully operational Celtic culture.

39. For some insights into this see Alan M. Kent, '"Drill Cores": A Newly-found Manuscript of Cousin Jack Narratives from the Upper

Peninsula of Michigan, USA', in Payton (ed.), 2004, pp. 106–43. See also Graham Shorrocks, 'Away to Go in the Southwest of England and in Newfoundland and the Question of Celtic Analogues', in *Canadian Journal of Linguistics/Revue canadienne de Linguistique*, 36:2, 1991, pp. 137–46; K. C. Phillips, 'Grammatical Conversion in the Cornish Dialect', in *Journal of the Royal Institution of Cornwall*, Vol. VI, New Series, 1971, pp. 233–5.

40. W. G. Orchard, *A Glossary of Mining Terms*, Redruth, 1991.
41. R. Morton Nance, *A Glossary of Cornish Sea Words*, Cornwall, 1963, p. 124.
42. See, for example, *An Gannas*, No. 341, 2005, pp. 13–14. Concepts being dealt with in this issue include capitalism [chatelydhieth], liberation theology [theologieth livreson], religious pluralism [liesplegieth kryjyansek] and abortion [erthylyans].
43. See Alan Pearson (ed.), *Cornish Dialect in Prose and Verse: A Selection compiled by the Federation of Old Cornwall Societies from the Prize-Winning entries of the Gorsedd competitions 1969–1980*, Cornwall, 1982.
44. Joy Stevenson in Les Merton, *Oall Rite Me Ansum!: A Salute to Cornish Dialect*, Newbury, 2003, p. 5.
45. R. Morton Nance, *The Cledry Plays: Drolls of Old Cornwall for Village Acting and Home Reading*, Marazion, 1956, p. 8.
46. Alan M. Kent (ed.), *Voices from West Barbary: An Anthology of Anglo-Cornish Poetry 1549–1928*, London, 2000, p. 84.
47. Alan M. Kent, 'Lamenting Loss in Cornish Literature', in Payton (ed.), 1998, pp. 183–7.
48. See Martyn F. Wakelin, *Language and History in Cornwall*, Leicester, 1975. Wakelin is still quoted extensively, especially by continental scholars working on Cornwall, but more accurate data is found in David J. North and Adam Sharpe, *A Word-Geography of Cornwall*, Redruth, 1980; and David J. North, *Studies in Anglo-Cornish Phonology*, Redruth, 1983.
49. A useful insight into this is given in Jan Gendall, *Scat-Ups, Scabs and Shagdowns: A Glossary of Community Nicknames*, Menheniot, 1995.
50. See Alan M. Kent, *The Hensbarrow Homilies*, Penzance 2002; *Ordinalia: The Cornish Mystery Cycle: A Verse Translation*, London, 2005.
51. Crystal, 2000, p. 124.
52. Hilary Keam, 'Great Expectations . . . !' in *Probus News*, No. 81, 2005, p. iii.
53. Will Coleman, *Madgy Figgy's Pig*, Cornwall, 2005, pp. 9–10. See also Will Coleman, *Lutey and the Mermaid*, Cornwall, 2005; *Tom and the Giant*, Cornwall, 2005.
54. Philip Payton, 'Identity, Ideology and Language in Modern Cornwall', in Hildegard L. C. Tristram (ed.), *The Celtic Englishes*, Heidelberg, 1997, pp. 100–23; Kent, 2000, pp. 278–84.
55. Mebyon Kernow, *The Real Future for Cornwall: Mebyon Kernow Policies for Cornwall*, Cornwall, n.d.

56. Bernard Deacon, Dick Cole and Garry Tregidga, *Mebyon Kernow and Cornish Nationalism*, Cardiff, 2003.
57. Gorseth Kernow, *Ceremonies of the Gorsedd of the Bards of Cornwall*, *Cornwall*, n.d. For background, see Dillwyn Miles, *The Secrets of the Bards of the Isle of Britain*, Llandybie, 1992.
58. Cheryl Straffon, *Pagan Cornwall: Land of the Goddess*, St Just-in-Penwith, 1993. See also *Meyn Mamvro: Ancient Stones and Sacred Sites in Cornwall* magazine.
59. See www.southwestrda.org.uk. See also the concerns raised in John Angarrack, *Breaking the Chains: Propaganda, Censorship, Deception and the Manipulation of Public Opinion in Cornwall*, Camborne, 1999.
60. Robert Penhallurick (ed.), *Debating Dialect: Essays on the Philosophy of Dialect Study*, Cardiff, 2000.
61. Nicholas Royle, 'Dialectology and Deconstruction', in ibid., pp. 112–15.
62. See the principles outlined in Jacques Derrida, and Gayatri Spivak (tr.), *Of Grammatology*, Baltimore, 1976.
63. See North, 1983; W.F. Ivey, *A Dictionary of Cornish Dialect Words*, Helston, 1976; K. C. Phillipps, *A Glossary of the Cornish Dialect*, Padstow, 1993.
64. Royle, 2000.
65. Royle, 2000.
66. Royle, 2000.
67. Royle, 2000.
68. Mufwene, 2001, p. 2.
69. Mufwene, 2001, p. 2.
70. Mufwene, 2001., pp. 4–6.
71. Mufwene, 2001, pp. 4–6.
72. See Markku Filppula, Juhani Klemola and Heli Pitkänen, *What's Celtic and What's English in the 'British Isles Englishes'?* Paper presented at the 4th Celtic Englishes Conference, Potsdam, Germany, 22–6 September 2004. For an interesting perspective on this, see Ignacy Ryszard Danka and Piotr Stalmaszczyk (eds), *Studia Indogermanica Lodziensia IV: Language Contact in the Celtic World*, Lódzkiego, 2002.
73. Cornwall County Council, 2004b, p. 18.
74. 4th Celtic Englishes Conference, 22–6 September 2004.
75. Mufwene, 2001, p. 4.
76. Alan M. Kent, 2000, pp. 14–16.
77. Jonathan Dollimore and Alan Sinfield (eds), *Political Shakespeare: New Essays in Cultural Materialism*, Manchester, 1985.
78. Ibid., p. vii.
79. See, for example, Peter Millington, 'The Truro Cordwainers' Play: A "New" Eighteenth-Century Christmas Play', in *Folklore*, 114:1, 2003, pp. 53–74; Simon Trezise, *The West Country as a Literary Invention: Putting Fiction in its Place*, Exeter, 2000.
80. See Alan Sinfield, *Literature, Politics and Culture in Postwar Britain*, Oxford, 1989; *Faultlines: Cultural Materialism and the Politics of Dissident Reading*, Oxford, 1992.

81. Itamar, Even-Zohar, 'The Literary System', in *Poetics Today*, 11, 1990, pp. 27–44.

82. See Kent and Saunders (eds), 2000, pp. 34–98, pp. 118–81 and pp. 212–17.

83. Daphne du Maurier, *Jamaica Inn*, London, 1992 [1936]; Charles Causley, *Figgie Hobbin*, Harmondsworth, 1985 [1970]; A. L. Rowse, *A Cornish Childhood*, London, 1982 [1942].

84. Anon. *Puskes, Sten ha Emmets: Satirical Humour for the Cornish*, Cornwall, 1997; Richard G. Jenkin (ed.), *Delyow Derow/Oak Leaves*, Nos. 1–15, 1988–96.

85. Itamar, Even-Zohar, 'Polysystem Theory', in *Poetics Today*, 11, 1990, pp. 9–26.

86. The proprietor of one shop in west Cornwall refuses to stack any books on Cornwall unless they are printed by Cornish publishers. This seems wrong-headed since, surely, writers in Cornwall want the 'Centre' to take notice?

87. Witness the debate on the publication of John Chynoweth, *Tudor Cornwall*, Stroud, 2002. Despite Chynoweth's name, his scholarship was perceived by several observers as being Anglo-centric.

88. Joan Tasker Grimbert (ed.), *Tristan and Isolde: A Casebook*, New York and London, 1995.

89. Peter Berresford Ellis, *The Celtic Revolution: A Study in Anti-Imperialism*, Talybont, 1985.

90. See, for example, Oliver J. Padel (ed.), *The Cornish Writings of the Boson Family*, Redruth, 1975.

91. Galicia is a good example of this. See Mercedes Quieixas Zas, *Breve Historia da Literatura Galega*, Galicia, 1999; Bietto Alonso Fernández, *Breve Historia do Nacionalismo Gelego*, Galicia, 1999.

92. See Graham Busby and Zoë Hambly, 'Literary Tourism and the Daphne du Maurier Festival', in Philip Payton (ed.), *Cornish Studies: Eight*, Exeter, pp. 197–313.

93. See *Poetry Cornwall/Bardhonyeth Kernow*, No. 1, 2002 and Simon Parker (ed.), *Scryfa: Celebrating Contemporary Cornish Writing*, Linkinhorne, 2003.

94. Tim Saunders, *The High Tide: Collected Poems in Cornish 1974–1999*, London, 1999. For his frustration with the form and content of the Revival, see Tim Saunders, 'Why I write in Cornish,' in *Planet*, No. 30, 1976; 'Cornish—Symbol and Substance', in Cathal Luain (ed.), *For a Celtic Future: A tribute to Alan Heusaff*, Dublin, 1983, pp. 253–8.

95. See Paul Newman, *The Life and Poetry of John Harris (1820–84)*, Redruth, 1994; Patrick Hutton, *I would not be forgotten: The Life and Work of Robert Stephen Hawker*, Padstow, 2004. For a perspective on this period, see Gerard Curruthers and Alan Rawes (eds), *English Romanticism and the Celtic World*, Cambridge, 2003.

96. Even-Zohar, 1990, p. 28.

97. Even-Zohar, 1990, p. 31.

98. Even-Zohar, 1990, p. 34–5.

99. See Judith Cook, *Daphne: A Portrait of Daphne du Maurier*, London,

1991; Margaret Forster, *Daphne du Maurier*, London, 1994; Richard Ollard, *A Man of Contradictions: A Life of A.L. Rowse*, London, 1999; Philip Payton, *A. L. Rowse and Cornwall: A Paradoxical Patriot*, Exeter, 2005.

100. John Hurst, Alan M. Kent and Andrew C. Symons (eds), *Jack Clemo: The Awakening, Poems Newly Found*, London, 2003.
101. Even-Zohar, 1990, pp. 36–7.
102. Even-Zohar, 1990, pp. 38–9.
103. Even-Zohar, 1990, pp. 38–9.
104. Even-Zohar, 1990, p. 43.
105. See Charmian Hussey, *The Valley of Secrets*, Cornwall, 2003. This was later re-published in London, 2004.
106. Even-Zohar, 1990, p. 39.
107. Even-Zohar, 1990, p. 39.
108. Even-Zohar, 1990, p. 40.
109. Even-Zohar, 1990, p. 40.
110. Even-Zohar, 1990, p. 40.
111. See, for example, Peter Lord, *The Visual Culture of Wales: The Industrial Society*, Cardiff, 2004; *The Visual Culture of Wales: Imaging the Nation*, Cardiff, 2004; Miles Glendinning and Aonghus Mackechnie, *Scottish Architecture*, London, 2004; Dorian Llywelyn, *Sacred Place, Chosen People: Land and National Identity in Welsh Spirituality*, Cardiff, 1999; Harold Carter and John Aitchison, *Language, Economy and Society: The Changing Fortunes of the Welsh Language in the Twentieth Century*, Cardiff, 2000.
112. Peter Ackroyd, *Albion: The Origins of the English Imagination*, London, 2002; Judy Giles and Tim Middleton (eds), *Writing Englishness 1900–1950: An Introductory Sourcebook on National Identity*, London and New York, 1995; Richard Weight, *Patriots: National Identity in Britain 1940–2000*, London, 2002.

WHY MOVE THE LIGHTHOUSE? VIRGINIA WOOLF'S RELATIONSHIP WITH ST IVES[1]

Michael Bender

INTRODUCTION

In this article, I argue that Virginia Woolf moved the setting of her novel *To the Lighthouse* from St Ives in Cornwall to 'the isles of Skye' in the Inner Hebrides. This argument is in itself not new, but in this article I look more closely at the problem, suggesting both the reason why she needed to move the location and the thinking behind the decision to situate the novel on a Scottish island.

Woolf (1882–1941) is now seen as one of the most important English novelists,[2] the best known of her ten novels being *Mrs. Dalloway* (1925) and *To the Lighthouse* (1927).[3] She is a leading figure among the modernist writers who utilized the stream of consciousness or interior monologue, such as Marcel Proust (1871–1922), James Joyce (1882–1941) and Dorothy Richardson (1873–1957). At the same time, she was also one of the most celebrated literary critics of her time, writing literally hundreds of reviews about classic texts and contemporary writers (anthologised in *The Common Reader* (1925) and *The Common Reader, Second Series* (1932)).[4] Her reputation diminished after her death but rose again with Quentin Bell's two-volume biography[5] published in 1972–73, the publication of the many volumes of her *Diaries* and *Letters,* and the early feminist writers' adoption of her and her political writings—notably *A Room of One's Own* (1929) and *Three Guineas* (1938).[6]

To briefly summarize the novel in question here, *To The Lighthouse* concerns a family and their friends during their summer holiday around 1910, when a sail to the nearby lighthouse has to be postponed because of strong winds. Ten years later, after the Great War, some members of the original party return, and a successful sail does take place. At both times one of the guests, Lily Briscoe, is painting in the garden.

RAW MATERIAL AND TRANSFORMATIONS

The raw material
Leslie Stephen (1832–1904), Virginia Woolf's father, was a successful essayist and the editor of *The National Dictionary of Biography*. Virginia was a product of her parents' second marriages, both their first spouses having died. Julia Duckworth brought three children from her first marriage: George, Stella and Gerard. Leslie brought one, a girl called Laura, who had what appears to be learning difficulties and was eventually permanently hospitalized. Together, Leslie and Julia had four more children—Vanessa, Thoby, Virginia and Adrian.

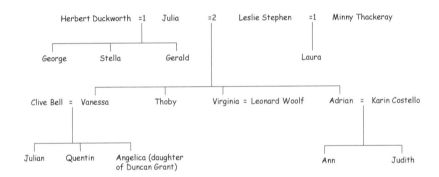

Family Tree
From Dell & Whybrow (2003)[7]

Leslie Stephen rented Talland House in St Ives from the Great Western Railway in 1881, a time when the artists' colony at St Ives was first becoming established[8] and the fishing industry—mainly pilchards —was already in decline.

Woolf wrote later that she never saw a successful use of the pilchard boats on the beach. As she observed, the pilchard boats were laid up for most of the year but in early autumn they were brought out in anticipation and anchored just off shore 'looking like black shoes, for each had a hood at one end, and a great coil of net at the other.'[9]

But the pilchards did not come. The huer in his hut at Carbis Bay watched in vain for the tell-tale signs of approaching shoals. The pilchards, it was said locally, had been disturbed by the introduction of steam trawlers, and this was why they came no more. 'Once', Woolf recalled, 'we thought we heard the Huer—a long clear wail sounded. All the sirens were shot. We could see the dotted circles of cork and the dark net beneath.'[10] But the distant mass of fish moved out of the bay again, leaving the fishermen empty-handed.

'All the years we were at St Ives the pilchards never came', said Woolf, 'and the pilchard boats drowsed in the bay ... It was a sight that made father gloomy. He had great respect for the fishermen. He minded their poverty'.[11]

The family came down to St. Ives every summer for their holidays, 'for two or two months and a half, along with invited friends',[12] roughly from July to October, until 1895 when the Porthminster hotel was built. The hotel restricted their view. Far more crucially, Julia Stephens died of influenza in 1895.

Transformations

Of course, Woolf was far too good a novelist just to give us a chunk of childhood memories. She also realised that interior monologues have to have a tension if they are not to appear trivially ego-centric, a problem that Woolf had correctly diagnosed as limiting Dorothy Richardson's work.[13] However, key characters clearly resemble members of her family, and friends are also recognizable.[14]

Woolf undertook a number of important transformations on the 'raw material' of childhood memories. To begin with, the setting became Skye—not St Ives. Also, there was temporal change, with 1895 being replaced by the period 1910-20. The locality itself was extremely limited, not the wider West Penwith hinterland that Woolf knew well and admired but a particular house in the town, together with the town itself and neighbouring Godrevy—on which island the actual lighthouse was set. Additionally, childhood reminiscences were transformed by Woolf in the novel into a coherent, extended life-review. There was an acknowledgment that key figures had died, and the whole narrative was seen through largely post-war eyes.

Woolf insisted that the story was set in 'the isles of Skye'.[15] Original readers had no reason not to take her at her word. Thus, Daiches,[16] writing in 1942, explained his own literary detective work in search of the precise location: 'The present writer, who knows the west coast of Scotland, has amused himself by trying to pin down the island, but had found that it is impossible to do so.' And yet, it is plain that the novel is really located at St Ives. This can be deduced from the actual descriptions.[17] Besides, there is Woolf's diary. On the day of the

Table 1: Characters and real-life equivalents in *To the Lighthouse*

Character in novel	Real person
Family	
MR RAMSAY	Lesley Stephens (source: Vanessa Bell, letter 11 May 1927 to VW)
MRS RAMSAY	Julia Stephens (Vanessa Bell)
NANCY RAMSAY	Stella Duckworth (Gordon, p. 47)
CAM RAMSAY	Young Virginia Woolf
JAMES RAMSAY	Adrian Stephens (Vanessa Bell)
ANDREW RAMSAY	Thoby Stephens
Servants	
KENNEDY, the gardener	Paddy (Dell & Whybrow)
MARTHE, the cook	Sophia Farrell
Guests	
WILLIAM BANKES	Lytton Strachey (Vogler, p.13)
LILY BRISCOE, artist	Vanessa Bell (Leonard Woolf)/ adult Virginia Woolf (Daiches, p. 84; Guiguet, p. 237)
Others	
Mr Paunceforte, the painter on the quay	James McNeill Whistler

Other sources: Schulkind; Zwerdling; Love; Lee.

publication of *Mrs. Dalloway*, Woolf was planning her next novel, as her diary entry for 14 May 1925 reveals: 'I'm now going all on the strain with the desire to stop journalism and get on to *To the Lighthouse*. This is going to be fairly short; to have father's character done complete in it; and mother's; and St Ives; and childhood; and all the usual things I try to put in—life, death etc.'[18]

Woolf did not, in fact, visit Scotland until 1938, only then acquiring first-hand knowledge of a country in which she had supposedly set her novel.[19] The transposition of St Ives to Skye was handled very casually by Woolf, which is surprising as she was a meticulous worker, revising both her fiction and non-fiction work many times and usually paying particular attention to detail and issues of authenticity. But in this novel there are several slips that let her down. Mr Banks is coming to

Skye from the right London terminus—Euston (not Paddington, the station for St Ives) but it would take him over a day to get up there; Paul says he will go to Edinburgh to replace Minta's lost ring, when Glasgow is much the nearer city. Moreover, Woolf (Letter to Vanessa, 22 May 1927)[20] accepted Lord Olivier's criticism that the Hebrides —the real location of Skye—have no rooks, elms or dahlias. Woolf, apparently, had not done her homework (though Olivier was wrong about the rooks).

With regard to the temporal changes, Hafley offers (un-controversially) the following dates.[21] Part One (The Window) is set in mid-September 1910. Part Two (Time Passes) is September 1919, and Part Three (The Lighthouse) is September 1919. So Woolf keeps the ages and characters of the family members as they were (when James/Adrian was six) but then moves them forward by twenty years. That the focus of the novel is purely on Talland House, together with the town of St Ives and Godrevy, is intriguing. The whole hinterland of West Penwith—its archaeology, its industrial landscape and so on—is untapped; the only material she uses are the flora, the sea and the lighthouse. And this is not because Woolf did not value or know the area.[22] Rather, the decision to geographically restrict the focus of the novel was a deliberate one. By restricting the narrative land-scape to the house, garden and the bay, the reader is forced to limit and focus his/her own imagination on the people populating that strip.[23]

The descriptions of Woolf's parents in *To the Lighthouse* are sharp and critical. This suggests that Woolf was not merely reminiscing about her childhood as, for example, Arthur Ransome did in *Swallows and Amazons*.[24] Rather, she is carrying out a life review[25] which, as we can see from the text, includes not just her relationship with her parents, but also the life success of her sister and herself. We should also note that the first act of sexual abuse that Woolf experienced (perpetrated by Gerald Duckworth) was in the hall of Talland House.[26] Moreover, Woolf was looking back some thirty years or more. During that period, of course, there had been many changes. There had, inevitably, been deaths; after each of which she had had some kind of breakdown. Her mother, Julia, died in 1895, to which event her father reacted with prolonged, hysterical grief: partly because he knew that her children blamed his constant demands for exhausting her. Her much loved half-sister, Stella Duckworth, died in 1897 after an unsuccessful operation; her father in 1905, and her beloved brother Thoby in 1907 from typhoid. Woolf reacted badly to loss, and each of these deaths affected her deeply and permanently. Thus, in writing about family members, albeit skilfully fictionalized, she was at the same time writing about people that she had lost—bereavements that were traumatic in the extreme and detrimental to her mental health.[27] Painful memories, both of loss but also of her own emotional distress, were being revived in her novel, against the wider background of the tragedy and uncertainty of the Great War.

THEMES

There are a number of important themes in *To the Lighthouse*. Among them are the nature of creativity and legacy, the qualities of male success, and—by far the most central and important theme—models of adult womanhood. What should the role of an intelligent (middle-class) adult woman be? This question links *Mrs. Dalloway* to *To the Lighthouse*, and may, at an unconscious level, mean that they are treated as a unity.[28] Perhaps it was for this reason that Woolf was able to proceed smoothly from finishing one to planning the next, without the 'usual' breakdown that accompanied the end of a novel.[29] It is surely not chance that her two most famous novels are essentially concerned with *female* consciousness; whereas, for example, her next novel, *The Waves*, published in 1931, is centrally concerned with a man's (Bernard's) perceptions, and is much less well regarded as a work of fiction.

Five models of the female role are provided. Firstly, there is Mr Ramsay's ideal of The Angel of the House,[30] the willingly subservient, passive wife. As Lehmann puts it: 'He is a monster of egotism, demanding as of right support and appreciation from all around him , thought secretly haunted by a sense of failure'.[31] For Ramsay, read Leslie Stephens. His demanding, neurotic behaviour was evidenced towards his wife Julia, Stella Duckworth and Vanessa, the sequentially conscripted Angels. His attitude had a sexual component, since he was unable to accept Stella's getting married—in a letter to her on her honeymoon, he cannot remember her husband's name.[32] Next there is Mrs Ramsay (aka Julia). She shows how a free-spirited woman makes the relationship work. She was a firm believer in marriage, and considered that marriage was the fulfilment all women should seek. Woolf had already explored this attitude in the character of Claire Dalloway. As Guiguet[33] has perceptively pointed out, there is a difference between Mrs Dalloway and Mrs Ramsay: Mrs Dalloway is a centripetal force—all lines of energy lead in towards her; Mrs. Ramsay is a centrifugal force—her energy radiates outwards from her to affect others. Woolf shows us how tiring such juggling behaviours are; and that they are part of a struggle to feel and connect.

Thirdly, there is Minta Doyle. She is encouraged to marry Paul by Mrs Ramsay. However, in Part 3, she is in a 'modern marriage', where certainly the husband, and possibly the wife, is unfaithful. The best this can offer is that they stay 'excellent friends'.[34] Lily Briscoe, the next character, although an independent woman, has no profession, and does not seem to be making a living out of being an artist. Although loving William Bankes, she has no long-term relationship, and there is the suggestion that that is the price one pays for an artistic career. At the end of the novel, when she can understand and make her peace with (the dead) Mrs Ramsay, she can now make the decisive brush-strokes to finish the picture and end the novel. She literally has the last words, but a careful reading shows considerable ambiguity:

> There it was—her picture. Yes, with all its greens and blues, its lines running up and across, its attempt at something. It would be hung in the attics, she thought; it would be destroyed. But what did that matter? She asked herself, taking up her brush again. She looked at the steps; they were empty; she looked at her canvas; it was blurred. With a sudden intensity, as if she saw it clear for a second, she drew a line there, in the centre. It was done; it was finished. Yes, she thought, laying down her brush in extreme fatigue, I have had my vision.[35]

We might see this as a triumph of artistic achievement, but the whole passage is riddled with doubts and self put-downs which contradict such a reading. In particular, note the following phrases: 'its attempt at something'; 'it would be hung in attics'; 'it would be destroyed'; 'it was blurred'; 'extreme fatigue'; 'I have had my vision'. The last statement suggests that she will have few further 'visions', and (as Moody points out)[36] the success is limited, both as to its validity—it has been achieved and nothing can be guaranteed as regards the future—and in terms of the scope of that achievement. It only concerns the artistic, leaving the personal sphere untouched. With 'It is finished', Lily Briscoe is repeating Jesus' last words. She too has been sacrificed, presumably on the altar of male definitions of reality and success, a theme also elaborated in *A Room of One's Own*.[37] But Briscoe and her creator Woolf are not identical in their beliefs. While Briscoe's uncertainty as to her artistic worth is reflected in Woolf's self-doubt, Woolf's view would have seen the need for a much stronger in-dependent identity, as shown by herself and her closest female friends, Vanessa Bell and Vita Sackville-West. Within such a view there was also a much more open demonstration of female sexual choice.[38]

However, Woolf, like Lily Briscoe, had fundamental doubts about her worth. This is perhaps not surprising. Despite Leslie Stephens' avowal in a letter[39] to his future wife that women ought to be as well educated as men, Virginia was educated at home and was the only child to receive no further education (Vanessa, although having to act as The Angel of The House following the deaths of Julia Stephen and Stella Duckworth, was permitted to combine this role with attending the Royal Academy and the Slade). Although her father recognized her ability as a writer, Virginia had to make do with his extensive library, with predictable effects: 'Owing partly to the fact that I was never at school, never competed in any way with children of my own age, I have never been able to compare my gifts and defects with other people's.'[40]

It is perhaps not surprising that both Lehmann (an editor at Hogarth) and Leonard Woolf[41] recognized that Virginia was most at risk of a breakdown on the completion of a novel, when '*it is finished*'. She circumvented publishers' comments on her texts by creating with Leonard her own press: the Hogarth.[42] But she could not avoid the critics. Also, she was aware of the cost of her chosen profession: it was significant that of the four great women novelists—Jane Austen, Emily Bronte, Charlotte Bronte, and George Eliot—not one had a child, and two were unmarried.[43] Virginia Woolf hoped to become the fifth childless great woman novelist. But this ambition was far from painless. Paradoxically, Woolf actually wanted children. Her friend, Violet Dickinson, had given her a cradle as a wedding present.[44] Leonard, nervous about Virginia's mental health, sought advice from her psychiatrist, the eminent Sir George Savage, who encouraged the couple to have children. But Leonard was unsatisfied with this reply. He consulted other doctors and the matron of the nursing home Virginia went to when she had 'her attacks': 'They confirmed my fears and were strongly against her having children. We followed her advice.'[45] This must have been a humiliating experience for Virginia, and hardly illustrated great trust by her husband. Male success was similarly difficult and elusive, and it is clear that Woolf saw her father's search for certainties both unsuccessful and misguided. In short, there is in the novel much emotional charge in the analyses of the basis of both male and female success. It is perhaps not surprising that Woolf moved The Lighthouse to give herself some 'distance' to work across. In St Ives, it would have been all too stifling and close-to-home.

VIRGINIA WOOLF AND INTERNAL COLONIZATION

It is interesting to note that Woolf's 'reading' of Cornwall was similar to the dominant discourse of our own time. Fifty years or so before she was writing, the idea of Cornwall as an exotic, non-industrialized peripheral area would have been nonsense. Flourishing tin and copper mines and continued innovation by Cornish engineers marked an energetic, industrial culture. There was also a very large fishing industry, centred on the pilchard and the herring. St Ives even had a fair-sized shipping line—Haines—while Hayle, across the bay, had its huge engineering works. But by the end of the nineteenth century both mining and fishing declined, with the pilchard disappearing altogether.[46] Much of what is associated with 'Cornwall' today is due to the very successful advertising campaigns and posters of the Great Western Railway in the decades before the Second World War, when Cornwall was comprehensively reinvented as a post-industrial tourist destination imbued with a Celtic exoticism.[47]

By the time Leslie Stephen brought his family down to St Ives, the 'artists' colony'[48] that would soon come to define the town was already emerging. The phrase is well-known today but the word 'artists' tends to hide or obscure the word 'colony'. For, leaving aside issues of light and landscape that (as far as the artists were concerned) legitimized their arrival and settlement at St Ives, their actions were essentially those of 'colonists'. This was not the external colonialism associated with imperial expansion but was rather an example of internal colonization: the exploitation of local resources and the organization of the infrastructure in a peripheral area of the country by its metropolitan centre, together with the attempt to create a hegemonic discourse to justify such an arrangement.[49]

Internal colonialization requires ready access to the periphery from the centre in order to both access its resources and to send controlling influences. The railways played a key role in allowing the new colonials rapid access to Cornwall, with the ability to return quickly to the centre when required. The Tamar was crossed by Brunel's Royal Albert Bridge in 1859; the branch line to St Ives was operative by 1879.[50] Reese has demonstrated the applicability of this internal colonization model to Brittany, where metropolitan influences attempted just such a hegemonic discourse, and the parallel example of Cornwall—and St Ives in particular—is a compelling one.[51]

We can still find contemporary attempts at achieving a hegemonic discourse. For example, in discussing the arrival of the artists, Dell and Whybrow write: 'The general consensus of the townsfolk on that first influx of artists was "Well, if they can work in the same conditions as us, they can't be too bad".'[52] Leaving aside the obvious question 'How do they know?', this is a remarkable statement, because artists and fishermen do not work in the same conditions. Artists can only paint outside in fine weather, since otherwise the paints would run. By contrast, the fishermen have to go out in any weather if they and their families are not to starve, which is presumably why the fishing boats perish as 'in the great storm last Christmas' noted in *To the Lighthouse*.[53] It seems that the authors are wishing to 'harmonize' the assumed and unspoken benefits of high culture with the worth of hard labour. This 'harmonization' of relationships between locals and in-comers is again noteworthy in Jane Brown's *Spirits of Place*. We are told:

> It is a quirk of St Ives's history that perhaps would not have appealed to Virginia that the real source of its twentieth-century fame was an inarticulate and wizened little dwarf of a failed fisherman [Alfred Wallis] . . . In August, 1928 two young painters Ben Nicholson and Christopher Wood, were having an interesting day exploring St Ives when they came upon Wallis' open doorway and his paintings. Nicholson, determined to escape from the stylish sophistication and fame of his inheritance, especially of his painter father, William Nicholson, was struck by Wallis's 'direct creative energy' and simple clarity.[54]

But this story about the creation of St Ives' fame is unfounded. The artists had started arriving some forty years earlier.[55] Nicholson was one of its most famous artists, and may well have been influenced by Wallis, but there were many, equally famous artists, most noticeably his wife, Barbara Hepworth, who were not.

Paradoxically, this colonization may initially have been seen as advantageous to the locals after the collapse of the pilchard fishery—as documented earlier, Virginia Woolf never saw the exciting shooting of the seine nets of the pilchard boats. Renting the upper storey of the fishing lofts as studios may have been important to the local economy, but this should not blind us to the nature of the relationship. It is this relationship, as it is represented in the novel, that I now wish to examine.

THE RELATIONSHIPS BETWEEN THE RAMSAYS AND THE LOCALS

What is striking is how minimal are the interactions—in thought as well as deed—between the house party and the locals. The guests, except when Mr Tansley accompanies Mrs Ramsay to visit a sick woman, have no interactions with the locals at all. Mrs Ramsay deals with the servants, who are locals, and is critical of them.[56] This negativity extends to the gardener, again a local man, who is only saved from the sack by his beauty: 'His beauty was so great, she said, beginning to speak of Kennedy, the gardener, at once he was so awful handsome that she couldn't dismiss him.'[57] In Part Three, Lily Briscoe remembers only Mrs Ramsay's irritation: 'But what was the look she had, Lily wondered, when she clapped her deer-stalker's hat on her head, or ran across the grass, or scolded Kennedy the gardener?'[58]

Mrs Ramsay's principal relationships with the locals—with the sick Elsie who she visits, and the lighthousekeeper's son 'with the tuberculous limp',[59] are founded on charity. Indeed, her first monologue concerns gifts for the lighthousekeepers:

> 'But it may be fine—I expect it will be fine', said Mrs Ramsay, making some little twist of the reddish brown stocking she was knitting, impatiently. If she finished it tonight, if they did go to the Lighthouse after all, it was to be given to the Lighthouse keeper for his little boy, who was threatened with a tuberculous limp; together with a pile of old magazines, and some tobacco, indeed, whatever she could find lying about, not really wanted, but only littering the room, to give those fellows who must be bored to death.[60]

This passage is interesting, because after we are led to admire Mrs Ramsay's industry and concern for the lad, the narrator then devalues that caring by the literally throwaway line, 'whatever she could find lying about, not really wanted, but only littering the room'. This relationship is continued after her death by Mr Ramsay, when, as the sail to the lighthouse is about to happen, he forces Nancy to wrap up some presents for the lighthousekeepers.[61]

Mrs Ramsay also sees it as her duty to support her husband against the perceptions of the locals. Her husband has the habit of shouting poetry out loud. When a local woman is scared by this, Mrs. Ramsay reacts by 'instantly taking his side against all the silly Giddingses in the world'.[62] She is thinking about her husband while at the dinner table:

> His understanding often astonished her. But did he notice the flowers? No. Did he notice the view? No. Did he even notice his own daughter's beauty, or whether there was pudding on his plate or roast beef? He would sit at table with them like a person in a dream. And his habit of talking aloud, or saying poetry aloud, was growing on him, she was afraid; for sometimes it was awkward—
>
> Best and brightest come away!
>
> —poor Miss Giddings, when he shouted at her, almost jumped out of her skin. But then, Mrs. Ramsay, though instantly taking his side against all the silly Giddingses in the world, then, she thought, intimating by a little pressure on his arm

that he walked up hill too fast for her, and she must stop for a moment to see whether those were fresh molehills on the bank, then, she thought, stooping down to look, a great mind like his must be different in every way from ours.[63]

But much sharper criticism of local people is still to come. In the short, middle section of the book ('Time Passes'), two cleaning ladies prepare the house for its re-opening after the war. The main voice, Mrs McNab, is described as a dissolute, brain-damaged alcoholic. She is dissolute in that two of her children were born out of wedlock, and one deserted her.[64] An alcoholic, she was always 'at the public house drinking' and her memory had gone: 'And the cook's name now? Mildred? Marian? Some name like that. Ah—she had forgotten. She did forget things'.[65] Mrs McNab is not to be trusted to report the key events—such as the deaths of three of the Ramsays. These unreliable statements are, therefore, put in square brackets.

Mepham,[66] in his study, equates these with the square of still living fish that the Macalister boy uses for bait, a description likewise enclosed in square brackets: [Macalister's boy took one of the fish and cut a square out of its side to bait his hook with. The mutilated body (it was alive still) was thrown back into the sea].[67] This may also be read as a moving metaphor for the maimed of the Great War, a painful memory too precious to be left to Mrs McNab and therefore given its square brackets.

Vogler is perceptive here: 'The Ramsays are *in* but not *of* the inhabitants. Mrs McNab is a representative of a minimal human consciousness . . . To decry her [Woolf's] failure to cover the full social spectrum in her work, as has often been done, is simply to wish she had been a different person or to lack an awareness of who she was.'[68] Woolf was not unaware of this criticism (see her 'Am I a Snob?').[69] But Vogler also makes the point that McNab's song from twenty years ago, which 'reflects her minimal but persistent consciousness', may as a literary device have the merit of providing a continuity across time and its tragedies.[70] Yet the viciousness of Woolf's description of Mrs McNab is paralleled in *Mrs Dalloway*, where a female beggar is singing outside Regents Park Tube station,[71] an example given by Carey[72] of Woolf's disdain for the masses. It is also noteworthy here that Mr Ramsay does respect the sailing and fishing skills of the boatman, Mr MacAlister, who takes him across to the lighthouse. Early on in the voyage he offers MacAlister tobacco.[73] Nearing the island, 'Mr Ramsay opened the parcel and shared out the sandwiches among them. Now he was happy, eating bread and cheese with these fishermen. He would have liked to live in a cottage and lounge about in the harbour spitting with the other old men, James thought, watching him slice his cheese into thin yellow sheets with his penknife.'[74]

Woolf also makes deliberate reference to this separation of house-party members from locals. At the supper table the conversation has been splintered, so Mrs Ramsay, with her will to create cohesion, orders the candles to be lit. There is an awareness of the native 'other', indicated here by italics:

> Now all the candles were lit up, and the faces of both sides of the table were brought nearer by the candlelight and composed, as they had not been in the twilight, into a party round the table, for the night was now shut off by panes of glass, which, far from giving *any accurate view of the outside world*, rippled it so strangely that here, inside the room, seemed to be order and dry land; there, outside, a reflection in which *things wavered and vanished, waterily.*
>
> Some change at once went through them all, as if this had really happened, and they were all conscious of making a party together in a hollow, *on an island*; had their common cause against *that fluidity out there.*[75]

Generally, interaction with only two groups of locals can be seen as in any way positive: the needy, who have reason to be grateful for Mrs Ramsay's charity, and those engaged in physically hard work. The rest, especially the servants, are viewed negatively. Indeed, Emery considers controversially that 'The case of *To the Lighthouse* . . . suggests that modern feminist women's writing may indeed become complicit in the constitution of a colonised Other'.[76]

CONCLUSION

Virginia Woolf's geopsychological centre was London, and her sense of 'the rural' was the Sussex Downs. It was at Monk's House, Rodmell, near Lewes in East Sussex, that she wrote this novel: 'Having a superstitious wish to begin *To the Lighthouse* the first day at Monk's House, I now think I shall finish it in the two months there'.[77] In fact, she lost the summer to her 'queer, difficult nervous system' (Diary, 5 September 1925).[78] It was not until 14 January 1927, again at Monk's House, that she recorded that: 'This moment I have finished the final drudgery. It is now complete for Leonard to read on Monday.'[79]

As we have observed, in the book Woolf's analysis of her parents is unflinching. Mr Ramsay is little more than an intellectual in his dotage, and who is apparently starting to dement. Mrs Ramsay exhausts herself maintaining her many children, her multiple roles in supporting the household and her husband's neurotic self-esteem. Lily contains elements of both Virginia and the person to whom she was closest, her sister. Yet, Lily Briscoe does not believe in herself enough to ever be successful as an artist or as a woman. *To the Lighthouse*, then, is not merely about Woolf's childhood memories of St Ives but is a penetrating and profound examination of complex, often difficult and unsatisfactory personal relationships, compounded by an acute sense of loss and the background of the Great War. It is not surprising, then, that Woolf found it necessary to create 'distance' and 'space' by moving the location of the novel to 'the isles of Skye'. The Scottish islands were at the opposite end of Britain to Cornwall, providing the distance she sought.

But the choice of 'the isles of Skye' was not merely one of distance. Having decided to move the lighthouse, Woolf also needed to find a location that mirrored aspects of the original situation in St Ives. As we have seen, the relationship between the main characters in the affluent house party and the locals is essentially colonial, suggestive of the internal colonization that was then more generally affecting St Ives with its 'artists' colony' and Great Western-sponsored tourism. Woolf needed to find another colonized 'Celtic periphery' inhabited by people who were also clearly 'other', in which the milieu of the metropolitan house party could be successfully transplanted. This made a Scottish island a 'natural' choice.[80] Yet, though maintaining this context, *To the Lighthouse* was not primarily about St Ives (or indeed Skye). Rather, it was about personal relationships, not place, and sought principally to consider that perennial question: What is successful adulthood?

ACKNOWLEDGEMENTS

I should like to thank Anthony Fothergill for his encouragement and support; and Professor Barbara Bender for her invaluable comments.

NOTES AND REFERENCES

1. An amended version of a paper delivered at the Cornish Audio-Visual Archive Conference, Cornwall Centre, Redruth, 15 May 2004.
2. For example, Mary Eagleton and David Pierce, *Attitudes to Class in the English Novel: From Walter Scott to David Story*, London, 1979.
3. *Mrs Dalloway*, London, 1996; *To the Lighthouse*, London, 1996. All page references for these texts will be from these Penguin Popular Classics editions.
4. *The Common Reader*, London, 1925; *The Common Reader, Second Series*, London, 1932.
5. Q. Bell, *Virginia Woolf, a biography. 2 vols. 1. Virginia Stephen 1882 to 1912*, London, 1972, *2. Mrs. Woolf, 1912–1941*, London, 1973.

6. *A Room of One's Own*, London, 1977; *Three Guineas*, Oxford, 1998.
7. M. Dell and M. Whybrow, *Virginia Woolf and Vanessa Bell: Remembering St Ives*, Padstow, 2003.
8. D. V. Baker, *Britain's Art Colony*, Bristol, 2000; T. Cross, *The Shining Sands: Artists in Newlyn and St Ives, 1880–1930*. Tiverton, 1994; M. Whybrow, *St Ives 1883–1933—Portrait of an Art Colony*, St Ives, 2002.
9. *A Sketch of the Past*, 112, in J. Schulkind (ed.), *Virginia Woolf: Moments of Being*, Sussex, 1976.
10. *A Sketch of the Past*, 112.
11. *A Sketch of the Past*, 113.
12. *A Sketch of the Past*, 112, footnote 9.
13. Dorothy Richardson, 188–92, in M. Barrett, (ed.), *Virginia Woolf: Women and Writing*, London, 1979.
14. Sources: D. Daiches. *Virginia Woolf, 2nd edn*, New York, 1962; M. Dell and M. Whybrow. *Virginia Woolf and Vanessa Bell: Remembering St Ives*, Padstow, 2003; L. Gordon. *Virginia Woolf: A Writer's Life*, Oxford, 1984; J. Guiget, *Virginia Woolf and her works*, New York, 1965; H. Lee, *Virginia Woolf*, London, 1996; J. Love. *Virginia Woolf: Sources of Madness and Art*. Berkeley, 1977; Letter from Vanessa Bell to Virginia Woolf, May 11, 1927, 572–73. In N. Nicolson (ed.) *A Change of Perspective, The Letters of Virginia Woolf, 1923–1928*, London, 1977; T. A. Vogler. *Twentieth Century Interpretations of To the Lighthouse*, New Jersey, 1970; L. Woolf. *Downhill all the Way: an autobiography of the years 1919 to 1939*, London, 1970; A. Zwerdling, *Virginia Woolf and the Real World*, Berkeley, 1986.
15. *To the Lighthouse*, p. 14.
16. D. Daiches, *Virginia Woolf*, 2nd edn, p. 83.
17. S. Reid, Reading Virginia Woolf and St Ives, 88–98, in E. Westland (ed.) *Cornwall: the Cultural Construction of Place*, Penzance, 1997.
18. A. Bell (ed.), *The Diary of Virginia Woolf, Volume Three, 1925–1930*, 18, San Diego, 1980.
19. J. Morris, *Travels with Virginia Woolf*, London, 1993.
20. In Nicolson, 1977. Footnote 12, 379.
21. J. Hafley. 'The creative modulation of perspective', 133–48. In M. Beja (ed.) *Casebook Series: Virginia Woolf: To the Lighthouse*, London, 1970.
22. She had used the hinterland in *Jacob's Room*, published by Hogarth in 1922; and describes it lovingly and in detail in her 1939 *Sketch of the Past* (Schulkind, footnote 9), for example:'We went for a walk each day', 114.
23. Other authors using this device include Hardy's use of Egdon Heath in *The Return of the Native*; and Daphne du Maurier of Gribbin Head in *The Birds*, a claustrophobic tension lost or at least lessened in Hitchcock's film version with its characters driving distances.
24. A. Ransome, *Swallows and Amazons*, London, 1930.
25. Life Review is a term coined by the American psychotherapist, R. N. Butler. 'The Life Review: an interpretation of reminiscence in the aged'. *Psychiatry*, 1963, vol. 119, 712–28. Reminiscence tends concern individual or group narratives, seeking positive values.. In contrast, a life review is most frequently but not necessarily undertaken towards the end of a life

(see M. P. Bender, *Bitter Harvest. Ageing and Society*, 1997, vol. 17, 337–48.) It involves the consideration of the major choice points in a life, major decisions and their correctness in the light of what one now knows. It can therefore be quite a painful process (see M. P. Bender, P. Bauckham and A. Norris, *The Therapeutic Purposes of Reminiscence*, London, 1999.)

26. *A Sketch of the Past*, 69. See Schulkind, Footnote 9.
27. Lee, 1996. See Footnote 12, especially Chapters 10 and 12 (pages 146–59 and 175–200).
28. The central question asked in these two novels is also the main concern of the two lectures given to female students at Cambridge in 1928, and published in 1929 as *A Room of One's Own*. I suggest that these three texts should be seen as an unified effort.
29. J. Lehmann, *Virginia Woolf*, London, 1975.
30. The term is attributed to Coventry Patmore in his 1856 poem of the same name.
31. Lehmann, 1975, footnote 27, p. 58.
32. See Lee, 1996, footnote 12, p. 137.
33. Jean Guiget, *Virginia Woolf and her Works*, 1962, Trans. Jean Stewart, New York, 1965, footnote 12, p. 235.
34. *To the Lighthouse*, p. 255.
35. *To the Lighthouse*, p. 305–6.
36. A. D. Moody. *Virginia Woolf*, Edinburgh, 1963, pp. 45–6.
37. Zwerdling, footnote 12, has documented in detail the conflict that Woolf had in resolving these issues.
38. See M. A. Caws. *Women of Bloomsbury: Virginia, Vanessa and Carrington*, New York, 1990; and V. Curtis, *Virginia Woolf's Women*, Stroud, 2003.
39. Quoted by Dell and Whybrow, 2003, footnote 7, p. 141.
40. *A Sketch of the Past*, p. 65 in Schulkind, footnote 9.
41. Lehmann, p. 32–3, footnote 27; Leonard Woolf, footnote 12, p. 55.
42. For the setting up of the Hogarth Press, see Lee, footnote 12, 362–64.
43. In *Women and Fiction*, published in *The Forum*, March 1929, and reprinted in Barrett, footnote 11, p. 45.
44. Lee, 1996, footnote 12, p. 334.
45. Leonard Woolf, footnote 12, pp. 55–6.
46. P. Payton. *Cornwall: A History*, 2nd edn, Fowey, 2004.
47. P. Payton and P. Thornton. 'The Great Western Railway and the Cornish-Celtic Revival', in Philip Payton (ed.), *Cornish Studies: Three*, 1993, pp. 83–103; C. Thomas, 'See your Own Country First: The Geography of a Railway Landscape', in Ella Westland (ed.), *Cornwall: The Cultural Construction of Place*, Penzance, 1997, footnote 15, 107.
48. A standard term for St Ives, e.g. D.Val Baker; and M.Whybrow, footnote 8.
49. See J. Reese, Internal colonialism: the case of Brittany, *Ethnic and Racial Studies*, 1979, volume 2 (3), 275–92.
50. Payton and Thorton, 1993; Thomas, 1997, footnote 44.

51. Reese, footnote 47.
52. Dell and Whybrow, 2003, footnote 12, p. 16.
53. *To the Lighthouse*, p. 240.
54. J.Brown, *Spirits of Place*, London, 2001.
55. See Whybrow, 2003, footnote 8.
56. Criticism of the Swiss maid, despite Mrs. Ramsay knowing that her father is dying of cancer, p. 45; of the cook, p. 124.
57. *To the Lighthouse*, pp. 100–1.
58. *To the Lighthouse*, p. 260.
59. *To the Lighthouse*, p. 13.
60. *To the Lighthouse*, p. 13.
61. *To the Lighthouse*, p. 214.
62. *To the Lighthouse*, pp. 107–8.
63. *To the Lighthouse*, pp. 107–8.
64. *To the Lighthouse*, p. 195.
65. *To the Lighthouse*, p. 204.
66. J. Mepham. *Figures of desire: narration and fiction in To the Lighthouse*, pp. 149–84. In G. Josipovici, (ed.) *The Modern English Novel: the Reader, the Writer and the Work*, London, 1976.
67. *To the Lighthouse*, p. 264.
68. Vogler, 1970, footnote 12, p. 14.
69. 'Am I a Snob?', pp. 181–98, in J. Schulkind, footnote 9.
70. Vogler, 1970, footnote 12, p. 25.
71. *Mrs. Dalloway*, footnote 3, pp. 90–2.
72. J. Carey, *The Intellectuals and the masses*, London, 1992.
73. *To the Lighthouse*, p. 239.
74. *To the Lighthouse*, pp. 299–300.
75. *To the Lighthouse*, pp. 146–7
76. M. L. Emery. 'Robbed of Meaning': the work at the center of To the Lighthouse, *Modern Fiction Studies*, 1992, vol. 38, 217–34.
77. Bell, 1972, footnote 16, p. 36.
78. Bell, 1972, footnote 16, p. 39.
79. Bell, 1972, footnote 16, p. 123.
80. I am indebted to the post-paper discussion at the CAVA conference for pointing out this transposition to me.

JACK CLEMO'S MYSTICAL-EROTIC QUEST

Andrew C. Symons

INTRODUCTION

During a literary career stretching over five decades, Jack Clemo tried to define and re-define himself as a mystic, an erotic-mystic, a Calvinist or neo-Calvinist, a Barthian, an evangelical-Catholic, and lastly simply as a Christian. Critics and reviewers have acknowledged only the label Calvinist; yet it is difficult to identify in Clemo's work a single idea emanating exclusively from the writings of John Calvin. Much more obvious are the influences of Robert Browning, D. H. Lawrence, Thomas Hardy, William Blake, the Powys brothers and various Catholic mystics. Clemo's literary-mystical theology is a singular product.

As with many twentieth-century Celtic writers, Clemo had a problematic relationship with his native land. He was reared in a dialect-speaking and working-class home, took not a single night's sleep across the Tamar until the age of thirty-four, and wrought his mystical vision from the industrial clayscape of Hensbarrow, in mid-Cornwall. Yet in 1968 he married an English woman, lived in Weymouth from 1983 until his death in 1994, and took his later imagery from English, Italian and other sources. This change of focus brought him into conflict with both Cornish and London critics. He died isolated and unrepentant.

Jack was born in 1916 to Reginald and Eveline Clemo in a clay-miner's cottage at Goonamarris. Overlooking the cottage is a white silt cone, and behind that a deep and streaming clay-pit. Clemo based the disordered family of Zachary Cruse, sunk in 'qualor and strife', from the novel *The Clay Kiln* (p. 17), on the Clemo family of St Stephens. Joel Cruse, the Reginald figure, achieves redemption through love, but Reggie's quest was brought to a premature close when he was drowned aboard H.M.S. *Tornado* in 1917. The loss of a husband and a mother in quick succession left young Eveline horribly exposed. Then in 1921 she observed a film covering Jack's right eye and trembled at the possibility of blindness—fortunately delayed for another thirty-four years. In despair, she climbed the stairs and flung her Bible onto the bed. Her eyes met Isaiah 54:

> . . . Fear not; for thou shalt not be ashamed . . . and shalt not
> remember the reproach of they widowhood . . . For thy Maker
> is thine husband . . . with great mercies will I gather thee . . .
> they children shall be taught of the Lord; and great shall be
> the peace of thy children . . .

The subsequent lives of Eveline and Jack Clemo were based upon this 'promise':[1]

> We can no longer find stability in any church. That's why I've
> stressed the individual experience, the 'personal covenant
> with God'. When you've had an amazing answer to prayer, or
> an overwhelming proof of divine guidance through a Bible
> text, you are no longer worried about church 'authority' or
> the lack of it! My mother's life and mine were based on her
> Isaiah 'promise': 'Thy children shall be taught of the Lord' . . .
> it has been literally fulfilled. (Letter, 4 October 1987)

Clemo believed that his religious conversion of 1937–38, his marriage to Ruth Peaty in 1968 and his visits to Italy in 1987 and 1993 with Fr. Benedict and Lilah Ramsden, were aspects of a predestined course, against which poverty, disability and literary rejection, often symbolized as 'fate' or 'fated nature', fought in vain. This intense sense of dualism, transcended only in the last years of his life, acted as his creative dynamic.

Jack Clemo's literary and mystical life divides itself into alternating periods of activity and drought. Each creative stage is associated with a specific type of mysticism:

1916–29	Wesleyan revivalism;
1929–37	Pantheism and early writings;
1937–40	Clayscape mysticism I, poetry and prose;
1940–45	Interregnum;
1945–55	Clayscape mysticism II, poetry and prose;

1955–68   Dark Night mysticism, occasional poems;
1968–93   Erotic mysticism, poetry.

Periods of intense mystical activity produced poems and novels. Autobiographical and polemical works usually revealed a slackening of mystical intensity. Critics have often tried to relate the poet's mysticism to disability, but the pattern was well established before the advent of blindness in 1955: 'Keep clear of the common pitfall of attributing my religious "vision" to physical handicaps. My ideas and emotional perceptions spring from an isolation of temperament; a streak of mysticism, which would have been much the same if my sight and hearing had stayed normal' (Letter, 17 June 1975)

HISTORICAL AND LINGUISTIC BACKGROUND
No understanding of Clemo's cultural and religious development is possible without reference to the historical and linguistic background of mid-Cornwall. Clemo's repeated attempts to reject the past as 'irrelevant and Pagan' (see Kent, *The Literature of Cornwall*, pp. 209–15)[2], following a 'Calvinist' conversion in 1937–38, has made this difficult. Critics have therefore assumed that the writer arose from a cultural vacuum which 'Calvinism' filled. In fact, mid-Cornwall possesses one of the most ancient continuous histories in Britain. Indeed, one has only to turn to the Cornish novels and short stories of Sir Arthur Quiller-Couch ('Q') to appreciate the cultural continuum Clemo's 'Calvinism' was attempting to repress.

Jack Clemo's isolated, working-class upbringing and lack of formal education meant that he heard little but dialect speech up until the time of hearing impairment. During the 1930s the writing of dialect stories provided the sole means of income. The tight speech rhythms of these stories, now collected in *The Bouncing Hills* (1983), contrasts with the longer vowels and more relaxed rhythms of lowland speech, as seen in the stories of Q. Extensive although unsystematic reading partly made up for Clemo's lack of education, and these works provided the models for his early writings. Poetry commenced in 1929 following a pantheistic experience at Penrose Veor farm, with prose following sometime afterwards. The earliest surviving poems, now published in *The Awakening* (2003), show a conflict between the poet's speech rhythms and the models of English versification, presumably taken from standard anthologies. Poems such as *Perranporth, August 15th, 1934* and *Sabbath* reveal the initial poetic structure coming under strain and subsequently disintegrating before a tight and staccato-like counter rhythm. Curiously, both the form and the content of Clemo's early poems leave the reader with a sense of unease. Some composers of the 1930's achieved the same result through certain developments of technique, but in Clemo's case there is no artifice. The tense and broken rhythms and staccato stressing of *The Burial, Good Friday, 1934,* make the poem dark, bleak and tortured. It is difficult to analyse using standard techniques.

As Leech and Crystall[3] have argued, metre in English poetry tends to follow the prose rhythms of English speech. Stress usually falls on the first strong syllable of a word and on the strong syllables of a line of poetry, with one, two or three unstressed syllables between. English poetry is *stress-timed*, with a *regular periodic beat.* Clemo's Hensbarrow intonation appears to conflict with English rhythms and poetic structures. Crystall points out that Celtic dialects of English do not usually stress the first strong syllable, but follow Celtic *delayed* or *postponed* stress. This, however, does not fully explain Clemo's problem of accommodation.

In *Confession of a Rebel* (1948/75, pp. 88–91) Clemo endeavours to dismiss the 'infinite remoteness' of the Cornish language and its associated 'legends, customs and pre-historic atmosphere', in spite of the language's continuance on Hensbarrow until about 1700 and an Arthurian folk tradition still existing today. In 1935 he was studying this material, but it was rejected following a Calvinist conversion in 1937–8. Even the heritage of Medieval Christianity, as with the anchorite cell on Roche Rock and the parish churches of Roche and St Denis, repelled him. Although Clemo relied heavily on his own religious instinct, it needs to be remembered that he was the first Clemo, possibly from the time of the Reformation, to actively embrace Christianity. Late (or Modern) Cornish, the language of his forbears, and post-Reformation Cornish culture, had been strongly secular. This tangled web of languages and cultures, therefore, needs to be teased out if Clemo is to be properly understood.

The transfer of language and culture from Celtic to Anglo-Cornish in the area of Hensbarrow can be dated with reasonable certainty. The process follows that identified at Constantine on the Lizard by Charles Henderson[4] and in West Penwith by P. A. S. Pool.[5] According to them, the English language expanded outwards from the towns, and down-wards through society from landowner to artisan, over a period of approximately two hundred years. Henderson's *Constantine in Corn-wall* identifies landowners, with the exception of the tragic Rescadens, as fully bilingual after 1550, and all but the least educated as bilingual after 1600. Interestingly, Pool[6] found in the Cornwall Record Office a probate document of *Francis John alias Trevallacke of Wendron,* who in 1622 could not pronounce English, yet was sufficiently wealthy to make a will. By 1700, according to Henderson, only the lowest orders of Constantine society possessed a meaningful knowledge of Cornish, with 1750 as a convenient date of closure. Pool dates language transfer in West Penwith as having taken place between 1550 and 1800.

LANGUAGE TRANSFER IN CONSTANTINE

DATE	*LANDOWNERS*	*TENANT FARMERS*	*ARTISANS*
1550	C — E	C	C
1600	E — C	C — E	C
1650	E — c	E — C	C — E
1700	E	E — c	E — C
1750	E	E	E — c

An interesting feature of parish records for Constantine and West Penwith, and to a lesser extent Hensbarrow, is that bilingualism produced in personal and place-names a conflict between delayed Celtic and initial English stress. This resulted in Cornish words and phrases:

1. Changing from Celtic to English stress, usually through the introduction of a
   plosive, for example Pen-gólva—Pédn-olva (St Ives)
2. Gaining or losing a syllable, for example Chy-gún—Chóonc (Newlyn)
3. Accommodating Celtic and English stress, for example
   Men-gwýn—Men-wídnan—Mídn-wídnion—Mén-wídden
          1678   1680   C20/C19

Henderson's section, *Local Pronounciation* for Constantine farms, shows a uniform Anglicization of stress. A detailed study of the subject can be found elsewhere.[7]

So-called 'Late Cornish', as spoken at Constantine and in West Penwith, was the Cornish of bilinguals not monoglots. The personal names of late monoglots retain a Celtic form on parish registers, while bilinguals show stress and syllable adaptation. The forward movement of stress, the introduction of an intrusive plosive and syllable accommodation can be clearly observed over time in the syllables 'pen' and 'gwyn' in personal and place-names.

1	2	3	4	5	6	7		1	2	3	4	5	6	7		1st	2nd
		G	W	Y	N						P	E	N			C	
		G	W	I	d	N					P	E	d	N		C	e
		G	W	Í	D	N					P	É	D	N		C	E
	G	W	Í	D	N	E				P	É	D	O	N		E-C	
G	W	Í	D	D	O	N		P	É	D	D	O	N			E	C

/ = STRESS

A rapid transfer of language from Cornish to English in the family group of Chygwýn (house white) can be seen in the Marriage Register of St Sithney on Mounts Bay.[8]

The Family of Chygwin in the Parish of St. Sithney

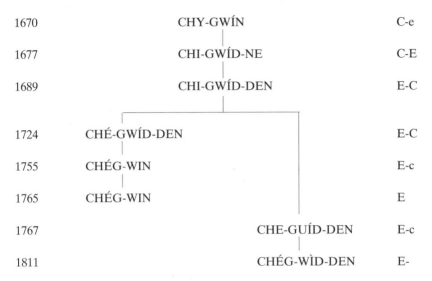

1670	CHY-GWÍN		C-e
1677	CHI-GWÍD-NE		C-E
1689	CHI-GWÍD-DEN		E-C
1724	CHÉ-GWÍD-DEN		E-C
1755	CHÉG-WIN		E-c
1765	CHÉG-WIN		E
1767		CHE-GUÍD-DEN	E-c
1811		CHÉG-WÌD-DEN	E-

The more extensive records available for the Lizard parish of Constantine show stress and syllable conflict at each level of society as English works its way down through local society from landowners to artisans. The Cornish speaking family of Chygwýn first appears on the Subsidy Roll of 1524–25. The Celtic form is retained until 1642, when John Chigwýn married Christian Walter and in 1659 took the lease of Meane Wartha. By 1660 the Subsidy Roll gives the upwardly mobile John Chigwýn and all nine males of that ilk who owned land as Chigwídne. John was becoming an English speaker. Already by 1649, however, the wealthy family of Trefusis, who probably only retained Cornish so as to converse with their tenants and servants, owned a field called Tregwídden Closes. Yet the 'Poor' on the Subsidy Roll of 1662–4 still retained the Celtic monoglot form of Chegwínn, evidenced by the -nn. During the 1740s, one hundred years after the family of Trefusis had used -gwídden, the Marriage Register records Chégwíddon as the standard form, thus indicating that even the artisans had English as a first language and Cornish as a second.[9]

The available evidence for language transfer from Cornish to

English in Clemo's home area of Hensbarrow, in mid-Cornwall, follows the pattern established further west but at a slightly earlier date. While the Prayer Book Rebellion of 1547 appears to have been the catalyst for change in Penwith and on the Lizard, the 1497 insurrection effected the same in mid-Cornwall. Bilingualism was recorded by 1595 in the adjacent western parish of St. Ewe, yet in 1644 trooper Symonds still heard Cornish spoken at Lostwithiel and Lanhydrock to the east—though possibly by west Cornishmen serving in Royalist army units.[10] The final decades of spoken Cornish are recorded on a series of Tin bounds documents, discovered by Charles Henderson, and dated to 1660 and 1685.[11] 1497 to 1685 provides for language transfer, a similar span to that found elsewhere.

This assessment can be further supported from the St Ewe Marriage Register. In the last years of the sixteenth century families were beginning to divide in terms of language, with women taking the lead. In the Tregwýn family we find: *Elizabeth Trédwine*, an English speaker; while *1606 Johannes Trewínne* was a Cornish one. Most revealing is a list of Cornish and English nicknames from 1582 to 1672 (Appendix).

Henderson saw the Hensbarrow documents of 1660/85 and map of 1696 as reflecting the speech of the last bilinguals. The Clemos and the Polmounters came from the level of society longest retaining Cornish. Exactly the same syllable and stress changes occur on Hensbarrow as in the mid-Late Cornish from Constantine and Penwith.

crows	gwýn	:	cross	white
'crouse wíden		alias	White	Cross'
Pen hal býghan		:		head marsh little = moor
'Péden Hal végan		alias		head of Halvégan Moor'

That Hensbarrow dialect follows mid-Late Cornish can be supported by Clemo's prose works. The dialect story *Maria and the Milkman* has Sammy Chégwídden as a central character. In *The Clay Kiln* (p. 84) Reginald Chégwídden is the Captain of the clay-works, while farm labourer Len Truscott speaks in *sing-song*, an accepted indicator of Late Cornish.

A tin-bounds document of 1685 gives amongst largely English names a few in Cornish. Henderson interprets *Mana Cart* as probably *Monhet-cam*, with monhet meaning mine or ore-ground. It appears that a few tinners still wished to name their works in Cornish. Even more remarkably, Henderson discovered on the map of 1696 evidence of a bilingual phrase, *Mene Flat in Pedan Halvegan*. The adjective *flat* comes from the noun *mene* (meneth–rock) as in Cornish and not in front, as in English, thus indicating a speaker whose grammar is still Cornish.

LANGUAGE TRANSFER IN HENSBARROW

DATE	LANDOWNERS	TENANT FARMERS	ARTISANS (Clemo/Polmounter)
1497	C — e	C	C
1550	E — C	C — E	C
1600	E — c	E — C	C — E
1660	E — c	E — c	E — C
1700	E	E	E — c

In proclaiming the 'infinite remoteness' of the Celtic past Clemo was obscuring one of his major achievements, the creation of poetic forms capable of conveying the rhythms, intonation and dissociations of Late Cornish and its wrecked culture. This process was not complete until the late 1940s when, after a period of literary drought, he brought forth *Christ in the Clay-pit* and *The Excavator*. The disturbing power of the clayscape poems, written at a time when Europe was surveying the wreckage of its own civilization, makes them peculiarly apposite.

CORNISH REVIVALISM AND THE POLMOUNTER INHERITANCE

John Polmounter (1845–1915) farmed the moorland tenement of Goonvean, where Goonvean clay works now stands. It lies to the north of the clay-miners cottage at Goonamarris where Eveline and Reggie Clemo set up home in 1913.

> Though the orchard fell the stable stayed;
> To this day it stands with its sweet warm straw,
> The black trucks baulked ten yards away.
> ('Goonvean Claywork Farm', 3.3–6)

The 'black trucks' symbolize the forces of disability and rejection which came within 'ten yards' of destroying the writer's own life.

John Polmounter, an illiterate drunkard, married Jane Bullen, a Bible Christian devotee, and through contact with the sect, which flourished only in Cornwall and Devon (and South Australia), was converted and became a 'local preacher'. Eveline remembered how his *face shone* when in the pulpit (interview, 1975). The Bible Christians accepted Wesleyan theology, which derived largely from High Anglicanism, but emphasized scripture and religious experience above liturgy and sacrament. After his conversion in 1937–38, Clemo came to interpret this emphasis as a return to the purity and simplicity of the

Early Church, as against the clericalism and apostasy of a later age. This is a central theme of *The Shadowed Bed*, a novel written in 1948–50 and published in 1986:

> In 'Marriage of a Rebel' I mentioned an allegorical novel I wrote in 1948–50, blending Barth and Lawrence. A dozen publishers refused it and when I went blind (1955) I laid it aside. Last spring Ruth (wife) read it, suggested a few revisions, and after praying for guidance I send the MS to Lion . . . Unless Lion change the title it's called 'The Shadowed Bed', symbolizing the shadowy movements of God and Satan on the human clay-beds. God appears as Potter, an exiled claywork owner, Satan as Beale, the sinister usurper who fools the village vicar. (Letter, 10 December 1988)

> and you felt the authentic experience even in my anti-church poems like 'Christ in the Clay-pit' and 'The Excavator'. It's in 'The Shadowed Bed' too. The sinners go straight to the Rock, Christ, and are told to build a little chapel 'for reading Potter's book, for prayer and breaking of bread' (pp. 217–18). This points to the simplicity of the first Christians, even though for them 'Potter's book' was only the Old Testament . . . (Letter, 4 October 1987)

> The Church was established on the fulfilment of Scriptural predictions, made centuries earlier, about the Messiah. (Letter, 4 October 1987)

Bible Christian revivalism was far from accepted by other literary figures.[12] A. L. Rowse records how his parents (especially his mother) thought Bible Christians less than respectable; although, curiously, Jack Clemo's Sunday school teacher, Sam Jacobs, was to become a close political friend of Rowse during the Labour anti-Appeasement campaigns of the 1930s. R. S. Hawker, vicar of Morwenstow, published a *devil hunt* satire of the denomination, while Arthur Quiller-Couch parodied Bourne's *Billy Bray, the King's Son* (1877) as *Jacky Pascoe, the King's Postman* in *The Ship of Stars* (1899). Hawker and Q saw revivalism as the release of repressed sexuality, even though William O'Brien, the denomination's founder, had been a close friend of Dr Jonathan Couch of Polperro, Q's grandfather.

Clemo counter-attacked in *The Shadowed Bed*. He portrayed the cultured and sophisticated vicar of Carn Veor, and his neurotic wife, as lacking: 'the elemental fire that would destroy the innate fastidiousness and reserve, the false delicacy, that estranged and deprived them' (p. 54). Behind Clemo's remark is the age-old Cornish distrust of Anglicanism. Clemo later broadened the target to include those forms of Catholic mysticism associated with mortification, religious vows and celibacy. The influence of William Blake is evident. Clemo's ideal was Billy Bray, the Bible Christian revivalist and Cornish miner, who combined spirituality with a robust sexuality. It was the decline of revivalism after the First World War which led Jack Clemo, and indeed Sam Jacobs, out of Methodism. Evelyn Clemo retained her Bible Christian faith even after the sect's absorption into larger bodies in 1907 and 1932. This led her to reject both the Modernist trends within Methodism and her son's supposedly Calvinistic reaction to them.

PANTHEISM AND EROTICISM
Clemo's rejection of the Church in 1929 led him to construct an alternative religion from pantheism, with Penrose Veor farm as his sacred grove, and eroticism, inspired by a local girl called Evelyn Phillips. The farm lies on the verdant border between Hensbarrow and the Goss moor, and within a triangle of probably Arthurian sites. Henderson and others[13] have identified Domellick as the *Domelioc* of Geoffrey of Monmouth's *Historia Regum Britanniae* (c.1139), with Carne Hill as the *Castle of Domelioc*, and Castle-an-Dinas to the north as the major stronghold. According to Geoffrey (Bk 8, 19–20), Uther Pendragon fell in love with Igraine, wife of Gorlois , Duke of Cornwall, and followed the couple to Cornwall. Gorlois sent Igraine to Tintagel (Castle-an-Dinas in the view of Henderson and Thomas) and died defending the *Castle of Domelioc* or Carne Hill. Uther used the magic of Merlin to seduce Igraine, with Arthur as issue. Clemo would have accessed Arthur legends through the Griggs of Penrose (see *The Arthur Legend and the Saint of the Parish* by Canon G. D. Doble).[14] Penrose and Carne Hill appear repeatedly in Clemo's earlier writings.

Clemo's first visit to Penrose Veor farm came in 1929. He was taken from the industrial wasteland of Goonamarris to the spring pastures at the moor's northern edge for a wedding reception. The sense of divinity within nature, a youthful infatuation with Evelyn and the brooding presence of Carne Hill, all combined to produce a mystical awe more potent than Church belief or secular education. *Confession of a Rebel* contains nearly a dozen references to the mystical power of Penrose.

Clemo was not the only Celtic writer struggling with such intuitions, as can be seen from the works of the Powys brothers. The first night Clemo spent out of Cornwall was in 1950 on a visit to T. F. Powys at Mappowder, in Dorset. In 1925 Professor of English

Literature at Cambridge, Sir Arthur Quiller-Couch, wrote to H. F. Stewart about re-exploring the 'real scene' of the *Tristan* romance from his home at Fowey.[15] *Memories and Opinions* relates his first discovery of the *exact site* of King Mark's abode to a mystical intuition.[16] 1925 saw Q commence the novel *Castle Dore* (completed by Daphne du Maurier), a re-enactment of the twelfth-century *Tristan* story as told by Beroul and Gottfried von Strassburg. The adulterous love of Amyot Trestane (Tristan) and Linnet Lewarne (Iseult), wife of Mark Lewarne (King Mark), is acted out around Castle Dore, on the lower Fowey. Henderson believed the original name of Castle Dore was *Carhurles*, a corruption of the *fort of Gorlois*.[17] The lovers are united in death in the vicinity of Castle-an-Dinas. After a *Calvinist* conversion in 1937–38, Clemo was to condemn such romanticism, much as the Catholic Ledru does in chapter seven of the novel. Yet before that, Clemo's passion for Evelyn, as set out in the poem *Midnight of the Flesh*, and conducted under the influence of the 'heretical pagan tide' of Penrose (COR, p. 65), was very much in the *Tristan* and *Arthur* mode.

By 1936 Clemo was facing romantic and literary rejection. He became increasingly disillusioned with the 'inhuman heart' of the Penrose visions (COR, p. 98). This led him back to the industrial clayscape of Hensbarrow, where another *Spirit*, in conflict with Penrose, took possession of him, producing a sense of being an Elect of God. Soon Clemo came into conflict with Q, whose novel *Ia* (1896) attacked the doctrine of Election and the mystical Calvinism Clemo was claiming to espouse.

CLAYSCAPE MYSTICISM

By Easter 1939, two years after the commencement of his clayscape experiences, Clemo regarded himself a Calvinist. A letter to H. J. Willmott, the staff columnist and later the editor of the *Cornish Guardian*, argued that only God's chosen elect stood secure against the depravity of approaching war. Poems like *Robert Browning*, started to include phrases such as *Calvin's stubborn creed* (4.5). A novel called *Private Snow*, begun in 1936 under the influence of Penrose pantheism, had its portrayal of man and nature adapted to his new creed. This did not please Q, who received the manuscript in January 1940 and promptly returned it. Clemo appeared unaware that *Ia* and *The Ship of Stars* ridiculed the very material he was presenting. Yet interestingly Q, who had become acquainted with Calvinism through his grandparents, the Fords of Newton Abbot, did not regard Clemo's manuscript as recognizably Calvinistic.

A public attack on Clemo's supposed Calvinism came in 1950, following the publication of *Wilding Graft* (1948), a novel which won an Atlantic Award for Literature. H. J. Wilmott in *London-Bodmin* (1950)[18] denigrated the work for advocating the 'eternal determinism' of Calvin's theology, and of supporting this through an obsession with human depravity. Although Clemo claimed in *The Invading Gospel* (1958, pp. 48–9) that he held only to modified or neo-Calvinism, Charles Causley's 1960 introduction to *The Map of Clay* again spoke of 'Clemo's uncompromising Calvinism' and his 'doctrine of Election'. Even in the posthumously published poem *Heretic in Florence* (1995), the poet is of 'Calvin's trend'. The poem *Pascal* (1993), in the phrase *Hippo Chronicle*, emphasizes the importance of St. Augustine of Hippo, a major influence on Calvin. Clemo is mapping out a theological line:

St Paul → St Augustine → Luther → Calvin → Barth → Clemo

At the Reformation Martin Luther, an Augustinian friar celebrated in Clemo's poem *Katherine Luther* (1971), built his teaching on Augustine's theology of Salvation, while rejecting Augustine's theology of the Church. Calvin developed this emphasis. Augustine has more recently been accused of never having fully freed himself from an early adherence to Manichean gnosticism; yet Calvin is at pains to distance himself from gnostic beliefs, especially those which pervaded the fringes of the Early Church and later arose in Manicheanism. Gnosticism, a dualistic system, regarded the created world as evil or under the influence of fate. Christ freed an Elect from the created realm through knowledge and a mystical experience beyond nature. The Early Fathers resisted gnosticism by emphasizing the goodness of creation, the doctrine of the incarnation and human free will. The theology of Clemo's clayscape literature, which is presented as Calvinist and Augustinian, appears instead to be closer to gnosticism.

The questionable content of Clemo's 'Calvinism' is evidenced through comparison with Calvin's *Institutes of the Christian Religion*:[19]

Creation
Creation is the *mirror* of God, making his *providence* known (p. 241), and contains *no random power* (p. 234), *fate* (p. 241) or anything *naturally bad* (p. 193). The beauty of creation is contrasted with the demonic (p. 210). However, God's revelation in nature is *insufficient* without revelation in Scripture because of man's perverted Will, yet the same Spirit inhabits both (p. 80). Manichean gnosticism denies God his *glory in creation* (p. 80).

Man

Man is not corrupted from nature (p. 295), nor is wicked by nature (p. 296), as Manichean gnosticism claims, but has a corrupted *Will*. As free will has, therefore, been lost, Salvation is God's sovereign decision. However, as the image of God in many has been *defaced* rather than destroyed, as the gnostics say, then man's natural gifts in the arts and sciences still evidence the Creator, even if the practitioners fail to recognize Him (p. 318).

Christ

Christ is fully God and fully man, the perfect image of the Father, and has atoned for the sins of the Elect, those predestined for salvation, as Augustine argued (Bk II, Ch. XXI).

Sexuality

Calvin opposed celibacy as alien to nature, which of itself is good.

Clemo's literary-mystical understanding of the Fall and human redemption is different from Calvin's doctrine. The poems *Christ in the Clay-pit* and *The Excavator* were written in 1945 as expressions of mature Calvinism. Unfortunately Clemo does not centre the Fall in man's WILL, but in the seductions of nature, especially as hymned by artists, scientists and priests. It requires the *excavator* to destroy beauty and free man for a mystical encounter beyond nature. In the words of the poems:

FALLEN	MEANS OF REDEMPTION	REDEEMED
creation	$\rightarrow$ *wrath*	$\rightarrow$ *God*
nature—fields, woods		*clay-desert, waggon*
	$\rightarrow$ *excavator*	$\rightarrow$
flowers, birds, bushes		*pit-props*
culture, intellect, poetry	$\rightarrow$ *blast, fire*	$\rightarrow$ *Christian art,*
		childhood foolishness
Churches, ritual, priest		*rite of baptism (in)*
	$\rightarrow$ *crucifixion*	$\rightarrow$
alter		*dripping clay,*
		doggeral (dogma)

The poems appear more gnostic than Calvinist. This is compounded when in *Confession of a Rebel* (p. 166) he claims that Calvin
regarded all knowledge of God through Nature as 'idolatry' in contra-
vention of the *Institutes* Bk. I.V.I., 'perfection of blessedness consists
in a knowledge of God . . . in the whole structure of the universe etc'
(p. 65).

Clemo's theological vision is fully argued in *The Clay Kiln* (pp. 58,
131–8, 194–6, 208, 244), a novel which reached its final form in 1951,
virtually at the close of his clayscape phase. Clemo presents a strict
Dualism symbolized by two clay streams flowing in opposite directions.
The stream of nature is governed by 'fate' and leads to destruction,
while the stream of 'predestination' is a divinely ordained plan. A
'leap of faith' is required to transfer from fated nature to
predestination-election. This results in a 'mystic otherness', particularly
experienced in sanctified sexuality. Christian mysticism exists where
'Nature is recognized as an instrument of Fate and repudiated', while
Christian sexuality is the product of 'election . . . beyond Nature'.

Again Clemo is in conflict with Calvin. Calvin rejected the gnostic
idea of Creation being allied to fate or any power other than God's
spirit. The Fall occurred in man's WILL. Salvation is grace rectifying
the WILL through God's sovereign choice, independent of mysticism,
sexuality or an Arminian 'leap of faith'. Grace elevates nature, it does
not abuse or destroy it. In investigating the creation, poets, artists
and scientists are proclaiming God's beneficence, even if by default.
Clemo's position appears to be an amalgam of a gnostic view of nature,
Arminian free will and a Blakean view of sexuality and science. This
does not invalidate his vision as mysticism is tolerant of contradiction.
It is not however Calvinist.

An even more extreme view of nature is evident in Clemo's
earliest clayscape verses. *The Token* speaks of 'nature's evil core' (II.3)
and the believer as 'Nature's foe' (14.1), while *Surrender* sees conversion as advancing 'past Nature' (I.25). The novel *The Shadowed
Bed*, completed 1950–51, continues the theme when calling Carn Veor
an 'evil thing' (p. 94) or 'pagan earth' (p. 122) which becomes 'unified
against' Maggie (p. 129).

Clemo's theology did not go unchallenged. While the views of
secular critics made little impression, the concern of his Wesleyan
mother and a Baptist fiancée of February to September 1949, did:
'When Eileen lectured me about my hatred of beauty in nature and my
nagging at organized religion, I had an uneasy feeling that she was
right, and when virtually promised to marry me I felt some hard crusts
inside me begin to melt' (Letter, 13 September 1983). They were, in
fact, questioning his whole understanding of nature; and probably his

indifference to the Eucharist. The Early Church Fathers rejected free-standing mysticism, regarding attendance at the Eucharist essential and the material side of the sacrament as a guard against gnosticism. Sometime in 1953–54 Clemo began to take the sacrament in his home from a local Methodist minister. Gradually the images of bread and wine percolated into his work, just as the more violent *excavator* type receded.

Clemo wrote *The Invading Gospel* (1958/1972) in 1954–55 in an attempt to clarify his theological position and to reply to the attack by Willmott in *London-Bodmin*. With white blindness descending upon him he was unable to revise the work, with the last section having to be dictated to his mother. He still rejected natural theology, any revelation in nature (p. 15), advocating instead a doctrine of total depravity affecting man and nature (p. 20). Salvation is presented as God's arbitrary decision, which inevitably follows (p. 28). Yet election is related only to a *bridgehead*, with the majority retaining free will (p. 119). How free will can be retained in a state of total depravity is not explained and cannot follow. This confusion becomes increasingly apparent when salvation is viewed as a leap of faith from 'nature to grace', a somewhat gnostic phrase, as against orthodoxy's under-standing of grace coming to an redeeming nature. The corollary is that once healed by grace, man is no longer alienated from God's creation, in the way Clemo's clayscape poems reveal the poet to be!

Any understanding of the doctrine of the incarnation appears absent from Clemo's clayscape works and makes but a brief entry into *The Invading Gospel*. Interestingly, it is the doctrine of the incarnation which the orthodox Sam Dekker uses against the gnostic Owen Evans in chapter nine of *The Glastonbury Romance* (1933) by J. C. Powys, a novel also incorporating *Arthur* and *Tristan* material and which Clemo would have read, being a fan of the Powys brothers. Clemo's in-carnational thinking seems to have grown out of an early Mariology, evidenced by the poem *The Divine Lover*, one stanza of which is included in *The Invading Gospel* (p. 49). It is the feminine, either in the physical presence of Evelyne Clemo, Eileen, Mary and Ruth, or in Mariology, that led him from a gnostic sounding mysticism of clayscape to the orthodox vision of his later work. Between the two lay the horrors of the *Dark Night*.

MYSTICISM OF THE 'DARK NIGHT'

Clemo's *Dark Night* phase probably began about 1951. After that his clayscape mysticism dried up, novel writing ceased and fewer poems were produced. The clayscape quest for a divinity *beyond/past Nature* had proved as illusory as a Penrose/pantheist one within nature.

Between 1955 and 1967 there is a record of only about thirty completed poems. These were published in *Cactus on Carmel* (1967), a year before his marriage. The *Carmel* of the collection's title is a reference to Carmelite spirituality, particularly to the *Dark Night of the Soul* of St John of the Cross and the *via negative* tradition of *The Cloud of Unknowing*. Although he eventually became critical of this material, it supported him at a time when little else did:

> I don't know much about St. Benedict, but I've read 'The Cloud of Unknowing' which has influenced many Protestants, including the American Fundamentalist A.W. Tozer . . . I still feel that the Negative Way is not the best, and that it leaves vital human relationships unexploited and unredeemed.

> I remain sympathetic to the Marian concepts, and was pleased recently when the BBC told me that they broadcast my poem 'Virgin Harbour' on Radio 4 on Christmas Eve.
> (Letter, 11 December 1989)

> The monk John thanked heaven for absolute
> Unbroken darkness . . .

> Did not some wedded Spanish artist
> Find a healthier way after baptism
> (*Beatific Vision*, I.3–4: 3.1–2, 1995)

Clemo possessed only a written Carmelite tradition and was not as fortunate as early Methodist and smuggler Captain Harry Carter of Prussia Cove, who while a prisoner in Britttany during the *Terror* encountered the living spirituality of a group of Carmelite nuns. From January to June 1794 he was frequently in the company of the niece of the bishop of St Pol-de-Leon, who always possessed the 'power to govern her own mind', a fact also true of Clemo in equally desperate circumstances.[20] Q satirized Harry Carter in the short story *King O'Prussia*.

The teaching on the *Dark Night* explains how the soul is purged of its sensual and spiritual faculties in anticipation of union with the *Spouse* in divine love. A Christmas gift from his mother of *The Browning Love Letters* in 1937 enabled Clemo to anticipate a human spouse, one 'granted by God' as the Browning–Barrett correspondence expressed it. That Elizabeth Barrett was a cripple and Clemo had threatened sight added special significance:

With my first Browning pages, read in crisis.

('Casa Guidi', 1 August 1995)

As Dante was let from purgatory to heaven by a transfigured Beatrice, so Clemo saw himself similarly raised, but by a physical wife, imbued with God's grace. The Very Revd. Fr. Benedict Ramsden, a close friend of Clemo during the last decade of the poet's life, made the point:

> This extraordinary man, as a boy, learned to construct such a vision of his unbelievably tragic circumstances as would make it, if not tolerable, at least significant. He arrived at his Browning pattern—in itself a remarkable construct, given his circumstances—at his awesome transformation of the clay symbol, and at the perhaps no less awesome erotic vision, linked to a divine promise of marriage. All this was a shaping of his life as much as it was of his writing. One can almost see his life as the primary artistic creation, and his poetry as a comment on it.   (Letter, 11 June 1999)

Clemo's vision of a future wife paralleled a developing Mariology. The idea of an immaculate conception led him to develop a theology of the incarnation, and with it the final refusal of gnostic influence. This then opened his Bible religion to the importance of the Early Church creeds and rites.

> The immaculate life, immaculate conception
> At the heart of creed and crucial rite.
>
> (*Massabeille*, I. 5–6)

The poem *Virgin Harbour* (1971) probably shows Clemo's Mariology in its final form. As regards the creeds he was able to write by 1993: 'I . . . breathe the Nicene marvels every day' (*Near the Race*, 5.1–2). Such a curious development is symptomatic of Clemo's literary-mystical mind. Yet it would have been mystical mumbo-jumbo had a wife not appeared.

EROTIC MYSTICISM

In 1967 Ruth Peaty of Weymouth, an admirer of Clemo's verse 'chanced' writing to him. A feminine breeze from 'psalms' and 'white chalk cliffs' blew west onto the ravaged scarps of Hensbarrow and say 'my face/Scarred, yet singing . . .' (*Wedding Eve,* 4.4–5, 6.5–6). The correspondence quickly matured into romance and marriage followed in October 1968, with fellow poet Charles Causley as best man. Seven years later Clemo said: 'I was torn inwardly. But it all became integrated. I could see a pattern in everything' (Conversation, 7 August 1975).

Clemo interpreted this as the fulfilment of his Browning vision of 1937 and 'My mother's . . . Isaiah "promise"' (Letter, 4 October 1987) of 1921. At the time, however, marriage gave every indication of being the ultimate fiasco of a tragic life:

> Ruth and I had opposite views on practical matters—she couldn't share my old-fashioned village domesticity, so I gradually adjusted myself to town standards. Even in mysticism we were not identical—Ruth thought some aspects of my mysticism were too much like D. H. Lawrence's. The unity required in marriage rests on basic commitment to Christ—there are bound to be areas of personality in which the couple must 'agree to differ'—and on practical points, as I've said before, I think it's the man who should change to make things easier for his wife. (Letter, 9 September 1987)

Its success and the erotic-mystical satisfaction resulting inspired two of his finest collections, *The Echoing Tip* (1971) and *Broad Autumn* (1975). The length and complexity of poems such as *Wart and Pearl* (56 lines) and *Katharine Luther* (58 lines) belies their composition complete within the poet's mind prior to typing. Clemo claimed perfect recall of all his poems. The collections were quickly followed by the autobiographical *Marriage of a Rebel. A Mystical-Erotic Quest* (1980, pb 1988). Courtship and marriage had transformed the *Dark Night* of 1955–67 into the erotic mysticism of 1968, with its progressive integration of Eros and agape, nature and grace. 'grace must invade nature before anything natural (sex, art or "religion") can enter the redeemed Kingdom. I no longer vilify natural beauty but merely show it's inadequate unless those who enjoy it have a Christian vision' (Letter, 9 July 1988)

Although the *Mystical-Erotic Quest* subtitle was unwisely deleted from the 1988 paperback edition, many, like Fr. Benedict Ramsden (conversation 24 September 2004), regard Clemo's erotic-mystical vision as making a significant contribution to contemporary Christianity.

The conflict between the two experiences of love symbolized by Eros, passionate and romantic love, and agape, divine love, and the unification of Eros and agape in Christian marriage, is a central motif of Clemo's quest. Written under the influence of Penrose, with its Celtic and romantic associations, the lost prose work of 1934 called *Christ or Eros?* (COR, pp.102–3) shows the embrace of Eros and the denial of agape. Disillusionment with Penrose mysticism in 1937 led Clemo to elevate agape and relegate Eros to the tender mercies of the 'excavator' and 'furnace fire'. Notary Ledru presents a modified version of Clemo's clayscape argument in chapter seven of *Castle Dor*. The Catholic Ledru condemns the troubadours for having transformed the adulterous assocation of Tristan and Iseult into a vision of 'deathless love' (p. 46); only to be refuted by Dr Carfax, who views Eros as a necessary adjunct to copulation and myth as embodying timeless truths about the human condition.

The symbol of Eros lay dormant through the clayscape and *Dark Night* phases. Then after thirty years it resurfaced in a poem of late 1966 called *Eros in Exile* (1967). The poem concludes a 'Lakeland' selection in *Cactus on Carmel* (1967) whose inspiration was Mary, an art teacher. Their romance lasted from January 1963 until December 1966, with the poem lamenting the failed quest of Eros and agape. Clemo later reflected in his down to earth fashion:

> mystical creative streak . . . I used to feel exasperated by the general misunderstanding and criticism. But I came to see the difference between beliefs and tastes that were essential to my true self and the whims and kinks that were mere unhealthy symptoms of loneliness . . . Eileen. . . . I let her straighten me out. But Mary tried to rid me of my basic theology I was adamant and would not yield an inch. I think it's important to recognize the distinction—to stand firm for one's true Christian integrity while being willing to have egoistic quirks and aberrations corrected by normal people—to say to a girl, 'Go ahead on my bachelor twists—I'll be meek and inherit the earth'!   (Letter, 13 September 1983)

Clemo's search was resumed through contact from 1967 with Ruth Peaty of Weymouth. The following collection, *The Echoing Tip* (1971), contained Eros in *Ste Gudule and St Agnes* and Venus in *Venus in Grace*, while *Broad Autumn* (1975) includes Aphrodite in *Wart and Pearl*. A climax is reached in *Porth Beach* (1975) where the poet describes himself as carrying Psyche's bowl. In Greek mythology Eros, at the instigation of Aphrodite, the Roman Venus, torments Psyche and ultimately falls in love with her. Eros, unbridled passion, and Psyche, or soul, remain united in love for eternity. Interestingly, it is Eros who drives Paris to Helen. These lovers Dante consigns to Hell, along with Tristram and Lancelot-Guinevere. After *Porth Beach* the Greek images disappear, with a final resolution of Eros-agape coming in *Marriage of a Rebel. A Mystical-Erotic Quest* of 1983. Unfortunately, through this Eros-agape phase from 1966 to 1975, Clemo continued to claim kinship with the school of Reformed theology, in which Eros is interpreted as self-centred love and agape as God-centred love, two mutually exclusive loves.

During the next twenty-five years of married life, Clemo set about exploring the parameters of the mystical life and of the nature of religious experience, with the relationship of human and divine love, Eros and agape, as a central theme. This led him particularly to the poems and novels of the Cornu-Irish Anne, Charlotte and Emily Bronte. His insights, which often conflict with standard Bronte scholarship, were set down in seven published poems: *Charlotte Nicholls* (1967); *The Islets* (to Emily Bronte); *Ste Gudule and St Agnes* (to Charlotte Bronte) (1971); *Emily Bronte, Haworth Keys:* 1840 (1993); *Anne Bronte, Foreign Idiom* (posthumously, 1995). Significant Bronte references are also found in works such as *After Billy Bray*, *Massabeilli* and *Salvaged*.

In *The Islets* Clemo recognized common 'Cornish blood stung by heaven's lash' (3.8) and in *Foreign Idiom* a parallel Celtic moorland vision. Yet in the latter poem he also noted that while his spiritual pilgrimage took him from the scars of Henbarrow to the Florentine palace of Casa Guidi, the apartments from 1847 of Elizabeth and Robert Browning, the Brontes remained shackled to the 'death-trap' (2.6) of Haworth.

The 'Cornish blood' came through Maria Branwell of Penzance, while the upbringing of the sisters fell upon the shoulders of Aunt Elizabeth after Maria's death. The Branwells of Penzance, like the forbears of Q at Polperro, and the Polmounters on Hensbarrow, were leaders of revivalist Methodism. Following the revival of 1813 the Branwells in Penzance and Dr Jonathan Couch in Polperro led the local Methodists out of Anglicanism. Although Clemo's mature religious vision remained sympathetic to revivalism and antagonistic to Anglicanism, he was aware that the sisters rejected Branwell revivalism and remained at least formally Anglican, as also did Q.

In his Bronte poems Clemo argued that the sisters suffered from organized religion, a boarding-school education, the hypocrisy of Victorian morality and sexual repression. This alienated them from their Celtic and mystical sensibilities, and from the Celts attraction to revivalism or Catholicism. Charlotte and Emily, even though teaching for a time in Brussels, were unable to appreciate Catholic mystics, while Charlotte—in the novel *Shirley* (p. 105)—dismissed Branwell type literature as 'mad, Methodist Magazines' steeped in 'ominous dreams, and frenzied fanaticism'.[21] (see *Salvaged*, stanza 7, 1986) Yet they were opened to 'Byron-twisted heats' (*Foreign Idiom*, 2.6). Clemo saw Byron, who possessed Trevanion blood, as an exponent of Eros in rebellion against agape, and used him as a symbol of pure evil (see *San Lazzaro* 1993). Emily was unable to advance beyond a Penrose-like 'bruised ecstasy' and an 'unsmiling heaven' (*Emily Bronte*, 3.5 and 6) because she had been desensitized to the 'Alert grace of hare's racing' (1.3)—an image of grace, nature and sexuality greatly in advance of the image of the 'excavator' of 1945.

In Stanza two of *Emily Bronte* Clemo accuses Aunt Elizabeth of having reared the sisters on a diet of Penwith mythology. Penwith, like Penrose, has an *Arthur* tradition, as Jenner explored in *Some Possible Arthurian Place-Names in West Penwith* (RIC 1912), while St. Michael's Mount appears on line 2733 of Beroul's *Tristran*.[22] *The Clay Kiln* (pp. 153–4) calls Zennor moor in Penwith an area steeped in ancient pagan associations, as did Q in the novel *Ia*. Zennor moor reminded Clemo of the plateau between Carne Hill and Roche Rock. Just as the witch Ia Rosemundy seduces the Calvinist minister Paul Heathcote above Zennor, so Olive Buzza, the village prostitute, who originated from west of Zennor, seduces the Methodist Charlie Crago near Carne Hill. Charlie Crago lived at Enniscaven, suggested by Jenner to be 'Enys Gawain',[23] while Olive Buzza's home was at White Moor, suspected by Q to have been *La Blanche Lande*, line 2653, of Beroul's *Tristran*. The Evelyn image of 1934, where the poet's Eros rises to the *Infinite* through sexual union with the beloved, has become by 1951 an Olive image of betrayal, madness and death, not dissimilar to the conclusion of *Tristan*. Clemo presents Eros without agape as tragic and fated.

The novels of Charlotte and Anne Bronte do not set Eros against agape, although St John Rivers in Charlotte's *Jane Eyre* could be seen as a corrupted symbol of agape, but in opposition to the formal religiosity and Victorian schooled morality Clemo despised and loathed. Yet, Emily, 'unshocked by evil' (*Anne Bronte*, 4.3), appears to have espoused the tradition of Eros in a specifically Celtic way, while agape, at least in *Wuthering Heights*, is consigned to the nightmare figures of Joseph and Jabez. Tristan and Yseut similarly reject agape, although in the more benign figure of Friar Ogrin (Beroul, 1362–1422). The relationship of Cathy and Heathcliff concludes with a union in death of the lovers on Peniston moor. When awaiting the final call from the ghostly Cathy, Heathcliff rejects the Christian religion, as does Tristran because of the power of *destiny* (2302), and cries 'My soul's bliss kills my body, but does not satisfy itself'. (Edinburgh, 1924,

p. 494)[24] The relationship of Amyot Trestane and Linnet Lewarne in *Castle Dor* ends with the union of the adulterous lovers in death below Castle-an-Dinas. Eros finds its ultimate meaning in death.

Q based this ending on the union in death of Tristran and Yseult, a conclusion also found in Wagner's opera *Tristan and Isolda*. The early writings of Clemo give two variations upon this theme: sexual gratification as the only 'paradise' desired in a song of 1936 called *Heaven number Eight* (COR, p. 124); and a spiritualized union with a divinity on Goonvean in *Christ in the Clay-pit* of 1945. Similar Celtic archetypes repeat themselves in *Tristram* and the writings of Emily Bronte, Q and Clemo (see appendices II and III).

Yet between 1967 and 1975 Clemo was able to achieve a resolution of unique importance. This is intimated in *Charlotte Nicholls* (1967), a poem clebrating the marriage in June 1854 of Charlotte Bronte and the Rev. Arthur Nicholls. The resolution of the conflict between agape and Eros in Christian marriage is extended to the union of creation and redemption in the sexual act. This is set against Emily's Eros inspired 'impassioned fantasy' and an 'artist-urge' to be 'self-fulfilled alone' (I. 10–11, 3.7). The argument is daring, as the spiritual vision resulting from marriage must be seen as justifying the death of Charlotte in childbirth nine months later.

A discussion of the literature relating to Eros, agape and mythology occurs in *The Mined and Heart of Love* (1962) by the Catholic academic M. C. D'Arcy S.J. It was written in response to *The Allegory of Love* by C. S. Lewis, *Agape and Eros* by the Lutheran theologian Anders Nygren and *L'Amour et L'Occident* by M. de Rougemont. D'Arcy's ultimate conclusion sheds considerable light on Clemo's post-1975 literary-mystical vision.[25]

In 1936 C. S. Lewis, in *The Allegory of Love*, chapter 1, challenged the commonly held view that *Courtly Love* and *Arthurian* romance were legitimate expressions of Medieval Christian society. This troubadour literature reached its apotheosis in *Lancelot, Erec and Enide* and the now mutilated *Tristan* by Chretien de Troyes. The twelfth-century Chretien adapted the *Matter of Britain* for a northern French audience; *Erec and Enide* was based on *Geraint and Enid*, and Tennyson's reworking restored the original title and Geraint's Dumnonian identity. Those familiar with Hernry Jenner's *Tintagel Castle in History and Romance* (RIC 1927), *The Tristan Romance and its Cornish Provenance* (RIC, 1914), *Review, 'Contributions a l'Etude des Romans de la Table Ronde'*, by J. Loth (RCPS, 1913), and *Dingerein and the Geraints* (RCPS, 1914), will recognize a distinctive Cornish provenance to much of Chretien's material, although Lewis and D'Arcy were unaware of this. The Christian ideal of marital faithfulness, Lewis argued, was subverted by the adulterous loves found in Chretien's work, to the point where romance and sexual passion formed a system working in opposition to the Medieval Church.

D'Arcy then explains how de Rougemont and Nygren develop Lewis' theme by suggesting how and why Christian love or agape and *Courtly Love* or Eros are in conflict. Although de Rougemont and Nygren differ in detail, they agree in essentials. Greek Eros symbolizes man's passionate desire for God or woman. It is ego-centred and demands satisfaction, something scarcely possible in this vicarious world, hence its tendency to seek for a reality beyond the material in a spiritualized or idealized love, which death alone can fulfil. Its religious expression divides into gnosticism or pantheism, although Platonism was the Greek form. When these Eros influences from the east met western Celtic myth, a synthesis occurred whose expressions were the songs of the troubadours and the poems of *Courtly Love*. The Lutheran Nygren argued that New Testament Christianity, with the exception of the writer of St. John's gospel, refused Eros. Yet the Neo-Platonism of early theologians, and especially Augustine, facilitated its entry, and its influence perverted the works of the Scholastics, Dante and John of the Cross.

Conversely, agape or Christian love is theocentric. It is God's selfless and supernatural love for fallen men. It cannot be merited, but is irresistible and comes to a predestined elect, independent of mystical influence. Sexuality is procreative, and not to be romanticized outside of the marriage bond. Nygren's perspective is that of Luther, Calvin and Karl Barth, all theologians Clemo eulogizes in *The Echoing Tip*.

If such an analysis is accepted, then Emily Bronte's *Wuthering Heights*, Q's *Castle Dor*, and the literatures of *Arthur, Tristan* and *Geraint*, fall under the heading of Eros. So must Clemo's Penrose, clayscape and *Dark Night* mysticisms, in spite of his claim to Reformed Protestantism. The Eros-Aphrodite-Psyche symbolism evades disguise, showing that Clemo did not view Eros and agape as opposites, but that Eros could be sanctified by agape. This is a new vision of Christian sexuality, taking a stand between the anti-mystical agape position of the Reformers and the mysticism of Catholic celibacy. D'Arcy finally unfolds an argument in *The Mind and Heart of Love* remarkably sympathetic to Clemo's stand.

D'Arcy rejects Nygren's Reformed view of man having lost at the Fall all powers of free will and an aspiration for God, as this would render him insensible even to election. Although supernatural grace is the prime mover, man's Eros rises as God's agape descends. The union of agape and Eros often necessitates a *Dark Night* of purgation, wherein the masculine anima and the feminine animus principles can rediscover an Edenic harmony, and subsequently a vision of the divine in supernatural joy. Such an analysis appears remarkably apposite to Clemo's life and mystical experience, with the marriage of 1968 as the pivotal point.

Clemo's literary mystical vision, therefore, was not the product of deprivation and disability. It lies at the heart of the European mystical tradition. The very Revd Benedict Ramsden, leader of the Community of St Antony and St Elias, a body ministering to the severely mentally disabled, makes the following statement.

> I have always thought of Jack not only as a poet but, as he thought of himself, a mystic. There is a tendency to assume that mystic insight simply 'comes'—a sort of visitation from on high, to which the recipient is entirely passive. This may be true in some cases, but there is another pattern in which, rather like an artist painting an icon, far from being passive, the mystic is himself involved in constructing his vision. I would have thought that, from a religious point of view, such co-creativity was more admirable than being merely passive to some sort of divine visitation. (Letter, 11 June 1999)

Fr. Benedict and Lilah Ramsden organized two visits to Italy: *Approach to Murano* (1993) was inspired by the visit to Venice in 1987; *The Cured Arno* (1995) was inspired by the visit to Florence and Venice in September 1993. Of the second Jack wrote:

> Few critics note my spiritual development—hence the 'Times' lament over the lack of 'fierceness' in my later work! A Christian can't remain stuck at his starting-point: he must expand with the fulfilment of God's promises. I was very much aware of this in Italy in September. Benedict took us to Florence first and we went to Casa Guidi palace, where the Brownings lived for 15 years. The place is now empty and closed to the public, but we were admitted after Benedict showed the curator a copy of 'Murano' and explained about Browning's influence on me! I was deeply moved, standing in the study where he wrote 'Christmas Eve' and 'Easter Day'. Ruther and I were photographed on the balcony where Robert and Elizabeth so often paced up and down. (Letter, 18 November 1993)

His tangle of key meanings, clues to God,
Led straight to the heart of my marriage.

Soon I shall stand on the balcony,
My wife's hand and mine on a roughly-caved cherub.
　　　　　　(*Casa Guidi*, for Benedict Ramsden, 4.4–5, 5.1–2)

When Clemo returned from Florence and Venice in September
1993 he only had ten months to live, and failed to see the publication of
The Cured Arno in 1995. Of his death in July 1994 Fr Benedict says:

I remember my last meeting with him. As I left the hospital
ward, I looked back and saw the ravaged man to whom I
had just tried to convey the homage I felt. He was utterly
transformed. He was lying on his pillow, his hands lifted
towards his wife, his lips pursed to kiss hers. For a moment, all
ravage fell away, and I was left with my last glimpse of him as
a lover. (Letter, 11 June 1999)

APPENDIX

Probable Cornish and English Nicknames from the Marriage Registers of St Ewe in mid-Cornwall and St Breage on Mounts Bay

Register Form: Date–Surname–alias–Nickname; & suggested meaning

St. Ewe	St. Breage
1582 @ Ownter–C. ewnter; uncle	1587 @ Kechen–E. kitchen or C. kegyn (kitchen), poss. Godolphin House
1603 @ Tentoren–C. den dorn; woman with man's fist	
1618 @ Sweet–E	1607 @ Danter–C. tanter; suiter
1623 @ Geare–Late C. gear; scribe or messenger	1609 @ Angove–C. an gof or gov; the smith
@ Anthorn–C. an dorn; the fist	1626 @ White–E
	1688 @ Full–C/E/ Fol/Foul/Fool
@ Geene–C. (Lh. Gen); chin	1690 @ Anhell–C. an hell; tardy
1645 @ Geene–gen: chin, family feature	C/E. the hall, poss. Godolphin
1646 @ Ounter–C. ewenter; uncle	1691 @ Anhell–as above
@ Gotha–C. goth; haughty	1690 @ Coach–C. cough; red
C. godhas; moles	1692 @ Touch–C. tuch or E. touch
1671 @ Pater–C. Lord's pravyer,	1697 @ Cunning boy–E. cunning boy
Rosary, a recuscant?	Or dial. Charmer
1672 @ Fadum–E. fathom; miner	1699 @ Cogden–C. cok(g); cuckoo C. den; man @ Uninformed–E
	1703 @ Tuck–C. tek(g); handsome
	1713@ Dissembler–E
	1717 (Clyes)–C. cleys: ditch

Marriage Registers, Phillimore & Taylor, 1904. Registers close 1812.

JACK CLEMO TEXTS REFERRED TO IN THE STUDY

Wilding Graft, London, 1948
Confession of a Rebel, London, 1949, 1975
The Invading Gospel, London, 1958, 1972
The Map of Clay, London, 1961
Cactus on Carmel, London, 1967
The Echoing Tip, London, 1971
Broad Autumn, London, 1975
The Marriage of a Rebel, London, 1980, 1988
The Bouncing Hills, Redruth, 1983
A Different Drummer, Padstow, 1986
The Shadowed Bed, Tring, 1986
Approach to Murano, Newcastle upon Tyne, 1995
The Cured Arno, Newcastle upon Tyne, 1995
The Clay Kiln, St Austell, 2000 (ed. D. Rowe)
The Awakening. Poems Newly Found, 2003 (ed. Hurst, Kent & Symons)

NOTES AND REFERENCES

1. E. Clemo, *I Proved Thee at the Waters. The Testimony of a Blind Writer's Mother*, Ilkeston, 1976. Conversation, Eveline Clemo & A. Symons, Whitsun 1975.
2. A. M. Kent, *The Literature of Cornwall*, Bristol, 2000, pp. 209-15.
3. D. Crystal, *Cambridge Encyclopedia of the English Language*. Cambridge, 1995. Syllable p. 246, Prosody pp. 248–9, Irish Stress p. 337, Phonetics p. 414. G. N. Leech, *A Linguistic Guide to English Poetry*, London, 1969, 1973, pp. 103–30.
4. C. Henderson, *A History of the Parish of Constantine in Cornwall*, ed. G. Doble, Truro, 1937. Rescadens pp. 82–5, Language p. 213, Local Pronounciation p. 236.
5. P. A. S. Pool, *The Place-Names of West Penwith*, Penzance, 1973, 1985.
6. P. A. S. Pool, *The Death of Cornish*, Penzance, 1975, 1982, p. 32.
7. A. Symons, *Stress and Intonation Patterns in Cornish Dialect, & Models of Language Transfer*, The Cornish Banner, ed. J. Whetter, No. 95, Feb. 1999 & No. 96, May 1999; P. A.S. Pool, Penzance, 1975/82.
8. Phillimore & Taylor, *Cornish Parish Registers. Marriages*, London, 1900.
9. Devon and Cornwall Record Society, *Subsidy Rolls, Muster and Hearth Tax Rolls & Probate Callendars of the Parish of St. Constantine, Cornwall*, ed. Tapley-Soper, London, 1900, Exeter, 1910.
10. P. Berresford-Ellis, *The Cornish Language and its Literature*, London, 1974, pp. 77–9.
11. C. Henderson, *Essays in Cornish History*, ed. Rowse & Co., Henderson, Oxford, 1935. *Blackmore*, pp. 130–34.
12. A. L. Rowse, *A Man of the Thirties*, London, 1979, pp. 31, 92, 124; R. S. Hawker, *Life and Letters of R. S. Hawker*, ed. Byles, London, 1905, pp. 56–62; J. Clemo, *Confession of a Rebel*, London, 1949 & 1975, pp. 77–8.
13. C. Henderson, Oxford, 1935. *Fowey* pp. 26–8 & p. 117; H. Jenner, *Tintagel*

Castle in History and Romance, Journal of the Royal Institution of Cornwall, vol. 22, 1926–8; C. Thomas, *Tintagel, Arthur and Archaeology*, London, 1993, pp. 23–4.

14. Contained in: Cresswell Payne, *The Story of the Parish of Roche*, Newquay, nd.

15. F. Brittain, *Arthur Quiller-Couch. A Biographical study of Q*, Cambridge, 1947, p. 117.

16. A. Quiller-Couch, *Memories and Opinions*, ed. Roberts, Cambridge, 1944, p. 65.

17. C. Henderson, Oxford, 1935, pp. 26–7.

18. *London-Bodmin. An Exchange of Letters between J. C. Trewin and H. J. Wilmott*, London, 1950, pp. 89–92.

19. J. Calvin, *The Institutes of the Christian Religion*, trans. H. Beveridge, Edinburgh, 1845.

20. *The Autobiography of a Cornish Smuggler (Captain Harry Carter, of Prussia Cove) 1749–1809*, ed. J. B. Cornish, Truro, 1894 & 1971, p. 90.

21. C. Bronte, *Shirley*, Edinburgh, 1924, vol. 2, p. 105.

22. Beroul, *Tristran and Yseult, Old French Text and Facing English Translation*, trans. Guy R. Mermier, New York, 1987.

23. H. Jenner, *Castle-an-Dinas and King Arthur*, Journal RIC, 1921–2. Also Tremodrett in Roche, the town of Modred.

24. E. Bronte, *Wuthering Heights*, Edinburgh, 1924, pp. 493–4.

25. M.C. D'Arcy S.J. *The Mind and Heart of Love*, London, 1945, 1962. See particularly Chapter 1; C. S. Lewis, *The Allegory of Love*, London, 1936, Chapter 1.

WILLIAM SCAWEN (1600–1689)—A NEGLECTED CORNISH PATRIOT AND FATHER OF THE CORNISH LANGUAGE REVIVAL

Matthew Spriggs

INTRODUCTION

The historiography of Cornwall is now quite diverse in approach.[1] We have English historians who do not see any distinctiveness for Cornwall beyond the level of any other 'English county', nationalist-oriented historians challenging whether Cornwall has ever been legally and constitutionally part of England, and Cornish historians full of angst about whether they or Cornwall are different from anyone or anywhere else and perhaps thus toeing a line seeking acceptance from the great metropolis (at least one of the two writers of books called *Tudor Cornwall* might be thought to fall into this category!). We also have some English historians who see Cornwall as clearly a land apart at least in the fifteenth to seventeenth century period (and presumably before), and expatriate-Cornish historians who want Cornwall to have been different from England but worry that they may be over-romanticizing a bit.[2] What links them all is that their positions are essentially 'political', or at least responsive to political debates about what it means to be 'British', or what it means to be 'English'. Also, all such histories respond to a feeling expressed by many Cornish people that their identity as 'Cornish' is constantly under attack from 'modernizing' or 'foreign' influences.

But as we shall see, it was ever thus with history and ever thus with Cornwall. Modern historical debate here is often passionate. It can sometimes sadly degenerate into name-calling, but overall such passion is generally positive. It shows that history matters in Cornwall; it shows that people care about the past. And one can also see that the extremes tend to influence each other unconsciously, so that a wider range of points of view, different perspectives, are brought to bear on issues that a lone opinionated historian of whatever hue would not have to think about unless pushed. Orthodoxies are challenged and that is, after all, what good original research always does. But there clearly are not enough historians of Cornwall, and I suspect some of the heat generated is due to a lack of critical mass.

The subject of this article, William Scawen (1600–1689), was in many ways a surprisingly modern historian. The different approaches to Cornish history I have outlined above would have been recognizable to him, engaged as he was in a particular patriotic and historical project towards the end of his life: on the one hand to record and on the other to revive, the Cornish language. He was among the first to see that it was in grave danger of dying out, and the first we know of who actively did something about it.[3] It was a patriotic project in that he saw the language as emblematic of the distinctiveness of the Cornish as the last representatives of 'the Ancient Britons in England', and as the heirs of one of the original pre-Roman kingdoms of Britain. It was historical in that he sought to explain how the present situation of the Cornish language (and indeed of the Cornish people) had come to pass.

'ANTIQUITIES CORNUBRITTANIC'
Scawen left at his death an essentially complete text of his thoughts on all this, which is in the Cornwall Record Office in Truro, entitled *Antiquities Cornubrittanic*.[4] You may think you know this manuscript well. A version of it was first published in 1777 and entered public consciousness particularly through re-publication of it by Davies Gilbert in his *Parochial History of Cornwall*.[5] This in turn is often quoted, for instance by Beresford Ellis in his 1974 book *The Cornish Language and its Literature*.[6] But this early draft—probably the second draft and dating to 1678—has little of the richness and detail of the much longer, fourth and final draft in the Cornwall Record Office which Scawen continued to add to until shortly before his death in 1689.

That final version has never been published—something I hope to be able to rectify—and it is because of this that historian Mark Stoyle has written:

> Scawen's monumental treatise . . . provides as rich a discus-
> sion of the question of Cornish identity from a contemporary
> Cornish standpoint as we are ever likely to get. Yet, strange

as it may seem, this fascinating document has been almost entirely neglected by previous historians of Cornwall.[7]

Stoyle also underlines my point about Scawen somehow seeming to be at home among the present diverse historiographies of Cornwall, when he says of his own research that he has 'followed in Scawen's footsteps' and that his book 'attempts to do very much what Scawen did: to tell the story of early modern Cornwall from the point of view of those who sought to perpetuate the Cornish sense of difference, rather than from the point of view of those who sought to undermine or suppress it'.[8] In discussing Scawen and other figures covered in his book, he continues: 'the tradition which they embodied has the right to be considered as a separate thread within the tapestry of the "new" British history'.[9]

WILLIAM SCAWEN'S LIFE

Stoyle's success in bringing William Scawen out of obscurity has been such, however, that he has created a problem for me in saying anything new about the subject. I will thus deal only very briefly with those areas of Scawen's life which are covered in detail by Stoyle, particularly his Civil War career, and talk more of Scawen as the father of the language revival. I want to show his hidden influence on the whole course of language recording and language revival in Cornwall up to the present.

Some background is needed, however, and I hope that Mark Stoyle will be indulgent when he recognizes much of his own research in the next few paragraphs. The Scawens were a gentry family who had been established at Molenick in the far north of St Germans parish since the fourteenth century, when it is said that a Scawen inherited the property through marriage. William Scawen, born in November 1600, was the son and heir of Robert Scawen (c.1562–1627) and his wife Isabella, the daughter of Humphrey Nicoll of Penvose.[10] Other younger sons included Robert Scawen, prominent in the Civil War on the Parliamentary side and who continued as a distinguished MP after the Restoration in Buckinghamshire.[11] Among the daughters was Elizabeth Scawen who married Martin Keigwin of Mousehole, and was the mother of John Keigwin the Cornish language scholar. We will meet him again later in this article.

William Scawen went to Queen's College, Oxford in 1617 and then to Lincoln's Inn in London for legal training in 1619.[12] He inherited Molenick and other estates in East Cornwall in 1627 upon the death of his father. Some time between January 1632, when a gap appears in the Fowey marriage register and the birth of their first child, baptised on 1 July 1634, he married Alice, third daughter of Nicholas Sawle of Penrice and his wife Alice née Rashley, also of Fowey. Alice Sawle was baptised in March 1604, and she and William had four girls and two boys. Strangely, three of the four daughters appear never to married although they certainly lived to marriageable age, and I can find no evidence that his two sons married either. One wonders what the problem was. William junior, the son and heir, was baptised in 1636 and was buried in October 1705, aged sixty-nine. The second son, Robert was baptised in 1641 and was certainly still alive in 1669 when he would have been twenty-eight. I have not been able to locate wills for either of them, nor for William senior.

From letters, we know William to have been a supporter of imprisoned Parliamentarian (and neighbour in St Germans) Sir John Eliot during Charles I's reign. He was one of the executors of Eliot's will after his death in the Tower of London in 1632. But after serving in the Short Parliament of 1640 as one of two MPs for St Germans, his re-election to what was to become the Long Parliament which followed was challenged by Sir Richard Buller and his family so that a more puritan candidate (one of the Moyle family of Bake) could be returned; William's short parliamentary career was over. He bided his time until the pro-Royalist uprising in Cornwall in October 1642 and then was active militarily on the Royalist side in Cornwall as Lieutenant-colonel to Colonel Piers Edgcumbe. This part of his career is particularly well-described by Stoyle and so I will not go into detail. He held administrative as well as military positions under the King, and was subsequently a member of the group that engineered the surrender of East Cornwall to Fairfax in 1646, so leading rapidly to the end of the Civil War in the west.

Like other Royalists he then had to compound for his property, something which he had thought that he would be exempt from under the terms of the surrender, but the agreement with Fairfax was only a verbal one and so 'not worth the paper it was written on'. Fairfax did, however, intercede on his and other East Cornwall Royalists' behalfs and this had some positive effect. Stoyle does not provide much detail of Scawen's later career, so I will attempt to start to fill the gap before going on to a discussion of *Antiquities Cornubrittanic* (henceforth *AC*).

Although the 1646 surrender can be seen as bowing to the in-evitable rather than simply treachery, it may not have stopped Scawen's continued support for the Royalist cause. He writes of being imprisoned in Pendennis when Charles Shrubsall was the Governor there, presumably on suspicion of Royalist plotting, and one would like to know more of this incident.[13] Shrubsall was never in fact the Governor, but is mentioned in December 1650 in the State Papers: 'the letter of Charles Shrubsall and Matthew Cozen, from Pendennis, concerning the state of their arms in that garrison'.[14] This certainly suggests a position of authority for Shrubsall—perhaps the position of Governor was a sinecure and Shrubsall as 'Captain' was in fact in charge of the day to day running of the Castle? Shrubsall is largely remembered for his destruction of the Mincamber logan stone and is also accused of destruction of religious buildings in St Buryan, seemingly part of a campaign of iconoclasm in Cornwall at the time carried out by the Puritans.[15] In July 1653 we read in the State Papers of 'Captain Cozins, commander of Pendennis Castle', which rather suggests that Shrubsall had moved on by that time. Tighter dating of Shrubsall's tenure might inform us of which particular Royalist plot Scawen was implicated in. The conditions of his original surrender in 1646 make it very unlikely that he was imprisoned at that time, so a time around 1650 seems most likely, given the records of Shrubsall that we currently have. The State Papers refer to prisoners at Pendennis, not all by name, during 1649–50.[16] With the Restoration in 1660 William Scawen was listed among those to receive the projected Order of the Royal Oak, and at that time his income was listed as £800 per annum.[17] The Order was never instituted as it was felt that it might stir up Parliamentary opposition by reopening old wounds. One wonders if it was for something more than just his war service that William was among the sixteen Cornishmen to be so honoured? He was appointed Vice-Warden of the Stannaries, a position of some power in Cornwall, and held that position it would seem until his death. In 1664 he was put in charge of the collection of Hearth Taxes for Cornwall, jointly with his son Robert. This Robert is confused in Basil Duke Henney's magisterial *The House of Commons 1660-1690* with William's brother Robert, then MP for Cockermouth, whom Eveline Cruickshanks erroneously claims 'was one of the first to run foul of the new Treasury Commission in 1667'.[18]

William and son Robert certainly ran foul of the Commission, deducting from Cornwall Hearth Tax receipts without formal certificates some £337 10s, or elsewhere £360, in respect of empty houses and of insolvent inhabitants such as 'pressed seamen and paupers' as William later described them. William continued to be hounded until at least December 1677 when he petitioned King Charles II on the matter, stating that he had 'done many considerable services to the late King for which in the late times he has very much suffered', and begged to be excused the debt. The petition produced the annotation 'Resolution thereon: Let my Lord of Bath speak to the King about this', and there is no further mention of it in the State Papers.[19] The Hearth Tax dispute certainly does not seem to have debarred William from participation in other potentially profitable administrative pursuits for central government during this period.[20]

It was in 1678 that Lord Chief Justice North, attending the Launceston Assizes, enquired about the Cornish language, chiding those present about its decay and enquiring whether there were any books remaining in the language. He was told confidently by one present that there were none. Scawen was clearly quite gleeful to disabuse him of this, revealing that he himself was in possession of the original manuscript we now know as the 'Passion Poem'—Harleian Ms. 1872 in the British Library. As Scawen recounts:

> I told him he was too bold in his negation, saying there may be such as you have not seen, and tis your own fault you have not seen an old piece thereof long in my keeping . . . His Lordship was earnest for a sight of it; This spoken by such a person, a stranger to our Country and having thereupon promised him it at his next coming in Circuit, it putt me into more sedulous thoughts concerning it than formerly, and to recall it out of those hands I had long before lodged it in for translation, they having turned it into verse as the Original was, but shorter and therefore more subject to error, they being conscious of their defects in so obscure a matter (though much pains bestowed therein) feared they should be laughed at, and were loathe to part with it.[21]

THE TRANSLATION OF THE PASSION POEM

Scawen set to work to prepare a copy with his attached observations but illness prevented him from attending the next Assizes and giving it to Lord North, and at the end of his life he had it still by him. He wrote at the beginning of his final text that: 'I have long had a proposal and a desire for the recovery of our pristine and primitive tongue, the Cornish, and had been very solicitous in it with many able persons to set about it, but they have been as deaf to my persuasions as dull towards their own interests therein. Proponit homo, disponit Deus'.[22] But for how long had Scawen had such a proposal? Stoyle has suggested it was during the Civil War that Scawen first took an interest in the language, 'initially kindled when he found himself fighting alongside men from the Cornish-speaking districts of West Cornwall in the Royalist army'.[23] The Cornish language would not have been heard in St Germans itself for somewhere between three and six hundred years before Scawen was born. In 1600 the nearest parish where it still might have been regularly spoken was St Austell. By Scawen's death it had retreated further west, beyond Truro.[24] A likely source of Scawen's interest in the language was Martin Keigwin, his brother in law, and a probable native speaker of Cornish. In AC he acknowledges the assistance of Martin and of his son John (Scawen's nephew).[25]

Martin Keigwin and Scawen's sister Elizabeth married on 27 December 1639 and Elizabeth gave birth to their son John in 1642.[26] It is thus likely that Scawen had the opportunity to develop his interests in the language pre-Civil War. However, Martin died in 1667. If he is the one referred to as translating the Passion Poem into verse but being too embarrassed to hand over his efforts, then it must have been a very early and now lost effort, presumably assisted by his son. John Keigwin's extant translation dates to 1682, and what is sometimes said to be the original of it is in the Lambeth Palace Library.[27] Further, it is not in verse but is a very literal prose translation, and so would represent a second attempt at translation.

Pertinent to this, we have the testimony of John Hicks' lost *History of St Ives*, transmitted through its quotation by C. S. Gilbert in his 1817 *Survey of Cornwall*. If we date forward from 1682 then we must assume that Hicks was writing around 1706:

> I remember about 24 years ago Mr Scawen, of Molenick, in St Germans delivered to me a manuscript in quarto written in the Cornish language in verse. It did concern the passion and death of our most blessed lord and saviour Jesus Christ . . . This book Mr Scawen desired me to carry to Mr Keigwin of Mousehole, to be translated by him into English. I also saw it after it was translated, and recollect that several verses were first written in Cornish, with the English written under it, but not in English verse.[28]

None of the extant manuscripts of the Poem dating to this time period have the English translation written under the Cornish. Generally, as in the Lambeth Palace Manuscript, they have the English on the opposite page to the Cornish. Hicks' memory may of course have been mistaken on this point. Andrew Hawke (following Astle) suggested that Scawen had given the poem to John Anstis to arrange for the Keigwins to translate it, but he was unaware of Hicks' statement and given the putative date of translation any involvement of Anstis would have been most unlikely anyway as in 1682 he was only thirteen years old![29]

Part of the acknowledgements given by Scawen for assistance reads thus:

> And as I have made my complaints, so let me also make my acknowledgements for those assistances, which I have had

from others in making those discoveries I have done, in letting in this little light into such an obscure Room, by the translating of the windows thereof, and that is first by Mr Martin Keigwin, and his son [John] my nephew, both of them pretty good grammarians. The father had lived in Brittany and some while also in Wales, whereby he was better enabled to compare those three different dialects, or words at least, with one another. They brought in also to their concurrence their neighbour Mr Boson of Newlyn.[30]

The 'Mr Boson of Newlyn' was most likely Nicholas Boson (1624–1708) although it could conceivably have been his cousin Thomas Boson (1635–1719).[31] Scawen's thanks might suggest that Boson assisted the Keigwins with the translation of the Passion Poem, but we have no corroborating evidence of this. But this still does not explain the shy translator of 'long before' 1678. Recall that it was said to be a verse translation. Perhaps the Keigwins, assisted by Nicholas Boson, had attempted an earlier verse translation? Or was it that Scawen's memory of it being a verse translation was faulty and it was in fact an early version of what became John Keigwin's prose translation?

Another possibility is given by what is known as the *Gwavas Manuscript* in the British Library, which includes a translation of two hundred verses of the Passion Poem claimed to be by one 'W.H.' and dated 1679–80.[32] This can only be that most notoriously inaccurate and downright mendacious of Cornish historians, William Hals of Fenton Gymps (1655–1737), and the handwriting indeed appears to be his. He would have had reason to be leery of having any Cornish translation by him made public as there is little evidence he had any but the most passing acquaintance with the language and certainly could not speak or understand it. He is not mentioned in Scawen's acknowledgements, and it would seem that he simply copied Keigwin's prose translation of 1682 and backdated it as his own. He would certainly have been capable of such a fraud.[33]

It is the translation of the Passion Poem attributed to John Keigwin which remained *the* translation for nearly two hundred years until Whitley Stokes' new text in the second half of the nineteenth century.[34] It was of course Scawen who had commissioned this translation. Scawen himself produced an English verse translation that is derived from and placed besides Keigwin's prose one in the final version of *AC*, but no one seemed to think it worthy of wider distribution and it was never reproduced. Of the named helpers, John Keigwin and the Boson family became vital links between Scawen, this first language revivalist, and the figures who really cemented the recording of the language in the eighteenth century and ensured that it could be revived at some stage: Edward Lhuyd, William Gwavas and Thomas Tonkin.

THE LINK WITH LHUYD

It has not been realized previously that Scawen himself was in direct communication with the pioneer Celtic philologist Edward Lhuyd. A note in Scawen's hand added to AC between 1687 and his death in November 1689 shows that he was eventually disabused of the idea that he possessed the only literary work surviving in Cornish:

> I have deferred the publishing of this the longer for that I was desired it might be communicated to the University at Oxford and did as much desire that I might know first what was in ye Library extant of ye Cornish and return being then made that there was nothing there, thereof have since by ye favour of ye Learned Dr Llyde [sic—Lloyd, as he then styled himself] upon search been informed that there is a Manuscript there given by Mr [James] Buttan [sic—Button] Ano 1615 written upon old vellum. The Subject whereof seems to be an abbreviation of the Old and New Testament contained in 87 Pages, two of which being sent to me, I caused to be translated, and will be found to be good Cornish, but not so old as this manuscript seems to be. Another such was since that accidentally found, the subject whereof (as I am told) seems to be only of ye Creation.[35]

The two works referred to are of course the *Ordinalia* and Jordan's *Creation of the World*. This passage also establishes the first indirect link between Lhuyd and John Keigwin, as it would doubtless have been Keigwin who translated the sample sent by Lhuyd for Scawen. Later it was Keigwin who was to be the translator of the works used by Lhuyd in his own researches.

Scawen had set up an indirect link which facilitated the translation of all then-known works in Cornish, and their dissemination to people such as Thomas Tonkin and from him to William Borlase, William Pryce, Davies Gilbert and others on up to the first generation of modern revivalists and beyond. But his importance may go beyond this link, important though it was, as there is no earlier reference than *AC* to Lhuyd having any knowledge of or interest in the Cornish language. Scawen appears to have been the instigator of Lhuyd's abiding interest in Cornish, and perhaps thereby his wider interest in comparative Celtic philology. Scawen seems to have completed AC in 1688 with only a short coda added to the end of it in 1689, by which time he seems to have been in seriously fading health if his handwriting is any indication. He was buried in St Germans on 18 November 1689.

Lhuyd's interest in comparative study of the Celtic languages has been suggested to have commenced under the influence of scholars such as John Ray and John Aubrey, or those he was in contact with even later such as William Nicolson and Edmund Wyld.[36] We can establish from surviving letters to and from Lhuyd that he was first in contact with Ray in June 1689 and with Aubrey sometime before February 1691, both most probably somewhat later than he was in communication with Scawen. In addition, Lhuyd's first communication discussing linguistic matters with Ray rather than botanical ones was not until November 1690.[37]

There is not much early evidence of any interest even in Welsh philology in Lhuyd's correspondence. The first extant Lhuyd letters from 1682 show knowledge of the Welsh names of plants, but no analysis of those names. A letter to Lhuyd sometime between January and March 1688 discusses a Welsh visitor to North America who claimed that the Indians could understand Welsh, and it was probably Lhuyd who communicated this to the Oxford Philosophical Society on 20 March of that year.[38] His first serious piece of linguistic research occurs as a four page Irish-Latin-British vocabulary included in John Aubrey's *Villare Anglicanum*, completed early in 1691, and said to be 'from Mr Edw: Lloyd of the Museum at Oxford 1689, writt by him'. This might suggest that the Lhuyd-Aubrey correspondence began in that year, but if so it is no longer extant.[39] There is also a letter sent to Dr Plot in May 1690 from 'Meredyth Owen', later admitted by Lhuyd to be himself, criticising 'Dr Bernard's censure of ye Welsh language' in a publication by George Hickes of 1689.[40] My search of the Lhuyd correspondence and other manuscripts has not been exhaustive, but on the evidence available I think that a claim that it was Scawen who may have first sowed the seed of Lhuyd's subsequent linguistic interests is one worthy of further investigation.[41]

SCAWEN'S INFLUENCE ON LOCAL SCHOLARS

Scawen certainly seems to be the originator of the idea of writing letters in Cornish between scholars as a means of practicing and reviving the language. This activity outlasted his death. Lhuyd, of course, addressed a missive to the Cornish people in the language in his 1707 *Archaeologia Britannica*,[42] and how many language enthusiasts today write to each other to hone their Cornish skills and demonstrate that the language is alive? Scawen wrote as reason 16 of 17 for the decline of the language that 'The want of writing is the great cause of its decay'. He continued:

> But I never saw a letter written in it from Gentleman to another, or by any scholar, which is to be wondered at and blamed as a thing very unbecoming such as ought to be studious of anything that is ancient. But since I began to set about this work I have caused some of those that [have] been my helpers therein to write me several letters which they contend at first to be very hard to be done, but after some practice it seemed easier. And I prescribed it to others to be a principal means to recover the Tongue to use in some good degree, at least in memory.[43]

Scawen seemed hopeful that the combination of publication of the Passion Poem (with its translation) and Cornish letter writing, could together save and revive the language. A passage on the next page underlines this:

> Had we but store of books written in ours . . . or but frequent letters interchanged with one another, according to that which we have in this one small piece, it might bring all into knowledge and into use, if men's industry and ingen[uit]y were set about it; and this I humbly advise as the fittest means, and the letters I have caused to be written to me I purpose shall remain as incitements to others to do the like.[44]

Sadly, none of these letters seem to have survived. But Scawen's contribution may have gone even beyond this. Sometime soon after the Restoration of 1660 Nicholas Boson wrote down the folktale of *Jooan Chei a Horr* (John of Chyanhor) in Cornish and also wrote for his children the romance in Cornish and English of *The Dutchesse of Cornwall's Progresse*. The first of these works has survived to the present and is still used in teaching Cornish language, and the second was known to William Borlase in its entirety but now sadly only survives in copied fragments.[45] What spurred Nicholas Boson into these sudden—and unique for the time—literary efforts? Surely it must have been the example and encouragement of William Scawen?[46]

OWNERS AND HANDLERS OF THE PASSION POEM

We have no idea where Scawen acquired the original manuscript of the Passion Poem, although it is clearly due to his assiduous efforts in recognizing its value that it has come down to us today. He tells us that he had had it long by him by 1678, and recounts several unsuccessful efforts to acquire other Cornish manuscripts such as the papers of Richard Angwin, who died in 1675.[47] William Hals claimed that the manuscript of the Poem had been found in Sancreed church in West Penwith, but that is as likely to be his own fantasy as to represent any real tradition.[48] We do have more idea of what happened to the Poem after Scawen's death. He had thought of donating it to the Bodleian Library in Oxford but had no guaranteed way to get it there safely from Cornwall, and also thought it would lay there unread. So his literary attempts were a more active scheme to get the manuscript known and circulated. In this, of course, he succeeded. Once he died it seems that the Passion Poem passed to his kinsman John Keigwin, perhaps along with at least one version of his manuscript of AC.

Both documents were borrowed by John Anstis (1669–1744) in 1693, who passed them on to Bishop Trelawny from whom the Poem passed to Edward Lhuyd and then back to Anstis. He seems never to have returned it and some time after June 1703, with or without Keigwin's approbation, the Poem entered the Harleian collection, later to become part of the British Library, as Anstis' donation.[49] There is a letter at the end of the Passion Poem by John Robyns, dated 1700, but this only means that he had access to it, not that he owned it himself as is sometimes claimed.[50]

THE FOUR VERSIONS OF ANTIQUITIES CORNUBRITTANIC

I have several times referred to various versions of AC. Here I must mention what got me on to researching William Scawen in the first place. It was a passage in that most useful of reference works on the Cornish language, Oliver Padel's 1975 catalogue of an exhibition of Cornish language manuscripts and books held as part of the Celtic Congress of that year in Cornwall. He noted the existence of three separate manuscripts of Scawen's work in Cornwall and a published version which was somewhat different than any of them. He further noted: 'The relationship of these three Mss. to Tonkin's full version and the printed abridgement has never been investigated'.[51] Intrigued and spurred on by this statement I have since undertaken that study. Elucidation of the history of the various versions can be used to trace further the influence of Scawen's work on those who owned or at least read one or other of the four manuscripts that must have once been in existence. Three of them are extant and the other is lost but known from its 1777 published version.

1. The earliest version, dating to 1678 is Cornwall Record Office Manuscript Dd.Enys. 1999.[52] A comparison with version two shows it

to be earlier. Indeed, Padel describes it as a 'copy of rough notes preliminary to Scawen's Antiquities'.[53] It is rather more than that, however, and includes at least two drafts of one page, showing it to have been a working copy made by a scribe and then amended by Scawen. There are fewer reasons given for the decline of the language (10 instead of 16 or 17 in other versions); it is much shorter than later versions; it leaves the date of death of Chesten Marchant blank, unlike other versions; and it has many remarks that are expanded upon in the second version. It includes the Lord's Prayer and Creed in Cornish, Welsh and Breton, as did Version 2 of AC in all probability, but not Versions 3 and 4. It occurs in a book of papers, some others of which too are by Scawen but include published newspaper material from *The London Gazette* dating from 1703–4 relating to the Stannaries.[54] It was in the possession of John Davies Enys by 1902[55] and was later placed in the CRO. This version does not seem to have been seen or used by later scholars until the twentieth century.

2. The second version, also probably dating to 1678 and intended ostensibly for Lord North, is now extant only in the version first published in 1777 'from a manuscript in the Library of Thomas Astle', which was then reprinted in 1779 and 1808 in *The Antiquarian Repertory*, and subsequently in Davies Gilbert's *Parochial History of Cornwall* in 1838.[56] This was not an abridgement of Version 3 as Jenner and others have suggested, but represents a separate manuscript tradition.[57] F. W. P. Jago reprinted the sixteen reasons herein for the decline of the Cornish language in his Cornish-English dictionary of 1887.[58] The later revivalists of the twentieth century also often refer to this version. It received prominence in Peter Beresford-Ellis' *The Cornish Language and its Literature*.[59] But it also affected a much earlier generation of scholars as a manuscript, through an abridgement of it (largely unacknowledged as to source[60]), sent by John Anstis to Bishop Trelawny as part of the materials used by Edmund Gibson to compile his expanded edition of Camden's *Britannia* in 1695. The original materials used in this compilation were in the St Paul's Cathedral Library for a time but were then transferred to the Bodleian Library in Oxford where they sit, generally unremarked by scholars of Cornwall. A comparison of Anstis' abridgement in that manuscript with the 1777 published version reveals them to be drawn from the same source,[61] but also makes clear that the 1777 publication was itself an abridgement of a somewhat longer manuscript.[62]

At the Anstis sale in 1768 many of his manuscripts were acquired by Thomas Astle (1735–1803), and it seems most likely that version 2 of *AC* was among them.[63] What happened to the manuscript after

Astle's death is unknown. It may still exist unnoticed somewhere, but it may not have been seen to have much value after publication had taken place. Many of Astle's manuscripts passed as a bequest to the Marquess of Buckingham and are now in the Stowe Collection in the British Library.[64] Other repositories of material from Astle's library should also be checked. Version 2, through incorporation of some of its conclusions in Gibson's *Britannia*, and through its publication some eighty-two years later and its several reprintings, has been the most influential of the manuscripts. This is a pity in some ways since Scawen's ideas continued to develop over the next eleven years until his death. This further development is much less known but—as we shall see—not totally ignored by early scholars.

3. The third version is in the Royal Institution of Cornwall. It is a copy in a scribe's hand-dated 1684 and includes subsequent additions in Scawen's hand between 1684 and 1687. As it currently exists it has some forty-four numbered pages, mirroring those in version 4 but finishing in the middle of reason 15 of the decline of the language.[65] In 1735 it was in the possession of Francis Gregor of Trewarthenick. He lent it to his cousin Thomas Tonkin whose transcription is in the British Library.[66] Tonkin also abridged it to be included in his *Archaeologia Cornu-Britannica*, and the abridgement is included with the partial manuscript of that work acquired by the RIC in 1999—the source of William Pryce's 1791 publication of the same name.[67]

When Tonkin examined the document there were apparently three additional pages, including reason sixteen for the decline of the language, which would have brought it up to the end of the section; and these exist in his transcription. But we can postulate that originally there would have been a further three pages: a title page for the transcription and translation of the Passion Poem, and two pages of introductory material about the Poem. We know this because the transcription and translation included in version 4 have two genera-tions of numbering scheme: 1–37 and 50–86. Neither of these would fit with its current placement in Version 4, which would demand that the first page should have been numbered 63. Clearly the transcription of the Poem, in a different scribe's hand than the main text of versions 3 and 4, has been moved from version 3 to version 4 after its original compilation (and numbering) sometime between 1682 and 1684.[68] It is also notable that this version does not contain the discussion of place names found in all other versions.

Francis Gregor also showed version 3 to William Borlase who refers to it in his Antiquities of Cornwall.[69] Before 1912 it was in the possession of Sir Lewis Molesworth (1853–?) of Pencarrow.[70] How he got hold of it was almost certainly from his mother Jane Frances, the daughter of Gordon W. F. Gregor of Trewarthenick, who married Sir Paul William Molesworth in 1849.[71] Sir Lewis Molesworth gave it to John Davies Enys in 1912 and it was later given to the Royal Institution of Cornwall in Truro.

4. The final version is that now labelled Fortescue Collection F2/39 in the Cornwall Record Office (CRO). The sixteen reasons for the decline of the language have now become seventeen. It is the only version to contain the transcription and translation of the Passion Poem, clearly moved from Version 3 in 1687, when the same scribe responsible for Version 3 was brought in again to prepare another fair copy, one incorporating Scawen's additions to that version. As we have seen, Scawen continued to add to this final version until his death in 1689. The first two sections are broadly similar in content to Version 3 with additions. They are entitled 'A Complaint for the Decay of the Cornish Speech' (actually a history of the Cornish people from Biblical times to the present) and 'The Causes assigned to the Cornish Tongues Decay' (the famous seventeen reasons). Section 3 is the Poem, and Section 4, called 'Observacouns on the Tongue' on Cornish proverbs and place names, as mentioned earlier does not occur in Version 3 but does occur in the earlier versions. At the end of the manuscript are Scawen's final additions dated 1688 and 1689.

Anstis' correspondence with Bishop Trelawny makes it clear that at one stage he had access to it, as it is the only version with Scawen's verse translation and he makes reference to that.[72]

On folio 28v is a later marginal note: 'Mem[oran]d[um] this Treatise was made by Mr Scawen of Moleneik & given me (J.M.) by that worthy sen[ior] Commissioner Sir Nic[holas] Trevanion the present possess[or] by Lease of that House An[n]o 1717 & now (1728) Commiss[ione]r of His Maj[esty]s Navy, residing at Plymouth'. It would seem, therefore, that Version 4 remained in the library at Molenick after the death of Scawen, and that of his son and heir William in 1705. Sir Nicholas Trevanion, a subsequent leaseholder of the estate, gave it to the mysterious J.M. in 1717 and in 1728 it was still in his possession.[73] I suspect that J.M. was one of the Moyle family of Bake in St Germans. John Moyle, Sheriff of Cornwall in 1737, would appear to be the most likely. He was born sometime between 1669 and 1682 and was buried in 1743 at St Germans, just in time for the manuscript to have passed to its next known owner. Perhaps less likely is his brother Joseph Moyle, born in 1679 at St Germans and known to be still alive in 1710.[74]

William Borlase also saw this Version. This was in 1748, and it was lent him by its then-owner The Reverend Charles Lyttleton, Dean of Exeter. There is a letter from Borlase about the contents inserted into the front of the CRO manuscript. The Morrab Library Borlase Letterbooks have further correspondence between the two men about Scawen.[75] How this manuscript came to enter the Fortescue collection I do not know, but there are singnificant connections between the Gregor family (who possessed Version 3) and the Fortescues (who at some stage owned Version 4 after Lyttleton). This is the version also used by Mark Stoyle most recently, so its influence continues.

This perhaps somewhat tedious listing of owners and scholars who have accessed the various versions of Scawen's AC over the years does I hope help to underline its continuing influence to the present day on scholarship. Indeed it would still be hard to go much beyond Scawen's (in his final version) seventeen reasons for the decline of the language, although of course some seem more pertinent than others today. But what recent research has shown is that Scawen had a much more direct effect in stirring the interest of John Keigwin and Nicholas Boson in recording the work of Edward Lhuyd. It appears to have been Scawen who got Lhuyd interested in Cornish in the first place, if not comparative Celtic linguistics in general. Lhuyd, the Bosons and Keigwin lead on directly to William Gwavas and Thomas Tonkin.[76] The latter leads on to William Borlase and to William Pryce, whose *Archaeologia Cornu-Britannica* of 1790 is nothing more than an abridgement of Tonkin's manuscript of the same name.[77] It was Pryce's publication that allowed Edwin Norris to learn enough Cornish to undertake his translation of the *Ordinalia* in 1859, which in turn gained the interest of Whitley Stokes and Henry Jenner, and the rest is history.[78]

'THE CLOVEN HOOF OF ANGLOPHOBIA'?

I thought I would conclude by addressing two issues in relation to Scawen. Was he anti-English? And was he a lone voice or did others share his views? The first issue is addressed by Mark Stoyle, who writes: 'despite Scawen's claim that he bore no malice towards the English, or indeed towards any other nation, the cloven hoof of Anglophobia is frequently to be discerned beneath the hemline of his text'.[79] It would be difficult to write about the death of a language and its replacement with another without expressing oneself negatively about the incoming language, so in that sense inevitably Scawen was guilty as charged. But in reading his text I was reminded of something the Scottish singer-songwriter Dick Gaughan once said: 'I'm not anti-English. Pro-Scottish yes, but never anti-English'.[80] In many ways Scawen could have claimed that sentiment in relation to the Cornish situation: pro-Cornish but not anti-English.

So much of history is opinion and reading between the lines. To an extent we might all be able to see the Scawen we want to see. We all bring the biases of our background and feelings about Cornishness, Englishness and Britishness to bear on a reading of his text, but along with any stridently anti-English reading we might make of Scawen there is definitely another more open sentiment which can also be read there. Right at the end of his life it seems he wrote an unpaginated epilogue: 'To my worthy Countrymen of Cornwall and all other who doe or may claime Descent from, or have the honour for the Brittish Blood, Prosperity and encrease of Renowne is wished.'[81]

The first point he makes there is that he never intended to derogate anyone who was not of Ancient British stock. Secondly, although he had extolled those gentry who had retained their British names he was not running down those who did not have Cornish names. Thirdly, he stated that he welcomed sympathetic non-Cornish people to settle in Cornwall, because after all the Cornish had long intermarried with English families. Fourthly, he notes that although he had complained about the lack of help he had received in trying to save the Cornish language he would encourage others to take up where he had left off, advising that (and it remains so true today) that to save and revive the language: 'the concurrences of the hearts and minds, the Tongues and Pens, the good wishes and prayers, are requisite and needful in my opinion'.[82] And finally if anyone is offended by what he may have said, he begs their forgiveness. He has said it only to restore what 'had been often spoaken, seldome written, and now almost lost, the Originall Cornish speech and Mother Tongue antiquated'.[83] Pro-Cornish certainly, but anti-English?

A NATION OF ONE?

Was he a lone voice in the wilderness, or perhaps with his ideas about Cornish identity as representative of the true Ancient Britons just slightly deranged? I think that in fact he was expressing a wider viewpoint that crops up again and again through to the present. The rumblings of the Cornish towards the end of the Civil War that they had never been conquered were reported in pro-Parliamentary sources and give a further hint of this feeling.[84] But if it was still true into the 1680s when Scawen wrote it is perhaps even more interesting to hear such sentiments expressed, admittedly from an unsympathetic source, as late as 1730 as being commonly held. There is a very interesting letter from William Borlase to Thomas Tonkin dated 17 November 1730. Tonkin had earlier written to Borlase about some ancient remains he interpreted to be of Roman origin in Gwendron (Wendron). Borlase replied:

One thing I am afraid of, which is that you will incurr the severe censure of some Antient Britons who value themselves above all things, like their brethren in Wales, upon their never having been overcome by the Romans; and yet nothing is more manifest than that where the Romans penetrated, built and bury'd they were certainly victors. For my part I am so far from being angry with you for having discover'd that the Romans pierc'd into this county even unto Gwendron, that I should congratulate my country thereupon . . . for submitting to a nation from which every part of their territories receiv'd improvements in the arts and conduct of life which more than overbalanc'd the loss of imaginary liberty, real wilderness & brutality.[85]

This was before either Borlase or Tonkin had read Scawen's work, so it is not a reference to his writings, but clearly pertains to people alive and expressing patriotic Cornish sentiments at the time. As I noted at the beginning of this article, it was ever thus in Cornish historiography!

CONCLUSION

The evening that I delivered the Caroline L. Kemp lecture to the University of Exeter in Cornwall at the Cornwall campus, Tremough, was also the occasion of the Cambridge launch of the sixty volumes of the *Oxford Dictionary of National Biography*. It was launched in Oxford the day before and at the National Portrait Gallery in London on 23 September. In the first edition of the *Dictionary*, over a century ago, William Scawen was absent, very much an unsung hero. I was very pleased to announce at the Lecture that this time around Scawen had been considered to merit an entry. A few years previously I suggested his inclusion to the Editors and was most happy that it was accepted.[86] I hope that in the Lecture, and in this article developed from it, I have helped add a bit of detail to the 500-word biography you can read there. I hope too that all will agree that William Scawen, as a notable Cornish patriot and the true father of the language revival, is indeed worthy of UK National attention.

NOTES AND REFERENCES

1. This paper was given as the Caroline L. Kemp Memorial Lecture for 2004 on 1 October at the newly-opened Tremough Campus of the Combined Universities in Cornwall. I thank the Vice-Chancellor of Exeter, Prof. Steve Smith for chairing the Lecture, Prof. Philip Payton of the Institute of Cornish Studies, University of Exeter for inviting me to give the lecture, staff of the Institute for making the arrangements for the lecture and the

audience for their helpful comments. My visit to Cornwall was as a British Academy Visiting Professor to the University of Exeter and I thank the Academy for their financial support. My research on Scawen has also been supported by the Faculty of Arts, The Australian National University. I have not changed the lecture as given except to add full referencing; in respect of the involvement of William Hals in the translation of the Passion Poem where subsequent research clarified his role; and in providing further evidence to back up my suggestion that Edward Lhuyd may have been stimulated to take up comparative Celtic philology by his correspondence with William Scawen. I would like to thank Jolyan Holmes, Joanna Mattingly, Oliver Padel, Philip Payton and Mark Stoyle for discussions and assistance pertaining to preparation of this paper, and also the archivists and librarians at the Cornwall Record Office, Morrab Library, and Royal Institution of Cornwall.

2. Examples of these different tendencies can be seen in works such as J. Angarrack, *Our Future is History: Identity, Law and the Cornish Question*, Padstow, 2002; J. Chynoweth, *Tudor Cornwall*, Port Stroud, 2002; J. P. D. Cooper, *Propaganda and the Tudor State: Political Culture in the Westcountry*, Oxford, 2003; P. Payton, *The Making of Modern Cornwall*, Redruth, 1992; P. Payton, *Cornwall*, Fowey, 1996; A. L. Rowse, *Tudor Cornwall: Portrait of a Society*, London, 1941; M. Stoyle, *West Britons: Cornish Identities and the Early Modern British State*, Exeter, 2002. I would include myself in the last category enumerated. P. Payton's *A. L. Rowse and Cornwall: A Paradoxical Patriot*, Exeter, 2005, elaborates the angst inherent in Rowse's struggles with Cornish 'difference'. J. Chynoweth, despite his Cornish-language surname, attempts to undo Cornish 'difference' in his book called *Tudor Cornwall*.

3. John Ray had earlier, after his 1662 and 1667 visits to Cornwall, concluded that the language was dying out, as recorded both in later publication of his notes on these visits and in his contribution to the 1695 Gibson edition of Camden: see J. Ray, *Select Remains of the Learned John Ray . . . with his Life by the Late William Derham*, London, 1760, pp. 279 fn, 281; reprinted in J. Ray, *Memorials of John Ray*, ed. E. Lankester, London, 1846, pp. 189 fn, 190; Camden's *Britannia . . . with Large Additions and Improvements*, London, 1695, Cornwall, column 16. That Ray is the source of some of the information about the decline of the language is shown by his original contribution in manuscript in Bodleian Ms. Eng.b.2042, folios 157–164, see especially fo. 164r. The other information on its decline used by Gibson came from William Scawen as abstracted by John Anstis—see footnote 61 below. Similar general sentiments to Ray as to the decline of the language were voiced earlier by scholars such as John Norden (in about 1584), Richard Carew, John Dodridge and Peter Mundy. References are given in M. Spriggs, 'Where Cornish was spoken and when: a provisional synthesis', in P. Payton (ed.), *Cornish Studies: Eleven*, Exeter, 2003, pp. 228–69, especially pp. 249–51.

4. CRO, Fortescue Collection Ms F2/39.

5. W. Scawen, *Antiquities Cornu-britannick; Or Observations on an Ancient*

Manuscript written in the Cornish Language, London, 1777. The original manuscript (now lost) of which this is a somewhat abridged version, 'from a Manuscript in the Library of Thomas Astle, Esq.' had once belonged to John Anstis and was summarized by him in his contribution to Gibson's 1695 edition of Camden—see footnote 3 above. The manuscript was presumably purchased by Astle at the Anstis sale in 1768. The 1777 version was republished in *The Antiquarian Repertory: A Miscellany intended to preserve and illustrate Several Valuable Remains of Old Times*, Vol. II, London, 1779, pp. 61–88 and again in *The Antiquarian Repertory . . .* chiefly compiled by Francis Grose Esq. F.R. and A.S., Thomas Astle, Esq., and other Eminent Antiquarians, Vol. III, London, 1808, pp. 208–34. Under the slightly different title of 'Observations on an Ancient Manuscript, entitled Passio Christi, written in the Cornish Language . . . with an account of the Language, Manners, and Customs of the People of Cornwall' it was printed as an appendix in D. Gilbert, *The Parochial History of Cornwall*, Vol. IV, 1838, London, pp. 190–221.

6. P. Beresford Ellis, *The Cornish Language and its Literature*, London, 1974, pp. 78, 80–85.
7. Stoyle, 2002, p. 146.
8. Stoyle, 2002, p. 182.
9. Stoyle, 2002, p. 182.
10. J. L. Vivian, *The Visitations of Cornwall*, comprising the Herald's Visitations of 1530, 1573 and 1620, Exeter, 1887, pp. 421–423; [J. Polsue/ W. Lake] *A Complete Parochial History of the County of Cornwall*, Vol. II, Truro, 1868, p. 55.
11. M. F. Keller, *The Long Parliament, 1640–1: A Biographical Study of its Members*, Philadelphia, 1954, p. 335; B. D. Henney (ed.), *The House of Commons 160–1690*, Vol. III, London, 1983, p. 404–5.
12. Information in this and the succeeding two paragraphs is taken from Stoyle, 2002, pp. 134–56 and Vivian, 1887, pp. 421–3, with additional information and corrections from the parish registers of Fowey and St Germans which are held in the Cornwall Record Office.
13. Cornwall Record Office(CRO), Fortescue Ms. F2/39, fol. 48.
14. Calendar of State Papers for 1650, p. 457.
15. Scawen in AC mentions the destruction of the Mincamber Stone—see CRO Fortescue Ms. F2/39, fol. 29v. For St Buryan see F. Hitchens and S. Drew, *The History of Cornwall*, Vol. II, Helston, p. 129.
16. See Calendar of State Papers for 1649–50, pp. 216, 478, and for 1653–54, p. 4. Joanna Mattingly is currently researching Charles Shrubsall or Shrubsole and has been able to discover that he was from a Kent family, as revealed in R. Hovenden (ed.), *Visitation of Kent, 1619–21*, London, 1898, p. 115. I am grateful to Dr Mattingly for this information.
17. T. Wotton , *The English Baronetage . . .* Vol. IV, London, 1741, pp. 363–4, quoting 'from a MS of Peter Le Neve, Esq.; Norroy, now among the collection of Mr Joseph Ames'. This is presumably the source of information for A. J. Rodway, in *The Western Antiquary* 2 (7), July 1887, pp. 38–9.

18. E. Cruickshanks in B. D. Henney (ed.), 1983, p. 404.
19. Calendar of Treasury Books, Vol. V, 1676–79, p.1368. The earlier stages of this case are documented in Vol. II, 1668, pp. 7, 267, 395, 585; Vol. III, 1669–71, pp. 117, 251, 533, 613, 616; See also Calendar of State Papers, 1675–76, p. 467; 1677–78, p. 522.
20. Calendar of Treasury Books, Vol. II, 1668, p. 399; Vol. IV, 1672–75, p. 543; Vol. V, 1676–79, pp. 251, 1004; Vol. VI, 1679–80, p. 110; Vol. VII, 1681–85, pp. 1071, 1192; Vol. VIII, 1685–89, pp. 34, 693.
21. Fortescue Ms F2/39, fol. 4v.
22. Ibid.
23. Stoyle, 2002, p. 142.
24. Spriggs, 2003, pp. 228–69. For another view concerning the Cornish language in East Cornwall, see J. Holmes, 'On the Track of Cornish in a Bilingual Country', in Payton (ed.), 2003, pp. 270–90.
25. Fortescue Ms. F2/39, fol. 32r.
26. CRO, St Germans and Paul Parish Registers. For details of John's life, see M. Spriggs, 'John Keigwin', *Oxford Dictionary of National Biography*, Vol. 31, 2004, p. 39.
27. Lambeth Palace Library, Ms. 806, Art. 17.
28. C. S. Gilbert, *An Historical Survey of the County of Cornwall*, Vol. II, Plymouth, 1820, p. 710.
29. For a study of the extant manuscripts see A. Hawke, 'The Manuscripts of the Cornish Passion Poem', *Cornish Studies* (1st series) 9, 1981, pp. 23–8. His remarks on Anstis are on p. 23. The original erroneous statement on this is in T. Astle, A Catalogue of the Harleian Collection of Manuscripts, Vol. I, London, 1759, entry on Harleian 1782 where Astle claims: 'I have heard Mr Anstis say, that he procured this Poem to be translated into English; and that he lent the Same Translation to Mr Lhwyd, who did not return it'. The confusion comes from the fact that it was indeed Anstis that secured translations of the plays of the Creation of the World and the Ordinalia to be made for Bishop Trelawny by John Keigwin in 1693. Bodleian Ms. Eng.b.2042, fol. 150r contains a letter from Anstis to Trelawny on this topic. Rather confusingly, transcipts of these translations in Bodleian Ms. Corn.e.2 give dates of 1691 and 1695 respectively while the title page of the former indeed mentions that it was done 'at ye request of the R[igh]t Rev[eren]d Fa[ther] in God Jonathan L[or]d B[isho]p of Exon'. The 'problem' that Hawke raises on pp. 26–7 of another lost manuscript of the Poem has now been solved by the rediscovery of Thomas Tonkin's *Archaeologia Cornu-Britannica*, albeit in mutilated form, which was generously donated to the Royal Institution of Cornwall (RIC) by Derek and Gussie Maker in 1999.
30. Fortescue Ms. F2/39 fols. 31v, 32r.
31. For details of the Boson family, see M. Spriggs 'The Boson Family', *Oxford Dictionary of National Biography*, Vol. 6, 2004, pp. 713–14.
32. British Library Additional Ms 28,554, fols. 51–8.
33. Further detail of Hals' language 'abilities' is given by A. Hawke, 'A Lost Manuscript of the Cornish Ordinalia?', *Cornish Studies* (1st series) 7, 1979,

pp. 45–60; see especially pp 46–7, 51–4. Some details of his life are given by J. Broadway, 'William Hals', *Oxford Dictionary of National Biography*, Vol. 24, 2004, p. 717, where his claim to have translated the Passion Poem is repeated.

34. There are twelve seventeenth- and eighteenth-century manuscript copies of this translation listed in A. Hawke, 1981, p. 26 (numbers 2–12, and Tonkin's, see fn. 29 above). Of these, no. 12, Bodleian Ms. Corn.c.3 actually dates to around 1750–1769 rather than 1800–1826 as Hawke has it and is in the hand of the Reverend H. Usticke and copied from Tonkin, as is Bodleian Corn.c.1 (no. 9). The very inaccurately transcribed first publication of the Poem by Davies Gilbert should be noted: D. Gilbert, *Mount Calvary*, London, 1826. Later publications include W. Stokes, 'The Passion', *Transactions of the Philological Society*, 1860–1, pp. 1–100, and most recently in facsimile and with a new translation, H. Woodhouse (ed.), *The Cornish Passion Poem*, Penryn, 2002.

35. Fortescue Ms. F2/39, fol. 5r.

36. F. Emery, Edward Lhuyd 1660–1709, Cardiff, 1971, pp. 70–75, dates his serious interest in comparative linguistics as mainly beginning in the 1692–3 period under the influence of Nicolson and Wyld, while noting his earlier contacts with Ray. C. G. Williams, 'The History of Welsh Scholarship', *Studia Celtica* 8/9, 1973–74, pp. 195–219, especially 209–10 attributes Lhuyd's linguistic interests more generally to his early contacts from 1682 onwards with Oxford scholars such as Thomas Hearne, Robert Plot, George Hickes and Humphrey Wanley. This may be so but no concrete proof except propinquity is offered and there is nothing that I can see in Lhuyd's early correspondence to suggest that this was the case pre-1689. D. R. Williams, *Prying into Every Hole and Corner: Edward Lhuyd in Cornwall in 1700*, Redruth, 1993, p. 7 suggests Ray and Aubrey. B. F. Roberts, 'Edward Lhuyd', *Oxford Dictionary of National Biography*, Vol. 33, 2004, pp. 710–12, highlights the connection with Ray.

37. Many of the extant original letters to Lhuyd can be found in the Bodleian Library, Oxford, Mss. Ashmole 1814–17, 1820, 1829, 1830 and from John Ray in Ms.. Eng.Hist.c.11. The earliest extant letter from Ray to Lhuyd is from Ms. Eng.Hist.c.11, fol. 36, that from Aubrey is in Ms Ashmole 1814, fol. 96; Many of Lhuyd's outgoing letters were published by R. T. Gunther, Early Science in Oxford, Vol. XIV, Oxford, 1945; The correspondence between Lhuyd and Ray is published in R. T. Gunther, *Further Correspondence of John Ray*, London, 1928, pp. 185–284. See B. Roberts, 'A Note on the Ashmolean Collection of Letters Addressed to Edward Lhuyd', *Welsh History Review* 7(2), 1974, pp. 179–85.

38. R. T. Gunther, *Early Science in Oxford*, Vol. XII, Oxford, 1939, pp. 327–8.

39. Ms. Aubrey 5, Bodleian Library, Oxford.

40. Gunther, Vol. XII, 1939, pp. 329–32.

41. B. F. Roberts gives some further hints as to Lhuyd's growing linguistic interests in the 1689–90 period in 'Edward Lhuyd and Celtic Linguistics', in D. Ellis Evans (ed.), *Proceedings of the 7th International Congress of Celtic Studies*, Oxford, 1986, pp. 1–9, especially p. 3.

42. E. Lhuyd, *Archaeologia Britannica*, Oxford, 1707, pp. 222–4.
43. Fortescue Ms. F2/39, fol. 30v.
44. Fortescue Ms. F2/39, fol. 31r.
45. The definitive editions of both are found in O. Padel, *The Cornish Writings of the Boson Family*, Redruth, 1975, pp. 8–23.
46. E. Lhuyd, *Archaeologia Britannica*, Oxford, 1707, p. 253, noted that *Jooan* had been written 'some 40 years since'. *The Dutchesse* was composed some time probably between 1660 and 1670 for the amusement of Boson's children who were born in 1653 (Nicholas), 1655 (John), 1659 (Mary) and 1661 (Benjamin). Information from Paul Parish Registers, CRO, and see also O. Padel, 1975, pp. 8, 28, 37.
47. Fortescue Ms. F2/39, fol. 31v. For the life of Richard Angwyn, see C. Henderson, 'Nicholas Boson and Richard Angwyn', *Old Cornwall* II(2), 1931, pp. 29–32.
48. British Library (BL) Additional Ms. 28,554, fol. 51r: 'found in Sacret [Sancreed] Church'.
49. In a letter from John Aubrey to Lhuyd dated Feb 20 1691/2 he recounts that a young Corrnish acquaintance of his had told him that John Keigwin had 'the History of ye Passion of our Saviour, entituled Mount Calvary, in Cornish verse [in the old Saxon character]'. He reiterates this statement in a further letter to Lhuyd of December 1 1692. The letters are found in Bodleian Ashmole Ms. 1814, fols. 96r, 101r . A year later the Poem was in John Anstis' possession. A letter from Anstis to Bishop Trelawny, undated but placed between letters from him dated December 11 1693 and January 2 1693/4, Bodleian Ms. Eng.b.2042 fol. 150r, transmits the original of the Poem to Trelawny and notes: 'The Cornish book is none of my own, but I am oblidged under hand & seal to return itt, & therefore desire your Lordship would not part with itt out of your hands; The translation into verse of the Cornish book is Mr. Scawens work which (if the book be printed) must be wholly omitted. Mr Scawen had collected some undigested notes relating to Brittain in generall, which he mostly had from Usher & Stillingfleets Antiquities of the British Church; but it is wholly to his Care that this book is preserved, & of whom I desire mention be made (if the book be printed) otherwise his Relations will take it amisse from me for parting with the book without their consents'. Bishop Trelawny apparently kept the Poem for several years, until Anstis arranged for it to be sent to Edward Lhuyd. See Bodleian Ms. Ashmole 1814, fol. 20r, where Anstis writes to Lhuyd that he lent it to Bishop Trelawny, 'who will send it (as you shall order itt but I pr[e]sume you will waite on his L[ordshi]pp while you are in the Country. This book belonged to Mr. Scawen (who was a kinsman to Mr. Keigwyn) who made some Colleccons in relation to Britain in g[ene]rall, which I can gett you'. The letter is dated 10 September 1700. Lhuyd clearly still had the Poem in his possession on 10 June 1703 when Anstis wrote to him: 'When you have ended with the Cornish Ms, I intend it for the Cotton Library'. This letter is in Bodleian Ms. 1814, fols 55–6. The Poem entered the Harleian Collection soon after and is numbered BL Harleian Ms. 1872. As the translation into verse

occurs only in AC Version 4, this must be the 'undigested notes' which Anstis refers to in his letter to Bishop Trelawny. A letter from John Keigwin's son Martin to Trelawny, dated 22 October 1693 (Bodleian Ms. Eng.b.2042, fol. 144r), similarly refers to what must be Version 4: 'There is a book in Mr Anstis hands, (which cost my father some considerable time in translating) together with several Cornish proverbs, and ye derivation of the names of Severall antient places in Cornwall, which hee hath promised to deliver to your Lordship'. There is no evidence Anstis ever sent this on later to Lhuyd and his letter of 1700 would suggest that he had earlier arranged for it to be returned to Scawen's relations. As that letter also separately discusses John Keigwin, the context would suggest that AC Version 4 was not in the latter's possession at the time.

50. The date of this (draft?) letter is 1 or 15 December 1700 and the content suggests it may be a letter to Edward Lhuyd who was at the time in Cornwall, about to embark for Brittany. It is reproduced in Woodhouse, 2002, p. 98.

51. O. Padel, *Exhibition of Manuscripts and Printed Books on the Cornish Language*, Redruth, 1975, p. 5.

52. CRO Ms. Dd.Enys.1999. AC occurs on pp. 1088–98, also numbered fols. 121–6. Also on pp. 1128–32 (129–31) is a list of names of old and extinct families of Cornwall by Scawen which appears to be later than that contained in Version 4 of AC. On p. 1124 (129) is an account of a deformed birth at St Germans in 1634, in Scawen's hand.

53. Padel, *Exhibition of Manuscripts*, 1975, p. 5.

54. Scawen's son William was the last of the family to live at Molenick and may have been the compiler of the manuscript. He was buried in St Germans on 19 October 1705 according to the St Germans Parish Registers in the CRO. Alternatively, the mention in the London Gazette among the Stannators of John Trevanion might suggest compilation by Nicholas Trevanion once he took over the lease of Molenick some time probably between the death of his first wife in Plymouth in 1715 and mention of his holding of the lease in 1717. See Vivian, 1887, p. 505 for the death of his wife, Elizabeth. See footnote 73 below.

55. This is clear from a letter to Enys from Thurstan Peter from Redruth, dated 9 April 1902 that is placed at the back of Dd.Enys.1999. Enys died in November 1912 as noted in Journal of the Royal Institution of Cornwall 19, Part 2 (60), 1913, pp. 179–80.

56. See footnote 5 for publication details.

57. Padel, *Exhibition of Manuscripts*, 1975, p. 5, believed it was an abridgement of Version 3; In this he is following Henry Jenner's opinion, given in various forms in Handbook of the Cornish Language, London, 1904, p. 17 and in a letter to John Davies Enys of 23 July 1912 pasted into the manuscript of Version 3 in the Royal Institution of Cornwall. A similar statement is made by Jenner in a typed note tipped in to the back of the manuscript, dated 28 August 1917.

58. F. W. P. Jago, *An English-Cornish Dictionary*, London, 1887, pp. iv–v.

59. P. Beresford Ellis, *The Cornish Language and its Literature*, London, 1974, pp. 78, 80–5.
60. This was commented upon by Thomas Tonkin, RIC Ms. *Archaeologia Cornu-Britannica*, p. 99 footnote: 'it is plain that S[i]r Jonathan Trelawney [sic] then Bishop of Exon, or whoever it was that communicated these things to Dr Gibson, had the perusal of this Ms. which ought to have been acknowledg'd, since so much use has been made of it'.
61. Bodleian Ms. Eng.b.2042, fols. 93rv, 130r–132v, 137v–138r, 141–2 on the Cornish language. Anstis includes further Scawen material throughout his topographic contribution, fols. 124–38. This manuscript consists of the notes of various correspondents which were collated for Devon and Cornwall by Bishop Jonathan Trelawny and then transmitted to Edmund Gibson for his additions to Camden's *Britannia*: E. Gibson, *Camden's Britannia, Newly Translated into English With Large Additions and Improvements*, London, 1695 (facsimile edition, Newton Abbot, 1971). The materials taken from Scawen appear in the Cornwall Section, cols. 16–18.
62. There are passages in Anstis' abridgement in Bodleian Ms. Eng.b.2042 which do not occur in the published 1777 version but which are similar, though often expanded, to passages in Version 1—see for instance on fol. 130v, passage beginning 'To which Gildas assents'. Wording in Versions 3 and 4 is often quite different and so these cannot be the source. It seems most likely therefore that the source is the manuscript of Version 2 that was then somewhat abridged for publication. Anstis also includes the Lord's Prayer in Cornish, Welsh and Breton on fol. 93r. In the printed version only the Cornish is given for this and the Creed, which—given that they occur in Version 1 in all three languages—would suggest that the manuscript of Version 2 also had them in this form. What must be a later addition to the printed edition of Version 2 is a passage with English translation from the *Ordinalia*, a point noted by A. Hawke, 1979, p. 49. As we have seen, Scawen was not aware of the existence of the *Ordinalia* until 1687–88, about 10 years after Version 2 was composed.
63. See Papers of British Antiquaries and Historians, Historical Manuscripts Commission Guides to Sources for British History 12, London, 2003, pp. 4, 6.
64. See Papers of British Antiquaries, 2003, p. 6 and R. Sweet, *Antiquaries: the Discovery of the Past in Eighteenth Century Britain*, London, 2004, pp. 236–37, especially footnote 21.
65. RIC Ms, Enys Collection. Padel, *Exhibition of Manuscripts*, 1975, p. 5–6 was mistaken in thinking that this version incorporated a copy of part of the Passion Poem. This error was repeated by B.O. Murdoch, *The Medieval Cornish Poem of the Passion*, Redruth, 1979, p. 8, but corrected by A. Hawke, 'The Manuscripts of the Cornish Passion Poem', *Cornish Studies* 9, 1981, p. 24.
66. BL Additional Ms. 33,420, fols. 108r–125v, originally numbered pp. 106–41. At the beginning of the manuscript Tonkin wrote: 'Of the following manuscript I can give no other account than what I received in part of a

letter from Cosen Gregor . . . and in confidence. "A manuscript about the antiquities, etc. of Cornwall communicated very lately, by whom writ I do not know; whether the kernel exceeds the shell you will be the best judge. When perus'd you will please return it. I am etc. Francis Gregor, Trewarthenick, June ye 18th, 1735'".

67. See footnote 29, above. I hope elsewhere to discuss Tonkin's manuscript and will demonstrate that it is the almost exclusive source of William Pryce's Archaeologica Cornu-Britannica, Sherborne, 1790, as well as being the source of Davies Gilbert's two works, Mount Calvary, London, 1826 and The Creation of the World, London, 1827, via partial transcripts made by the Reverend Henry Ustick and now Bodleian Mss. Corn.c.1 and Corn.c.3. Tonkin's manuscript disappeared for 200 years after the death of Pryce in 1791 until it turned up again on a market stall in Totnes in the early 1990s.

68. In CRO Ms. Fortescue F2/39, fol. 32r he writes: 'Afterward when I had cast it into the form & Mold proposed and much time spent therein, and my turning it into English Meeter, w[hi]ch was necessary, the Transcribeing often being tedious to old age, There came in seasonably to my aid one John Read a man intellingent in the Tounge'. This suggests that John Read may have been the scribe for the Poem and English and English verse translations that occur in Version 4. He is presumably the same person mentioned in a letter from John Anstis to Lewis Stephens, Vicar of Menheniot, on 19 October 1700, during Lhuyd's visit to Cornwall. Referring to Lhuyd, Anstis writes: 'Tis probable he may consult John Read the Quaker of St Kayn who pr[e]tends skill in our Tongue'. See Bodleian Ms. Ashmole 1814, fol. 23r.

69. *W. Borlase, Antiquities Historical and Monumental of the County of Cornwall*, London, 2nd edition, 1769, p. 414, fn. c. The first edition was published in 1754. Borlase's Ms. Letterbooks Vols. I and III in the Morrab Library, Penzance include letters from Gregor between Feb. 1744 and October 1758. W. M. M. Picken was mistaken in his suggestion that Version 3 was also seen later at Trewarthenick by Richard Polwhele, in 'A Tonkin MS. in the British Museum', *Devon and Cornwall Notes and Queries* 29 (part 10), July 1964, pp. 281–2. Perusal of his source shows that it is a quotation from Borlase and not penned by Polwhele: See R. Polwhele, *A Cornish–English Vocabulary*, Truro, 1808, p. v continuation of footnote from pp. iii and iv. This forms Vol. VI of Polwhele's *History of Cornwall.* In the facsimile edition of this work (3 Vols, Dorking, 1978) a title page dated 1808 is included but the relevant part of the footnote is missing from p. v and the main text on p. vi does not occur in the original 1808 edition. This is explained by the date at the bottom of page vi as given in the facsimile which reveals the real date of the particular edition of Vol. VI that was used as 'May 1836'.

70. A pencilled note inside the cover, presumably in J. D. Enys' hand states 'Given me by Sir Lewis Molesworth 1912'. As can be seen from the letter mentioned in footnote 57, Jenner examined the new acquisition in July of

that year. Sir Lewis died in Torquay in early June: information from Angela Broome, RIC Librarian.

71. Vivian, 1887, p. 329.

72. As discussed above, footnote 49.

73. According to J. L. Vivian, 1887, p. 505 Nicholas was '9th in remainder to the estates under the entail created by the will of John Trevanion of Carhayes 1737', the latter being a rather distant relative. Nicholas was 'a Captain R.N., Commissioner of His Majesty's Yard at Portsmouth', died 16 Nov. 1737. He married three times, his last wife, Catherine, being the daughter of William Eliot R.N. of St Germans and great-granddaughter of Scawen's friend Sir John Eliot.

74. Vivian, 1887, p. 335.

75. A letter to Charles Lyttelton from Borlase is tipped in to the front of CRO Ms. Fortescue F2/39, dated January 5 1748. Lyttelton had recently sent the manuscript to Borlase to aid in his researches. By this time it was bound in its present form and Borlase notes that the transcription and translation of the Poem were missing several pages, as now. Further correspondence between the two on the Cornish language occurs in the Morrab Library Borlase Letterbooks and in BL Ms. Stowe 752.

76. There is extant correspondence of members of the Boson family and John Keigwin with William Gwavas. Gwavas in turn collaborated with Thomas Tonkin in the preparation of *Archaeologia Cornu-Britannica*: see BL Additional Ms. 28,554 ('The Gwavas Manuscript') and Biblioteca de la Diputacion Foral de Bizkaia, Bilbao, Spain, Ms. Bnv-69 ('The Bilbao Manuscript'). Lhuyd and Tonkin also maintained a correspondence, first printed (unpaginated) at the end of W. Pryce, 1790. For details of Gwavas' life see, M. Spriggs, 'William Gwavas', *Oxford Dictionary of National Biography*, Vol. 24, 2004, pp. 339–40. For Tonkin see L. Douch, 'Thomas Tonkin, An Appreciation of a Neglected Historian', Journal of the Royal Institution of Cornwall N.S. IV (Part 2), 1962, pp. 145–80.

77. Correspondence between Tonkin and Borlase can be found in the Morrab Library, Borlase Letterbooks. Borlase also had access to various of Tonkin and Gwavas' manuscripts—See Borlase's manuscript on the Cornish language, CRO Ms. Dd.Enys.2000, and also Douch, 1962, pp. 160–72 for the Tonkin manuscripts which Borlase examined in 1761. He had earlier had access to *Archaeologia Cornu-Britannica* in 1748, as is clear from the letter to Lyttelton of 5 January 1748 discussed above, footnote 75, and this volume was later in Pryce's possession, from which he published his abridgement under the same title.

78. Edwin Norris (1795–1872), the noted Assyriologist, acknowledged his debt to Pryce's publication in *The Ancient Cornish Drama*, Vol. I, Oxford, 1859, p. vi. He in turn was influential on the great Irish Scholar of Celtic languages, Whitley Stokes (1830–1909). Stokes acknowledged Norris' assistance in his first substantial Cornish language publication, a new transcription and translation of the Passion Poem in *Transactions of the Philological Society* 1860–61, p. 3, as well as that of the Reverend Robert Williams (1810–81), who published his Cornish dictionary, *Lexicon*

Cornu-Britannicum, in 1865 in Llandovery and London. Williams in turn in the Preface (unpaginated) notes that his dictionary would never have been completed had it not been for Norris' 1859 publication of the *Ordinalia*. The first paper of Henry Jenner (1848–1934) on Cornish, 'The Cornish Language', *Transactions of the Philological Society* 1873–74, pp. 165–86, noted his debt to Norris, Williams and Stokes on p. 185. His own *A Handbook of the Cornish Language*, London, 1904 is the cornerstone of the modern Cornish language revival.

79. Stoyle, 2002, p. 150.
80. He said this on a British TV documentary series aired on SBS in Australia sometime during the late 1980s, called 'How to be Celtic' in film of a live concert.
81. CRO, Fortescue F2/39, fol. 67r.
82. CRO, Fortescue F2/39, fol. 67v. The entire discussion is contained in fols. 67rv. Another significant passage is worth quoting in this regard, found on fols. 67rv: 'For those who have come in to us of late, or may hereafter we are willing to give them both invitation and encouragement, that bringing Wealth & good nature with them, they are upon easy terms admittable to be equall Sharers with us without grudging of any thing that is honourable among us. The Cornish blood & honour being soon to be diffused & spread to them, for hardly can there be any genealogy found among us any way ancient, that doth not participate with of the rest sooner or later. Which is, or should be a good means to link all firmly together, in Religion to God, in Loyalty to his vice-regent, & in unanimity to ourselves, & the good of our Country, that so we may be as the virtues are printed in Tables, all conjoyn'd together, giving and receiving mutual help & comfort to & from one another, the way to make us to be as the old Jerusalem was, a City at unity in itself, & as the new Jerusalem will be, to which God conduct us.'
83. CRO, Fortescue F2/39, fol. 67v.
84. P. Q. Karkeek, 'Fairfax in the West 1645–46', *Transactions of the Devonshire Association* 8, 1876, pp. 117–47. The 21 March 1645[/6] quotation of Hugh Peters is given on p. 144: 'I answered a common murmuring amongst them, that their country was never conquered.' Similar rebellious sentiments of a separate ethnicity were recorded throughout the previous century: see references in M. Spriggs, 'The Cornish Language, Archaeology and the Origins of English Theatre', in M. Jones (ed.), *Traces of Ancestry: studies in honour of Colin Renfrew*, Cambridge, 2004, pp. 143–61, especially pp. 152–4.
85. Morrab Library, Borlase Letterbook Vol. 13, fol. 24r.
86. M. Spriggs, 'William Scawen', *Oxford Dictionary of National Biography*, Vol. 49, 2004, pp. 195–6.

STAGING THE STATE AND THE HYPOSTASIZATION OF VIOLENCE IN THE MEDIEVAL CORNISH DRAMA

Paul Manning

INTRODUCTION

Medieval European drama, particularly Cornish drama, is notable for graphic depiction of extreme violence and cruelty. Its blurring of the boundaries between real and realistic violence is so pervasive that one commentator has dubbed the genre 'Medieval Snuff Drama'.[1] The staging of violence in medieval drama elicits conflicting responses from a modern audience. On the one hand, it seems to confirm the general opposition by which the Medieval stands to the Modern as a world in which violence is omnipresent in everyday life, in contrast to a modern world where violence seems generally to have been 'confined to barracks' by a civilizing process.[2] On the other, the way in which the medieval plays dwell on the realistic, even grotesque, depiction of violence, reminds us of our modern selves, who live in a world in which violence, when and where it appears, is found in ever more extreme forms, and represented ever more realistically.[3] I argue that the Cornish miracle plays, and in particular their detailed staging instructions, provide material of great interest to historical anthropologists and sociologists who are interested in the way that violence is imagined in relation to the emerging notion of a state as an entity with a monopoly on violence, or a civilizing process in which violence is increasingly displaced from everyday life and 'confined to barracks'.

The stage diagrams of Cornish plays are microcosmic representations of a broader macrocosm, a map of a medieval cosmos, in which all the components of the modern state are represented and made visible. And given that alongside such obviously important entities such as God and the Devil, Kings and Bishops, there are unchanging stage positions for agents of violence, Torturers, it seems that violence itself is highlighted in these stage diagrams as an integral part of a medieval cosmology. In this paper, then, I argue that the staging of violence is central to the staging of the state itself in Medieval Cornish drama. Since no actual political arrangement at that time 'on the ground' corresponded to our notion of a state, it can be argued that the idea of the state may have emerged in the imagination long before it corresponded to anything 'real'. If the modern state is an imagined entity, a 'state idea', rather than something 'out there', what better place to study its rise than in the medieval imagination? If 'the state is not the reality which stands behind the mask of political practice. It is itself the mask which prevents our seeing political practice as it is',[4] then the theatre would seem to be as good a place as any to start studying the idea of the state. Violence and media of power are quite real, of course, 'but it is their association with the idea of the state and the invocation of that idea that silences protest, excuses force and convinces all of us that the fate of the victims is just and necessary.'[5]

I am not so much interested here in the way that the pre-modern or modern state *displays itself* dramaturgically through public exhibitions of pomp and power, as Geertz's famous analysis of the Balinese 'theatre state' or the many discussions of 'state spectacles' in the anthropological literature.[6] I am interested in how relatively autonomous ritual or theatrical occasions act to represent a timeless and distantiated cosmology in which the legitimacy of the state and violence are a major part of the narrative argument. As Abrams points out, 'the state is a unified symbol of an actual [political] disunity', and (unified) states are things you *believe in,* in much the same way you believe in God.[7] As an invisible cosmological principle and a symbol unifying existing visible practices of power, it must be *displayed somewhere* to be understood and imagined as a unity, often in tandem with the rest of the cosmological order in which it is embedded, which is no more obvious to the naked eye. While the power of the pre-modern state was undoubtedly 'made visible through signs displayed in the form of theatre, with processions, progresses, royal entries, coronations and funerals, and rituals which guaranteed the well-being and con-tinued power of the rulers',[8] alongside this 'state theatre', the state idea was equally represented as part of other dramatic representations of a broader medieval cosmology, dramas that were narratives of salvation extending across all of time, including as part of their argument the genesis of the state, its separation from the church, and its final integration, and at the same time the integration of violence, into a

Christian state. An ordinary peasant in a place like Cornwall might well have encountered very concrete power, violence, as well as scattered instances of pomp, in their everyday life, but need not have experienced them as being part of a unified state unless they were presented in some way as being graspable as part of one. And this might as easily have been accomplished by watching a dramatic spectacle *about the state* as it would have been accomplished in watching a *state spectacle*.

The medieval theatre may be a good set of texts through which to apprehend medieval cosmologies, including the state idea, but why Cornish theatre in particular? Cornish plays are noteworthy in that they not only have full texts available (the recent discovery of a new play makes the cycle of Cornish plays almost unique), but also their stage diagrams and staging instructions are well-preserved, making them a uniquely detailed resource for studying the way that these plays 'stage the state'. In the staging of these plays three factors emerge which I argue must be understood in tandem and in relation to the staging of pomp and power:

1) First, the stage diagrams of the plays do not portray arrangements in physical space as might a modern stage diagram, but rather, divisions in social space in which the feudal estates are given a special place and are separated from the locus of their activity and aligned with an unchanging cosmological order. The stage diagrams amount to a microcosmic model of a whole medieval cosmology. Part of this organization of space separates the agents of violence (torturers) from their principals, implying that violence is an unchanging part of a cosmological system, apart from the persons who employ it and upon whom it is employed.

2) The staging of these plays are peculiar to the modern spectator in that they involve a great deal of what has been called 'pointless to-and-froing', during which characters who are separated from the playing space by the conventions of the stage diagrams (1) 'act at a distance' through complex arrays of mediators. Much of the action of the plays involves 'mediational routines' that, far from being pointless, enact both pomp and power as the ability to 'act at a distance'.

3) Among the mediators, the most peculiar are the figures called the torturers, who are clownish characters who have a monopoly on the portrayal of all that is grotesque, most particularly realistic violence. Medieval plays are noteworthy for the way they restrict dramaturgical realism to grotesque realism, in particular realistic displays of violence. Torturers are not only separated from their

principals and located as an unchanging principal within the stage diagrams (1), they also serve as intermediaries within mediational routines (2), routines that involve a specific form of performance that they monopolize, a 'grotesque' materiality of staged violence contrasts with other forms of activity.

My argument, then, is that a central theme of the Cornish miracle plays is the cosmology of the state, and the torturers are the incarnation of the principle of monopolization of violence upon which states depend. The plays produce a cosmological reconciliation of violence and the state. They do this by providing an alibi for violence as technical means for the moral ends of the state; violence becomes 'socio-technical'.[9] This is a process that Zygmunt Bauman calls the *adiaphorization* of violence, a process by which violence and other forms of social action, is rendered indifferent, *adiaphoric,* that is, 'neither good nor evil, measurable against technical (purpose-oriented or procedural), but not moral values'.[10] Adiaphorizing actions, including social actions like violence, requires 'articulation of [social] action into the hierarchy of command and execution: once placed into the "agentic state" and separated from both the intention conscious sources and the ultimate effects of action by a chain of mediators, the actors seldom face the moment of choice and gaze at the consequences of their deeds'.[11] This is an important aspect of modern forms of power as 'action at a distance' with moral consequences including the 'banality of evil'.[12] Ironically, the adiaphorization of violence, a consequence of modernity, is itself a partial product of the civilization process, which according to Elias attempts to separate violence from everyday life, thereby producing both the formation of the state with a monopoly on violence and the concomitant 'pacification of society' and civil life. As I will show below, the articulation of social action into component parts of command and execution produces a sense of power as 'violence at a distance'. Such mediational performances in other domains are also constitutive of ceremony and pomp as well as power, both of which are characteristic of the medieval play.[13]

I argue that a focus on the staging of pomp and power turns these plays into a valuable resource for studying medieval political imaginaries. In particular, subtle differences in political imaginations of the correct use of power can be discovered by careful attention to the differences between individual plays. Subtle changes in the staging of torturers and other characters between earlier (the *Ordinalia* c. 1350–75) and later plays (*Beunans Meriasek*, c.1504) articulate broad differences in models of the relation of violence and legitimate political authority. In earlier plays, violence is a legitimate means if its ends are legitimate within a Christian kingship, while in the later plays the dualistic opposition within political authority between tyrants and kings associates violence in the form of the torturers only with illegitimate, tyrannical, political authority.[14]

Weber famously locates the relationship of real physical violence, its abstraction as a property from diverse real relationships, its incarnation, accumulation and monopolization as a general *means* for diverse *ends*, as being the very stuff of the state. Whatever else states do (and of course, this includes many things), this they must *specifically* do in order to be called a state.[15] At the same time, as Elias notes, as violence is aggregated and monopolized to serve a specific set of masters in the process of state-formation, violence must at the same time be banished normatively from other domains, 'confined to barracks'.[16] And the anonymous dramaturges of the Medieval Cornish stage implicitly made just such an argument four hundred years before, in the way they represented the position of violence in the cosmology of estate and state represented in the stage diagrams of the Cornish stage. The special position of the torturers, separated from the activity of the play (confined to barracks) until they are called to perform their special task, their monopolization of staged violence, all anticipates on the stage the attempted monopoly of violence central to the formation of states.

This may seem remarkable, since the medieval world is distinguished from the modern, for one, by the lack of the very idea of distinct sphere of the 'state'. And even if there is a medieval idea of the state, it is one that lacks the monopoly of violence that is central to any definition of the modern state. Unmonopolized, unspecialized violence was a ubiquitous, pervasive, immanent aspect of medieval realia, but there is a difference between sporadically violent actual relationships, and the relationship of potential violence that the state attempts to wrest from other actors. This relationship, violence, and its agents, become a specific form of unilateral mediation constitutive of states and their subjects. In the Cornish miracle plays, there is, in fact, a *represented* monopoly on violence as a pure technical means abstracted away from any moral ends to which it may be put. The torturers, ubiquitous characters honoured with their own position in the stage diagrams, embody this principle, possessing a monopoly on actual depicted violence, even if the agents for whom they are the means are as diverse as the moral ends they are put to. The torturers stand apart in the stage diagrams, and stand out in the way they enact realistic violence on the stage, as a constant separated from, and yet ubiquitous in, the rest of the dramatic universe.

If the birth of the state, or the idea of the state, lies in the monopolization of violence as technical potentiality, then surely logically prior to this is the abstraction of violence from actual social relations (in which violence exists, but is not rationalized, functionalized as a homogenous means that is 'multifinal' with respect to ends) as a purely technical potentiality that can be monopolized.[17] Not yet monopolized, the torturers still represent monopolizable violence, violence as such, violence as means, violence as cosmological functional principle, alongside kings, priests, god and devil. The Cornish miracle plays, if they cannot yet be said to be 'about the state', contain within them all of the cosmological primes from which the modern idea of the state can be built, and all of them are presented as just that, cosmological primes, invariant positions in the stage diagrams of the plays, which at the same time are diagrams of the cosmos.

In medieval Cornish drama, the figure of the torturers, ever-present characters who specialize, as it were, in the representation of enacted violence, has drawn a fair degree of attention in the past, connected as it is to the pervasive themes of violence in medieval theatre. What is particularly peculiar about the torturers in Cornish drama is their omnipresence (not a single play lacks them), as well as their prominent and invariant position in the stage diagrams. Like violence, the torturers stand out, indeed, stand apart, from the performance in which they play a singular functional role. The distinctive and unchanging position of the torturers in the north-east corner of all stage diagrams in all Cornish plays draws our attention to the semiotic principles underlying the staging of these plays. Why do such minor characters as the torturers warrant a special position in the stage diagrams alongside Heaven, Hell, Kings and Priests? Bakere proposes the following explanation in her discussion of the *Ordinalia*:

> It is, at first sight, surprising that the Torturers should be considered important enough to have their own permanent tent while major characters like Noah and Moses do not have any. The reason is, presumably, that the Torturers stand for the constant elements of cruelty and brutality in man, and thus must have a permanent place in the microcosm of the stage as they do in man himself.[18]

Bakere here suggests that the *invariant* character of the staging of the torturers represents some timeless human capacity for evil and violence. This is in keeping with her view that the themes of the Cornish plays are strictly religious, with no secular concerns whatsoever. However, Olson has recently suggested that the central theme of the later cycle 'Beunans Meriasek' is a historically positioned critique of tyranny.[19] Following her lead, I consider the changing symbolism of seemingly invariant formal elements, such as staging and the position and role of the torturers, to explore the political cosmology and ontology of the state that is an ever present theme in a cycle of plays whose thematic always includes the articulation of secular and spiritual authority, and the relation of legitimate authority of kings and the illegitimate authority of tyrants. In these matters the shifting allocation and valorization of an otherwise invariant element of violence, embodied in the torturers, produces a kind of theodicy of violence, by which the specific employment of violence in a given case is diagnostic of legitimate kingship or tyranny, but violence itself is elevated to an invariant cosmological principle. The plays thus produce a moral critique of specific instances of the employment of violence, but at the same time violence itself and its agents, and by extension, the state's monopoly on violence, is hypostatized as a technical invariant irrespective of the moral ends to which it is put. By exploring the semiotics of staging, I will argue that the figure of the torturers represents in the first earlier cycle of plays (the *Ordinalia*, c.1350–75) in effect a theodicy of the state's monopoly on violence, while in the later cycle of plays (*Beunans Meriasek*, c.1500) it becomes in effect synonymous with illegitimate state power that must resort to coercion rather than consent. Other changes in the stage diagrams between these cycles, particularly in the position of kings, parallel changing political orientations to the role of violence in the constitution of the state. In the *Ordinalia*, we see represented over the period of three days the historical process that Perry Anderson, in his *Lineages of the Absolutist State*, called the 'upward displacement of coercion'. This process has two historical phases, the first being the 'centralisation and coordination of feudal domination . . . a shift from individualised to concerted coercive subjection of rural populations'.[20] This is represented as an idealized project in the way that violence moves from being something used directly by one ordinary character on another (Cain killing Abel), to something monopolized by a special group of characters who have no other function other than violence (the torturers), and secondly that the torturers (coercion personified) are commanded only by seated characters (nobles) and perform acts of violence only on characters that lack seats (rural populations). The second stage of the process is one in which this upward displacement of coercion (which produces and articulates the difference between estates as a function of violence) is combined with centralization of violence, and the king emerges as a monopolist of violence (and violence moves from producing estates to producing the state).[21] The parallel on stage is when torturers move from being at the beck and call of a rather diverse group of rather lowly feudal characters (bishops, characters like Pilate and Prince Annas) to being monopolized by the Christian Emperor at the end. This process happens in *Beunans Meriasek* with the defeat of tyrants by legitimate emperors and the abolition of torturers for knights.[22]

In order to properly assess the changes in the position and role of various invariant formal elements, we need to describe the relatively invariant contexts in which they appear. The peculiarity of the torturers only emerges against a backdrop of normal expectations, from which they differ systematically in both behavior and staging conventions. Therefore, we must delay our discussion of their position until we have a normal context in which their insistent abnormality becomes visible.

STAGING ESTATE: THE DRAMATURGICAL REPRESENTATION OF FEUDAL ORDERS

There are two Cornish miracle plays for which we have full stage diagrams preserved, these are the 14th century *Ordinalia*, a play designed to be played over three days, with separate diagrams for the play of each day: *Origo Mundi* (the Creation of the World), *Passio* (the Passion play), and *Resurrexio* (The Resurrection play, c.1350–75), and *Beunans Meriasek* (the life of Saint Meriasek, c. 1504), designed to be played over two days, with separate diagrams for each day. The *Ordinalia* stage diagrams show a circular arrangement dividing a central playing area (*platea*) surrounded by eight peripheral *sedes* (seats) associated with named characters. The diagrams show certain commonalities, in that there is a seat for Heaven in the top (which is East, as in most medieval world maps, the location of the altar in a medieval church), the Torturers in the NE corner, and all, except the Passion play, have Hell in the North:

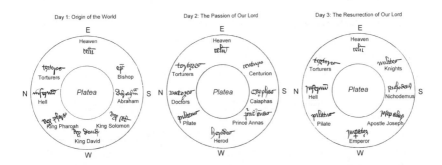

The *Beunans Meriasek* (henceforth BM) stage diagrams again show an identical distinction between *platea* and *sedes*, but the number

of the latter is much larger and varies considerably, forcing some seats like Heaven and Hell to be 'scrunched' into a small space, it being unclear whether this is an artefact of scribal representation or actually the disposition of the seats in playing space. The stage diagrams of BM show some of the same properties as were found across the days of the *Ordinalia*, with Heaven in the East and Hell (roughly) in the North and the only seat intervening between them being the torturers (see below for the diagrams from BM).

These two plays, coming perhaps from different areas of Cornwall over a century apart, on widely different themes, nevertheless show important parallels in staging that point to a shared tradition of staging in formal terms irrespective of dramatic content in terms of plot. Perhaps the most striking is the constancy of position not only of Heaven and Hell, but also the position reserved in all plays for the torturers, which is the point of ultimate interest in this paper. I will discuss the category oppositions that inform these stage diagrams beginning from those shared across most, if not all medieval drama, moving from these to those categories that are specific to Cornish staging. I will look at the diagrams as static elements of positional symbolism before I look at how they affect performance.

Throughout the discussion it should be obvious that Cornish stage diagrams are not well served by a methodology which assumes that they served dramaturgical ends of performance first and foremost, at least not in the modern sense. Modern stage diagrams, and modern stages, are 'addressed' to the problem of showing a narrative to an audience, whereas these stage diagrams not only make no provision for a space for the audience, they seem to be addressed, rather, to the problem of fitting or orienting the action in the play into a larger cosmological system, making the stage diagram a microcosmic representation of the macrocosm. In this sense, medieval drama resembles ritual.[23]

SEAT AND PLATEA

Cornish miracle plays were played 'in the round', a round being divided in turn into *sedes* ('seats', also *loci* 'places') and *platea* ('place'), the former in this case forming a raised amphitheatre where (presumably) the audience sat and where the seats of certain players were placed, surrounding the place where the principle action of the play was conducted.

This central dramaturgical distinction between *sedes* and *platea* in the theatrical space of the Cornish miracle plays, rather than the opposition between the stage and the audience in modern theatre, is the central organizing opposition of most medieval drama, however it is expressed in physical terms:

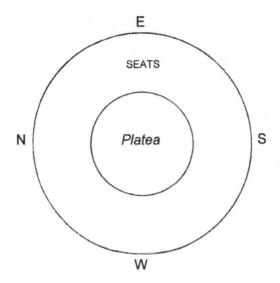

The *locus*, or *sedes*, is recognized as the unit of specified place, often sacral in significance, like the crib or Easter Sepulchre, the focus of performance analogous with the altar, the focus of worship . . . The area between and around the *loci*, where commuting and other non-specifically localized action takes place, is known as the platea . . . The *platea* is the location of movement and action, of transition between those pictures [represented by the *loci*].[24]

First of all, this opposition is one between semiologically marked (*sedes, loci*) and unmarked (*platea*) terms: the elevated seats are associated with specific named persons or places, and have specific ('marked') values, while the platea is effectively defined as simply the lowered empty space between these seats with no positive properties ('unmarked'). Having no intrinsic properties, it can serve simply as an empty space between the seats, for transitions or movement, or it can be given specific dramaturgical values by setting up scenery representing specific places within this space.

At the same time, as King notes, the opposition between seats and platea spatially articulates a kind of cosmological presupposition of the feudal order, with 'the movement or disorder of the *platea* alternating with the order presented by the *loci*'.[25] As we will see, the seats are the point of origin of violence, but never its end point, violence is a unidirectional relationship between seats and platea. As King notes, the specified places represented by seats represent essentially a miniature diagram of status positions within a cosmological and feudal order, rather than specific locations or sets as in a modern play.[26] There can be no question that seats, on the whole, are given to characters who are 'important' in an absolute sense (in spiritual, secular or cosmological terms), regardless of the relative dramaturgical importance of the role they play in the narrative itself (which is often vanishingly minor). Unlike the occasional pieces of moveable scenery that dot the platea, seats do not have a directly 'representational' function, rather, they represent social stations, estates, in the first instance, and only residually do they represent those places, like towers, castles, heaven, hell, associated with such social or cosmological stations.[27] Moreover, the asymmetric opposition between lowered place and raised seat resembles (is iconic of) social hierarchy.[28] Therefore, the allocation of seats, as well as the opposition between seats and platea, produces a diagrammatic icon of the feudal order, between secular and spiritual authorities and an unclassifiable residue of peasantry.[29] In the Cornish plays, then, the spatially encoded opposition between unseated characters and seated characters is essentially an icon of a social opposition of symmetric community (since the level platea allows no spatial distinction of rank between characters), and asymmetric hierarchy (since the seats themselves represent 'hierarchy' in relation to the 'community' of the place, and, amongst themselves, hierarchical relations are coded both by static value of seats and dynamic interaction).[30]

The characters themselves in many of the plays can be classified into three groups, 'platea' characters, 'seated' characters, and characters who mediate on behalf of seated characters in the platea (messengers, for example). So this opposition in staging is also a principle of social classification, the characters of biblical drama are classified in terms of this representation of a hierarchical feudal order. Taking the first two groups, characters with any sort of feudal rank (either secular or spiritual authorities: kings, princes, earls, knights, popes, bishops) will always have seats, while the groups of characters who begin in the platea (the unclassifiable residuum) tend to be relatively egalitarian (Adam and Eve, Noah and his family) or tend to be groups that are 'low' with respect to some feudal personage (Moses and his people versus Pharoah and his [seated], Jesus and his disciples versus Herod, and so on).

STAGING POMP AND POWER: MEDIATIONAL PERFORMANCES

Since spatial seatedness and social rank are identical, interactions between seated characters present problems for performance, for the rigidity of the staging forces all interactions into hierarchical grooves. For one seated character to interact with another, either they must happen to meet on the neutral ground of the *platea,* or one must *descend* from his seat and accede to the presence of the other who is seated, or a messenger or other mediator must be used to summon one seated character into the presence of another. This leads to the multiplication of mediating figures in medieval drama. The opposition between seat and platea makes momentary relations of hierarchy unambiguous, and a good deal of the dramaturgy of the plays is geared to overcoming these oppositions, generating not a little 'to-and-froing' of mediators between principals.

There is little question that these questions of hierarchy are extremely important and 'real' for the playwright and audience. Interactions between rulers and their subalterns should ideally be asymmetric, with one seated and the other in the platea, particularly when the former is issuing a command to the latter. There are occasions when a 'seated' character who is on the platea will ascend to his seat solely to issue a command, as if the asymmetry of the speech act of command must be replicated in the asymmetry of the positions of the characters engaging in it. King David, standing in the *platea,* must 'ascend' to his seat specifically to summon and command his messenger, who is presumably located, waiting, at the seat or in the platea nearby:

[ascendit rex dd.]	[King David goes up]
messyger my bel aber	Messenger, my fair servant,
dus thy'mmo ketoth ha'n ger	Come to me soon as the word,
rag colenwel voth ov brys [31]	To fulfil the wish of my mind.

At the same time, if a seated character must go into the presence of another seated character, the temporary asymmetry produced by the apparent accession of one ranked character into the other can be mitigated. For example, the seated character can invite the character to sit with him, so that symmetry is restored (as does Caiaphas for Annas, whom he has summoned with a messenger).

PRINCEPS ANNAS	PRINCE ANNAS
me a thotho yn lowen	I will go to him joyfully,
del ywe ow syre da	As he is my good sire,
rak dyswythyl an bylen	To despatch the villain,
mar kevs erbyn a laha	If he speaks against the law.

[*et tunc iet ad episcopum descendit*]

[*And then he shall go to the bishop*]
[*He goes down*]

hayl cayfas syr epscob stovt
dek can quyth thy's lowene

Hail Caiaphas, bold sir Bishop;
Ten hundred times joy to thee!

CAYPHAS
wolcom by mahommys blout
dues nes hagh yse gene
[ascendit annas][32]

CAIAPHAS
Welcome, by the blood of Mahound;
Come near and sit with me
[Annas goes up]

In the same fashion in BM, Pope Silvester, summoned into Constantine's presence by a messenger, shows that he will not 'incline' to Constantine by ascending to his throne (tower) without permission. The act of equalizing their position by ascending is taken to directly encode this:

SELUESTER
Hayll constentyn in the dour
me a wor ty a wetsa
bones grueys dyso enour
ha the gregyans a pe da
ny an gressa
rag the voys in dysgregyans
awos ovn gothe mernans
inclenya dys ny vanna
[*ascendit*]

SILVESTER
Hail, Constantine, in thy tower!
I know thou deservest
That Honour be done to thee,
And if thy faith werc good
We would do it.
Because of thy being in unbelief,
For fear of suffering death,
Incline to thee I will not.
[*He goes up*]

CONSTANTINUS
Seluester wolcum owhy
nynsyw awos drokcoleth
ythogh kerhys dymovy[33]

CONSTANTINE
Silvester, you are welcome
It is not on account of an ill deed
That you are fetched to me.

The Emperor Tiberius, when Pilate (a near equal as a seated character) is led unceremoniously into his presence by torturers, still has the grace to descend to greet him in the platea as an equal, all of which upsets the torturers, since it is in conflict with the expectations of how someone summoned by torturers should be treated (certainly in the Passion no one descends from their seat to greet Christ when he is brought with torturers).[34]

All of this leads to a certain amount of the plays being taken up in representations of ceremony (an extreme example being the immense amount of time devoted to portraying pomp in the second day of the newly discovered play *Beunans Ke*): status is not merely represented in the static oppositions between seated characters, but also in their interactions in performance. Many characters have no other purpose than the mediate between seated characters. On the one hand, there are the multitudinous messengers and their functional equivalent, who presumably are to be found initially seated near the principals for whom they act as agents. These characters allow seated characters to interact with other seated characters and characters in the *platea* alike without themselves moving. On the other hand, there are figures like the torturers, who sit apart from their principals in a special seat, and are specialized for violent interactions between estates and the platea. In the middle are characters like knights, who may be seated with or apart from their principles, and are used to suggest the possibility of violence, enacting instead coercion without actualized violence.

This classification of mediators is at the same moment a classification of types mediational performance, in terms of power (persuasion, coercion, and outright violence), and it is also a classification of the proper *addressees* for each kind of performance. Messengers (and their functional equivalents) can be used to allow a seated character to interact with anyone, seated or not, but their special purpose is to interact with other seated characters, to summon them when going oneself would imply self-abasement. Torturers, on the other hand, are generally used on 'low' characters, characters of the platea, but even when they are used on seated characters, this can only happen when the seated character is in the platea. Knights, though they may not use real violence, are essentially hybrids of messenger and torturer, using threats and some physical coercion (but no blood!), when interacting with platea characters. Interactions between seated characters are typified by the peaceful intercourse mediated by the messenger, interactions between seated characters and the platea are typified by violence represented by the torturers.

This mediation is, however, not merely a functional response to dilemmas for performance produced by the rigidity of the stage diagrams. Rather, mediation is an end in itself, multiplying mediation, separation between the command of the seated, unmoving principal and his mobile agents, itself produces, dramatizes and poeticizes how authority can be translated into *power*, that is, the ability to 'act at a distance'. Commentators on Medieval plays of various kinds are frequently mystified by the large amount of time and personnel devoted to representing the fact of mediation, valued seemingly in itself as a means of representing pomp and authority.[35] However, important as this was for the medievals, it plays little role in the modern analysis of the plays: 'The issuing of commands, accompanied by ceremonial entrances and exits to repeat them, forms the basis of action at Herod's court. This pompous and unnecessary to-and-froing is evidently a dramatic end sought in itself, for it complicates and slows down the plot'.[36]

This to-and-froing, so pointless to the modern eye, that characterizes medieval drama forms a kind of performance that R. Bauman has termed a 'mediational performance'.[37] A mediational performance is one that breaks down a single act (whether of speaking or other act) into component parts or roles, resolving simple acts performable by a single actor into complex ones involving many participants. Mediational performances highlight the way a simple act is now transformed into the ability to 'act at a distance', 'they place the complexities of participation structures on display, inviting the contemplation of the analyst and participant alike'.[38] If mediational performances serve the ends of pomp, by poeticizing and magnifying every action as an end in itself, they also serve the ends of power, for an important basis of modern notions of power is the ability to 'act at a distance'. Ironically, then, mediational performances in the service of pomp seem peculiarly medieval, while those in the service of power seem quite modern.

Mediational performances are in effect the flip side in performance of the division of theatrical space into seats and platea. For some seated characters, the ability to act within the platea comes about only through mediating characters, who represent them in the platea while they remain seated (for example, God in the *Ordinalia* does not frequently descend from heaven after the first day of the play, and never in BM, presumably to preserve his otherworldly majesty; there are similar arrangements in Hell). Some seated characters lack mediators, variously Knights, Torturers, Doctors; this is because they are *themselves* mediators for other seated characters. The remainder of the seated characters have such 'mediators' who perform services for them in the platea, whether or not these mediators have seats of their own. For example, kings have entourages of various sizes and descriptions, as do Bishops, as do God and the Devil. These last two characters provide interesting analogs to the opposition between messenger and torturer, for just as the messenger primarily deals in speech, the torturer in material violence, so too the angels deployed by God act primarily as messengers, the demons deployed by the devil act both as messengers, but also as violent counterparts to the torturers, whose duty is to drag souls or bodies of the dead to hell. Messengers and angels act primarily on incorporeal signs and souls (spiritual authority), torturers and demons act on corporeal bodies (temporal authority); the former manifests itself through decorous speech, the latter through corporeal violence and grotesque realism of speech and action.[39] The dualism dividing temporal authority in the play BM, which I discuss below, again reveals itself here cosmologically, torturers and tyrants worship the Devil, just as legitimate authorities worship God.

In spite of all this apparent diversity, there are basically two opposed kinds of mediator (and mediational performance) based on different types of power, messengers and torturers (with knights in between). Unlike torturers, messengers as figures are typically seated with the principals for whom they are agents, and hence (unlike the torturers) are specialized depending on their principal. Kings and emperors employ messengers, while God employs angels (whom he sometimes calls 'messengers') or saints, Satan employs devils, bishops employ crozier-bearers. Again, unlike torturers, messengers do not, in general, coerce their target; if coercion is to be done, knights, jailors or torturers are used instead. But it is important to stress that only torturers can actualize their potential for violence on their targets, the knights, jailors and others coercively escort them from place to place, but do not kill. Torturers in the *Ordinalia* complain bitterly when they are summoned merely to invite Pilate into the Emperor's presence, just as if they were messengers.[40] Indeed, the only characters in the *Ordinalia* who kill, other than the torturers, include the first murderer, Cain, and Pontius Pilate, who kills himself (saving either the torturers or the emperor himself from killing him, an act from which the Emperor has to be restrained).[41]

Most importantly, messengers are the only mediator that can be used for symmetric intra-estate interactions, interactions between two seated characters, while torturers and knights are alike in that they are usually characteristic of asymmetric inter-estate interactions between seated characters and 'commoner' characters in the platea. In BM, moreover, messengers are *only* used by secular authorities (seated in the West or South West) to summon spiritual authorities (typically seated in the South East). Interactions involving messengers seem to imply symmetry, here, coordinate and complementary authority between Imperial and Papal hierarchies. When messengers are addressed to non-seated characters, they use the language of command and issue threats of violence.[42] Similarly, as messengers mediate within and between estates, angels and devils or demons mediate between cosmological orders, allowing their principals, God and Lucifer, to remain in Heaven or Hell. The primary difference is that devils seem to work both as messengers and as physical agents of coercion, dragging bodies or unsaved souls of the dead to hell,[43] while angels work primarily as messengers (Gabriel to King David, for example).[44]

Modern critics have found fault with medieval drama in the

'pointless to-and-froing' of these messengers, but I would argue that their existence not only solves important dramaturgical problems of hierarchy encoded in the stage diagrams, but also, by creating a distinction between principal and agent that is displayed in this mediated communication, encodes the authority and power of the principal, who can act therefore 'at a distance'.[45] The basic distinction between seat and platea is an icon of static hierarchy, but when placed in motion in performance through mediation it becomes a distinction of *power* between the immobile principal (seat) and the platea as the scope or field of their actions carried out by agents. Both messengers and torturers serve to magnify the power of the seated character by displaying an opposition between principal and agent, seat as locus of conception and platea as locus of execution, but in different ways, on the one hand in words, in the other deeds.

The most distinctive difference between messengers and other types of mediators is in seating: messengers are always seated with the figure they mediate for, torturers are always seated apart (knights, once again, can be apart or together with their principal). Violence appears to be separated from the person who commands it not only in mediational performance, but also in the stage diagrams themselves. Violence, at once very common and very gruesome on the medieval stage, is nevertheless 'confined to barracks' when not in use. In order to explore this dimensions of power, we need to know how violence in the form of the torturers fits into the diagram of the cosmos represented by the arrangement of seats on the stage.

STAGING COSMOLOGY: *THEATRUM MUNDI*

The seats and their functions in the play are articulated to the points of the compass, an orientation which makes the medieval Cornish stage is a microcosm of the world itself, a *theatrum mundi*. Stevens has persuasively argued that medieval stage diagrams (*theatrum mundi*) are replicas in miniature of the world as a whole (*mappa mundi*), a 'cosmic stage', just as the iconography and architecture of the medieval church follows a similar plan with an identical orientation. All three, stage, map, church, serve as parallel images of the world. The first parallelism is the circular form of the stage and the medieval T-O map. The other is a series of parallels in orientation to the points of the compass. The East (the location of the altar in a church) is pervasively associated with Heaven or Paradise in both stage diagrams and *mappa mundi*, just as the North is associated with Hell. Interestingly, the North East, the location of the torturers in Cornish stage diagrams, is associated with the walled region inhabited by Gog and Magog, 'where the unclean semi-human monsters roamed' in many *mappa mundi*.[46] In short, just as the temporal cycle of the plays spanned all time producing a complete map of the economy of salvation from genesis to the resurrection or beyond, so too the plays themselves in their stage diagrams 'replicate . . . a plan of the universe'.[47] Not merely a miniature plan of the universe, the stage diagrams by their orientation are part of, point to, that same universe they replicate.

The seats most important to articulating the changing stage diagram of each play to a broader unchanging cosmological scheme are those oriented to the cardinal directions. Cardinal seats such as Heaven (East) and Hell (North) (the Torturers, although non-cardinal (NE), fit in here too) remain unchanging both in position and occupants across all plays. These seats represent basic 'anchors' for the whole medieval cosmology. The other cardinal seats link the cosmological order to the anchoring points of the feudal order: seats like West (Kings and Emperors), and South (priests and bishops) do not change position, and are reliably typological, that is, they have the same *type* of occupant across all plays, even if the name of that occupant changes.[48]

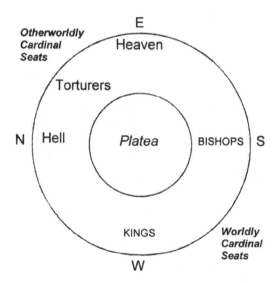

This is the case in the *Ordinalia,* but the situation in BM is slightly more complex. In BM the larger number of seats guarantees that while Heaven is insistently in the Eastern position (and the Heaven seat appears to be the 'anchor of anchors', the seat most consistent across all existing medieval stage diagrams), Hell and the Torturers are forced into a small space in the NNE corner. Moreover, the 'cardinal' Western and Southern cardinal positions are not occupied, rather they form *boundaries* between mirror image opposite forms of authority. The Southern position faces off a Bishop (the bottom of a Christian ecclesiastical hierarchy terminating in the Pope adjacent to Heaven) with a Duke or an Earl (the bottom of a Christian secular hierarchy terminating in the Emperor). The Western position faces off a Pagan Tyrant (the acme of a pagan secular hierarchy) with a Christian Emperor (the acme of the Christian, secular hierarchy). The Western position is still the summit of worldly power, but disputed, and the southern seat still is associated with ecclesiastical power, but the summit of ecclesiastical power is nearer heaven. The opposition between these two pairs of cardinal seats is at the same time the opposition between an unchanging set of eternal, otherworldly seats (Heaven and Hell) and their historical, worldly equivalents (Bishops adjacent Heaven and Kings adjacent Hell).

Lastly, there are seats, always associated with non-cardinal directions, that change both in position, number and location (ranging from one to three seats between the cardinal seats) and type of occupant, though the type of occupant will be in general similar to one of the adjoining cardinal seats. The situation in BM roughly follows this pattern as well, except that the adjoining non-cardinal seats are formed into recognizable hierarchies. The seat of the torturers is extremely odd in this respect, being the invariant and only permissible NE seat between Heaven (E) and Hell (N) in *all* plays. It is the only non-cardinal seat that shares in all the properties of cardinal ones, it is the only 'worldly' seat that is as eternal as the otherworldly seats of Heaven and Hell that stand to the left and right of it.

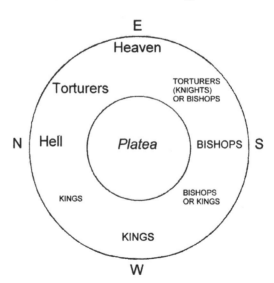

Seats can therefore be divided into two groups according to whether they serve a *typological* or *cosmological anchoring* function across all plays (what I will call *cardinal* seats, since most of these are aligned to cardinal directions, plus the NE seat occupied by the torturers) versus those that have values that are more variable typologically (based often on semi-fortuitous associations with adjacent *cardinal* seats), and in number (a varying number of such seats between one (*Ordinalia*) or up to three or four (*Beunans Meriasek*) are possible), which are always non-cardinal points of the compass (hence *non-cardinal seats*). Cardinal seats are invariant across all stage diagrams in all plays (with one exception), they are cosmologically and paradigmatically anchoring positions in terms of which the more variable seats take their syntagmatic values.[49] The cardinal seats have a typological function, establishing relations of equivalence of type between successive occupants of a given seat over each day of the play, hence they establish typological relations of equivalence between 'kings' (W) and 'priests' (S), respectively.

As noted, the cardinal seats are further organized into two opposed sets. Heaven (E) and Hell (N) are 'otherworldly' powers standing opposed to their 'worldly' equivalents, representatives of spiritual authority (priests in the S seat) and temporal authority (kings in the W seat), respectively. This delineates a mirror-image arrangement in which the division of unchanging otherworldly authority between Heaven (spiritual) and Hell (temporal) is reflected in the division of temporal authority between spiritual and temporal powers (priests and kings, respectively), an immutable set of first principles opposed to a mutable temporal order (composed of changing occupants of the same eternal seat). Again, the NE position of the torturers, standing as the only seat between Heaven and Hell in all plays, has an ambiguous position as an immutable cosmological prime in a non-cardinal position.

Other than the torturers, the non-cardinal seats are all unambiguously worldly seats. These seats are doubly mutable: not only are their occupants variable at the individual token level, but the type represented is itself also variable, and, indeed, the number of such seats is also variable, ranging from one to many. These seats take on their typological values by association with adjoining, typologically invariant, cardinal seats: the NW position (adjacent to the W position of kings) can contain only (usually) tyrannical figures of temporal authority in the *Ordinalia* (respectively Pharoah and Pilate). The SW position, between the S associated with spiritual authority (Abraham, Bishop Caiaphas, Nichodemus) and the W associated with temporal authority, contains either 'kings' or 'priests' (Solomon, Prince Annas,

Joseph of Arimathea). The SE position, standing nearest either the torturers (ignoring Heaven for the moment) in the NE or priests in the S, can contain either 'priests' or quasi-torturers (respectively a Bishop, a Centurion, and Knights).

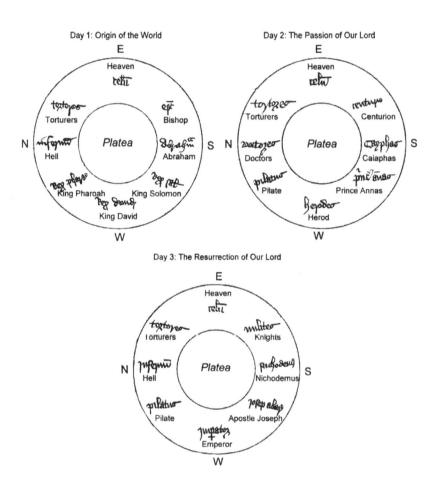

This is the pattern in the *Ordinalia*. In BM there are instead multiple seats between each cardinal seat (with the exception of the NE seat of the torturers), and dividing the round into three sectors of mirror image hierarchies. On the first day of the play, from N to W runs an ascending hierarchy of secular authorities up to a Tyrant figure nearing the W position (Respectively Outlaws, the Earl of Rohan, the Duke of Cornwall and Emperor Teudar), all of these are figures of temporal authority associated with Cornwall, good or evil; from W to S is a descending hierarchy of legitimate secular authorities from the Emperor Constantine (Constantine, King Conan, the Duke of Brittany, all associated with non-local secular authority); from S to E is an ascending hierarchy of spiritual authority from a Bishop of Kernou in the S to the Pope Silvester nearest heaven in the E (These images are modified from the transcriptions of Whitley Stokes, with the positions of characters more nearly approximating the relative positions indicated in the original Peniarth manuscripts):

BM Day 1

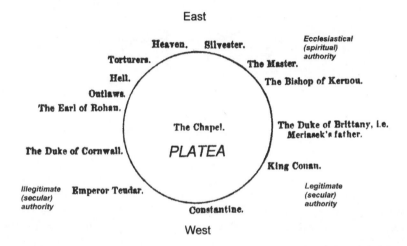

On the second day, the axis from N to W begins with a minor character (the woman's son), through the (pagan) Bishop of Pola, through two pagan characters, Duke Magus 1 and 2, the good Earl Globus, with the generic Tyrant Emperor in the W; from W to S we begin again with Constantine, followed by King Massen, to the Earl of Vannes; from S to E we again ascend from the Bishop of Kernou, to the second bishop, to Pope Silvester.

BM Day 2

Just as cardinal seats in all plays seat up a parallel series of mirror-image oppositions, such that Heaven (E) and Hell (N) stand as 'that world' to the seats of temporal (W) and spiritual (S) power of 'this world', on the one hand, and on the other E and S pair off as 'spiritual' to N and W with pair off as 'temporal', in this play the non-cardinal seats are each linked to the non-cardinal seats as a set of mirror-image hierarchies. These hierarchies parallel one another in content (each

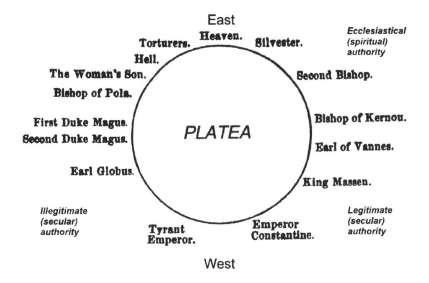

one having a parallel system of ranks from bishops to popes; earls, dukes, kings and emperors), just as they are mirror image reflections of one another in precisely this way, so that the Christian secular hierarchy terminating in Constantine is a mirror image reflection of the Christian spiritual hierarchy terminating in Pope Silvester, and the parallel secular hierarchy in the NW terminating always in a Pagan tyrant emperor figure is in turn a mirror-image reflection of the Imperial hierarchy of Constantine, producing an image of each as equivalently structured mirror images, a common medieval motif articulating different orders, using the 'mirror' trope as a semiotically organizing principle (see the diagrams from BM above).

> To each ecclesiastical power there corresponds a lay power, governed by the *saeculare jus* [Secular law]; hence are derived the pairs *papa-imperator, primates-rex, episcopus-comes, sacerdos-miles* [Pope-Emperor, *Primate*-King, Bishop-Duke, Priest-Knight] . . . [T]he unified physiognomy of culture . . . is reflected in each microstructure in exactly the same way as—to take up a simile much used in the Middle Ages—the same image is reflected in a mirror, or on a smaller scale in each of the fragments of the same mirror once it has been shattered.[50]

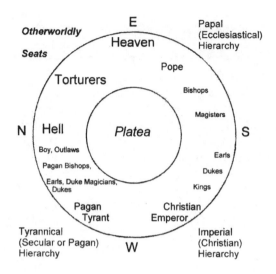

But these close parallels between the two plays belie an important difference. In the *Ordinalia* there is only, in effect, an opposition between *all* secular authority (centered in the Western seat, nearer to Hell) and *all* spiritual authority (centered in the Southern seat, nearer to Heaven). In *BM*, in addition to a general opposition between spiritual authority centering in the SE opposed to secular authority in the West, the secular authority is itself divided into two. In the NW secular authority (associated with Cornwall, that is, local political authority, on the first day if not the second) terminating in a tyrant, is characterized by a lack of cohesion, a chaotic confusion, between its hierarchically ordered members, some of whom are pagan or devil-worshippers, others of whom are Christian, and consists of an odd mixture of commoners (Outlaws, the Boy), Pagan spiritual authorities (Bishop of Pola), secular authorities (dukes and earls, some of whom are Christians), and even mixed types (the Dukes Magi are simultaneously the pagan equivalents of Dukes and Bishops). This confusion is mirrored by *legitimate* and *cohesive* secular Christian hierarchy in the SW headed by Constantine. The West position is unique in the *Ordinalia*, in which secular authority, for good or ill, is unified, and episcopal authority is generally more malign than regal authority in a set of plays in which Herod, though evil, is mild mannered, even understated. This same position appears divided into a manichean opposition in the later play between a Tyrant and an Emperor. Corresponding to this division of secular authority is a functional division in the principals who can command torturers. In the former play all kinds of authorities (spiritual or secular) can command the torturers, while in the latter play only tyrants can do so.

STAGING THE STATE: TYRANTS AND EMPERORS

The organization of the stage diagrams, then, presents a feudal order of estates (the *sedes*) opposed to a residual order represented by the *platea*. These seats are doled out on the basis of character status, regardless of relevance to story (some seated characters have little or no role in the plot): emperors, kings, popes, bishops, priests, and subaltern potentates, and sometimes knights all have seats. This feudal order is at once a cosmological order, the stage is a *imago mundi*, representing the entire universe from Heaven to Hell. The cosmology presents the temporal order as being at once a reflection of the cosmological order, and is invariant in itself in the sense that there will always be *sedes* for kings and priests, even if the specific occupants are variable. And, moreover, there will always be violence, for the NE position of the torturers is presented as a cosmological given, an invariant type as necessary as Heaven, Hell, Kings and Priests. The stage diagrams then, make an almost Weberian argument about definitional role of violence to the proto-state. At the same time, differences in the organization of the stage diagrams can show us different models of kingship, and different models of the role of enacted violence in the political and cosmological order.

As noted, the main difference between the *Ordinalia* and the later play *Beunans* Meriasek is that the Western position, the position of secular authority, kingship, is unitary in the former plays, and is bifurcated in the latter. That is, in the *Ordinalia* the W position is unambiguous, while in BM the W position is usually composed to two emperor like potentates, one a Tyrant Emperor slightly to the N, the other an Emperor slightly to the S. Moreover, these two opposed types of 'emperors' each stand at the head of mirror-image hierarchies of feudal authority.

This minor change produces a distinction between two models of secular authority, which corresponds to very different models of the role of violence, personified by torturers, in the medieval 'state'. In the *Ordinalia* Kingship (W) as a whole is legitimate, with Tyrants relegated to a non-cardinal position (NW). Consequently, torturers (who serve both good and evil characters), when they come to be in the service of Christian kings, are legitimate expressions of power. In the later plays, instead, there is an equipollent manichean opposition between tyrants (who employ torturers) and kings (who employ knights), represented in the stage diagram by having the western position divided between opposed tyrants and kings.

In the *Ordinalia*, the first occupant of this position is King David, who as the *sacerdos-rex* contains within his person both the typologized functions (king and priest) which render his rule legitimate. Solomon occupies this seat after the death of David, changing from his non-cardinal seat as heir apparent (SW) to the cardinal seat of true king (W) upon his coronation. Herod inherits from Solomon the title of 'secular king' as opposed to 'divinely legitimated emperor'. Finally, the emperor Tiberius reconciles secular with spiritual authority by accepting Christianity. Therefore this seat (with its succession David, Solomon, Herod, Emperor) is associated with the line of David, and with legitimate kingship as such (as each king is in some sense legitimated by the Jewish, and later Christian, God). It stands opposed to the position in the NW, which are unified in opposition to this seat by including only 'Pagan' kings (Pharoah and Pilate) who, unlike Herod, are completely divorced from legitimating cosmological principles. In this play, the torturers are first employed at the service of evil characters in the first two plays, in both cases evil bishops, until in the final day of the play they come to be in the service of the Christian king Tiberius. Violence in the service of evil is associated not with kings, but with subaltern potentates, specifically evil priests, while violence redeemed in the service of good is associated with Christian kingship.

It is in B*eunans Meriasek* where this opposition (implied in the *Ordinalia*) between 'legitimate, Jewish or Christian' (W) and 'illegitimate, Pagan' (NW) king is brought to the fore, for here at first glance it appears that we have no single 'Western seat', but rather the Western seat is bifurcated into two seats, side by side. As Olson argues, the unifying theme of this play is tyranny, or more specifically, the opposition between illegitimate and legitimate temporal power (tyrants and emperors), with possible linkages to Cornish hostility to the English monarchy following the 1497 rebellions (with the redaction of the play dated at 1508).[51] This dualistic conception of secular authority is reflected in the modifications of the stage diagrams. The western seat closest to Hell is associated with evil 'tyrants', who are presented as doubly illegitimate rulers (having no clear title ('usurper') and being pagan rather than Christian), who worship the devil, employ torturers instead of knights, and lack legitimacy or mercy, and whose own servants show no loyalty.[52] The western seat closest to Heaven is occupied by legitimate 'emperors' (or rulers who are to be legitimated later, notably Constantine, who is converted on the first day of the play), who show all of the opposite tendencies.[53] Therefore, the unified position of the *Ordinalia* is broken down into a sub-typology of 'temporal authority' into 'Tyrants' and 'Emperors'.

In fact, Constantine himself makes the transition from tyrant to emperor on the first day of the play.[54] Since, according to Olson, the struggle between illegitimate 'tyrants' and legitimate kings and emperors is a basic dynamic of these plays, this bifurcation of the single position into a Manichean equipollent opposition is part of the rhetoric of the individual play. Therefore, the 'bifurcation' of the Western position may in fact be only apparent, for it seems that the Cardinal Western position is not only a position of temporal authority, but in this play, temporal authority is typically evil, rather than good.

Here, then, we have a situation where a specific change in the stage diagrams (the bifurcation of a once unitary cardinal position into two opposed positions) produces in itself a new view of the nature of political authority and power. In the *Ordinalia* kingship is ultimately unitary and legitimate in its use of violence, while in *Beunans Meriasek* the position of kingship is in turn divided into Tyrants and true Kings. What is crucial is the valuation of the torturers. In the *Ordinalia* the torturers are ultimately neutral personifications of violence, capable of being employed by evil bishops or good kings. In BM good kings have knights (characters who represent the potential for violence), evil tyrants have torturers, these being the only characters who are allowed to *enact* violence on the stage. In the *Ordinalia* kingship and violence are ultimately legitimate, while in BM there is a dualistic view of the legitimacy of the state and violence.

Reconstructed (hypothetical) stage diagram for Beaunans Ke

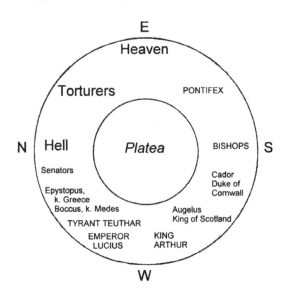

A similar set of oppositions between tyrants and emperors can be gleaned from what little information we have for the newly discovered Cornish play *Beunans Ke* (BK). Internal textual evidence indicates the presence of a certain number of 'worldly' seats, and given the presence of the torturers, we can reconstruct a sense of the 'otherworldly' ones as well (remembering that Heaven and hell seats are consistently present even in plays that make little use of them). The first day of the play features a Tyrant Teuthar (presumably in the NW), replaced on the second day by the Roman Emperor Lucius, who is opposed to King Arthur (presumably in the SW), each with their allied kings and potentates (NW and SW, respectively). There are also signs of separate seats for bishops and a pontifex. On this basis, we can provisionally reconstruct something like this as the general stage diagram for this play:[55]

STAGING VIOLENCE: THE FIGURE AND PLACE OF THE TORTURER

The figure of the torturer and his valuation within the larger staging conventions becomes part of very different models of the role of violence in the state in these two plays. In this final section I want to sum up some of the marginal features of the torturers that makes them central to the imagining of the relation of violence to the polity in the medieval plays.

First, the torturers are marginal characters in staging. They have a seat of their own in the NE, a seat that in almost all respects behaves as an entity of a cosmological order rather than a feudal one. The seat of the torturers is consistently the only seat between Heaven and Hell, corresponding to the location of Gog and Magog in Medieval *mappa mundi*, who are also uncomfortably poised between being historical and cosmological agents (waiting to serve as the armies of the antichrist), the torturers seem to represent not concrete historical characters like David, Caiaphas, and Solomon as much as they represent violence itself, elevated to a cosmological principle. While they seem to be 'worldly' characters in most dramaturgical respects, notably that they can be freely approached in their seats and summoned by other worldly characters (unlike Heaven and Hell), their staging seems to imply that they instead belong along with Heaven and Hell to cosmology. Secondly, the torturers are the only 'low' characters to be given a seat of their own, they are not so much estates of the feudal hierarchy like those represented by the other 'worldly' seats (kings, priests, knights) as abstract presuppositions of that feudal hierarchy. In this respect they differ from other 'low' characters who serve as mediators, such as sundry messengers, crozier bearers, demons and angels, whose incessant to-and-froing makes up much of the action of the plays, in that unlike messengers and the like, who are seated with those they serve, they have a seat of their own, presenting special problems when they are summoned. Not only do they separate their principals, those who command them, from the violence they command, but they also are separated physically from those who command them in the seating. Lastly, while messengers can mediate between different estates, between seated characters as with characters in the platea, the torturers represent a specific articulation of the seats and the platea: the torturers always act on behalf of seated characters against characters whose current location is the platea, and, moreover, only torturers can actually enact violence on those characters.

The torturers are not merely deviant in terms of their staging, they are marginal and monstrous in other respects as well, their portrayal embodying a familiar set of aesthetic conventions that link them to the lowly, the comic, the bodily and material, and the grotesque. In general, the aesthetic of realism is linked to that of the grotesque, and both of these to evil, just as schematic and ideal images are linked to holiness and good, this particularly applies to images of realistic grotesque violence and its perpetrators, as Camille notes for the iconography of the period as a whole: 'This equation between realistic depiction and evil is interesting in terms fo the dialectic in medieval art between the abstract schematic forms of the good—the frontal hieratic figures of saints—as opposed to the vigorous, lively gestures of their tormentors'.[56]

The torturers' grotesque realism resemble other forms of performance that rely exclusively on embodied performances with no transcendent verbal element, *histriones* (mimes) and *meretrices* (prostitutes):

> What brings the two *status* [of *histriones* and *meretrices*] together, then, is primarily the use made of the body and of parts of the body exclusively within the existential sphere, as if the world of *res* [material things] could hope to be complete in itself. What is more, *histriones* and *meretrices* make use of complementary signs of purely bodily message: make-up, disguise, masks, all elements which themselves become charged with the vital and corporeal. A realism, and a grotesque one at that, appears as a form of communication which is antithetical to that the cultural codes offer, codes for which the parts of the human body have no value unless in function of something else which is not corporeal, on the basis of the general principle *per visibilia ad invisibilia*.[57]

For the torturers of the Cornish plays, Cross draws attention to their motley dress, their grotesque embodiment and fascination with scatology and sex, their 'amoral and antisocial' character, and their lack of ability to assimilate or reflect upon evil, part of a general disjuncture between 'reality and reflection' that they display.[58] To this list we could add their other 'grotesque' features, notably their fascination with the literal 'gorey details' of their actions, the accidents of bodily mutilation and disfigurement, over the transcendent meaning or teleology of their actions as they inscribe power on the bodies of their victims. This is parallel to their general fascination with their own embodiment, as they draw attention to their various bodily processes, such as sweating, trembling, exhaustion. As Cross points out, 'The torturers . . . are in that peripheral position, entering the scene to perform an act which is not related to any moral or ethical commitment to their victim. Torturing is their vocation rather than their ethic'.[59]

The general way that torturers (and devils and demons) embody a general aesthetic register of the comic, bodily-material and grotesque across speech, action and appearance, a kind of medieval equivalent of modern 'splatstick' horror film violence,[60] has been explored by Veronica Plesch for the French Passion Plays, and her conclusions are worth quoting at length. In essence, all this aesthetic of the comic, bodily-material and grotesque does not imply that torturers and demons are carnivalesque spirits of resistance, rather, they produce an aesthetic disconnection between the agents of violence and their principals:

> The community has recourse to specific techniques to emphasize its disconnection from the executioner . . . [T]he community engages in a 'comedy of innocence' in order to deny any responsibility in the decision and the implementation of the murder. The executioner thus belongs both to the community and is rejected from it: hence the fundamentally human nature of the tormentors in these plays, with their very down-to-earth reactions, of pleasure, fear, pain, tiredness . . . At the same time, the playwrights emphasize their lowliness, and this in particular through comic and grotesque effects, which then contribute to produce alienation.[61]

In dramaturgical terms, too, the torturers occupy a unique and marginal position. In the *Ordinalia* the torturers have a monopoly of enacted violence: not only do they embody a cosmological invariant of violence, they monopolize *embodied violence*. If actual enactments of beatings, torture, and death are to be inflicted on other players, frequented attended by grisly special effects technologies, only the torturers can display this violence. The realism of this violence, as opposed to the conspicuous lack of realism anywhere else in these plays, again links the torturers and their function to the register of the grotesque. Other characters who represent a *potential* for violence (knights, squires, others) can never actually *actualize* this violence (unless it is inflicted on these self-same torturers, for torturers can receive, as well as give, violence). In BM, where the torturers represent the violence enacted by tyrants, knights in the service of kings acquire some of the attributes of torturers in this respect, but for the most part they are employed in battle against these self-same torturers.

The torturers, moreover, represent a specific form of mediation in the plays: the torturers enact violence against characters in the *platea* commanded by seated characters, they delineate a vector of violence between the *sedes* and the *platea*. In those rare circumstances where violence must be done against a seated character, the torturers will not perform this violence until the character is in the *platea,* and not even then, because in this circumstance the seated character (Pilate) kills himself. The torturers, then, are not like other seated characters who are principals of their actions, rather, they serve a very specific subtype of the same general dramaturgical function of *mediator* as the host of other mediating figures that populate the medieval stage, sundry knights, messengers, crozier bearers, demons, angels, and so on.

Virtually all seats that represent priests or kings have mediators of one kind or another directly associated with the seat. The only seats that lack mediators, in fact, are those seats that are seats of characters that themselves *are* mediators (torturers or knights). Naturally, mediators who are seated with, or standing near, the seat they serve, can be ordered about by a seated character without further ado. However, a problem arises when a seated character wishes to summon torturers, who are themselves seated, and at some distance. One cannot approach them (this would be self-abasement, though tyrants routinely do this in BM), nor does one summon them by messenger (which presumably would magnify them by using a mediator to summon a mediator, treating them as status equivalents of other seated characters). How, then, does one summon them?

Like messengers and other mediators who are seated with those they serve, the torturers are summoned by direct command by a seated character. This is the one example in the plays in which two seated characters are allowed to interact directly with one another. Since commands, as we have seen, should be issued to subalterns from a seat, it is impossible that such a command be delivered from the platea.

Moreover, since the torturers are seated until they come, it is impossible to accede into their presence without the ruler subordinating himself to the subaltern character (though this does happen to tyrants in BM, see below). At the same time, sending a messenger to them would be in effect treating them as if they were coordinate potentates, and not distant servants, so this too is unacceptable.

This logical impasse generated by the logic of seating is 'solved' by allowing seated characters to bellow their commands from their seat to the torturers at some distance away. For the most part, in both plays, the characters who issue commands to torturers are seated, and some, like Teudar, specifically ascend to their seat to issue the command to the torturers.[62] This is, in fact, the only time in the plays that seated characters are allowed to speak to each other while seated, as if the physically distantiated seats were in fact co-present (but note, again, the torturers reply only when they accede to the presence of the summoner).

This summoning is structurally similar to the way a command is given to a near-by attendant, like a messenger, who is presumably seated with the character (such as the example of David and the messenger given above). But given the maximally large distance between the seated character (often in the W or S) and the torturers (in the NE), the command would have to be quite loud to carry across the entire *platea*. The dialog itself continuously draws attention to the loudness involved in commands issued to the torturers, as well as the distance travelled by this loud command. The torturers, in their replies in the *Ordinalia* draw specific attention to the fact that their summons is bellowed (and oblique reference is made in BM to their summoning as being 'cried'). Reference is made to the loudness of the summons on two separate days of the *Ordinalia*, once in response to a summons from Caiaphas (S) in the *Passio*,

heyl volaueth volaueth	Hail, high priest, high priest,
uthyk mur yv the areth	**very loud is thy speech**
leman worth agan gylwel[63]	now calling us

And once in the *Resurrexio*, when the torturers reply to a seated Tiberius, the torturers reply that his cry was so loud it caused them fear,

melord anon her we buth	My lord, anon here we be;
agas clewas o pur uth	**Of you very loud was heard**
crye mar bras	**The cry so great**
lemmyn worth agan gelwel	But at calling to us,

rak ovn desefsen merwel	From fear I would have desired to die;
me a crennas[64]	I trembled.

In the next summoning in the same play, attention is drawn in the Torturers' reply to the almost absurd distance over which the summoning is conducted. The torturers reply indicates that they were 'coming from Spain, in Germany, at a tavern' when called. In the final summoning by Tiberius, the command itself draws attention to this aspect of summoning, complaining about loudness of the cry needed to call them, their apology implies that they tend to wander away when they have nothing to do.[65]

a pur harloth ple fugh why	O very rascals, where were ye?
pur vth o clewas an cry	**Very loud was heard the cry**
genef orth agas gylwel[66]	by me to you calling.

The torturers, then, are summoned in a way that is very similar to the way that, for example, messengers are summoned (that is, by a seated character). The main difference is that the torturers have their own seat, while messengers are generally seated with the character they serve or on the platea nearby. Therefore, commands to torturers must be bellowed to overcome the distance. Commanding the torturers in this way allows seated characters to interact directed with seated characters without sending a messenger or going themselves to fetch them. Functionally, messengers and torturers alike respond *directly* to commands as if they were equally present, but torturers are seated apart and distantly.

This is as true in BM as in the *Ordinalia*. Constantine summons his torturers by simply shouting at them from his seat, as if they were present. Their answer does not make anything of the loudness of his voice, but it is clear from the first time they are summoned that they are being summoned from their seat (they engage in an action of 'parading' (*pompare*) which is typical of seated characters when they first appear):[67]

CONSTANTINUS	CONSTANTINE
tormentoris guesyon fol	Torturers, mad lads
tormentoris dugh thym ol	Torturers, come ye all to me
aberth mahum ha soly	On behalf of Mahound and Sol
[*hic pompabunt tortores*	[*Here the torturers shall parade*
[*w swerdys*	[*with swords*
heyl constenten the nobil	Hail Constantine the Noble!

del onny the lel bobil	As we are thy loyal people
devethys ython warbarth	Come are we together.

As Constantine becomes Christian, control of the torturers passes on to his tyrannical counterparts, to whom, however, the torturers are *not* loyal. One sign of Teudar's tyrannical impotence in BM as a ruler is that the torturers do not pay any attention to his commands shouted in the proper style from his seat. As a result, Teudar must *descend* from his seat to find them and beat them in order to get them to obey. Teudar, after speaking with Meriasek and desiring to demonstrate his power, ascends to his seat to call the torturers; since the torturers are paying no attention to him, he descends again, and says that he needs to fetch them, making a mockery of himself, he and his men then go to the torturers to beat them, and then returns home (to his own seat) when they agree to obey.[68]

TEVDARIUS	TEUDAR
mahum darber hardygrath	Mahound, provide hard grace
Ze neb a ruk ov trobla	For him who hath troubled me!
[*ascendit*	[*He Ascends*
Tormentoris dugh in plen	Torturers, come into the field.
tormentoris marsogh len	Torturers, if ye are loyal,
tormentoris dugh dym scon	Torturers, come to us at once!
ay ay ay dar ny regh vry	Ay, ay, ay, ruin, you don't regard!
[*descendit*	[*He descends*
reys yv age herhes y	Need is it to fetch them
pan yv mogh ol ov duwon	since all my grief is a mockery
[*her yerdis aredy for teudar and hys men*	[*Here staves ready for Teudar and his men.*
Hov hov pythesogh matis	How, how, where are ye, mates?
y besche reb your patis	I will baste ye (?) by your pates.
pendra reny dar napya	What shall we do, nap? (??)
ay num clewugh ov kelwel	Ah, you hear me calling?
tannegh honthsel kyns sevel	Take handsel before rising.
go to dalethugh frappia	Go to, begin striking!
[*et verberabunt eos*[69]	[*And they shall beat them.*

Teudar beats his servants when they do not respond to his call, and when they fail at their assigned task, he descends from his seat to beat them again.[70] Similarly, the torturers descend from their seat to hide from the Tyrant Emperor of the second day of the play in an adjacent tent (the tent of the woman's son, now become a tavern), because their wages are not paid.[71] Their drudge, whom they have sent to spy on the tyrant, instead rats them out and the tyrant is forced again to descend, search their vacated seat and eventually find his hiding servants and beat them.[72]

It is the nature of tyrannical power that each Tyrant must in fact go to the seat of his own torturers and beat them to get them to beat others, just as it is in the nature of legitimate power that legitimate kings have their commands obeyed, and their servants, in turn, need never actually use the force that lies behind their commands. The critique of tyrannical power in BM works by inversion of the model found in the *Ordinalia*. In the latter play, torturers are employed by both legitimate and illegitimate authorities, while in the latter torturers are diagnostic of illegitimate authority. Moreover, in the *Ordinalia* the torturers are used alongside messengers by the same set of authorities for *functionally* discrete ends (torturers act on characters in the *platea*, while messengers act both on seated and unseated characters, torturers enact violence between estates, messengers communicate between and within estates). In the play BM, torturers are the exclusively province of tyrants, paralleled by knights and messengers amongst legitimate authorities (Constantine, while still a pagan tyrant, uses torturers, but eschews their use upon becoming a Christian king). Lastly, while the torturers are always obedient in the *Ordinalia*, magnifying the power of the king by displaying a mediated model of agency distinguishing between seated principal and mobile agent in the platea, in BM the principal must often undermine his own authority by inflicting violence directly upon his own agents of violence, in effect effacing this distinction between immobile principal and mobile agent.

CONCLUSION

The special position of the torturers seems in general to decouple them from any specific principal, so that they become a hypostasis of violence as such, the differential capacity for which is constitutive of temporal power. Their essential function is violence: torturers represent in the purest form of actual violence (and the knights the subdued form of potential, but never actual, violence), and whose inherently asymmetric mediating function can only be directed by a seated character against a character currently in the platea (unlike messengers, who may approach either sort of character). Their separated seating segregates the instrument from the power it serves, as if to insulate power from the pollution of the means of its realization (violence), as well as to hypostatize violence as something unto itself, that can be invoked for good or evil, legitimate or illegitimate ends. The torturers, the bearers of 'actual violence', cannot, given their at once comic and horrifying grotesque bodily features and tendencies, be seated with the power they serve without somehow assimilating it to that power, polluting it (unlike knights, for example, who, like messengers, never actualize their potential for violence). Indeed, in the Ordinalia, the good Emperor wishes to descend from his throne to kill Pilate himself, but his underlings restrain him from an act that would at the same time diminish his kingly power by refusing to divide agency into immobile principal and active agent, but would also pollute him with the bloody deed. Moreover, the pollution of the sin of Cain (the only other character in the plays shown to kill) that accrues to them because of the fact that they are actually shown to kill their victims means they must be kept apart from those they serve. They are summoned by word to perform unspeakable deeds. They are bearers of 'violence as such', the very political basis of the economic order in question is hypostatized as a force that stands (or rather, is seated) apart as a purely technical aparatus of violence independent of its teleology. My analysis parallel's Bakere's here, although Bakere sees this hypostasis of violence as being essentially of psychological moment, a fact about 'humanity', rather than as being a sort of attempted theodice of temporal power that separates the teleological from the technical apparatus of power, as I am arguing.

In the *Ordinalia*, then, there is as part of a general economy of salvation presented in that play a historical theodice of power and violence. The torturers are introduced in the service of evil to produce martyrs and ironically, the means of salvation (in crucifying Christ), but it is in the *Resurrexio* that they are recuperated as being part of the new divinely legitimated imperium, and they do this by attempting to avenge the death of Christ on the body of Pilate (Pilate kills himself, alleviating the need to depict actual violence on a seated character). They must, however, remain (physically) separate from power partially because they serve and constitute different temporal powers (good or evil) indifferently, and partially because in this way the pollution of the agents of the deed that constitutes power is separated from the principal on whose behalf it is done, or lastly because the means of power (actual or potential violence in the form of the torturers or the knights) must be seated apart from the order it serves (the temporal order, legitimate or otherwise).

At the same time, the order of estates is itself reinforced dramaturgically, in that intra-estate interactions between seated characters is typified by the mediating figure of the messengers, just as inter-estate interactions between seated characters and the platea are typified by violence incarnated in the torturers. Since estates are multiple and coordinate in seated characters, each such seated character must possess his own proximate mediating figure to mediate intra-estate interactions (as well as, of course, non-violent inter-estate interactions), variously messengers, crozier-bearers, angels, demons. But in the *Ordinalia,* inter-estate interactions between seated characters and platea characters are general, and there is, in essence, only one mediating figure, the torturers, that stands as it were between all the seated characters and all the platea characters. The exception here is Pilate in the third play, who, in contrast to Maximilla of the first day and Christ of the second, cannot be killed by the torturers and kills himself in prison.

In BM, by contrast, the torturers (actualized violence) become a figure of pure and unmitigated evil, whose employment is, by virtue of a kind of miasma, a diagnostic of tyrannical, rather than imperial, authority. This opposition in the staging diagrams is also found in the function of the torturers, who no longer exclusively bring violence from seat to platea (inter-estate), but also intra-estate violence between seated characters on either side of the divide between legitimate and illegitimate temporal authority. The fact that tyrannical authority is based on actual violence and coercion is emphasized because the torturers themselves must occasionally be beaten in order to get them to beat others, while the legitimate imperium is ruled within by authority, rather than coercion, and hence knights are only needed to coerce those outside its domain (like tyrants), and remain symbols of potential violence in other respects.

All medieval plays share a formal dramaturgical arrangement that not only multiplies and rigidifies the status distinctions between characters by encoding them directly into the staging itself, but also by multiplying the number of mediating figures, such as messengers and torturers, who further represent the power that is concomitant between such estate distinctions by creating distinctions between immobile principals and mobile agents. On this level, then, the 'pointless to-and-froing' of medieval drama as a whole is anything but pointless, it is integral to the staging pomp, 'staging of estate' (directly encoded in the invariant spatial arrangement of the stage diagrams), and, one might argue, to representing formally the nature of power itself, 'staging the state' by representing dramaturgically the basic distinctions between immobile principals (seats) and mobile agents (platea) which allow the representation of projectable and magnifiable power and authority as being essentially about mediation of agency. All this 'to-and-froing' decomposes a single act of communication, command or violence, into discrete roles and distributes them across characters, magnifying the social, spatial and temporal gap between the principal, his agents and his targets, displaying dramaturgically the nature of pomp and power alike as being proportional to the distance between command and execution.

But these two plays do more than this. In the changing allocation of the figure of the torturers, these plays make very different arguments about the kinds of power and authority that are typical of the emerging model of state. In the *Ordinalia*, state-like activities are essentially unitary, the torturers are spread as agents across a diverse array of spiritual and secular authorities, legitimate and illegitimate, though they serve only one master on any one day of the play. In BM, the torturers are specifically diagnostic of tyrannical authority, and far from magnifying this authority, they in fact undermine it, for the tyrant lacks authority over his own subalterns. He must coerce his coercers, coercion is diagnostic of tyranny 'all the way down', just as for a legitimate king, except when in battle with tyrants or dragons, his peaceable authority 'goes all the way down'.

But lastly, the decomposition of action (command or coercion) into a dramaturgically mediated complex not only allows the pro-jectable power and authority of the principal to be magnified by the gap between himself and the locus of realization of his power or authority, it also allows the *means* (incarnated in the agent) to be separated from both *principal* and *ends*. Monopolizable violence, the very stuff of states, as such emerges incarnated in a single figure, the torturers, standing outside the system of estates as a cosmological prime, and separated from them as an unclean, almost demonic or monstrous, means to diverse ends.

This brings us finally to the position of violence in the cosmology of the plays. As notes, the torturers are ambiguously staged, located between Heaven and Hell, they seem to be an eternal seat of a cosmological principle. At the same time, they are thisworldly enough to be summoned by emperors and bishops from their seats, they are lowly mediators of kings and bishops who happen to be seated apart. They are liminal, therefore, sharing in properties of two kinds of seats, at once worldly and otherworldly. It's worth suggesting that this positioning does not merely have the function of separating torturers from their principals, *adiaphorizing* violence by separating it as a purely sociotechnical apparatus from its moral sources and moral ends, but it also contains an argument that violence is eternal, and even part of the cosmological economy of salvation the way Heaven and Hell are. How? The four torturers (there are always four) can be linked allegorically to another 'four torturers (the jail of earthly life, misery, death and worms)'.[73] If that is correct, then the torturers stand as the cosmological entity that has power over, or most characterizes *this world*: violence, misery, death, and worms. Standing between Heaven and Hell, they are also the powers that take living beings from this world represented by the *platea* to one or the other of those other worlds. By killing them. This positioning makes them cosmological mediators between life (the platea, this world) and death (Heaven and Hell, that world), just as they are worldly mediators between worldly principals and worldly victims.

But these torturers also have a changing position within the economy of salvation of the plays. In the *Ordinalia*, these figures of violence are ultimately recuperated within a single logic of kingship and economy of salvation, themselves recuperated at the same time as legitimate secular authority is reconstituted when the pagan emperor becomes a Christian. In BM, there is a dualistic logic in which coercion is once and for all separated from the legitimate arts of kingship, torturers are forever associated with tyranny.

ACKNOWLEDGEMENTS

Thanks to Richard Bauman, Steve Coleman, Michael Silverstein, Rupert Stasch, for encouragement and comments on various drafts of this paper. I would like to thank Anne Meneley and Veronique Plesch for providing especially detailed comments, for which I am indebted. Errors are my own.

NOTES AND REFERENCES

1. Jody Enders, 'Medieval Snuff Drama', *Exemplaria* 10:1, 1998, 171–206.
2. Norbert Elias, 'Violence and Civilization: The State Monopoly of Physical Violence and its Infringement', in J. Keane (ed.), *Civil Society and the State*, London, 1988, pp. 177–98; J. Fletcher, *Violence and Civilization*, Cambridge, 1997.
3. On the portrayal of violence in medieval plays see John Gatton, '"There must be Blood": Mutilation and Martyrdom on the Medieval Stage', in Redmond (ed.), *Violence in Drama*, Cambridge, 1991, pp. 79–100; Veronique Plesch, '*Etalage Complaisant?* The Torments of Christ in French Passion Plays,' *Comparative Drama* 28, 1994–95, pp. 458–85; Veronique Plesch, 'Notes for the Staging of a Late Medieval Passion Play', in Clifford Davidson (ed.), *Material Culture and Medieval Drama*, Kalamazoo, 1999, pp. 81–4. Michael O'Connell persuasively argues that this grotesque realism of the portrayal of blood and physical violence is related to the focus on embodiment and materiality of medieval 'incarnational drama' (which echoes the centrality of the incarnation of Christ in Medieval Christianity), and therefore should be central, rather than peripheral, to our understanding of the genre, as opposed to the 'textualization' of God's body in more modern drama, Michael O'Connell, 'God's Body and Incarnational Drama', in his *The Idolatrous Eye: Iconoclasm and Theater in Early-Modern England*, New York, 2000, pp. 67–88.

4. Philip Abrams, 'Notes on the Difficulty of Studying the State (1977)', *Journal of Historical Sociology*, 1:1, 1988, p. 58.

5. Abrams, 1988, p. 77.

6. Clifford Geertz, *Negara: The Theatre State in Nineteenth Century Bali*, Princeton, 1980; Bernard Cohn and Nicholas Dirks, 'Beyond the Fringe: The Nation State, Colonialism, and The Technologies of Power', *Journal of Historical Sociology* 1:2, 1988, 224–9; For a period example of 'state spectacle' for comparison, see Gordon Kipling, *Enter the King: Theatre, Liturgy and Ritual in the Medieval Civic Triumph*, Oxford, 1998.

7. Abrams, 1988, pp. 77–79.

8. Cohn and Dirks, 1988, p. 224.

9. Elias terms the monopoly on violence and its attendant specialists a 'sociotechnical invention of the human species' (Elias, 1988, p. 179). Technical here normally refers to human interactions with nature, hence sociotechnical, yet at the same time social and yet technical, in the sense that violence is separated from its moral ends or goals (part of what Bauman (below) calls 'adiaphorization'), as if, for example, torture were simply a technical skill with its own specialists like drilling for oil and its experts.

10. Zygmunt Bauman, 'The Social Manipulation of Morality: Moralizing Actors, Adiaphorizing Action', *Theory, Culture and Society* 8, 1991, p. 144.

11. Bauman, 1991, p. 145.

12. Zygmunt Bauman, *Modernity and the Holocaust*, Cambridge, 1989.

13. Richard Bauman, 'Mediational Performance, Traditionalization and the Authorization of Discourse', in Hubert Knoblach and Helga Kotthoff (eds), *Verbal Art across Cultures: The Aesthetics and Proto-aesthetics of Communication*, Tubingen, 2001, pp. 91–117.

14. For the *Ordinalia* (c. 1350–75) I use the standard edition of Edwin Norris, *The Ancient Cornish Drama*. 2 volumes, Oxford, 1967 [1859], citing by line number, using the following abbreviations, O*[rigo Mundi]*, R*[esurrexio]*; the Passion Play is usually abbreviated as *D* to prevent it from being confused with another Conirsh passion text abbreviated using P; *Beunans Meriasek* (BM, c. 1504; Whitley Stokes, *Beunans Meriasek: The Life of St Meriasek, Bishop and Confessor: A Cornish Drama*, London, 1872); *Bewnans Ke* (BK, c. 1500, O. J. Padel, *'Bewnans Ke': The Life of Saint Ke*, 2003 available at http://www.asnc.cam.ac.uk/resource/ BewnansKeText-20March03.pdf.

15. 'The claim to the *monopoly* of the *legitimate* use of physical force' (original emphasis), Max Weber, *Economy and Society: an Outline of Interpretive Sociology, Volume 1*, Berkeley, 1978, p. 54; Elias, 1988.

16. Elias, 1988; Fletcher, 1997, p. 36.

17. Bauman, 1989, p. 100; Elias 1988, pp. 177–9.

18. Jane Bakere, *The Cornish Ordinalia: a Critical Study*, Cardiff, 1980, p. 153.

19. Lynette Olson, 'Tyranny in Beunans Meriasek', in Philip Payton (ed.), *Cornish Studies: Five*, Exeter, 1997, pp. 52–9.

20. Perry Anderson, *Lineages of the Absolutist State*, London, 1974; cited in Abrams, 1980, p. 80.

21. Abrams, 1980, p. 81.
22. Olson, 1997.
23. Paul Manning, 'The Word Made Land: Incarnationalism and the Spatial Poetics and Pragmatics of Largesse in Medieval Cornish Drama', *Semiotica* 146:1, pp. 237–66, and references there. For the general relation between theatre and ritual, see William O Beeman, 'The Anthropology of Theater and Spectacle', *Annual Review of Anthropology* 22, 1993, pp. 369–93. For a classic discussion of the historic relation in Europe, see O. B Hardison, *Christian Rite and Christian Drama in the Middle Ages*, Baltimore, Maryland, 1965.
24. Pamela King, 'Spatial Semantics and the Medieval Theatre', in *The Theatrical Space*, London, 1987, p. 47.
25. King, 1987, pp. 45–6.
26. King, 1987, p. 53.
27. The dialog makes it clear that these are sometimes understood to be castles or palaces of those characters, and are elevated. There is one exception to the rule that 'seats' are not 'sets', the seat of a minor character of the later play BM is transformed into a tavern, that is, from a medieval 'seat' to a modern 'set'.
28. Throughout I will occasionally be using the terminology of Peircean semiotics. The division of possible relations between signs and their objects I will be employing includes ICONS (iconic relations), INDEXES (indexical relations) and SYMBOLS. Icons are those signs which stand for their objects by virtue of RESEMBLANCE. Diagrams are simplified icons, whereas portraits are fuller icons. Indexes are signs that stand for their object by virtue of some really existing relationship in space, time or causality. So a weathercock points in the direction of the wind because the wind makes it do so, a bullethole points to the bullet that made it. Any sign that lacks these two relations is a symbol, a sign that stands for its object by convention. Mixed signs are possible, and in particular I will speak of 'indexical icons' (Manning, 2003), signs that both resemble their objects (icon) and are really connected to them too (index). The stage diagrams are an example, they are both models of the universe (icons) and they are part of it (indexes): their orientation in space in terms of the directions makes each part of the diagram 'point' to its notional location in real space. A diagrammatic icon is something like a road map, or a stereo diagram, where none of the individual parts of the sign resemble their objects (dots do not resemble cities), but the relationship of the parts of a diagram resemble the relationships between the parts of the object (the relationship between dots in a road map resembles the relationship between cities in the universe in terms of relative distance).
29. On the contrast between classifying typology of higher social orders and unclassifiable residuum of lower social orders associated with a grotesque materiality, embodiment and realism in medieval social models, see Maria Corti, 'Models and Antimodels in Medieval Culture', *New Literary History* 10, 1979, pp. 352–3.
30. 'The open playing-area at the foot of the church steps, the *platea* . . . , and

the audience were on the same level . . . the platea is associated both with earthly and diabolical activity, and assumes different identities as need arises.' William Tydeman, *The Theatre in the Middle Ages: Western European Stage Conditions c. 800–1576*, Cambridge, 1978, p. 123; also Robert Weimann, *Shakespeare and the Popular Tradition in the Theater*, Baltimore, 1978, p. 84.

31. O. 2270–3.
32. D.569–576.
33. BM.1759–1769.
34. R.1802–1827.
35. A limiting case is represented by the newly discovered play *Beunans Ke* (BK), in which the back and forth movements of assorted messengers, legates, senators and kings between two emperors and their respective subjects leading up to a rather short battle form the bulk of the action of the day.
36. Richard Axton, European Drama of the Early Middle Ages, Pittsburgh, 1974, pp. 78–9.
37. R. Bauman, 2001, p. 96.
38. R. Bauman, 2001, p.96. 'Participation structures' for instances of talk typically involve decomposing a unitary speaker into a number of sub-roles, minimally, the *principal*, the person responsible for the text, whose position the text expresses, *author*, the person who composes the text, and *animator*, the person who performs the text, for other kinds of actions our terminology is reduced primarily to the opposition between principal and agent, see Erving Goffman, *Frame Analysis*, Cambridge, Mass., 1974, p. 516–37; for further discussion see Adi Hastings and Paul Manning, 'Acts of Alterity', *Language & Communication* 24:4, pp. 291–311.
39. For the opposition between immaterial signs and corporeal things, and grotesque realism as being the sphere of the latter, see Corti, 1979, pp. 352–3. For other parallelisms between devils and torturers in French plays of the same period, including comic grotesqueness of speech, action and appearance, see Veronique Plesch, 'Killed by Words: Grotesque Verbal Violence and Tragic Atonement in French Passion plays', *Comparative Drama* 33, 1999, pp. 22–55. The same parallelisms are found on these levels in the Cornish plays. For general iconographic parallelisms in other visual media between torturers and other monstrous entities, including demons, Jews, and Saracens, see Deborah Strickland, *Saracens, Demons and Jews: Making Monsters in Medieval Art*, Princeton, 2003.
40. R.1823–5.
41. R.1965–1976.
42. O.2297–2302.
43. R.1906–1955, Belsebuc to Pilate's wife; O.541–70 (Abel), O.881–916 (the soul of Adam), R.2307–2360 (the body of Pilate).
44. O2229–2254.
45. Z. Bauman, 1989; see R. Bauman, 2001, for an account of 'action at distance' that focuses specifically on verbal mediators.

46. Martin Stevens, 'From *Mappa mundi* to *Theatrum Mundi:* The World as Stage in Early English drama', in John Alford (ed.), *From Page to Performance: Essays in early English drama*, East Lansing, 1995, pp. 32–5. For a classic discussion of the 'stage-world' (The 'little O, the Earth' and the 'wooden O', the stage) relation, see Thomas Stroup, *Microcosmos: the Shape of the Elizabethan Play*, Lexington, 1965.

47. Stevens, 1995, p. 37

48. The Western King position must always be occupied, and when its occupant dies, as happens at the end of *Origo Mundi*, Solomon ascends to the Western seat of King David upon coronation.

49. See King, 1987, p. 54 for a parallel distinction within the pageant plays.

50. Corti, 1979, pp. 342–3.

51. Olson, 1997, p. 56.

52. On these traits see Olson, 1997.

53. Olson, 1997, p. 55.

54. Olson, 1997, p. 55.

55. The newly discovered Cornish play, the Life of Saint Ke (BK), has no stage diagram associated with it, but from the stage directions it can be concluded that the play features seats for characters similar to the ones in these plays. The Tyrant Teuthar has a seat (explicit references include BK.19, 43–44, 50–1, 60, 72, 151, 158), including a full retinue including a counselor, jailor and servant, and two messengers. There are also torturers serving the tyrant (for example, 84ff), but the section in which they are summoned is missing, though when they leave his presence it is implied they return to their seat (BK107). A very large assortment of other feudal personages have their own seats or are associated in some way with the seats of others (there are several dozen kings and assorted potentates, who cannot possibly all have their own seats). These counts are based on explicit references to seats or actions involving seats in either character speech or in stage directions: 4 soldiers (*armiger*, BK 181, 186), Cador the Duke of Cornwall (BK. 182–3), Augelus King of Scotland (184), a pontifex (187–8, 392–3, 396), the second bishop (191); Arthur King of Britain, Gwynvwer and Mordred together (202, 211, 225–6, 229–30, 263, 265, 276–7, 280, 286–7, 356, 359, 385, 401, 410, 430), Lucius Emperor of Rome (231–4, 235, 244, 338, 355), Boccus, King of the Medes (315), Epystopus, King of Greece (316), 2 Senators (326, 331, 370).

56. M. Camille, *The Gothic Idol: Ideology and Image-making in Medieval Art*, Cambridge, 1989, p. 65.

57. Corti, 1979, pp. 352–3.

58. Sally Joyce Cross, 'Torturers as Tricksters in the Cornish "Ordinalia"', *Neuphililogische Mitteilungen* 4, 1983, pp. 448–55; see also Hans Jürgen Diller, 'The torturers in the English mystery plays', in Meg Twycross (ed.), *Evil on the Medieval Stage, Medieval English Theatre* 11, 1992, pp. 57–65.

59. Cross, 1983, p. 454.

60. The term 'splatstick' is a blend word that was coined by horror film actor Bruce Campbell to describe his genre: '"Splatstick" is physical comedy (slapstick) that involves evisceration (things that go "splat!")'

(http://www.pro-researcher.co.uk/encyclopaedia/english/splatstick_film). It would not be going too far to use this term to describe Medieval grotesque realism in violence.

61. Plesch, 1999, p. 47.
62. BM.949–52.
63. D.953–5.
64. R.1767–72.
65. R. 2148–2240.
66. R.2242–4.
67. BM.170–1177, 1521–1532.
68. BM.949–55.
69. BM 848–961.
70. BM.1053–1065.
71. BM.3245–3280.
72. BM 3281–3345.
73. Andrzej Dabrówka, 'Medieval Theatre of Schools: Educational Beginnings of Early Drama', Miskolc, Hungary, 2002 (http://www.mediewistyka.net/dab/miskolc.htm).

'TOO RARELY VISITED AND TOO LITTLE KNOWN': TRAVELLERS' IMAGININGS OF INDUSTRIAL CORNWALL

Cynthia Lane

INTRODUCTION

It is axiomatic that Cornwall's experience of industrialization from the early eighteenth to mid-nineteenth centuries was highly distinctive, resulting in social, economic and cultural characteristics and an assertive identity of 'industrial prowess' that were themselves also distinctive.[1] These attributes were readily apparent to literary visitors, those contemporary travel writers who provided commentaries as they journeyed around Cornwall observing the local scene. Cornwall was not connected to the national railway system until as late as 1859.[2] Before that date relatively few people were persuaded to visit what was considered a remote and forbidding region. The journey by coach or coastal steamer was lengthy and tedious. Many English men and women knew more about Paris than about Bodmin or Truro. Mention of 'Cornwall' conjured images of smuggling and wrecking, and of a rocky, dangerous coastline and a harsh interior of fogs and mists and barren wastes and crags. This was the imagery of 'West Barbary', as Cornwall was known by its detractors.

As Bernard Deacon has argued, this unsavoury picture was complemented and at length supplanted by an alternative image of 'Industrial Civilization', one prompted by the predominance of mining and industrial modernity discovered by visitors to Cornwall during the eighteenth and nineteenth centuries.[3] And yet, as we shall see in this article, this industrial civilization, though indisputably 'modern', was often also outlandish in the eyes of external visitors—emphasizing

Cornwall and the Cornish as 'other'. Despite the onset of modernity, Cornwall remained 'different'.

Travel writers, struck by the 'difference' that they had found in Cornwall, provided a range of observations and impressions that we may neatly categorize as those of *space, livings* and *people.*

SPACE:
WEST BARBARY?

As Drew has argued: 'Space frequently mirrors the values of a culture —its social relationships, power structures, religious and cosmological ideas—and re-enacts patterns of place'.[4] Space thus defined is constituted by the interaction of the 'shape' and 'form' of geology and topography as articulated in patterns of settlement and economic activity in the landscape, as well as in the meanings and readings attributed to physical features. Here 'space'—as expressed, for example, in towns, coastal scenery or mining landscapes—is closely related to notions cultural identity: as Drew puts it, 'a fingerprint that brands a culture as unique'.[5]

When travellers encountered this space in eighteenth- and, especially, nineteenth-century Cornwall, they increasingly found not the backwater that tales of 'West Barbary' had led them to expect but rather a resourceful, fully operational independent economy involved in mining, engineering, fishing and agriculture. The degree to which this was so depended initially on the route a traveller chose to enter Cornwall. The most direct route was across the Tamar from Devon via Exeter and Okehampton, following the road that is now the A30. This way took the traveller through Bodmin Moor, along the spine of Cornwall, a route that on first acquaintance would seem to possess to the full all the forbidding attributes of 'West Barbary'. An alternative approach was from Plymouth in Devon and along Cornwall's southern coast, a gentler and more welcoming landscape. Given that there was not, before 1859, an efficient network of railways, and that the roads were very poor and potholed, visitors could also choose to enter Cornwall by sea, usually through either Falmouth or Hayle and so straight into the commercial and industrial heartland that epitomized 'industrial Cornwall'. In this way, the 'space' of industrial Cornwall was itself uneven and far from homogenous, with visitors often proffering what they imagined to be valid Cornwall-wide generalizations that in fact reflected their reactions to particular localities, rather than a reading of Cornwall as a whole.

For example, in 1778 William Gilpin entered on the main thoroughfare to Launceston and then proceeded across the moor to Bodmin. His preconceived notion of a dreary wasteland was confirmed by this route and he imagined that all of Cornwall was similar: 'We travelled . . . through a coarse naked country, and in all respects as uninteresting as can well be conceived. Of wood, in every shape, it was utterly destitute. Having heard that the country beyond Bodmin was exactly like what we had already passed, we resolved to travel no farther in Cornwall'.[6] Two years later the Rev. John Swete, who travelled on the same road in 1780, realized how misleading was this first impression of Cornwall. He too had encountered a 'bleak and exposed situation . . . [which] gave me a more unfavourable opinion of the county than I afterwards found it in general deserved'.[7] Thirty years later, when Rev. Richard Warner went over the same road the message of wild Cornwall had obviously not changed for first-time travellers: 'We had at length a specimen of the denuded scenery which we had been taught to expect through a journey of many days'. The use of the word 'taught' is telling. Warner, like others before and after him, held a preconceived image of Cornish space based on what he had been told beforehand.

In contrast, James Forbes was conscious of the myth of 'West Barbary' but found the reality different when he entered Cornwall in 1794 along the alternative southern route from Plymouth. He was very surprised as it was 'much superior to what I had been prepared to expect'. He explained that 'the different features the country assumes, in quick succession, from these soft and woody scenes, to rude un-cultivated heaths and unbounded views, finely contrast each other, and are peculiar to this county'. Forbes mused: 'I am most surprised in Cornwall to see the fertile valleys and rich woody glens . . . because most travellers represent it only as a heathy, bleak, barren country.'[9] This, as we have seen, was because many travellers entered into central Cornwall on the main thoroughfare through the moor, and had little opportunity or did not take the trouble to get to know Cornwall better. Hence Wilkie Collins in his letter of introduction to the readers of his book *Rambles Beyond Railways*, written in 1850, spoke of Cornwall as 'too rarely visited and too little known'.[10] Travellers like Collins were beginning to appreciate the complexity of 'space' in Cornwall.

Additionally, visitors were increasingly ready to interpret this complexity as yet further evidence of 'difference', emphasizing (para-doxically) the notion of 'otherness' already inherent in constructions of 'West Barbary'. At the same time that they criticized West Barbary, they nonetheless reinforced its basic assumptions. Industrial Cornwall, though a product of modernity, was still a foreign country for those outsiders who encountered it. In 1865, for example, Walter White wrote that 'frequently did I fancy myself out of England while in Cornwall, and anyone able to use his eyes may well be pardoned for the illusion'.

Moreover: 'Under the influence of . . . strange names, the peculiarities of the people, and unfamiliar landscape features, it seemed to me more than once that I was in a foreign country, and I caught myself saying in conversation—"When I get back to England"'.[11]

MINING

Mining tended to dominate space—or perceptions of space—in eighteenth- and early nineteenth-century Cornwall, and therefore generally took precedence over observations that travellers might make about agriculture or other activities. Although mining had always been an important element in shaping the economy and character of the Cornish people, it was given a dramatic boost in the early 1700s with the advent of new technology such as the steam engine and improved methods of ore separation, leading to a rapid transformation of the mining landscape as huge beam engines and engine houses appeared everywhere. When Celia Fiennes visited Cornwall before 1700 she found that water was still a major source of power, with many water-wheels used to drain mines in the St. Austell district.[12] She wrote in 1698 that there was 'great labour and great expense to drain the mines of water with mills that horses turn and now they have the mills or water engines that are turned by the water, which is conveyed on frames of timber and trunks to hold the water, which falls down on the wheels, as an over shot mill'. As she continued west, she 'passed by one hundred mines, some on which they were at work, others that were lost by the waters overwhelming them'.[13] Fifty years later, however, the scene had been transformed. In 1750 Dr Richard Pocock saw tin works at Polgooth and Chacewater which each employed a 'fire [steam] engine to pump the water out'.[14] These engines, designed and constructed by Thomas Newcomen, were two of the first three operating in Cornwall, the first of many as they swiftly supplanted the less efficient water technology. A century later and steam technology was ubiquitous in Cornwall, as Walter White noted in his visit to the St Austell copper mines in 1854:[15]

> Then come paths across flats of dirty water; the noise of the ore-crushing machinery—thump, thump, thump—heard for miles; and you see iron rods stretching away furlongs in length . . . what could they be? Suddenly some unseen power gives one of them a pull a yard or two to the right or left, with a jerking clank, followed by a watery gush. It is a pump-rod . . . impelled by the engine, which is too far off to be visible, and keeping the workings beneath your feet free from water. The

hill beyond presents a curious medley of machinery and trees;
a spectacle for one unaccustomed to the mining districts.[16]

Boulton and Watt dominated Cornish mining for a quarter of
century from 1775 until the expiry of their patent in 1800.[17] Thereafter,
there was a great era of experimentation and improvement as the
Boulton and Watt engines were progressively replaced by what became
known as 'the Cornish beam engine'. Cyrus Redding, writing in 1843,
was fascinated by these engines and championed their superiority: 'we
shall presently state the enormous power and duty [efficiency] of the
existing steam engines of Cornwall, of which so little is known out of
the county, and which have no parallel elsewhere'.[18] One hundred and
fifteen Lancashire engines were not the equal of two Cornish engines,
he insisted, an assessment which mirrored Cornwall's rapid rise in that
period as an international centre of engineering expertise.[19]

When James Boswell visited the mining districts around Redruth
in 1792, he thought that from a distance the great heaps of earth
thrown out of the mines seemed like huts, while 'The country has a
waste appearance by the soil being pared for fuel'.[20] Warner, writing
sixteen years later, was more descriptive. Mining, he said, for all its
technical innovation and wealth production, produced a blighted landscape. It:

> levels the little wood . . . penetrates into the earth, and covers
> the neighbouring soil with unproductive rubbish. It proceeds
> to poison the brooks around with its mineral impregnations,
> spreads far and wide. The sulphurous smoke of its smelting-
> houses blasting vegetation with their deleterious vapours,
> obscuring the atmosphere with the infernal fumes of arsenic
> and sulphur. . . . It appeared to us like a district filled with
> extinguished volcanoes, which, having exhausted their fury,
> could now only be traced in the universal desolation they had
> occasioned.[21]

Earlier, Fiennes had visited the same locality and rode 'over heath
and downs which was very bleak and full of mines'.[22] Forbes, in 1794,
thought the country to be barren, with no tree visible: 'hill and dales,
heaths and commons were covered with heaps of stones, ore, and
ashes, blackened by the smoke from the adjacent smelting houses . . .
full of mines'.[23] More than fifty years later, in 1854, White described a
similar scene:

All around the horizon . . . is mines. A hungry landscape,
everywhere deformed by small mountains of many-coloured
refuse; traversed in all directions by narrow paths and winding
roads, by streams of foul water, by screaming locomotives
with hurrying trains; whirling and vibrating, the forest of
tall beams, make up an astonishing maze of machinery and
motion. Giant arms of Steam-engines swing up and down; and
the stamping-mills appear to try which can thunder loudest,
proclaiming afar the progress made in disembowelling the
bountiful old earth.[24]

So far the travellers had been observing space above ground.
Boswell also described the deep mines where 'miners go down sometimes perpendicularly in iron buckets, sometimes by steep ladders from
one depth to another, descending transversely'.[25] An extraordinarily
deep mine extending under the sea-bed was Botallack, near Cape
Cornwall in the far west. Botallack was visited by Redding in 1842 who
described it as an 'astonishing undertaking' where an 'enormous steam
engine had to be lowered 200 feet down a rocky cliff . . . and here mules
and their riders may be seen trotting down tracks that the pedestrian
stranger trembles to pass'.[26] Walter White in 1854 was impressed by the
air of busy-ness and bustle at Botallack, 'for here the labour goes on as
in a factory'. He observed tramways and trains of wagons running to
and fro where once donkeys and mules did the carrying.[27] Once again,
even in such difficult terrain, steam power had replaced animal power.
However, Botallack was beginning to suffer the signs of what was to
become of the rest of Cornwall's copper industry from the 1860s.
Collins in 1850 commented on Botallack's struggles: 'The price of
copper has fallen of late years, the lodes have proved neither so rich
nor so extensive, as at past periods; and the mine when we visited
Cornwall, had failed to pay the expenses of working it.'[28] As visitors to
Cornwall began to divine, as a result of the 'all-consuming passion for
mining affairs, there was an unhealthy lack of diversification in Cornish
industrialization, an 'overspecialization' that was already making itself
apparent.[29] Indeed, it is likely that the overall sale of ore from mines in
Cornwall never did repay the total investment in the industry.[30]

However, despite this unpromising picture, industrial space in
Cornwall did include a relatively new industry: one which absorbed
some of the technology, methods and manpower from the declining
mines. This was the china clay industry, which was destined to become
by the early twentieth century the most important industry in Cornwall.
Most of the china clay came from the St. Austell area. As early as 1854
White described this district as busy with 'pumps working, wheels

revolving, white torrents flowing . . . extending far into the dreary
district north to St. Columb'. Here '[t]he white paths, banks, and levels
made strange chequer-work among the dark patches of heath'.[31] This
was an imagery that complemented that of the tin and copper mines,
reinforcing the sense of industrial space in Cornwall experienced by
visitors. Agriculture, when its was discussed, was normally in the
context of its relationship to mining. Thus, for example, White in 1854
noticed much 'improvement' in the cultivation of the heathland in
Penwith, the work of miners with small holdings:

> You see numerous small holdings; some under good
> cultivation, others but partially cleared. With good manage-
> ment they grow good crops of potatoes, barley and wheat.
> Should this continue, West Penwith will cease to look
> desolate; and a succession of fruitful fields will be seen even
> to the Land's End. In other parts of the county the miners,
> each taking a little patch, have cleared much of the waste.[32]

These improvements had been made since Fiennes' visit in 1698, when
she had commented that 'to the Land's End is stone and barren'.[33]
The improvements were due largely to the reclamation of wasteland
encouraged by landowners such as Sir Christopher Hawkins and Sir
Francis Basset (created Baron De Dunstanville in 1796).[34] Miners were
encouraged to build cottages and enclose a few acres of these lands.
Approximately 25,000 to 30,000 acres of wastelands were reclaimed
between 1700 and 1860.[35] Such enclosure often existed cheek-by-jowl
with the paraphernalia of industry and mining. In 1794 Forbes thought
that, although the hills around Penryn and Falmouth were heathy and
barren, they were more cultivated than he had expected.[36] Sixty years
later, White found that in the reaches of the Fal 'here and there a few
pleasant snatches of scenery remain, where the hill-sides have been
left un-mutilated' by the mining industry. Typical was the scene that
confronted him at Perran Wharf:

> Perran Wharf, and its noisy foundry, occupy the bottom of a
> shady hollow, which might be taken for a broad glade in
> a forest. You will perhaps be as much surprised to find that
> industry need not always be associated with ugliness, as by
> the beauty of the place itself. Piles of manufactured iron lie
> about, and heaps of coal and refuse, and vessels are loading
> and unloading at the wharf, but the scene is romantic, and
> the woods of Carclew, Sir Charles Lemon's domain, come

sweeping down in masses of foliage that triumph over smoke, and all the roar of bellows and furnaces![37]

An important component of industrial 'space' was the mining and engineering towns such as Hayle, Camborne, Reduth and St Austell, and Cornwall's urban growth between 1700 and 1850 was duly commented on by travellers. In 1724 Daniel Defoe thought Redruth to be of 'no consideration'.[38] In 1750, however, Pococke saw that the town held a great market for provisions once a week where four to five thousand people attended, an indication of the growing importance of Redruth in supporting its mining hinterland.[39] By the time Warner visited Redruth in 1808, it had become 'a town, if not of surpassing beauty, at least of intercourse, activity, and population'.[40] Redruth's population in 1811 was 5,903.[41] Warner explained that because the town was situated in the heart of the mining country it was considerably enriched by the mining concerns, with conveniences and comforts flowing from the retail trade.[42] Redding wrote that Redruth had increased six fold in the last eighty years. He said it was the most important town in the mining districts, 'standing in the midst of a bleak and irregular district, the earth turned inside out by ancient and modern workings for tin and copper'.[43] Redruth had grown to 11,504 souls by 1861.[44] And yet, this was still small-scale compared to the new conurbations elsewhere in Britain, testament to the particular quality of Cornish industrilization. Birmingham, for example, had grown from 25,000 in 1740 to 232,841 in 1851, Leeds from 17,000 in 1775 to 101,000 in 1851, and Liverpool from 5,000 in 1700 to 376,000 in 1851.[45]

Though later to develop as a commercial, ecclesiastic and administrative centre, Truro was for much of this period a comparable mining town to Redruth, a result of its strategic position alongside the mining districts and it proximity to important producers such as Great Wheal Busy. From Fiennes' visit in 1698, when she thought Truro had a good quay and used to be a good trading town, but had become 'disregarded', Truro grew to become the capital of Cornwall.[46] It also cultivated a reputation as a stylish town: 'the people of this town dress and live so elegantly, that the pride of Truro is one of the bye-words of this county; and the quarter-sessions . . . being generally held here, it is pretty well stocked with attorneys'.[47] In 1842, Redding announced it to be 'one of our finest country towns of its size, its population and buildings are on the increase'. He estimated the population to be about 10,000 at the time.[48] *Kelly's Directory 1856*, states that the population in 1851 was 10,733.[49] Again, this figure seems somewhat modest when compared with the growth of Manchester in the North from a population of 8,000 in 1700 to 95,000 in 1801, to 365,000 by 1850.[50] *The*

Directory of 1856 attributed Truro's growth to its situation on an arm
of the Falmouth harbour and its position in the mining district, with
three main roads running to St. Austell, Bodmin and Redruth.[51] Its
trade continued to consist of exporting tin and copper, and it also
imported coal, and timber from Norway. White commented on this
when he saw 'Norwegian ships discharge their cargoes of timber, for
use in the mines; the demand being incessant'.[52]

Further east, by contrast, was Liskeard, a major agricultural town
but also an important supplier for the adjacent mining areas, particularly after the discovery of copper on Caradon Hill in 1836. In 1874
Defoe described Liskeard as well built, with a 'very great market' and
'people of fashion'.[53] Forbes in 1794 noted that Liskeard contained a
few genteel houses, although 'the situation is very hilly . . . dirty and
badly paved'. And Collins in 1850 thought Liskeard—by now also a
major mining centre—an 'abomination of desolation, a large agricultural country town. Modern square houses, barren of all outer
ornament; wide, dusty, deserted streets'.[54]

THE COAST

Notwithstanding the pre-eminence of mining in Cornish 'space' during
the industrial period, Cornwall remained a quintessentially maritime
region. Some of the trading ports were integral to the mining industry—such as Hayle, Portreath and Par—and even old ports (such as
East Looe) which had long maintained a mix of activities, including
fishing, became involved in mining-related activity. However, despite
the intimacy of this link, coastal Cornwall—and in particular fishing
villages from Cawsand, Portwrinkle and Polperro to Mevagissey,
Newlyn and St Ives—provided a powerful alternative conception of
'space'.

Along the southern coast the travellers came across plunging
valleys and steep cliffs. Celia Fiennes in 1698 was astounded by the
very steep descent and ascent in and out of Looe, three times steeper
than she had come across before.[55] Warner had to dismount and lead
his horses in some parts of the narrow, steep lane of about seven miles,
which he said was a precipitous zig-zag of a track with an abrupt
descent of about 100ft in depth.[56] Over time many of these steep tracks
leading into these isolated villages were improved. As Redding stated
in 1842, a new road into Looe had been built making the town more
accessible by land. Significantly, these coastal space descriptions by the
travellers were mainly concerned with the fishing ports and villages,
prefiguring the later pre-occupations of the tourist industry.

For example, the fishing village of Looe was frequently
commented on by visitors. In 1724 Defoe saw Looe as a good trading

town in merchandise and fish. However, less than 100 years later in 1808 Warner saw a completely different picture. Looe was, he said, 'a small miserable town, and despoiled of its trade by war, exhibits little else at present than poverty and discontent'.[57] Looe relied on its trade in pilchards to Europe, which had come to a standstill during the Napoleonic War, and Warner bemoaned this 'shutting up of the Mediterranean ports'.[58] Trade had improved in Looe by the time of Collins' visit in 1850:

> One of the prettiest and most primitive places in England. . . . The houses of the town straggling out towards the sea along each bank of the river, in mazes of little streets; curious old quays project over the water at different points; coast-trade vessels are being loaded and unloaded . . . hills, harbour, and houses thus quaintly combined together. . . . No such thing as a straight street in the place.[59]

White, in 1854, described Looe as 'romantic and striking to the stranger', as 'gardens and cottages line the hill-sides, filled with shrubs, flowers, and fruit trees; literally "hanging gardens"'. The species of flowers, White said, generally grew in more southern European climates, but were well suited to this protected port, 'warmed by the southern sun'. This, White added, gave Looe that 'foreign aspect' which English visitors could detect in many towns in Cornwall.[60] This, in turn, helped to create the sense of the exotic that by the second half of the nineteenth century was already building an important tourist industry in Cornwall. By the 1870s visiting Cornwall for one's health had become very fashionable, and Penzance in west Cornwall had become especially popular. With the help of the new railway services, more tourists were visiting Penzance for its 'Mediterranean' climate and for the benefit of their health. Hotels followed, Penzance becoming the tranquil, almost genteel holiday resort that Thomas Mills encountered in 1863:

> The spacious walk was thronged with young ladies, in expansive crinoline, and with book or crochet-work in hand; young men, bearing a spy glass under their arms . . . adorned every seat, and, in fact, the whole length of the promenade seemed a complication of gay-coloured bonnets, spy-glasses, fascinating hats, dainty boots, short-tailed coats, Crimean beards, Dundreary whiskers, envious veils, bright sunshine, white, hot sand, bathing machines, boats, stately ships, and blue water in the distance.[61]

But Penzance also remained an industrial port. In the last quarter of the eighteenth century, Penzance—with its large, relatively safe bay—became an important port for the import and export of materials such ore, coal and timber. In his visit in 1724, Defoe was surprised by the bustling activity and the large number of ships at anchor in what he imagined was such a remote spot. Forbes in 1794 and Warner in 1808 also noted that Penzance was responsible for the export of tin, there being many mines nearby. Moreover, the port exported pilchards, herring and fish oil to the Mediterranean, and imported timber, planks, iron, and hemp from Russia and Norway for use in the mines.[62] Forbes claimed that 'many persons at Penzance have within these last fifty years acquired fortunes from twenty to sixty thousand pounds, and during that period the town has been much improved; and all its good houses, as well as many pleasant seats in its vicinity, have been erected'. White arrived in 1854 and found 'signs of growth and fertility'.[63]

Falmouth and Fowey on the south coast were the largest harbours in Cornwall. Falmouth dominated the export trade in pilchards: this was due mainly to its many trading contacts with the Mediterranean, as there was little fishing in the harbour itself. In 1808 Warner thought that Falmouth had the potential to become the best trading port in the whole country. He said that although it was 'a place of great population, wealth, and respectability [it] deserves a much larger portion of the attention and encouragement of the government than it has been honoured with' due to its magnificent harbour.[64] Falmouth exported salt pilchards, tin and corn, and imported timber and iron and coals for the tin works. Similarly, in 1854 White thought Fowey a comparable harbour to Liverpool yet, 'judging from appearances, the trade is nothing like commensurate with the natural advantages'. And yet Liverpool was once 'a mere fishing village—and now!'[65] Like Falmouth, Fowey had much unrealized potential. And in the comparison with Liverpool was a sense that Cornwall's industrialization had remained too narrow, that by the mid nineteenth century the 'over-specialized' and 'incomplete' characteristics of that industrialization were already becoming apparent to external observers in their contemplation of Cornish 'space'.

LIVINGS:
MINING

In observing 'space' in Cornwall the travellers revealed a relatively mixed economy: an industrialized region engaged in intensive and extensive mining but also an agricultural hinterland and a littoral engaged in commercial fishing and international trade. Instead of finding the subsistence rural society that many travellers expected, visitors discovered that a large number of people depended mainly on the contract of their labour for a livelihood, the hallmark of a modern industrial economy. 'Livings', then, is about how people earned their livelihoods in industrial Cornwall, and how this was observed and interpreted by visitors and travellers.

About thirty thousand people depended on Cornish tin mining in the first half of the eighteenth century, with half the total being wholly dependent on the mines for their livelihood, and the other half also involved in cultivating smallholdings or taking part in the seasonal pilchard fishery.[66] The mining population grew substantially in the first half of the nineteenth century, with 36,284 copper mine employees alone recorded in the 1851 census out of a population of approximately 345,000. Inevitably, therefore, any consideration of 'livings' in Cornwall was dominated by commentaries on the working lives of the mining population.

As early as 1698 this was evident in the observations of Celia Fiennes. A mile and a half from St Austell (probably Polgooth), she came upon men digging in tin mines, at 'least twenty mines all in sight', which employed about 1,000 men working 'almost night and day' seven days a week to prevent their mines being flooded with water.[67] Pococke in 1750 said the miners worked six days a week, eight hours a day underground.[68] Redding showed not much had changed by 1842, when he reported that the men worked eight-hour shifts ('cores'), in the deepest mines, often taking an hour to reach the surface. And in 1850, Collins still found the men to be working eight-hour days and rotating night shifts.[69]

The working miner ranged from the 'free' miner working his own tin-stream or small mine, to casual labourers working in the larger mines for a weekly or daily wage. From medieval times free miners had been declining, yet they still survived, while wage-earners had appeared to undertake a multiplicity of labouring tasks about the mines. Cornish mines, however, remained dominated by 'tribute' and 'tutwork' contracting, in which part of the entrepreneurial function was performed by the miners themselves. Tutwork contracts were concerned with the volume of ground mined (often in the sinking of a shaft or in driving a level), while tribute was concerned with the value of ore extracted. Redding commented favourably on the tribute system. He attributed the 'harmony and equality' that seemed to prevail between miner and employer to the positive aspects of the system. But not all observers were so sure. Collins was not impressed by the system when he encountered it in 1850. He thought the bidding between rival groups of miners ('pares') for the contract did not always ensure a fair or productive bargain, due to the speculative risk of many poor lodes.[70] Indeed, as Collins thought, tributing was as likely to lead a miner to destitution as it was to wealth and prosperity.[71]

But despite his criticism of the tribute system, Collins in 1850 thought there was sufficient work to be had and that 'comparing the rate of wages with rent and the price of provisions; setting the natural advantage of the county fairly against its natural disadvantage, it is impossible not to conclude that the Cornish poor suffer less by their poverty, and enjoy more opportunities of improving their social position, than the majority of their brethren in many other counties of England'. He felt the 'general demeanour' of the people supported his claim. The Cornish were 'a cheerful, contented race'. Indeed, '[t]he views of the working men are remarkably moderate and sensible—I never met with so few grumblers anywhere'.[72] Collins was fortunate enough to witness what Rowe describes as the 'Indian Summer' of the Cornish copper mining industry. In the 1850s the fortune of copper mining still seemed bright with high copper ore prices, having recovered from the depression and famine time of 1847, and before its eventual decline in the 1860s and beyond. Earlier, in the first and second quarters of the nineteenth century, many miners struggled to make a living wage, with scarcely enough to set aside for the proverbial rainy day. The poorer miners were nearly always in debt to local tradesmen and shopkeepers, and larger ones suffered too during the Napoleonic wars and in their aftermath.[73]

Travellers referred occasionally to the miners' housing. Warner considered that the miner lived comfortably in a small cottage he had built himself, often with a garden.[74] Due to the plentiful availability of moor land, the miners typically occupied cottages scattered over the picturesque locations, often on cliff tops, with white-washed walls which suggested to the travellers more comfort than a closer inspection would have revealed. They were very small and often overcrowded, with earth floors, cob walls, no proper foundations, and suffering badly from dampness. The pretty gardens disguised dung heaps and un-sanitary septic mudpools.[75] Ayton in 1813 detected that the cottages in the St Agnes mining area were substandard. There were 'a few houses which proclaim defiance to every appearance of comfort and convenience, a few inclosures, called gardens, in which even weeds disdain to grow, and a few other things for the service of man, in the same whimsical style of unfitness'.[76] However, Fiennes had had an agreeable visit to a cottage in 1698. She thought the cottages were like barns, 'much like those in Scotland—but to do my own country its right the inside of their little cottages are clean and plastered, and such as you might comfortably eat and drink there, and for curiosity sake I drank there, and met with very good bottled ale'.[77]

By the middle of the nineteenth century only a small proportion of the total mining population of Cornwall possessed smallholdings or gardens of any size.[78] They had become less common as the mining population expanded. Many lived in overcrowded and unsanitary cottages, hovels of cob and thatch, with a low life expectancy. Measles, smallpox, diphtheria, typhoid, and (in males) mining diseases such as silicosis and phthisis, were prevalent. Rowe maintains that in Cornwall poverty, dirt, and malnutrition killed more than did occupational diseases. Mining accidents also claimed more than a few victims, and conditions in smelting works such as those at Hayle were fearful. 'The processes of roasting and refining the ore at Hayle, during which it passes through six or seven furnaces, are highly interesting', wrote Warner in 1808, 'but the pleasure arising from a sight so curious . . . is greatly damped by the appearance of the workmen engaged in it. Nothing can be more shocking than this scene.' As he put it, 'Some of the poor wretches who were lading the liquid metal from the furnace to the moulds, looked more like walking corpses than living beings.'[79] But by the time Redding visited Hayle in 1842 the copper smelting works had been abandoned. Hayle, he wrote, 'now possesses iron works in which the largest steam engines are manufactured, with a degree of good workmanship equal to that in any other place of the like manufacture in England'.[80]

In the St. Austell area, increasing numbers of former tin and copper miners sought employment in the expanding china clay works, despite their traditional disdain for clay. White in 1854 spoke to miners in the Carclaze mine, just north of St Austell. 'There isn't as much tin as there used to be', said one of the miners, 'and we go to work at the clay because it pays best'.[81] From his observations White in 1854 estimated that there were more than 7,000 people employed in china clay production and transport, raising 80,000 tons of clay for export.[82] His estimate of the number of clay workers was almost certainly exaggerated but it does indicate the impact of this fast-growing industry upon White, who was clearly impressed by its scale and extent.

THE SEA

Surrounded by the sea, Cornwall had long supported the fishing of mackerel, herring, crab, and lobster, as well as the seasonal pilchard catch. Travellers witnessed the fluctuations of affluence and poverty in the fishing industry, with the ebb and flow of the annual run of pilchards, scarcity of salt, the salt duties and outbreaks of war, all of which had characterized that industry for centuries. Collins noticed in 1850 that traditional methods of fishing had not altered over time. The seine net and the huer on the hill, who gave warning of approaching shoals of fish, were still in use, as were the drift nets in deeper waters.[83]

In 1827 there were 10,500 people employed in the Cornish fisheries, but only 1600 drift-men could be regarded as permanently employed, the remaining being employed for the seasonal work of seining or curing the pilchards.[84] In 1850 Collins estimated 10,000 persons—men women, and children—derived their living from the fisheries, not only the inhabitants of the coast, but also, during the pilchard season, many farm workers.[85] The uncertainty of employment was a feature of the fishing industry due to the seasonal run of the pilchards which appeared for only a few weeks a year. As Daniell elucidates: 'but for some occult cause, their [the pilchards] numbers are never certain, and the hopes of the fisherman are as precarious as those of a farmer before harvest'.[86]

The prominence of women in the fishing industry workforce reflected the wider position of women in Cornwall, not least in the mines. Pococke in 1750 saw women and children separating the earth from the ore in Chacewater. Boswell in 1792 witnessed 'men, women, and children employed in beating and sorting and otherwise preparing the ore and stone'. Forbes in 1794 commented on the gender mix he saw working around the tin streams: 'I am pleased to see so many women and boys engaged in the latter parts of this work as I always am with any manufactory that gives employment to the female sex whose province is too often intruded on by the other.' In 1808 Warner also noted that many women and children prepared the ore after it was raised.[87] Likewise, he learned at Marazion that in the fishing trade the 'bulkers' generally were women who prepared and piled the pilchards into the curing house. Daniell in Portwrinkle in 1823 watched the occupation of a number of men, women, and children in the various processes of washing, salting, and pressing fish, together with the manufacture of nets, ropes, and casks.[88] In the coastal trade in 1850, Collins thought, 'the women take a very fair share of the hard work out of the men's hands'. In Looe he saw women carrying coals from the vessels to the quay in hand-barrows. Moreover, while the women toiled, '[a]s to the men, one absorbing interest appears to govern them all. The whole day long they are mending boats, painting boats, cleaning boats, rowing boats, or, standing with their hands in their pockets, looking at boats'.[89] Similarly, at Port Isaac in 1813 Ayton watched women loading slates into a small sloop. He commented that their labour was equal to that of men, but that their wages were considerably less because they were women.

PEOPLE:
'A KIND OF BARBARIANS'?

> The game called the Hurlers, is a thing the Cornish men value themselves much upon; . . . it is a rude violent play among the boors, or country people; brutish and furious, and a sort of an evidence, that they were, once, a kind of barbarians.[90]

These words of Daniel Defoe's in 1724 were an indication of most travellers' pre-conception of the people of Cornwall and their expectations of their behaviour. Bernard Deacon has described Cornwall's narrative of achievement between 'West Barbary' and 'Industrial Civilization'. 'West Barbary' was represented by the Cornish reputation for drunkenness, violence and lawlessness symbolized in hurling, wrestling and wrecking. 'Industrial Civilization' was the image the Cornish adopted to represent the technical progress dominant in industrializing Cornwall, together with the moral upheaval encouraged by Methodism. But as Deacon explains: 'in the retelling of this myth in the nineteenth and twentieth centuries West Barbary became more barbarian and Industrial Civilisation more civilised'.[91] Travellers went to Cornwall in expectation of West Barbary and came away impressed by Industrial Civilization. Yet this Industrial Civilization, based as it was on an assertive Cornishness and pride in industrial prowess, was also perceived as 'different' by visitors, the Cornish marked now by a sturdy individualism and independence. Cornwall had changed but had remained 'different'.

The appeal of Methodism in eighteenth- and nineteenth-century Cornwall reflected in part the weakness of the Anglican Church. A gap had appeared between church and people, as James Forbes noted in 1794. He reported that 'too many of the farmers in Cornwall, especially near the Land's End, where spirits are extremely cheap, are very fond of drinking, and set a bad example to their families and dependants'. He blamed this on 'another great evil', which was the non-residence of the clergy among their parishioners.[92] The Methodists enlivened and invigorated Cornish religious life, and were considered by many—then as now—to have played a central role in the supposed transformation from West Barbary to Industrial Civilization. Many travellers attributed to the Methodists the apparent moral improvement of the Cornish people. The Reverend Warner considered that the Wesleyan

Methodists had had a purifying influence, combating wrestling and stamping-out cock-fighting, inter-parish battles and other riotous revels.[93] Similarly, Redding also supposed 'the humbler classes in Cornwall were much softened and civilised by the preaching of Wesley'.[94] As Warner concluded:

> Their dangerous wrestling and hurling matches are now of much rarer occurrences than heretofore; the spirit of sport has nearly evaporated, and that of industry supplied its place. The occupations in the mining countries fill up the time of those engaged in them too effectually to allow leisure for prolonged revels, or frequent festivities; and in other parts of Cornwall, the constant pursuits of steady labour have banished the traditional times and seasons of vulgar riot and dissipation.[95]

Collins, visiting Redruth in 1850, was aware of the impact of this 'civilizing' modernity, notable especially in the industrial heartlands such as Redruth with their allegedly more urbane, sophisticated standards:

> People became less curious to know who we were, stared at us less, gossiped with us less; gave us information, but gave us nothing more—no long stories, no invitations to stop and smoke a pipe, no hospitable offers of bed and board . . . We had left the picturesque and the primitive, with the streets of Looe and the fisherman at the Land's End, and had got into the commercial part of the country, among sharp, prosperous, businesslike people.[96]

One hundred and fifty years earlier, in 1698, Celia Fiennes had had a different reception. She had remarked about the curiosity of the people in Redruth and west Cornwall, who asked questions as to where and how far she was going and from where she had come from, but knowing little beyond their home and maybe the market town they frequented.[97] But the changes Collins had discerned were confirmed by White, who in 1854 detected the 'improved' qualities of the Cornish miner—even when compared to the neighbouring agricultural labourer:

> Though in the main . . . 'a rough lot', you will see . . . a marked difference between miners and field-labourers. The intelligence gleaming in their eyes, and their general expression, denote a habit of thinking for themselves, as you

will find by their shrewd remarks, if you get into talk with them. In daily conflict with rude circumstances, their native resources are developed and multiplied. Their ingenuity is manifest in the numerous improvements they have made in their tools and machinery.[98]

White and Collins had eminent allies in their advocacy of the worth of the Cornish miner. J. S. Mill, liberal and utilitarian thinker and champion of 'the market' in economic life, approved of tribute and tutworking and the general social tenor of industrial Cornwall. In 1845 Mill reported that for 'intelligence, independence, and good conduct as well as prosperous circumstances, no labouring population in the island is understood to be comparable to the Cornish miners'. Mill wrote highly of a system he thought raised the condition of the Cornish miners, who were invariably joint-adventurers, 'far above that of the generality of the labouring class'.[99] In Mills' estimation, West Barbary had indeed given way to Industrial Civilization.

However, the miners' sometimes 'outlandish' appearance and 'foreign' manners elicited mixed reactions from travellers from outside. Ayton in 1813 came across some miners who had just come up from a mine in St. Agnes, men 'whose manners betrayed strong evidence of having been formed at least twenty fathoms below the surface of the earth. They have a very unhealthy appearance, which is easily accounted for . . . resulting from exposure to bad air, and sudden and violent changes in its temperature'.[100] A decade later, Daniell spoke of miners in the St. Austell area: 'The sallow and gloomy aspect of these men increase the feelings of melancholy and distrust with which a stranger is beset when he enters upon this dreary region; and it is difficult in the first instance, for the mind to associate the idea of honest and useful labour with an occupation carried on far from the light of day, in the secret recesses of the earth'.[101] And yet Collins thought that the 'miners are a fine-looking race of men—strong and well proportioned'. He did not think the hard work and bad air affected them much, but pointed instead to the 'pure air of the cliffs and moors on which their cottages are built, and the temperance of their lives (many of them are teetotallers)'.[102]

'A STRONG SPIRIT OF DISTINCT NATIONALITY'

These 'positive attributes' of the mining population by the early nineteenth century were being projected onto the Cornish working class as a whole. In particular, visitors frequently fancied that they detected a pervading sense of equality and a general lack of class consciousness in Cornwall, especially when compared to the deference shown to them by the lower classes elsewhere in Britain. The impact of Methodism, the effect of industrialization—which in Cornwall threw people from different classes into common speculative ventures—and the absence of a powerful aristocracy combined with an ambivalent attitude to law and order (as evidenced in smuggling and wrecking) to reduce deference in social relations.[103] Moreover, early industrialization also provided opportunities for social and economic mobility, perhaps more so than occurred elsewhere. Even at the time of Defoe's visit in 1724 there was evidence that the wealth accrued from the mining had set the beneficiaries up very well. When Defoe arrived in Penzance 'the great many good families of gentlemen' surprised him, as he had expected such provincial people to be underprivileged. 'They are supposed to be so poor', he said, due to their remoteness from London. He concluded, rightly, that the wealth was due to the tin and copper ore found in abundance in the area.[104]

The travellers were also astonished to find a general lack of reverence afforded them as gentleman and members of the better sort. Ayton explained his surprise at the lack of respect shown toward himself and William Daniell when they were trying to arrange for a fisherman to sail them along the coast from St Ives for a few hours in 1813. They found the demands of the boatmen 'extravagant':

> The pilchard fishery has put a few shillings into their pockets, so that they could afford to be insolent, and affected a most galling indifference whether they obliged us or not. . . . The boatmen never condescended to flatter, but cheated us with an air of assurance that was almost respectable. They are a fine bold set of fellows, and as their common occupation of fishing, laborious and perilous as it is, returns them but a scanty subsistence, they may, perhaps, be excused for now and then hooking a stray gentleman . . . who, they suppose, travels from his home for the express purpose of scattering his money about him with heedless profusion.[105]

Likewise, James Forbes in 1794 was 'forcibly struck' by the outspokenness by a serving maid about her master, after whom he had enquired. He thought 'few servants in the metropolis' would have testified in such a manner.[106] Thomas Mills in 1863 also noticed this lack of servility when he spoke generally about the Cornish:

> The men of Cornwall . . . are what is [sic] popularly known as 'regular bricks'. There is nothing like servility about them. The labourer or peasant you pass in the road . . . wishes you a

frank and courteous 'good morning', but does it with an air of independence and in a manner that shows he thinks himself quite as good as you . . . no 'cringing' is there in his demeanour like I have seen nearer home, and neither does he 'sir' you at every pause in his discourse. And then, again, there is a greater seeming of equality among the different classes . . . which, without lowering any, adds to the good feeling of all.[107]

In all this, as Collins reminded his readers, 'Cornwall is a county where, it must be remembered, a stranger is doubly a stranger, in relation to provincial sympathies, where the national feeling is almost entirely merged in the local feeling; where a man speaks of himself as Cornish in much the same spirit as a Welshman speaks of himself as Welsh.'[108] Likewise, White also acknowledged that 'a strong spirit of distinct nationality is still cherished in Cornwall'. The people of Devon and Cornwall were quite different from each other in their character and accents, he insisted. Upon entering Cornwall from Devon in 1854, he wrote that 'at once you are struck with the difference between the county you are in and the one you have left'.[109]

CONCLUSION

Cornwall's experience of industrialization was distinctive, if not unique. Although it changed Cornwall to the core in many respects, it did not mean that Cornwall had become like other areas of industrial Britain. On the contrary, Cornwall's 'difference' was re-invented anew. Travellers visiting Cornwall in this period were often surprised that they encountered not the West Barbary they had been led to expect but rather an Industrial Civilization that bore all the marks of the 'improvement' that Methodism and other agencies of modernity had provided. But beneath this veneer of modernity, and sometimes because of it, Cornwall remained 'different'—sometimes outlandishly and frighteningly so—with travellers thinking themselves in a land apart from England where the locals exhibited a fierce local patriotism and a non-deferential individualism and independence in the face of outsiders.

Paradoxically, although one of the first regions of Britain—and thus Europe and the world—to industrialize, Cornwall's experience of industrialization remained 'overspecialized', 'imperfect' and 'incomplete'. This contributed further to the contrasts between Cornwall and industrialization as observed elsewhere in Britain, and helps to explain the often complex (and sometimes contradictory) observations of those literary travellers who visited Cornwall in the eighteenth and nineteenth centuries. Inevitably, perhaps, these visitors' perceptions of Cornwall were influenced by the dominating presence of mining in Cornish 'space' but this did not blind them entirely to other dimensions —from farming and fishing to gender and tourism—in their consideration of 'space', 'livings' and 'people'. These visitors are interesting because they brought with them preconceived ideas of what Cornwall might be like. Sometimes their assumptions seemed to be confirmed but more often than not they needed considerable modification, or were rejected altogether. And yet, despite their general approval for the changes wrought by Methodism and other agencies of modernity, they remained wary of the Cornish as a provincial 'other'. These travellers were, by and large, the mouthpieces of an educated, literary, metropolitan elite. Their words, therefore, are a priceless insight into the way in which Cornwall was regarded by that elite as it industrialized in the eighteenth and early nineteenth centuries. Cornwall might have embraced modernity but it remained a world away from the culture, standards and norms of the English metropolis.

NOTES AND REFERENCES

1. See Philip Payton, *The Making of Modern Cornwall: Historical Experience and the Persistence of 'Difference'*, Redruth, 1992.
2. A. Shorter, W. Ravenhill, K. Gregory, *Southwest England*, London, 1969, p. 4.
3. Bernard Deacon, 'The Hollow Jarring of the Distant Steam Engines: Images of Cornwall between West Barbary and Delectable Duchy', in E. Westland (ed.), *Cornwall, the Cultural Construction of Place*, Penzance, 1997, p. 17.
4. Philip Drew, *The Coast Dwellers*, Ringwood, 1994, p. xi.
5. Drew, 1994, p. xii.
6. William Gilpin, Observations on the Western Parts of England, Richmond, 1973, p. 192.
7. Rev. John Swete, 'A Tour in Cornwall in 1780', *Journal of the Royal Institution of Cornwall* 6, 3, 1971, p. 194.
8. Rev. Richard Warner, *A Tour Through Cornwall in the Autumn of 1808*, London, 1809, p. 84.
9. James Forbes, 'Tour into Cornwall to the Land's End', *Journal of the Royal Institution of Cornwall*, 4, 2, 1983, p. 160.
10. Wilkie Collins, *Rambles Beyond Railways*, London, 1982, p. 2.
11. Walter White, *A Londoner's Walk to the Land's End*, London, 1865, p. 179.
12. John Rowe, *Cornwall in the Age of the Industrial Revolution*, St Austell, 1993, p. 6.

13. Christopher Morris, *The Illustrated Journeys of Celia Fiennes 1685–1712*, London, 1982, p. 205.
14. James Joel Cartwright (ed.), *The Travels Through England of Dr. Richard Pococke Vol II*, London, 1965, p. 109.
15. Rowe, 1993, p. 42.
16. White, 1865, p. 184.
17. Rowe, 1993, p. 72.
18. Cyrus Redding, Illustrated Itinerary of the County of Cornwall, London, 1843, p. 216.
19. Payton, 1992, p. 75
20. James Boswell, 'Jaunt to Cornwall August to September 1792', privately printed papers from the *Journal of James Boswell*, prepared by G. Scott, and F. Pottle, 1934, p. 21.
21. Warner, 1809, p. 106.
22. Morris, 1982, p. 206.
23. Forbes, 1983, p. 190.
24. White, 1865, p. 293.
25. Boswell, 1934, p. 21.
26. Redding, 1843, p. 174.
27. White, 1865, p. 280.
28. Collins, 1982, p. 112.
29. Payton, 1992, p. 81.
30. Payton, 1992, pp. 78, 80.
31. White, 1865, pp. 186, 191.
32. White, 1865, p. 275.
33. Morris, 1982, p. 207.
34. Edwin Jaggard, *Cornwall Politics in the Age of Reform 1790–1885*, Woodbridge, 1999, p. 12.
35. Rowe, 1993, p. 225.
36. Forbes, 1983, p. 171
37. White, 1865, p. 207.
38. Daniel Defoe, A Tour Through the Whole Island of Great Britain, Harmondsworth, 1971, p. 242.
39. Cartwright, 1965, p. 113.
40. Warner, 1809, p. 240.
41. Rowe, 1992, p. 184.
42. Warner, 1809, p. 240.
43. Redding, 1843, p. 186.
44. Payton, 1992, p. 109.
45. www.geocities.com/localhistories
46. Morris, 1982, p. 209
47. *Universal British Directory*, 1793–1798, p. 217.
48. Redding, 1843, p. 117.
49. *Kelly's Directory*, 1856, p. 144.
50. W. T. Selley, *England in the Eighteenth Century,* London, 1964, p. 247.
51. Kelly's Directory, 1856, p. 143.
52. White, 1865, p. 205

53. Defoe, 1971, p. 228.
54. Forbes, 1983, p. 160, Collins, 1982, p. 16.
55. Morris, 1982, p. 203.
56. Warner, 1809, p. 86.
57. Warner, 1843, p. 87.
58. Warner, 1809, p. 93.
59. Collins, 1982, p. 7.
60. White, 1865, p. 175.
61. Thomas H. Mills, *A Week's Wanderings in Cornwall and Devon,* London, 1863, p. 74.
62. Forbes, 1983, p. 175, Warner, 1809, p. 147.
63. Forbes, 1983, p. 175, White, 1865, p. 268.
64. Warner, 1809, p. 111.
65. White, 1865, pp. 196, 182.
66. Rowe, 1993, p. 28.
67. Morris, 1982, p. 205.
68. Cartwright, 1965, p. 112.
69. Redding, 1843, p. 199, Collins, 1982, p. 112.
70. Collins, 1982, p. 112.
71. Rule, 1987, p. 125.
72. Collins, 1982, p. 40.
73. Rowe, 1993, pp. 164, 305.
74. Warner, 1809, p. 301.
75. Rule, 1987, p. 83.
76. Ayton and Daniell, Vol I, 1978, p. 20.
77. Morris, 1982, p. 208.
78. Rowe, 1993, p. 153.
79. Warner, 1809, pp. 135–6.
80. Redding, 1843, p. 185.
81. White, 1865, p. 194.
82. White, 1865, p. 191.
83. Collins, 1982, p. 88.
84. Rowe, 1993, p. 291.
85. Collins, 1982, p. 39.
86. Daniell, 1978, p. 26.
87. Cartwright, 1965, p. 110, Boswell, 1934, p. 21, Forbes, 1983, p. 163, Warner, 1809, p. 276.
88. Warner, 1809, p. 193, Daniel, Vol VIII, 1978, p. 39.
89. Collins, 1982, p. 9.
90. Defoe, 1971, p. 243.
91. Bernard Deacon, 'The Hollow Jarring of the Distant Steam Engines: Images of Cornwall Between West Barbary and Delectable Duchy', in E. Westland (ed.), *Cornwall, the Cultural Construction of Place,* Penzance, 1997, p. 11.
92. Forbes, 1983, p. 168.
93. Warner, 1809, p. 301
94. Ayton and Daniell, Vol I, 1978, p. 28, Redding, 1843, p. 188.

95. Warner, 1809, p. 359.
96. Collins, 1982, p. 119.
97. Morris, 1982, p. 207.
98. White, 1865, p. 294.
99. Rule, 1987, p. 124.
100. Ayton and Daniell, Vol I, 1978, p. 20.
101. Daniell, Vol VIII, 1978, p. 48.
102. Collins, 1982, p. 112.
103. Jaggard, 1999, p. 19.
104. Defoe, 1971, p. 233.
105. Ayton and Daniell, Vol I, 1978, p.17.
106. Forbes, 1983, p. 174.
107. Mills, 1863, p. 31.
108. Collins, 1982, p. 47.
109. White, 1865, pp. 202, 166.

BRIDGET CLEARY AND CORNISH STUDIES: FOLKLORE, STORY-TELLING AND MODERNITY

Philip Payton

INTRODUCTION

> Are you a witch or are you a fairy,
> Or are you the wife of Michael Cleary?[1]

As Angela Bourke records in her important book *The Burning of Bridget Cleary*, published in 1999, this children's rhyme is still well-known in South Tipperary in Ireland. It is an echo of an extraordinary event that gripped Ireland (and Britain) more than a century ago: the torture and eventual killing in March 1895 of Bridget Cleary, a twenty-six-year-old woman from Ballyvadlea in rural County Tipperary. Likewise, the house where Bridget died, still inhabited today, is known locally as 'the place where they burned the witch', while Bridget herself is remembered as 'the last witch burned in Ireland'.[2] But Bridget was not a witch, nor was her death connected with witchcraft as is generally understood. Rather, Bridget Cleary died because her husband Michael had become convinced that she was a 'changeling', that the fairies had stolen his real wife away and substituted a lookalike from the other-world. Michael had had to take drastic action, first to be sure that the woman in his house was indeed a changeling, and then to see to it that his real wife was restored to her home and husband.

At first glance, the story is remarkable because it illustrates the survival in Ireland until at least the eve of the twentieth century of a 'superstitious belief' strong enough and prevalent enough to provoke or even legitimize the taking of a human life. But on closer analysis the story is more remarkable still for, as Angela Bourke has argued, it reveals a folk-culture that had endured beneath—even despite—the veneer of 'rational', civic administration exercised by political and religious authorities in Ireland. As Bourke puts it: 'just out of sight of the solid new Catholic chapels, with their paved yards and stout iron railings, and underneath the orderly grid which Victorian officials and administrators were conscientiously laying over every corner of the land, another world continued to exist'. This was a world 'whose ways of thinking were based on oral tradition, not on the printed word'.[3] And as Seamus Deane has added, the story of Bridget Cleary is also 'a parable of the cultural and political relationship between Ireland and Britain at the end of the last [nineteenth] century'. Within it '[a] modern world of newspapers, courts and railways, and an old world of folklore and fairy-belief tradition are brought together with such force that we can feel the antagonisms and the incomprehensions of the 1890s still reverberant within our own disputes about modernity and colonialism, [and] cultural memory'.[4]

As the Irish language had been steadily replaced by English, so the oral tradition had become increasingly supplanted by the world of print and documentary record: '[a] whole world of wakes, herbal cures, stories of kings and heroes, and legends of the fairies—the culture of those who had not learned to read and write—became increasingly marginal'.[5] It survived, by and large, in the lives of those individuals who were themselves marginal in the new society that had emerged —men like illiterate, lame and poorly-sighted Jack Dunne, a fifty-five-year-old labourer who had a reputation as a *shanachie* or story-teller with a particular knowledge of the fairy world. As Bourke remarks, Dunne was 'a man who might have commanded respect in an earlier generation . . . but who had become marginalized and isolated in an increasingly modern society'.[6] It was Dunne who had first suggested to Michael Cleary that Bridget might be a changeling, and it was he who had recommended the remedial actions that Michael was to take later with such dramatic consequences.

But in the wider, modern world Jack Dunne counted for little. He and others like him, argues Bourke, 'still lived in a symbolic universe very different from the one mapped by the R[oyal] I[rish] C[onstabulary [the agent of British administration in Ireland]: centralization and uniformity had little relevance to their daily lives'.[7] Likewise, the folk-religion of such people—with its reverence of holy wells and local saints, and its traditional songs and prayers based on kinship groups and the home—was at odds with the formal Catholicism that had developed in nineteenth-century Ireland. Bourke again: '[t]he

Catholicism the priests propounded in the towns and chapel-villages of County Tipperary was modern-minded, outward-looking, literate, and essentially middle-class. It sternly opposed attendance at wakes, and had no time whatever for stories about fairies'.[8]

THE DEATH OF BRIDGET CLEARY

When Bridget Cleary first fell ill (with a fever, a result of catching cold when out selling eggs) her husband sought the help of priest and doctor. But neither offered a convincing remedy, and Michael Cleary turned from the modern world to the traditional. On Jack Dunne's prompting he had obtained a herbal medicine, which he force-fed Bridget with a violence that presaged what was to come later. It may be that there was already some difficulty between Michael (a cooper) and his wife, for she was clever and attractive. She had trained as a milliner, in which trade she was successful, and she liked to dress well and colourfully—to the evident disapproval of some observers locally. She was also said to be haughty, and made a point of keeping hens: an assertion of female independence in traditional Irish society. More-over, there was a hint of sexual indiscretion. It was rumoured that Bridget Cleary had had a liaison with one William Simpson. The fact that Simpson was an 'emergencyman', a member of a despised group of opportunists in rural Ireland that had taken on the lands from which tenants had been recently evicted, made the alleged affair even worse in the eyes of local critics. It had been evident for some time that there might be trouble ahead for Bridget Cleary, and the thought that she might be a changeling seemed not unreasonable.

When the herbal medicine recommended by Dunne appeared not to work, Michael Cleary was spurred to adopt more desperate measures. Dunne himself had been shocked when he had first seen the ailing Bridget in bed, exclaiming, 'That is not Bridgie Boland!' (her maiden name).[9] This was not merely a suggestion that Bridget did not look herself but was rather a serious accusation which insisted that this person was *not* Bridget Cleary. Thus, as the *Cork Examiner* was to observe, 'his remark set all the fairy machinery in motion'.[10] Dunne was now convinced that the person supposed to be Bridget was in fact a changeling planted by the fairies. Bridget herself had unwittingly given credence to this interpretation, when she had mentioned to her cousin Johanna that her fever had come on when she 'took like a trembling coming by Kylenagranagh'[11]—a 'fairy ring' or 'fairy fort' in the locality, typical of many across Ireland that were remains of ancient settlements but had become subsumed into local folklore as the places where fairies dwelt.

When Bridget had been given her medicine, she had been taken from her bed and held above the fire in the kitchen as part of the cure. She had not been burned, save perhaps for a small blemish on her forehead which may have been the result of brandishing a red-hot poker too close to her skin. Now, however, a more stringent remedy was called for if the changeling was to be unmasked and the real Bridget Cleary returned. Iron and fire were traditional weapons in confrontations with fairies. Dunne had heated the iron poker that had been used to encourage Bridget to swallow her medicine. Now he and Michael Cleary returned to the fire itself, for there was suddenly a sense of urgency which insisted that if the matter was not resolved by midnight the 'real' Bridget might be lost for ever. Fire was the last resort in dealing with a changeling. Amongst others who had gathered at the Cleary house for the impending crisis was Bridget's father, Patrick Boland. As Bridget was held above the fire-place, he implored: 'Are you the daughter of Patrick Boland, wife of Michael Cleary? Answer in the name of God'. Bridget answered pitifully, 'I am, Dada.'[12] As midnight passed, Bridget appeared to be in a confused and deranged state, with eyes rolling, and those present seemed satisfied that the changeling had indeed been exposed. She was returned to her bed, her nightclothes singed.

Next day, Bridget was quieter and got up from her bed to drink some tea in the kitchen. Michael insisted that she should eat three pieces of bread before she be allowed to drink. She ate the first two but refused the third: a willfully subversive act so typical of a changeling that Michael Cleary flew into a rage. He knocked her to the ground and grabbed a red-hot stick from the fire, shouting and waving the stick so close to Bridget that within seconds her calico chemise was ablaze. As Angela Bourke concludes: 'this does seem to have been the moment when he became convinced that she really was a changeling left by the fairies'.[13] At any rate, he doused Bridget in paraffin from the oil-lamp and let her burn.

Michael Cleary buried Bridget's remains in a shallow grave. For the moment the word was that Bridget had 'disappeared' from her home, and Michael assured a distraught Patrick Boland, Bridget's father, that his real daughter would be restored on the following Sunday night. She would be seen at Kylenagranah fairy-fort, riding on a white horse. He would grab the horse, cut the straps and so rescue her from the fairies. Michael appeared to believe his own story, and spent three nights at Kylenagranah in the genuine expectation that his wife would emerge from the fairy-fort riding a white horse. Bridget did not appear but her charred body was uncovered by the Royal Irish Constabulary, and the full force of British justice swung into action. Remarkably, Michael Cleary was found guilty of manslaughter, not murder, evidence of a certain ambivalence among the jury which took account of Cleary's apparently unshakeable belief in the fairy world. But when Cleary and his accomplices had been marched from the county gaol in Clonmel to the court-room they had been 'greeted with yells, hisses and groans'[14] from the crowd—not all believed that his motives were other-worldly.

Although none sought to justify Michael Cleary's actions, there was a marked divergence in the ways in which the events of the case were read. Before it was apparent that Bridget had been killed, the Clonmel *Nationalist* newspaper—in its usual romantic nationalist language—spoke of her disappearance 'as a kin to the fairy romances of ancient times in Erin . . . The Land of the Banshee and the Fairy'.[15] But when the full horror of the facts became known, the Tory-Unionist press took the affair as yet further evidence of the inability of the Irish to govern themselves, the Irish peasantry being no better than 'Hottentots' or savages from 'Dahomey'. The *Nationalist*, in turn, condemned this 'Tory Slander', with its attempt 'to stir up racial and religious passion and prejudice, and if possible to damage the cause of Home Rule'.[16] Thus at the same time that traditional belief remained a means by which ordinary folk resisted the intrusion of centralized modernity, so it was being politicized by the middle classes in the promotion of (or resistance to) self-government.

Moreover, as part of this politicization, this traditional belief was increasingly co-opted and repackaged as part of the construction of 'Celtic Twilight' Ireland, a romantic nationalist project in which folklore was deployed as part of the armoury of 'difference' and as a central element of Irish national identity. William Butler Yeats, for example, had published his *Fairy and Folk Tales of the Irish Peasantry* in 1888, half a dozen or more years before Bridget Cleary's death, to be followed by *Representative Irish Tales* in 1891, *Irish Fairy Tales* in 1892, and *The Celtic Twilight* itself in 1893. The product of an educated, literate, English-speaking elite, part of the modernity that had clashed with the traditional world, this work nonetheless appealed not only to nationalist sentiment but to a middle (and upper) class already tired of industrialization and urbanization. By the end of the nineteenth century, therefore, folklore had come to enjoy a complex role in Irish life, on the one hand still an alternative belief system current beneath the veneer of centralized modernity, but on the other an important reservoir of cultural capital to be tapped by romantic nationalists in their advancement of 'Celtic Ireland'.

'CELTIC CORNWALL'

Notwithstanding the efforts of Cornish-Celtic Revivalists, now as in the late nineteenth century, to make comparisons between 'Celtic Cornwall' and 'Celtic Ireland', it would be wrong to draw too close or uncritical a comparison between the two territories. Although a sense of Cornish ethnicity endured, 'Cornishness' in the nineteenth century was entwined in a complex world of 'Englishness', 'Britishness' and Imperialism to a degree that 'Irishness' was not. The Cornish thought themselves 'Ancient Britons', as the Welsh did, but only slowly was this reinterpreted as a form of 'Celticity'—and even then one which emphasized the 'aboriginal British' quality of the Cornish, in marked contrast to Irish 'Celticity' which stressed its non-British and indeed anti-British character.

To this was added the fact that most Cornish were fiercely Protestant, many of them Methodists or other Nonconformists highly suspicious of Irish Catholicism. Moreover, Cornish identity in that period was essentially industrial—the Cornish were 'industrial Celts'— and it was the iconography of industrialization that informed most assertions of Cornishness: not least on the international stage where the Cornish were 'Cousin Jacks', the world's foremost miners as they liked to argue. Irishness, by contrast, was essentially rural. Outside of Ulster (where industrialization was an important component of an alternative Protestant Unionist identity) industrial expansion had been patchy, leaving much of the island deeply rural, while the romantic nationalism forged by the likes of William Butler Yeats and later given political expression by De Valera wallowed in its rural idyll and was positively anti-industrial.[17]

And yet, there were important comparisons and similarities between Cornwall and Ireland. As in Ireland, so in Cornwall the indigenous Celtic language had been under great pressure from English. In Ireland, by the time of Bridget Cleary's death, Irish had retreated by and large to the remote Gaeltacht of the west and north-west. In Cornwall, John Davey of Boswednack, near Zennor in the far west, reputedly the last person to have had more than a smattering of traditional Cornish, had died just a few years previously, while Cornish as a community language had disappeared more than a century before that. As in Ireland, the retreat of Cornish and the advance of the English language—and with it growing literacy and documentary forms of communication—meant that an older oral tradition had been increasingly marginalized. The 'droll' (story) tellers that had been lately an important part of Cornish life had all but disappeared. Where the oral tradition remained—manifest in the rich collections of folklore recorded in the mid- and late nineteenth century—it was principally in the far western peninsula of West Penwith, where the Cornish language had lingered longest and where outside influences were more easily resisted. But even here, as in Ireland, there was an intruding modernity which swept the oral tradition before it, or at least forced it below the surface. At Zennor, home parish of John Davey in the fastness of West Penwith, Henry Quick (1792–1857)—a local doggerel poet, in his own way a latter-day droll-teller—lamented the demise in his lifetime of the old ways:

> The Cornish drolls are dead, each one;
> The fairies from their haunts have gone:
> There's scarce a witch in all the land,
> The world has grown so learn'd and grand.[18]

As in Ireland, an older informal folk-religion of holy wells (with their charms and miracle cures) and local saints was in the nineteenth century under pressure from a formal and increasingly centralized religion of modernity which frowned upon traditional activities. Paradoxically, this was Methodism—theologically oppositional to Catholicism—and yet which in its ideology of modernity had in Cornwall much in common with Catholicism in Ireland. Just as Catholicism in Ireland disapproved of wakes and other exhibitions of uncontrolled emotion or exuberance, so in Cornwall Methodism—especially Wesleyanism—sought to control the behaviour of its adherents. Cornish wrestling and hurling, for instance, were abhorrent to the Methodists. One correspondent in the *West Briton* newspaper in November 1821 noted with satisfaction 'the conversion of many miners, who are men of experimental religion and practical godliness' (i.e. Methodism). But he also warned 'that they could not attend such sports [as wrestling and hurling], without violating the dictates of their judgment, without trampling on that sacred command, "Whether therefore ye eat or drink, or whatsoever ye do, do all to the glory of God".'[19]

In fact, such sporting events became battlegrounds between advocates of the new and defenders of the old, where contests between modernity and traditional belief were acted out. In May 1823, for example, it was reported in the *West Briton* that '[t]he annual feast of [Saint] Germoe, in the western part of this county, was held last week. This feast is the only one (*sic*) at which the ancient sport of hurling is kept up'. But even as the parishioners prepared to throw their hurling ball, 'a body of Brianites, a sect lately sprung up from among the Wesleyan Methodists, made their appearance at the time of the hurling, and attempted to put a stop to the diversion by commencing their devotional exercises, but without success'.[20] Later, in 1829, a further correspondent in the *West Briton* made an explicit link between wrestling and paganism, and between wrestling and the opponents of 'progress' and 'improvement'. Wrestling was 'a sport which everyone must allow to be a relic of paganism . . . a very humiliating contrast to the general progress of the community in religious and intellectual improvement'. Especially disturbing, he wrote, was that the civic leader of one Cornish town had lent his support to the sport: not at all what one would expect from such an entrusted guardian of modernity, morality and order: 'The part which the civic chief . . . is reported to have recently taken in rewarding and eulogizing wrestlers will not, it is hoped, find many imitations.' Wrestling, the correspondent concluded, was an 'evil', and it encouraged 'idleness, folly and vice'. Moreover, 'God has forbidden it.'[21]

But at the same time that the Methodists had tackled the evils of 'paganism' with their evangelical zeal, so beneath the surface in Cornwall—as in Ireland—traditional belief endured. As in Ireland it was often amongst the marginalized that such belief flourished, as in the case in September 1829 of '[a] poor man named John Rowe' who lived at Tremoor in the parish of Lanivet. Rowe, who was 'far advanced in life' had 'by industry and economy' scraped together some twenty pounds, quite literally his life's savings. One Sunday, however, counting his treasure, he found that not all the pieces were alike, and that sovereigns had been replaced by farthings, a shilling and a button. He had a shrewd idea who the thief might be. But instead of turning to the police or magistrates he resolved instead to seek the advice of one Johnny Hooper, a 'conjuror' and 'cunning man' who would be able to identify and name the burglar, and perhaps to punish him as well as restoring the treasure to its rightful owner.[22]

'THE CELTIC POWERS WHO HERE HOLD SOVEREIGN SWAY'

Quick had mourned the disappearance of traditional belief. But perhaps he protested too much. As late as 1890, on the eve of the decade in which Bridget Cleary met her death, M. A. Courtney opined that '[f]ew Cornish people are probably aware how wide-spread still with us is the belief in charms and charmers, ghosts, and all other superstitions'. Moreover, she continued, many did not realize 'that there are witches in our county, shunned and dreaded by some who fear their supposed power to ill-wish those who offend them, and sought by others who want by their aid to avert the evil eye, or by their incantations to remove spells already cast on them'.[23]

It may be that Courtney, who had collected her material in a

populist book *Cornish Feasts and Folklore*, had more than a
commercial eye to a burgeoning tourist trade which sought Cornish
'difference' and encouraged constructions of the Cornish as an exotic
'other'. She might also have seen her work as a Cornish patriotic effort,
rather like Yeats' strivings in Ireland at the same time, a romantic
proto-nationalism that anticipated the activities of the Cornish-Celtic
Revivalists in the years ahead. Indeed, by the 1890s the industrial
culture that had epitomized nineteenth-century Cornwall was in crisis,
with copper abandoned and tin in trouble, with many thousands of
Cornish miners and their families having emigrated to the better
prospects of the New World. In such circumstances, the Cornish-Celtic
Revivalists looked back to an older, pre-industrial Cornwall, one that
was essentially rural and not far removed from the Irish imaginings of
Yeats and De Valera.

Robert Hunt, writing in the 1860s and, like Courtney, an
enthusiastic collector of Cornish folk-lore, had been ambivalent about
all this. A product of a technocratic age, Hunt approved of Cornwall's
industrial might, eulogizing the role of mining magnate John Taylor in
promoting the cause of modernization in Cornish mines and publishing
British Mining: A Treatise in 1886. However, he recognized that
beneath the veneer of scientific and technological progress so typical of
mid-nineteenth-century Cornwall, there was an older, traditional belief
that for him defined the authentic if somewhat disturbing, primeval
Cornish character:

> Those wild dreams which swayed with irresistible force the
> skin-clad Briton of the Cornish hills, have not yet entirely lost
> their power where even the National and British Schools
> are busy with the people, and Mechanic's Institutions are
> diffusing the truth of science. In the infancy of the race, terror
> was the moving power; in the maturity of the people, the dark
> shadow still sometimes rises, like a spectre, partially eclipsing
> the mild radiance that Christian truth shines upon the land.[24]

Hunt acknowledged that 'England, with many people, appeared to
terminate on the shores of the Tamar', and he was sure that in West
Penwith '[n]othing but what the Briton planted remains, and if tales tell
true, it is probable that long years must pass before the Englishman can
banish the Celtic powers who here hold sovereign sway'.[25] He wore his
ambivalence on his sleeve, however, for while he approved of those
National and British Schools and Mechanic's Institutions—with their
scientific and Christian 'truths'—so he also regretted the passing of that
faintly disturbing but certainly appealing culture that lurked beneath

the surface. He was in no doubt that this culture was 'Celtic' and, despite his own ambivalence, his treatment of traditional belief anticipated the romantic proto-nationalist tone evident in Courtney later in the century, together with the more overtly nationalist themes elaborated by W. B. Yeats.

Be that as it may, Courtney—like Robert Hunt and William Bottrell before her—had also seen her work as a genuinely scholarly project, a serious attempt (mirroring those elsewhere in Ireland and Britain as well as in continental Europe) to record folklore that was still extant but in danger of fast disappearing in the face of modernity. Indeed, most of her material had first appeared in the *Folk-lore Society Journal* between 1886 and 1887, scholarly contributions to a scholarly publication. Robert Hunt's *Popular Romances of the West of England* (subtitled *The Drolls, Traditions and Superstitions of Old Cornwall*) had been first published in 1865. William Bottrell's *Traditions and Hearthside Stories* appeared in 1870, his *Stories and Folklore of West Cornwall* following in 1880. Together, these formed an important corpus of recorded Cornish folklore—much of it drawn from West Penwith in the far-west where the oral tradition (like the Cornish language) had survived the longest. Collected by and large before the crisis of de-industrialization that progressively overtook Cornwall after the late 1860s, they were—and remain—testament to the survival of an extensive oral tradition beneath the surface.

As much as in Ireland, such folklore was also evidence of the fascinating juxtaposition of modernity and traditional belief. The Cornish mining industry, at least until the crisis of the 1860s, was regarded as the most advanced in the world, with the Cornish beam engine seen as the perfect application of high-pressure steam engineering in mastering the problems of deep mining. Technologically advanced and industrially complex, Cornwall was nonetheless far removed in distance and culture from the urbanized, metropolitan centres of Britain. The industrial landscapes that had emerged in Cornwall resembled not the large conurbations of the Midlands or North of England but were rather a patchwork of small towns, scattered villages and countryside—industrialization in a rural setting. Moreover, the spread of mining was by no means even or homogenous, for although mining was to be found across Cornwall, quite literally from the Tamar to Land's End, there were relatively few centres of concentration. Much of Cornwall remained extremely remote, a remoteness accentuated by the topography of Cornwall and its tortuous landward communications—including the fact that Cornwall was not joined to the UK rail network until 1859.

'THERE ARE MANY OTHER TALES OF CHANGELINGS'

It was against this paradoxical background of industrial modernity and survival of traditional belief that stories of changelings—in several respects strikingly reminiscent of that of Bridget Cleary—survived in popular memory in Cornwall until at least the end of the nineteenth century. Courtney, echoing the work of Bottrell, told the tale of Jenny Trayer, who lived under Chapel Carn Brea, 'on the old road from Penzance to St Just in Penwith'. According to this story, a spriggan (a type of fairy) took the place of Jenny's baby one evening when she was in the fields helping with the harvest. On her return, she was surprised to find the child not in its cradle but 'in a corner of the kitchen where in olden days the wood and furze for the then general open fires were kept'. However, exhausted from her labours in the fields, Jenny Trayer did not dwell upon the surprise but went straight to bed and slept soundly to the next morning. Thereafter, there was to be no rest:

> From that time forth she had no peace; the child was never satisfied but when eating or drinking, or when she had it dandling in her arms. The poor woman consulted her neighbours in turn as to what she should do with the changeling (as one and all agreed that it was). One recommended her to dip it on the three first Wednesdays in May in Chapel Uny Well, which advice was twice faithfully carried out in the prescribed manner.[26]

On the third Wednesday, however, as Jenny made her way to St Uny's holy well, the fairy-folk as if from nowhere hailed their changeling brother, who 'made answer in similar voice' that he had no intention of returning to the spriggan world. Understandably rattled, Jenny consulted another neighbour, who—in an echo of Jack Dunne's advice to Michael Cleary—told her that:

> the best way to get rid of the spriggan and have her own child returned was 'to put the small body upon the ashes' pile, and beat it with a broom; then lay it naked under a church style; there leave it and keep out of sight and hearing till the turn of night; when nine times out of ten the thing will be taken away and the stolen child returned'.[27]

Jenny did exactly as she was bid, and at the church style 'next morning the woman "found her own dear cheeld sleeping on some dry straw", most beautifully clean and wrapped in a piece of chintz'.[28]

Significantly, Courtney added that '[t]here are many other tales of changelings, but they resemble each other so much that they are not worth recording'.[29] Belief in changelings, then, so Courtney would have us believe, was commonplace in nineteenth-century Cornwall. So too, she added, was a further charm for outing a changeling and restoring a child to its parents. This was an echo of the hot 'ashes pile' method employed by Jenny Trayer in her attempt to retrieve her child but it was also more than reminiscent of the hearthside ordeal endured by Bridget Cleary. As William Bottrell had recommended to those determined to banish a changeling: 'Make by night a smoky fire, with green ferns and dry. When the chimney and house are full of smoke as one can bear, throw the changeling on the hearthstone; go out of the house, turn three times round; when one enters, the right child will be restored'.[30]

As in Ireland, so in Cornish lore fire was an important last resort in dealing with a changeling. So it was in dealing with a witch (shades of Bridget Cleary, as her story metamorphosed in the years after her death), Courtney noting that in 1890 the game of 'Burning the Witch' was '[s]till played' by children in Cornwall. In this, an effigy of the witch in question was placed in a slit made at the end of a long stick, and burnt with the flame from a candle.[31]

'THE PARENTS SUPPOSE THEIR CHILD TO HAVE BEEN CHANGED'

Despite the common presence of heat and fire in the stories of Jenny Trayer and Bridget Cleary, there were important distinctions between the two tales. Most significant, of course, was that—as the mass of historical documentation attests—Bridget Cleary was a real person, her suffering and death a human tragedy that horrified informed opinion in Ireland and Britain. Jenny Trayer was, by contrast, at least as far as we can tell, a fictional character in a folk-tale, her story emblematic of the widespread belief in changelings, the deployment of familiar place-names such as Chapel Carn Brea and Chapel Uny Well designed to lend authenticity and realism to the story as it was told and re-told to the people of West Penwith.

However, that is not to say there were not documented cases of changeling belief in Cornwall. In July 1843, for example, the *West Briton* reported the case of J. Trevelyan of 'the Orchard', Penzance, who was brought before the Mayor and Borough Magistrates on a charge that he had 'very shamefully ill-used one of his children'. Now almost three years of age, 'the child was frequently punished by the servants by being put out upon a tree in front of the house, where he was often compelled to remain for hours together'. Specific accusations were that 'he was, on a cold winter's day, at Christmas, 1841, when he was only fifteen months old, put out on the tree, and kept there for two hours and a half, that he was frequently kept a long time without food, and sometimes kicked and beaten'. As the report continued, '[m]any other facts of a similar nature were spoken to, showing a long course of vile treatment'. And as the *West Briton* revealed: 'the reason assigned for it was, that the parents were said to suppose their child to have been changed [by the fairies]'. The Bench, however, could find no evidence to 'legally connect' Trevelyan to 'the infamous treatment of his child', and the case was dismissed.[32]

Others, though, were less forgiving, and Trevelyan was forced to leave town the next day: 'the populace followed the carriage and assailed it with yells and hisses, and other indications of hostility'.[33] However widespread the belief in changelings, there was also, as the anger of the crowd demonstrated, suspicion in such cases that the appeal to changeling lore by the likes of Trevelyan was in fact an excuse for the abuse of a particularly vexatious child. But then again, the existence a particularly vexatious child was often—as the story of Jenny Trayer showed—a sure sign of a changeling presence! As in the case of Bridget Cleary, actual behaviour was seen to reinforce traditional belief, especially when that behaviour was itself predicted by the belief or considered symptomatic of a particular condition.

In Cornwall, as the story of Jenny Trayer and the case of J. Trevelyan both suggested, changelings were usually children: the fairies having replaced the sweet abducted babe with an ugly, screeching, obnoxious brat. In Ireland (as Bourke has noted), changelings also tended to be children, so that the case of adult Bridget Cleary was to a degree an exception to the rule. Small children could not answer back or confound their abusers in a way that older victims might, especially if they suffered from congenital or other disabilities that contributed to their 'vexatious' state. But as the tension between traditional belief and modernity became more acute, in Cornwall—as in Ireland—it became progressively more difficult to argue convincingly that a 'problem' child (or a 'problem' wife) was a changeling, and other facets of traditional folk-lore were likewise rendered less credible or less acceptable.

'A NEW CHUM TO HIS FRIENDS IN CORNWALL, NEAR ENGLAND'

It was this decline in credibility—as well as currency—in the face of modernity that Henry Quick had mourned. It may be, as argued above, that Quick protested too much, and the evidence is that traditional belief continued to survive beneath the surface of modernity. However, traditional belief also metamorphosed in response to change in a way that Quick had not foreseen, so that while 'droll-telling' as he understood it did indeed appear to fade away, other forms of story-telling emerged.

As Alan M. Kent has argued persuasively, while traditional drolls might well have disappeared, new types of story-telling appeared, to respond to and make sense of modernity. This was especially so as the 'Great Emigration' sped the Cornish—Cousin Jack and Cousin Jenny—to the ends of the earth in response to the expansion of the international mining frontier in the nineteenth century. As Kent explains:

> There were a number of socio-cultural and geopolitical reasons why the drolls of previous ages started to decline in the nineteenth century. Certainly, the growth of mass literacy, revivals in Methodism, and alternative pastimes contributed to decline. But it might also be postulated that these drolls were being replaced in Cornish culture by the Cousin Jack Stories whose success and popularity reflected their essential modernity; that is, they were products of a complex industrial society . . . Put another way, it can be argued that as traditional pre-industrial Cornish culture was eroded in the nineteenth century, so the Cousin Jack story took on a function as the new droll of modernism.[34]

To make his point, Kent has examined a rich collection of such 'Cousin Jack narratives' from the Upper Peninsula copper-mining country of Michigan in the United States of America. The result is impressive—a large body of Cousin Jack stories that reveal much about the Cornish in their dispersal and subsequent impact in the New World—and Kent concludes that students of Cornish folk-lore should recognize that the narrative's 'popularity over one hundred and fifty years demonstrates its centrality in the corpus of populist telling and writing emerging from Cornwall'.[35] Moreover, this re-invigorated story-telling reflected the realignment of Cornish folk-lore in North America, as Paul Manning argues elsewhere in this volume. Here, for instance, the old 'Jew' of Cornish mining legend had become transformed into the 'Tommyknocker' of American frontier lore.

Michigan, of course, was but one home of the emigrant Cornish, and similar Cousin Jack stories emerged from other areas of Cornish concentration across the globe. One such district was the northern Yorke Peninsula of South Australia, where extensive copper deposits had been struck in 1859–61, leading to the rapid development of the area—Moonta, Wallaroo and Kadina—as 'Australia's Little Cornwall'. Among the body of 'new' droll-tellers that emerged on the Peninsula was one Jan Rogers, a Cousin Jack who insisted upon his essential Cornishness by explaining that he 'warn't born out Horse Downs for nothing . . . I caant be nothen else but a Cornishman'.[36] Rogers contributed to the *Yorke's Peninsula Advertiser* during the 1870s, in one especially telling contribution—in the form of a dialect letter from 'A New Chum to his Friends in Cornwall, near England'—addressing the confusion many Cornish newcomers had experienced with regard to the trade unions that had become established on the Peninsula. In Cornwall, attempts at unionism—similar to those attempted by Welsh coal-miners at much the same time—had come to little (unlike their Welsh counterparts), the collapse of copper and subsequent decline of tin leading to the emigration of would-be leaders of men and failing to create a climate conducive to the growth of trade unions. 'New Chums' arriving in South Australia from Cornwall, therefore, were confused about 'the Union' that they found out there.

For the average Cousin Jack, 'the Union' meant the Poor Law Union and Workhouse back home. Hence the New Chum's confusion: he knows the miners' Union is nothing to do with the Poor Law and perceives (but does not understand) the various attitudes concerning the legitimate (or otherwise) functions of trade unionism:

> Sum time ago wen waages was cut ere, the men ad a strike, and thare was sum fine doins wat I can heer; and ever sense they av got a Union. Now a Union out here esnt zaccly like a Union es ome, for ome tes for peepel wen they do git ould an caant git a livin for to go in. You knaw ould Jan Rekerd an Mary Thomas and Maary Joans went in the Union wen they got ould an cud only crawl bout. But this ere Union out ere in Munta es a different kind or thing—tis a kind of club in wich men do pay sum munny evry week (wot for, I doant zaccly knaw). Sum do say tes for to keep a good plaace for a man they do caall a Prisidunt—that es a little king, like a thing—an sum do say tes for to git cheep things, for the shopkeepers es too deer, an sum do say that tes for to ave munny to strike agen wen they do cut the waages, but I doant knaw myself. Ime goin to ave a chat with Mary Jane bout et sum ov these days an then sheel make me understand things a little better, for shees a wunnerful sharp wommun, wich you hall do knaw.[37]

'THE ANCIENT CORNISH LANGUAGE IN THE COLONIES'

Jan Rogers' 'letter', with its wry humour and the use of Cornu-English dialect as a badge of Cornishness, is an excellent example of the new type of Cousin Jack story-telling identified by Kent, mediating and negotiating as it does the boundary between existing knowledge back in Cornwall and the demands of New World modernity on the international mining frontier. In Cornwall itself, similar developments were observable. When the third volume of William Bottrell's folk-lore collections—*Stories and Folk-lore of West Cornwall*—appeared in 1880 it contained an intriguing piece on 'The Ancient Cornish Language in the Colonies'. This was a classic exposition of what historians have called 'the myth of Cousin Jack', the means by which Cornish emigrants asserted and defended their position as the world's premier hard-rock miners. Significantly, as Bottrell's story showed, the deployment of Cornu-English dialect—including words (like *myryan*, 'ant') inherited from the Cornish language—was an essential part of this strategy. That the story was considered appropriate to include in a collection of *traditional* tales was an indication of the impact of the Great Emigration, and with it international modernity, upon the repertoire of Cornish story-telling by the 1880s.

As Bottrell explained:

Cornishmen's clannish propensities are well known and are most apparent when they meet in foreign lands. At the goldfields of Australia, as elsewhere, they stand by and support each other 'through thick and thin'. Cornishmen are also preferred for many kinds of work which require some degree of engineering skill . . . Consequently, many persons from other shires who have never been west of the Tamar try to pass themselves off as Cornishmen, and sometimes succeed in being received into the fellowship of 'One and All'.[38]

However, Bottrell added, this ruse did not always succeed, and if someone was considered guilty of appropriating Cornish credentials in a manner of which was not approved, then language would be deployed to expose him or her:

If . . . the stranger be suspected of 'sailing under false colours', when they are all in familiar chat about nothing in particular, 'Cousin Jackey' will take occasion to say to the new chum 'My dear; ded 'e ever see a duck *klunk a gay*'? If the stranger be up to the intent of the question he will probably reply, 'Learn thy granny to lap ashes', which is the West Country equivalent for teaching the same venerable dame to suck eggs; but, if ignorant of what the question means, he is given to understand that they regard him as an interloper and will be no more deceived by him than a duck can be made to *klunk* (swallow) a *gay* (fragment of broken crockery).[39]

Similarly, in another such test:

> A Cornishman will come behind the stranger who wishes to pass for a genuine Cornishman and say, quite natural-like, 'Mate! There's a green *myryan* on thy *nudack'*. The venomous bite of a green myryan (ant) being much dreaded, a Cornish-man would either put his hand to the nape of his neck, to brush it off, or show in some other way that he understood the meaning—looking 'as dazed as a duck against (on hearing) thunder' the while.[40]

In another tale in his 1880 collection, Bottrell again tackled the issue of the Cornish overseas. In his lengthy story 'Hallantide: or A St Just Feast Fifty Years Ago', Bottrell provided an important insight into the preoccupations and concerns of Cornish people in the early and mid-nineteenth century. Among those 'San Tusters' (St Justers) gathered on 'Feasten Eve' was one Nanny, whose son Tom was anxious to join the emigrant throng that was already making its way to the lead mines of Wisconsin and Illinois: 'Her boy, Tom es roving mad sometimes to get married and be off overseas to a place where many of his comrades went some years ago, and are doing well there, so Tom says. "What's the place called Nancy, that thee art always dreaman about?" "Dodgeville", replied the younger; "es near Mineral Point".'[41]

Once again, it is significant that attitudes to emigration are deemed important enough to be included in a quintessentially traditional portrait of Cornish life, to take their place alongside and as a part of traditional Cornish lore. Indeed, as if to emphasize the point, it was asserted in the same story that in many St Just homes was hung 'that red-hot picture of Vesuvius and the Bay of Naples', a favourite souvenir for Cornishmen returning from abroad 'to let their friends know something of the wonders they have seen'. The Feast's host wanted to know more: '"Come here, Dick, and the rest of 'e, and tell us about this picture and other foreign things that Cousin Jack brought home on his return from his first voyage abroad". Dick looked at the picture and said, "This is the same that one may see in almost every house in Capens Row, and in many on Sandy Bank".'[42]

In his 'Zennor Hearthside Stories' in the same volume, Bottrell recounted a conversation 'with a very intelligent old miner'[43] in which, once more, the overseas Cornish were seen to occupy an important place. Like many others, the 'old miner' had been out in America, and might have stayed there if it had not been for the outbreak of the Civil War. But although he had returned to Cornwall, the experience of being abroad had—he admitted readily—broadened his horizons and altered him for the better:

> a spell of bad times came, and sent me and a good many other Cousin Johneys [*sic*] off to the Lakes [Upper Michigan] and Mineral Point for a time, where I believe many of us would have stopped and sent home for our families if it were not for the cursed kick-up the Yankies made about their darkies, and old Virginia's shore. Well, before we crossed the herring-pool [the Atlantic] I was as bad as the old woman down in St Ives, who was four score and had never been farther than the top of the Stennack, before Whitfield [a colleague of the Wesleys] came one Sunday to preach on Trecoben [*sic*], when all the town went to hear him. The old dame, among the rest, reached the top of the hill, and looking round, declared she never thought the world was half so large, and supposed the hills she could see far away must be France, or Spain, or perhaps some of the foreign countries she had read of in the Bible.[44]

It was significant that it was a Wesleyan preacher (Whitfield), an agent of modernity, who had first challenged the belief system of the 'old dame', albeit unwittingly, the evangelical demands of this new style of preaching forcing her for the first time in her life to travel beyond her immediate environs. Likewise, the 'old miner' himself had benefited from his exposure to the modernity of the New World. But when he returned to Cornwall, he was dismayed that many of the old drolls that he had known as part of the oral tradition of his youth were now being committed to print. His discomfort was two-fold. Now a well-travelled man of the world, there was some embarrassment for him in these quaint stories—'foolish drolls',[45] as he described them—being made available for the amusement of more sophisticated strangers. But there was also real anger that some Cornish people—equipped now with the ability to read and write, the fruits of modernity—were betraying their traditional lore by writing it up deliberately for the delectation of outsiders. His response revealed all the angst of this clash of the old and the new, between traditional belief and modernity:

> I found when I came back from Yankee-land that a lot of our Cousin Johneys who learned to read and write a little had

been telling what they call Cornish stories to enlighten strangers; but, the traitors, they have been telling such a lot of stuff as is only likely to turn their own country and comrades into ridicule. Those who try to make fun of their mates for the amusement of strangers, or for the sake of showing off their fancied superiority, should have their windpipes slit, or their bread-bags ripped up, the dastardly crew.[46]

'A WHITEMAN WHOSE FAMILY WAS FROM CORNWALL'

In Bottrell's stories the distinction between traditional belief and modernity had now become blurred, his final volume—published in 1880—beginning to take account of not only the fast-disappearing drolls of old Cornwall but also the new Cousin Jack narratives that had by then emerged. But as 'old miner' had intimated, in this contact between traditional belief and modernity, the Cornish overseas were in a particularly ambivalent and ambiguous position. They were, like 'old miner', equipped by experience to observe, comment on, and even negotiate the boundaries between traditional belief and modernity. But more than this, they were also part of the 'problem'. On the one hand, as highly-skilled hard-rock miners, they were the very epitome of modernity. But, on the other, they cultivated a protective ethnic exclusivity based on traditional beliefs, values and usages imported from home. Similarly, just as 'new chums' newly arrived from Cornwall —like the individual in Jan Rogers' 'letter'—could be bewildered by the degree of modernity encountered in the communities abroad, so the emigrant Cornish were themselves agents of modernity.

This was not only a result of their superior knowledge and techniques as miners and engineers but because they were, both consciously and unconsciously, foot-soldiers of European intrusion and British imperialism in the new lands. Just as the tragic case of Bridget Cleary reflected the explosive contact between traditional Irish culture and the modernity of British rule, so in Mexico, Cuba, the United States, Australia, New Zealand and elsewhere there are documented cases of similar contact—sometimes explosive, often hostile, almost always uncomprehending, occasionally well-meaning or even altruistic, routinely exploitive—between the Cornish and the indigenous populations of the countries to which they had ventured.[47]

A recent testament to that contact is contained in Boori (Monty) Pryor's book *Maybe Tomorrow*, an early twenty-first century account of the clash between European modernity and traditional Aboriginal culture over several generations in Queensland, Australia. Pryor, an Aborigine, is in part descended from Bert Gribble, the son of Father John Gribble, a Cornish clergyman who in 1892 had founded the

Yarrabah mission for Aborigines. In an affair typical of its time and place, an encounter between colonizer and colonized, young Bert made pregnant fifteen-year-old Jinnah, an Aboriginal orphan girl at the mission. And just as the story of Bridget Cleary has continued to resonate among her kinfolk in County Tipperary down to our own time, so that of Granny Jinnah continues to affect her twenty-first-century descendents in Queensland, finding its place in contemporary Aboriginal story-telling and song. When, in the 1990s, Pryor was shown a photograph of Bert Gribble, his reactions confirmed the enduring impact of that culture clash so many years before: 'Looking at this photo . . . a whiteman whose family was from Cornwall, I had mixed feelings'.[48]

CONCLUSION
With the tale of Bert Gribble and Granny Jinnah, the exploration of the relationship between modernity and tradition has come full circle, revealing both the complexity of the Cornish experience in the nineteenth century and the ability of events long ago to continue to affect individuals and communities today. In an important sense, the early twenty-first-century obsession, academic as well as popular, with the Great Emigration is further evidence of that continuing resonance. The detailed elaboration of numerous family histories—together with the more extended scholarly treatment afforded Cornish emigration—reveals an enduring Cousin Jack grand narrative as significant today as it was in the 1880s when first noticed by Bottrell.

Be that as it may, it is clear from this cursory examination that Cornish folklore—and in particular the fascinating juxtaposition of industrial modernity and traditional belief in the nineteenth century —is a subject ripe for further study. Today, Cornish folklore is generally relegated to traditional stories repackaged in glossy booklets for the tourist trade, or facsimile editions (without the benefit of introductions to set the scene for the modern reader) of the collections by Hunt, Bottrell and Courtney. Regrettably, the innovative and provocative treatment of Cornish folklore initiated by Charles Thomas in the 1950s, which seemed to promise much productive work in the field, has generally not influenced contemporary Cornish Studies practitioners. It is time, then, to return to this overlooked but rich reservoir of material. And in doing so, we can do no better than to take our comparative cue from Angela Bourke, who in her nuanced, inter-disciplinary approach to the story of Bridget Cleary has produced a brilliant model for those wishing to penetrate and understand the interface between modernity and traditional belief.

NOTES AND REFERENCES

1. Angela Bourke, *The Burning of Bridget Cleary: A True Story*, London, 1999, p. 203.
2. Bourke, 1999, p. 203.
3. Bourke, 1999, p. 24.
4. Seamus Deane, dustcover notes, Bourke, 1999.
5. Bourke, 1999, p. 5.
6. Bourke, 1999, p. 58.
7. Bourke, 1999, p. 9.
8. Bourke, 1999, p. 9.
9. Bourke, 1999, p. 62.
10. Bourke, 1999, p. 62.
11. Bourke, 1999, p. 64.
12. Bourke, 1999, p. 82.
13. Bourke, 1999, p. 108.
14. Bourke, 1999, p. 118.
15. Bourke, 1999, p. 21.
16. Bourke, 1999, p. 126.
17. For a discussion of the complexity of Cornish identity in this period see Philip Payton, 'Industrial Celts? Cornish Identity in the Age of Industrial Prowess', in P. Payton (ed.), *Cornish Studies: Ten*, Exeter, 2002, pp. 116–135.
18. P. A. S Pool, *The Life and Progress of Henry Quick of Zennor*, Redruth, 1994, p. 43.
19. *West Briton*, 2 November 1821.
20. *West Briton*, 9 May 1823.
21. *West Briton*, 24 July 1829.
22. *West Briton*, 25 September 1829.
23. M. A. Courtney, *Cornish Feasts and Folklore*, 1890, repub. As *Folklore and Legends of Cornwall*, Exeter, 1989, p. iii.
24. Robert Hunt, *Popular Romances of the West of England*, 1865, repub. Lampeter, 1993, pp. 24-25.
25. Hunt, 1865 & 1993, pp. 22–3.
26. Courtney, 1890 & 1989, pp. 126–7.
27. Courtney, 1890 & 1989, p. 127.
28. Courtney, 1890 & 1989, p. 127.
29. Courtney, 1890 & 1989, p. 127.
30. Courtney, 1890 & 1989, p. 128.
31. Courtney, 1890 & 1989, p. 208.
32. *West Briton*, 14 July 1843.
33. *West Briton*, 14 July 1843.
34. Alan M. Kent, '"Drill Cores": A Newly-found Manuscript of Cousin Jack Narratives from the Upper Peninsula of Michigan, USA', in P. Payton (ed.), *Cornish Studies: Twelve*, Exeter, 2004, pp. 106–43.
35. Kent, 2004, p. 137.
36. *Yorke's Peninsula Advertiser*, 3 March 1876.
37. *Yorke's Peninsula Advertiser*, 25 February 1876.

38. William Bottrell, *Stories and Folk-lore of West Cornwall*, 1880, repub. Felinfach, 1996, p. 183.
39. Bottrell, 1880 & 1996, p. 183.
40. Bottrell, 1880 & 1996, p. 184.
41. Bottrell, 1880 & 1996, p. 52. Nanny is apparently Tom's mother; Nancy is a younger woman.
42. Bottrell, 1880 & 1996, pp. 52–3.
43. Bottrell, 1880 & 1996, p. 80.
44. Bottrell, 1880 & 1996, p. 81.
45. Bottrell, 1880 & 1996, p. 80.
46. Bottrell, 1880 & 1996, p. 81.
47. See Philip Payton, *The Cornish Overseas: A History of Cornwall's Great Emigration*, Fowey, 2005.
48. Boori (Monty) Pryor, *Maybe Tomorrow*, Melbourne, 2004, p. 126. I am grateful to Ann Trevenen Jenkin for kindly drawing my attention to this book.

JEWISH GHOSTS, KNACKERS, TOMMYKNOCKERS, AND OTHER SPRITES OF CAPITALISM IN THE CORNISH MINES

Paul Manning

INTRODUCTION

The Cornish were so stereotypically associated with hard rock mining during its golden age in the American West that one joking definition of the word 'mine' was 'a hole in the ground with a Cornish man at the bottom'.[1] A mine was the intersection of natural geological features (a hole in the ground) and cultural ethnic ones (the Cornish man at the bottom). For the Cornish, too, what it meant to be Cornish stood at the intersection of ethnicity and geology, nature and culture. The Cornish diaspora turned their ethnicity into a claim on technical expertise in hard rock mining that in the nineteenth century made a Cornish miner a necessary adjunct to mines all over the world.[2] Nor was the claim entirely ungrounded. Cornwall was the place where hard rock mining was pioneered in all its aspects; not merely technical, but also financial and even superstitious ones. The institutions associated with Cornish mining went wherever Cornish miners went, which is to say, every-where and anywhere there was a hole in the ground, for the Cornish were a very migratory people.[3] Cornish identity was a very saleable commodity, a set of claims of expertise over hard rock mining, that guided the movements of the Cornish throughout the world.[4]

In this article I am concerned with the superstitions of mining, specifically folkloric ideas about Jews and Fairies and Jewish fairies in Cornish mines. I am also interested in the changing social ontology that underlies these beliefs, including changing forms and formulations of anti-Semitism, as well as changing notions of nature and economy, from medieval to modern Cornwall that underlie these superstitions.[5] But, in a move that will surprise no one, I will argue that these beliefs are embedded in technical and financial and other institutional aspects of their mining context. Part of this context is the rise of Cornish-style capitalist modernity. It includes changing ideas about nature and exchange that would bring dead Jewish miners to life as nature spirits, and then later, banish them from nature to the hazy supernatural half-life of folklore.

Cornish mining developed and spread with capitalism, or rather, was developed and spread as a specific local form of capitalism, a 'culture of capitalism'. This culture of capitalism included both things we now tend to think of as technical and natural, those relating to industrial production, as well as those social and non-natural things we think of as being essential to capitalist exchange, such as specific forms of capital and wages. But it also included things that were not so immediately pragmatic and utilitarian, things that belonged not to the natural world of brute facts, but some other world of beliefs and stories. These beliefs and stories involved certain kinds of spirits, specifically the ghosts of Jewish miners who were also fairies. In this article I will bracket specific problems of causation between these seemingly different and incommensurable worlds of production, exchange, and superstitious ideology, because such problems are vexatious and possibly artefactual, and simply discuss each sort of thing alongside all the others. The story is interesting enough, I think, to tell it in an unprincipled and eclectic way.

Viewed in retrospect, then, Cornish 'mining culture' included what we capitalist moderns think of as purely technical matters, involving the socialization of nature, a labour process of production determined by the natural realities of hard rock mining, in which the Cornish were key innovators.[6] Cornish mining culture also included matters we think of as purely conventional or social, matters of exchange such as indigenous methods of adapting this labour process of production to capital. In Cornwall, innovations in the organization of production and exchange included both unique methods in recruiting capital (the cost book system)[7] and unique wage contract systems (the tribute system). According to this common sense view of capitalism production is divided from exchange as nature from culture. Both of these things, production and exchange, however, stand together in our common sense view as a kind of natural, real 'base' to a superstructural category of interesting but basically unreal' things we call the supernatural. In this case, this includes beliefs in spirits and supernatural agents, spectral 'others', associated with the production process.[8]

The Cornish culture of capitalism included all these different kinds of things, and this culture proved able to move along with Cornish miners wherever hard rock mining was to be done. In terms of production, Cornish miners of the diaspora came to be known as 'Cousin Jacks', and Cousin Jacks were found in mining communities across the New World.[9] A hole in the ground could not be dignified with the term 'mine' anywhere in the world unless a Cousin Jack miner was at the bottom of it. Ethnic identity and skill were one in the figure of the Cousin Jack miner. In matters of exchange, too, the cost-book system and the wage systems of Cornish mines, piecework systems like the tribute system, which shared risk between labour and capital, were introduced elsewhere in Britain and all over the world throughout the nineteenth century.[10] Lastly, Cornish mining spirits followed Cornish miners throughout the world, creating an Atlantic 'faerie diaspora' that mirrored, or even exceeded, the real one.[11] Here, I trace the mutations in Cornish identity and self-definition and the identity of their spectral others in relation to changes both in the labour process and the valorization process of capital.[12]

But first, I need to introduce the basic folkloric narrative that I am trying to locate in terms of a changing culture of capitalism. I am going to give a short overview of this story. It begins in the sixteenth century with Cornish tinners alleging that the most ancient miners, what are usually called 'the old men', were Jews; in the nineteenth century, as mining moves underground, so do these mining Jews, but they become associated with ghosts and fairies called 'knackers' in the process; lastly, as these miners take their ghosts to the mines of the new world, they adopt the Ellis Island name of 'Tommy knockers' and their Jewish ethnicity disappears.

GOING UNDERGROUND
First of all, there is the problem of Jews becoming miners, then ghosts, and then fairies, in Cornish mining. It is frequently claimed that beliefs in underground mining spirits are basically universal, and there may be something to this.[13] This is usually linked to the universally uncanny experience of the 'anti-world' of mining, the subterraneanness and danger of mining leads to all manner of superstitions, just as it is often said that sailors, vulnerable to the whims of the high seas, are very superstitious. The simplicity of the analysis does not mean it is wrong. If it is true it would be simply the natural, technical aspect of mining that is relevant to the analysis: when you go underground, perhaps deep underground as with hard rock mining, you begin to establish different, and opposed, norms for behaviour compared to that which exists above ground, and perhaps opposed belief systems. Taboos appear that oppose the surface world to the mining world, such as bans

on whistling, the presence of women, making the sign of the cross, and so on, common amongst later Cornish miners.[14] Maybe it is just because mines are frightening, dark and dangerous. It could be as simple as that.

Now, Cornish tinners have had beliefs about 'others' involved in production, called 'the old men' and often identified with 'Jews' and sometimes 'Saracens', long before mining itself went 'underground'. The immediate evidence for these predecessors was the wooden picks and shovels found in streaming (mining in streams), which were attributed to 'Jews' just as the ruins of old smelting houses (called 'Jew's Houses'), old styles of ingots, old mining works and in general all evidence of older styles of mining by 'the old men' (earlier miners using different technologies) were summarily attributed to Jews or Saracens.[15] However, it was only when mining went underground, a move from streaming to lode mining, that these Jews moved from temporally displaced deceased predecessors, the old men, to spectral contemporaries, nature spirits or ghosts. But they remained Jews. As Ghosts, they were uncannily both predecessors and contemporaries, ghosts of dead Jewish miners. Just as their technology (same function, different substance) was both similar and different, so too they were themselves present and absent, self (miner) and other (Jew). In the old world, these ghosts remained the ghosts of Jews even as they were assimilated to the world of fairies. In the new world, they ceased being Jews and ceased being fairies, and moved from being the anonymous spirits of the old men to being the spirits of the recently dead miners, specifically, those that died mining. Presently, they ceased to be anything at all, and died the second death of all spirits in a disenchanted world.[16]

So the Jews became by turns ghosts, fairies and then nothing at all. But how did the old men, the anonymous mining predecessors, come to be identified with Jews? And why are the Jews always imagined as *workers*? We find 'Jews' as spectral others (whether natural predecessors or supernatural contemporaries engaged in the same activity as the self), in Cornish mining from the very start. As Victorian commentators historicized and naturalized these Jewish miners as real historical Jews, the fact that these were Jewish *workers* bothered them a great deal. By the nineteenth century, 'Jew' and 'Worker' were supposed to be non-intersecting sets. Therefore, Folklore must have 'got it wrong'. Victorians offered rationalizations of the Cornish beliefs that insisted that the Jews must have been involved in Cornish mining not as *producers*, that is, as engaged in the *labour process* of mining (that is, the actual concrete technical process of work), as the Cornish stories implied. Rather, the story goes, because they were Jews, they must have been involved in the tin industry as merchants and usurers, in the *valorization* process (under mercantilism, this would presumably mean advancing risk capital against future earnings, and in general the buying, selling and smelting of the tin).

All of this assumes that when these stories arose an essentially capitalist working class of 'tinners' could be distinguished from the other 'tinners' who engaged in other aspects of the process. The folklore makes no distinction, just as everyone is a tinner who has to do with tin on any level, so we find spectral 'Jews' from the 'point of production' all the way to the market, where the Victorians felt Jews would more properly 'belong'. My argument here is not only that the earlier system did not have a clear distinction between production and non-production, workers and others (capitalists, for example, or merchants), but further, that the relevant distinction is a similar one, based on the distinction between a natural economy of farming (against which miners in Cornwall seem to have always opposed them- selves, even if, as is likely they engaged in it 'part time') in which the product is an immediate use-value, and the 'unnatural economy' of mining, in which everyone who is engaged is only interested in the product as an item to be exchanged for money. Hence, it makes sense for everyone involved to stand to the 'natural economy' of the farmers as 'Jews' to 'Christians', money to useful things.

RISK: WEALTH AND DEATH

So, in this article I am interested in the supernaturalization of the stories of Jews so that Jewish miners come to be nature spirits. I am also interested in how Jews ever got to be involved in Cornish mining at all. And lastly, I am interested in how Jewish spirits are associated with different kinds of risk in mining. Roughly, Jewish spirits, called 'knackers', are good omens, guardians of natural wealth, indicating the presence of ore, lucky strikes and mother lodes, in Cornwall. In the new world, they are no longer imagined as Jews, or fairies, and they no longer guard wealth. These new spirits, the Tommyknockers, instead are often the ghosts of miners who died from mining accidents, and they are portents of the risk of death.[17]

As mining becomes specifically capitalist and moves underground, the 'Jews' are assimilated to the world of ghosts and faeries, and begin to be called 'Knackers', Knockers' or 'Tommy knockers'. While the earlier 'Jews' were indicators, I suggest, of a 'unnatural' economy of mining, a whole trade that ran all the way from the Cornish stream- works to London, every link of the chain being at once an act of production and exchange, in the capitalist period production comes to be opposed to exchange within this unnatural economy (which is still opposed to the natural agrarian economy in which it is embedded).[18] In a productivist ideology of capitalism, the production process is imagined as being a relatively natural metabolism between nature and culture, but fettered and subordinated to an entirely unnatural logic of exchange.[19] The erstwhile spirits of exchange come to be associated with production *within* exchange, or production *for* exchange, nature spirits who represent the sorts of risks inherent in a labour contract that involves both natural variables and contractual ones. Accordingly, the spirits move from being associated with exchange to being associated with material production and material wealth, that is, the presence of lodes.

This brings us to a third change: the personalities and moral character of the spirits varies with the nature of the wage contract system. Miners working tribute systems (a species of internal contract piecework system in which the wage is directly proportional to production at some rate of shillings paid to pound value of ore raised), who therefore share the risk of the capitalist and have an interest in finding ore, have different views of the nature of spirits than those who work an simple time based system.[20] In the former, the spirits tend to be associated as signs or portents of wealth, in the latter, they are signs or portents of danger.[21] In the former, they express a category of risk with components that are both natural (the whereabouts of lodes) and conventional (the contract struck that month), accordingly the spirits themselves are hybrids, nature spirits and the ghosts of Jews. In the latter, with a time based contract, the spirits express the only variable that is likely to interest a miner working on the clock: danger and death. The category of risk associated with the supernatural does not change, but the question is what the risk is, wealth or death, spirits of wealth (tributing) or spirits of danger (time wages). The spirits become more malevolent as the miner's relation to production is increasingly alienated.

ALL ABOARD: COUSIN JACKS AND TOMMYKNOCKERS IN THE NEW WORLD

The last change in the spirit world is simply the one in which all the Old World associations are lost, and these spirits, now called 'Tommyknockers', move into every mine with the same authority as the Cornish miner, losing all attributes of fairies and Jews.[22] As the Cornish move to the New World, Cornish identity in the New World becomes essentially an expression of technical experience.[23] Cornish immigrants not involved in the Cornish pastime of hard rock mining quickly assimilate; those involved in mining retain ethnicity since this ethnicity is a claim on essentialized technical experience and skills.[24]

Just as Cornish farmers and fishermen generally disappear into other ethnicities in the New World, so too their associated spirits (Piskies, Spriggans, associated with farmers, mermaids associated with fishermen) disappear. But the tenacity of Cornishness as a category of production ('Cousin Jacks') is identical to the tenacity of the mining spirits, who are also associated with production. The Tommyknockers come to control the mines on a supernatural plane as the Cousin Jacks do on the natural plane. Even non-Cornish ethnic miners can be found with Tommyknocker stories.[25]

Now that I have told the story in outline, I should like to go into a little more detail about each of these transitions.

JEWS

> 'An ancient story I'll tell you anon,
> Which is older by far than the days of King John;
> But this you should know, that that red-robed sinner
> Robb'd the Jew of the gold he had made as a tinner.'[26]

Stories of Jewish miners appear with the very first narrative reports about Cornish tin-miners, generally called tinners, dating from the late sixteenth and early seventeenth centuries. In any area in which mining has been pursued over long historical period, at any point in history, contemporary miners are going to encounter evidence of previous workings, what are generally called 'Old Men's works', the mining predecessors generally being called 'the old men'. In Cornwall, however, from the very start, these old men are identified with Jews. The very first chapter of the first description we have of the Cornish tinners is entitled 'Of the working [of] Tinworks by the Saxons which tinners call Jewes working.'[27] The evidence of these Jewish predecessors itself was empirical, the presence of working implements in old works made not of iron, but of wood. In this period tinning was primarily for stream tin (stream works), and not mined deep underground. Our earliest author, Thomas Beare writing in 1586, disagreed with the tinners, believing that the old men were not Jews, but another heathen people, perhaps Saxons (I have modernized the spelling for the convenience of the modern reader):

> It appears by working of our tinners in Cornwall that the Saxons, being heathen people (when they inhabited our country) were skilful workers and searchers for black tin, which in those ancient days wrought not with spades and working tools made of iron as we have now in our time but all

of the hart of oak, they as got their tin and their blowing
houses hard by their works and so made it white, for proof
whereof diverse workers of our time have found their shovels,
spades and mattocks made all of oak and holm in diverse and
sundry places as they have searched for tin in old waste
ground they have found white tin blown likewise. . . . But
whatsoever they were either Saxons or Danes or any other
nations our tin workers . . . call and term their places by the
name of the working of Jews.[28]

Thomas Beare disagreed with the tinners that the earlier miners
had been Jews, on the grounds that it did not make sense historically:
first, all Jews were exiled from England in 1291, second, they were
never granted any liberty to search for tin, and third, they never
showed any interest in leaving cities.[29]

This account is paralleled a generation later in Carew's *Survey of
Cornwall*, of 1602. Echoing a tinners' myth ('a strong imagination') also
mentioned in Beare's account to the effect that the distribution of tin is
the result of Noah's Flood,[30] Carew goes on to explain the way in
which stream and moor tin lead to tin lodes, and the correspondingly
different methods of working tin. Under this rubric he adds:

(The Cornish tinners) maintain these works to have been very
ancient, and first wrought by the *Jews* with pickaxes of Holm,
Box and Hart's Horn: They prove this by the name of those
places yet enduring, to wit, *Attal Sarazin*, in English, the *Jew's
offcast*, and by those tools daily found amongst the rubble of
such works . . . There are also taken up in such works, certain
little tools heads of brass, which some term thunder-axes, but
they make small showing of any profitable use.[31]

Some such story about Jewish involvement in Cornish mines is
repeated in every subsequent account, and Beare's doubts notwithstanding, it is transposed from a belief of the tinners to a historical
fact by the nineteenth century. But even as the Jewish tinners are
transformed into a historical fact, there remained something potentially
bothersome about the story, summed up in the apparent oxymoron
'Jewish workers'. Nineteenth-century anti-Semitism could easily see
Jewish involvement in the financial end of the tin works, perhaps in
the 'natural' Jewish role as usurers and merchants, but certainly not
working (unless they were slaves!). Some accepted the alleged fact of
Jews in Cornwall, suitably emended from diligent workers to usurious
merchants. The natural historian Borlase seems to be the first to

emend the account to see British workers exploited by Romans or Jews (the former engrossing the mines under direct supervision, the latter acting, like the Phoenicians and Greeks before them, in a more indirect mercantilist fashion) always on the basis of natural historical evidence, never referring directly to folkloric evidence:[32]

> In one of the workings here were lately found, about eight feet under the surface, two slabs, or small blocks of melted tin, of about twenty eight pounds weight each, of a shape very different from that which for many years has obtained in Cornwall; as they have no stamp on them, probably as old as the time when the Jews had engrossed the tin manufacture in the time of King John.[33]

> So by their coins, sepulchres, and sacrificial instruments found in and near the ancient tin-works, (whither nothing perceivable could tempt them, but the riches of those mines) it is as apparent that the Romans worked those mines, or at least with their soldiers superintended the workmen. At this time the Britons had likely little or no property; they were working miners under their conquerors, but what regulations they were subject to is uncertain.[34]

By the nineteenth century, such accounts are continued, partially with reference to folkloric traditions. For example, Hunt's account of 1881 accepts the reality of the Jews, but stresses that they were not workers, but merchants:

> Tradition informs us that the Christian churches upon Dartmoor, which are said to have been built about the reign of John, were reared by the Jews. Once, and once only, I heard the story told in more detail. They, the Jews, did not actually work in the tin streams and mines of the Moor, but they employed tinners, who were Christians; and the king imposed on the Jew Merchants the condition that they should build churches for their miners.[35]

Others accepted Jewish workers, but added that they were enslaved under the Romans. Still others, notably the linguist Max Muller, insisted that this was a 'verbal myth', like many others, a 'disease of language' resulting from false etymology:[36]

There is hardly a book on Cornish history or antiquities in which we are not seriously informed that at some time or other the Jews migrated to Cornwall, or worked as slaves in the Cornish mines. Some writers state this simply as a fact requiring no further confirmation; others support it by that kind of evidence which Herodotus, no doubt, would have found sufficient.[37]

Using the new methods of philological science, Muller explained away each of these verbal myths as mutations of ordinary words. Offering a true 'natural history' of discourse, Muller grounds these myths in an appropriately geological metaphor, explaining that languages change by a *metamorphic process*, which

> consists chiefly in this, that words, as they cease to be properly understood, are slightly changed, generally with the object of imparting to them once again a more intelligible meaning. This meaning is mostly a mistaken one, but the word in its new dress and with its new character is frequently made to support facts and fictions which could not be supported by other evidence.[38]

Using philological arguments and verbal metamorphic processes, he dispenses with the Jewishness of such alternate places names as *Marazion* and *Market Jew*, as well as the Jews of *Jew's Houses* and the Saracens of *Attal Sarazin* , finding instead English reinterpretations of opaque Cornish etymologies: 'Thus vanish the Jews from Cornwall.'[39]

From all these varied responses we see that, one way or another, the Jewish tinners were turned into creatures commensurate with historical fact and natural history, most especially the latter, their behaviour was brought into line with the canons of 'natural' occupations for Jews according to nineteenth-century anti-Semitism. Beginning with the natural historians of the eighteenth century and continuing into the nineteenth century, in elite accounts, the behaviour of the Jews of Cornwall is made concordant with beliefs about the stereotypical position of Jews within a European economy, and the Jews are historicized and taken from a mythic or folkloric order into a natural, historical order. The result of these historicizations is that the Jews are reconciled with natural history, and the Cornish Jews are either explained away or their customs and habits reconciled with notions of appropriate Jewish behaviour.

What was it that is so distressing about 'Jewish workers' that caused some to turn them into ante-diluvian merchants? The problem seems to be not so much the territorial incongruity of Jews in Cornwall, but rather that these Jews appear rather insistently as figures involved in *production* and not *exchange*. Nineteenth century political economy and industrial capitalism differs from mercantilism in that the structure of industrial relations clearly is divided into two great spheres, one of production, one of exchange. Production was understood to be human technical interaction with nature, 'industry', while exchange was understood a largely conventional world of purely social forms, 'the market'. As involvement with production came to be a general measure of social worth, those spheres of the economy more distant from production, for example finance capital, were increasingly seen as unnatural and parasitic fetters on the real source of social wealth and thence social worth, production. This particular set of ideologies that links social worth to natural, material production is generally called productivism. The emerging productivist narrative of anti-Semitism places the figure of the Jew squarely in the parasitic world of exchange, and freeborn Britons in the intrinsically valuable role of production.

Anti-semitism changes as the interpretation of the economy does: nineteenth century anti-semitism was not medieval anti-semitism. Later rationalizers, living within a productivist universe, insist that what this account 'must' mean is that the Jewish tinner, a non-productive figure of monetary exchange and usury par excellence, among other things, was involved in mining as a mercantile interest, not as what we would now call 'immediate producers'. But as we will see, the only constant factor in the figure of the Jewish tinner and his later supernatural form is that he is a figure of production.

But in these earliest accounts, before the Jews follow the miners underground and become sprites or ghosts, it seems we have a rather different opposition at work, embedded in a different understanding of economic relations, a mercantilist one in which production or technical aspects of labour process are not discretely separated and mediated once and for all from the social, conventional, economic aspects of exchange. In short, the opposition between industrial *production* (implying a uniquely identifiable group of productive workers) and monetary *exchange* (implying a group of owners, shareholders, merchant interests in opposition to the former group), is not easily identifiable and has no relevance to this distinction. This is partially because the different groups involved in tin production cannot be easily opposed to other another, and all activities involving tin, both 'production' and 'exchange', fade one into the other, forming a whole 'trade' of tinning. Different 'technical' aspects of the trade, from getting the tin, and processing it, and smelting it, and so on, are distributed across different groups mediated by a series of relations of monetary exchange as well: tinners dig for black tin and sell it to smelters who smelt it and sell it to tin merchants and so on. A tinner, then, is anyone engaged in the 'trade' of tinning from start to finish. The prototype definition offered by Beare is someone who by themselves does 'the whole trade', that is, takes the tin from the ground to the market, doing everything by himself. But under this definition, Beare complains, there would be few if any tinners. He then follows the tin-working from the ground all the way to London, and finds all those along the way to be tinners.[40]

Nor is there a divide in industrial organization at this stage between workers and owners at the point of production. A given tin concern is divided into shares called doles, at a rate of one dole per participant. The contributions of partners in the concern is at this point measured not in money, but in labour, each dole representing the labour of one participant, and at the same time, representing a right to one share of the wealth realized by that work.[41] This labour can be given in kind or via a representative who stands in for the owner of the dole for the entirety of the year. In turn, one who is working the right or dole of another can put in another form of labourer, a day labourer called a Spaliard, to replace his labour on a daily basis.[42] The relationship between labour and capital does not oppose adventurers or owners in the aggregate to workers in the aggregate, but rather, each share represents both an obligation to labour and a right to the proceeds, and each wage contract essentially involves *delegating* the labour represented by a single dole to some other worker over a longer or shorter period of time.[43] The captain, in latter-day mines exclusively representative of capital, a manager, is ambiguous in function at this period, likely reflecting a highly uneven situation on the ground during the period, with enterprises ranging in size from small partnerships to large enterprises with something more clearly resembling an emergent capitalist form of organization. According to Beare, the captain must be a tinner working a dole, appointed by his fellows, and effectively acts as a representative of the mining group, dealing with the sale of tin, and equitable division of proceeds, which includes some managerial functions like assigned spales (fines) for missed work.[44] According to Carew, writing not long after, the captain is a figure found exclusively in quasi-capitalist larger mines where there appears to be one adventurer with many shares: 'If the worke carrie some importance, and require the travaille of many hands, that hath this name, and they their Overseer, whome they term their Captaine.'[45]

With the exception, perhaps, of these larger concerns, the organization of production does not serve to identify any specific group of people who resemble labour or capital, and the main form of exploitation of surplus value at this period is mercantilist, involving advances of risk capital to working miners for subsistence by smelters, black tin merchants or white tin merchants. Therefore, the primary way that surplus value is realized is, in effect, usury, and this happens at each stage in the production and exchange process.[46]

So if the image of the 'Jewish tinner' is not keyed to a productivist opposition between material production, that is, industry, versus exchange, that is, the market (as it would be, for example, in National Socialist ideology), this is because the opposition between 'production' and 'exchange' is not 'visible' under this pre-capitalist social formation. Instead, we find spectral 'Jews' attending the entire tinner's trade from production to market (Jewish wooden tools, Jewish smelting houses and Jewish ingots), but most especially in the production end. What then does the figure of the 'Jew' oppose itself to?

My best guess is that the Jewish tinner is the opposite of the Christian peasant. The activity of the tinner, understood as every branch of the tin trade from production to market, is opposed to agricultural activities as unnatural to natural economy in the Aristotelian sense. That is, the goal of a natural economy, such as farming, is not value (expressed in the money form) but use-values (often immediate consumption). For such an opposition to exist it is not necessary for farming or mining to be exclusive full-time occupations or unchanging status, rather, it is much more likely that prior to industrial capitalism tinning was a side activity engaged seasonally: 'Each year, with spring ploughing and lambing past . . . [a farmer-miner] would set off each day from about the middle of April . . . [and] toil in the shallow trenches which represented his workings until July or August when the call of the harvest would return him to full-time work on his farm.'[47] Farming differs from tinning as activities, in that the one has as its goal production of immediate use-values, production leads immediately to consumption, whereas the other production leads to exchange, the tinner desires money, not tin, unlike the farmer. Hence, all aspects of the tin trade exist under the sign of money, they are all related to exchange in that their goal is exchange and not consumption. As Beare and Carew make clear, the tin trade is shot through with usury as well at each link in the chain. Moreover, since norm is based on the economy of use-values, whose ends, human needs, are qualitative and finite, the economy of the tinners seems unnatural in that its ends, money, is measured quantitatively and infinite. Hence, we will see, the figure of the devil comes to be associated with tin-work as a figure of uncanny productivity. But it is more particularly the local tinners who must distinguish themselves and their activities from those of 'normal' Christian farmers. Other aspects of the subculture of the tinners reported by Beare, including an 'anti-language' called 'tinner's language' and various rituals expressive of solidarity, indicates that tinners and tin-work were at that time opposed as a marked activity.[48] Presumably this is why the tinners claimed that the original tinners must have been Jews, because in a late medieval form of anti-Semitism, Jews were in effect not merely signs of usury, but money-oriented ('monetized') economies in general, including both what we later think of production and exchange.

The figure of the Jew, then, sums up and condenses the opposition between a 'Christian' natural economy, consisting primarily of diverse agricultural and pastoral labour processes that are united by a common teleology of autarchic subsistence, use-values produced for consumption, over and against an equally various set of 'Jewish' labour processes that are each performed not for use-values but as part of exchange. The former appears as a 'Christian' way of life, the latter 'Jewish'.

GIANTS

This would have been the case in the pre-modern period, in which involvement in the monetary economy would have been more anomalous. The tinners of Beare's period are forced to view themselves and their activities from the perspective of the hegemonic viewpoint of non-monetized peasant subsistence activities, standing as outsiders, 'Jews' to the backgrounded and unremarkable status of 'Christian' peasants.[49] By the nineteenth century we encounter a series of stories in which the tinners are represented by a positive figure, Jack the Tinkeard (or Tinker), who stands in opposition to farmers who are identified with a race of pre-human Giants. The giants of these stories seem to represent undifferentiated agricultural labour expressible in strength as opposed to skilled labour represented by Jack the Tinker.[50] Jack the Tinker is a kind of culture hero who comes to Cornwall from a land far away in a mythic time when Cornwall is inhabited by Giants. The land Jack comes from is also inhabited by giants, but these giants are tinners, unlike the farmer giants of Cornwall. Indeed, these far away giants seem to have been taught to engage in tinning by certain 'wise men' (Bottrell calls them 'merchants') who engage in what is a fairly obvious form of mercantilist exploitation:

> He was bred in a country more than a month's journey to the East . . . [H]e well remembered . . . living on the moors amidst the hills with a company of men, some called them giants, who streamed for tin in those cold regions, where the hills were covered with snow a great part of the year. Merchants from a

city at no great distance, often came to the moors to purchase tin, and they brought the tinner's tools and food in exchange.[51]

In this land [whence Jack came] there were many giants, who digged for tin and other treasures . . . Many, many more strange things did the tinkeard tell. Amongst other matters, he spoke of wise men who came from a city at no great distance from this land of tin for the purpose of buying the tin from the giants, and they left them tools, and other things, that the diggers required in exchange.[52]

The Cornish giants, by contrast, are dumb, strong, and use only the simplest of implements, knowing nothing of money, tin or tools. Jack is forced to teach them over and over how skill and dexterity will beat strength, and how the raw materials that surround them can be converted into wealth by skill: 'Tom [the Giant] won the prize in all games in which brute force was more required than science: the tinkeard was always the victor in such as depended more on dexterity and trained skill than mere strength.'[53] The Cornish giants are figures representing a kind of natural economy, they are ever satisfied with what they have, and see no reason to aspire for more, they clearly represent agricultural workers and farmers. These giants both do not 'know tin', and their desires are simple, limited ones that can be satisfied without recourse to monetized economies:

'Look here you, Jack,' says Tom [the giant]; 'whatever could possess the old fools of giants to heap up such a lot of black and gray mining-stones against the wall? wherever could they have found them all?'
Jack carefully looked at the stuff thus laid bare, clapped his hands together, and shouted—
'By the gods, it's all the richest tin!'
Now Tom, poor easy-going soul, 'didn't knaw tin;' so he could scarcely believe Jack, though Jack had told him that he came from a tin country.
'Why, Tom,' says Jack, 'thee art a made man. If these banks are all tin, then there is enough to buy all the land, and all the houses, from sea to sea.'
'What do I care for the tin; haven't I all a man can desire? My lands are all stocked with sheep and horned cattle. We shall never lack the best beef and mutton, and we want no better than our honest homespun.'[54]

In fact, Tom and his wife find this whole notion of unlimited wealth, represented by the discovery of a form of wealth, tin, that was not immediately useful, but of unlimited value, to be extremely upsetting: 'Tom and Jane professed to treat lightly the discovery of the tin, it was clear that they thought deeply about it, and their thoughts spoiled their appetites. It was evidently an accession of wealth which they could not understand.'[55] Tom's notions of wealth are rooted in immediate use values, not monetized in terms of exchange value. Moreover, this autarkic wealth of use-values is reckoned in having sufficient quantities of simple foods and goods, beef, mutton and homespun cloth, not unlimited quantities of qualitatively different goods, fancy foods clothes purchased with tin at market that Jack will teach them to desire by the end of the story.[56]

Aside from being simple in their tastes, ignorant of tin and generally suspicious of money, the giants are also quite strong, a feature which again opposes them to skilled workers like Jack the Tinker. Their first combat illustrates the principle that skill beats strength, though Tom believes that Jack is the devil:

> The tinkeard showed Tom that he had no cloven foot, and told him that it depended more on handiness than strength to conquer with the single-stick; and that a small man with science could beat a big man with none. The tinkeard then took the clumsy bar of the gate from Tom, gave him his own light and tough blackthorn, and proceeded to teach him to make the easiest passes, cuts &c.[57]

Throughout the nineteenth century agricultural activities and physical strength defined occupations that were the bottom of any Victorian labour hierarchy. The properties that made an agricultural worker were natural properties that humans shared with animals, primarily physical strength and undifferentiated labour, while those that made a skilled industrial worker were those properties, skill and technique, that had to be learned and separated humans from animals. Such an opposition that opposed raw animal physical strength with agricultural workers ('farmers') and skill and dexterity with skilled industrial workers ('miners') is found across variety of skilled occupations on both sides of the Atlantic.[58] These included sets of occupational myths by which skilled workers defined themselves over and against the undifferentiated, purely quantitative labour and strength of agricultural workers and unskilled workers called 'Navvies'.[59] These Cornish stories that oppose the Tinner culture hero Jack the Tinker to the simple and strong Tom the Giant resemble Paul

Bunyan myths of Western extractive industries, which, as Nancy Quam-Wickham shows,

> reveal the folk and class values of Western workers, values that downplayed physical prowess in work processes reinforcing workers' belief in skill as the most important and distinctive attribute of a competent, successful, and manly worker. Paul Bunyan, for all his superhuman strength, often failed in his efforts to harvest the wealth of the forests or bring in a successful producing oil well. In both settings, Paul's actions often become blunders, and his persona borders on buffoonery.[60]

The older occupational mythology that opposed Jewish tinners implicitly to Christian farmers seems to revolve around the opposition of ends between a labour process whose goal is an 'artificial' goal of money (tinning, associated with Jewish predecessors), and one whose goal is a 'natural' economy of directly consumable use-values. The newer occupational mythology of Jack the Tinker also features a culture hero, a mythic predecessor, who comes from far away to civilize Cornwall, bringing with him changes not only in production (tinning and all manner of other skills), but also newer concepts of limitless consumption based on money and the market. Both of these innovations are confusing to the old order (the natural agricultural economy of farmers represented by Tom the Giant), who cannot see how skill can defeat raw undifferentiated strength, any more than they can understand a world of limitless desire, both in quantity and qualitative differentiation, brought by monetary forms of wealth. In this mythic world, it is the farmers' turn to feel a bit out of place, assimilated to a dying race of stupid giants imagined from the perspective of a civilizing process wrought by a tinner culture hero.

KNACKERS

If eighteenth and nineteenth-century elites showed a tendency to rationalize, historicize and naturalize the Jewish tinners as being creatures that could be understood in the terms of a 'natural history', the miners themselves went in the opposite direction, 'supernaturalizing' the Jews by assimilating them to other forms of supernatural alterity. By the arrival of the natural historians and Wesleyanism to Cornwall, elite and lay accounts, the account of the parson or the historian and the account of the tinner, begin to move in opposed epistemic directions, towards naturalization and towards supernaturalization, respectively, always with a sideways glance at the other.[61] As one tinner told the folklorist Bottrell in the late nineteenth century: 'I know the strangers . . . and grand learned folks like our [parson], don't believe in [spirits] we [call] knackers workan in the bals [mines], and say that the noise, made by these old ghosts of tinners, is caused by water oazin out of a lode and drippen into a pit.'[62]

Ironically enough, with the advent of a unified concept of nature as a relatively monolithic, homogenous entity opposed to human artifice, *nature* spirits themselves would be banished from the realm of *nature*, replaced with natural explanations in elite accounts or banished to the realm of the supernatural in lay accounts.

As mining went from streamworks to underground lode works, and as the structure of the mines became more or less a recognizably capitalist sort of venture, the Jews of the mines also changed, they came back to life. Moving from being mythic old men knowable only through their tools and works, they came to be supernatural presences, and attracted to themselves all manner of supernatural attributes of ghosts, demons, and fairies. In the earliest period the 'old men', predecessors in the mining world, presented themselves only indirectly through material signs of their work, old tools, old mines, each of which was uncanny in the sense that they both resemble and differ from the tools and works of contemporary miners. The miners themselves were 'other' in two senses, that they were definitively dead and gone, and that they were ethnic 'others' who differed from miners in that they were Jews, but were similar in that, like miners and unlike peasantry, they were related to the unfamiliar and uncanny world of exchange.

We hear little of these Jews until the nineteenth century, when they reappear, sometimes through the same material signs, wooden tools, as before, but now they have followed the miners underground, and they have become associated with supernatural, spectral alterity. They are still dead, but not gone. For they are present in different spectral forms, assimilated in different ways to different forms of 'supernatural' presence, including ghosts, fairies, supernatural evils as well as empty superstititions. This oft-cited passage from Charles Kingsley's novel *Yeast: A Problem*, shows the ways in which all these different features of fairies, Jews, ghosts and the devil (supernatural evil and hell) had become bundled together by the nineteenth century:

'Well, sir, I got into a great furze-croft, full of deads (those are the earth-heaps they throw out of the shafts), where no man in his senses dare go forward or back in the dark, for fear of the shafts; and the wind and the snow were so sharp, they made me quite stupid and sleepy; and I knew if I stayed there I should be frozen to death, and if I went on, there were the shafts ready to swallow me up: and what with fear and the howling and raging of the wind, I was like a mazed boy, sir. And I knelt down and tried to pray; and then, in one moment, all the evil things I'd ever done, and the bad words and thoughts that ever crossed me, rose up together as clear as one page of a print-book; and I knew that if I died that minute I should go to hell. And then I saw through the ground all the water in the shafts glaring like blood, and all the sides of the shafts fierce red-hot, as if hell was coming up. And I heard the knockers knocking, or thought I heard them, as plain as I hear that grasshopper in the hedge now.'

'What are the knockers?'

'They are the ghosts, the miners hold, of the old Jews, sir, that crucified our Lord, and were sent for slaves by the Roman emperors to work the mines; and we find their old smelting-houses, which we call Jews' houses, and their blocks of tin, at the bottom of the great bogs, which we call Jews' tin; and there's a town among us, too, which we call Market-Jew —but the old name was Marazion; that means the Bitterness of Zion, they tell me. Isn't it so, sir?'

'I believe it is,' said Lancelot, utterly puzzled in this new field of romance.

'And bitter work it was for them, no doubt, poor souls! We used to break into the old shafts and adits which they had made, and find old stags'-horn pickaxes, that crumbled to pieces when we brought them to grass; and they say, that if a man will listen, sir, of a still night, about those old shafts, he may hear the ghosts of them at working, knocking, and picking, as clear as if there was a man at work in the next level. It may be all an old fancy. I suppose it is. But I believed it when I was a boy; and it helped the work in me that night. But I'll go on with my story.'[63]

As this story shows, in the process of becoming spirits, the erstwhile Jews, now called 'knockers' or 'knackers' (after the sounds which form their main sensory manifestation), and their wooden tools, become associated with virtually every form of supernatural alterity, all forms of superstition and 'old fancy' are all rolled into one story. First and foremost, the knockers are cosmological others, associated here with the fires of hell. Elsewhere they are indirectly associated with the devil who shows uncanny levels of productivity with his wooden tools in one Cornish song which goes 'Here's to the devil with his wooden pick and shovel, digging tin by the bushel, with his tail cock'd up!'[64]

Importantly, this rather famous quote occurs in the midst of a conversion narrative, and the Knockers are associated with all the forms of supernatural alterity and false belief that are opposed to the righteousness of Wesleyanism (and, indeed, the sort of superstition that both Wesleyan supernaturalism and elite naturalism tended to eradicate). That is, they are not merely supernatural agents of the devil, they also stand ambiguously for phantasms conjured up by fancy and superstition as opposed to the beliefs of right religion. The narrator, a Cornish miner, goes on to make this connection between Knockers and the devil, as well as superstition in general, clear:

> 'And I shook like a reed in the water; and then, all at once a
> thought struck me. "Why should I be a coward? Why should I
> be afraid of shafts, or devils, or hell, or anything else? If I am
> a miserable sinner, there's One died for me—I owe him love,
> not fear at all. I'll not be frightened into doing right—that's a
> rascally reason for repentance."'[65]

As well as being associated with the devil, knockers or knackers are predecessors who are contemporaries, that is, ghosts. However, they are not the named, known individuated familiar ghosts of the recent dead, they are a tribe of ghost of prior inhabitants, collective and unknown. They are also humanized attributes of animistic nature, like fairies.[66] Like other fairies, these Jewish-fairy hybrids live in liminal spaces opposed to the everyday world, underground in mines. Mines are both spatially inversions of the normal world, resembling other haunts of fairies like piskies or pixies associated with meadows, swamps, wastes and unenclosed and uncultivated land, 'places frequented by goats', the natural world beyond the cultivated world of nature.[67] Knackers are fairies here in their guise as 'nature spirits'. Knackers are also associated with inscrutable signs of prior inhabitants, the ancient mines of the old men, who worked them before Noah's Flood are analogous to the stones and ruins raised by giants that are haunted by spriggans and bukkas.[68] Lastly, knackers, like all fairies, guard treasure.[69]

In genre, too, knackers are like other fairies and spirits in being epistemic others: unlike flesh and blood 'natural figures', persons who are as at home in face to face contact as they are in reports and gossips about them, fairies can be encountered in first person unlaminated narratives only indirectly, through signs such as noises or their tools. Their special haunt is narrative. They can be seen only through the eyes of others, in narratives that are always laminated by quotation, hearsay, and tradition. As narrative others, they are ever guests in the speech situation, only at home in the narrated situation. As evidentiary others, they are never at home in eyewitness account, only indirectly perceptible in evidentiary modes from auditory, to circumstantial, to hearsay. As epistemic others, they are doubtful figures between belief and disbelief, fact and fancy, very much unlike normal flesh and blood humans. This quality of fairies, their distance from narrative and epistemic directness, is itself one of the strongest motifs of the fairy narratives themselves. Fairies hate visual contact, they hate prying and spying, universally punishing, often by blinding, those who seek a more direct epistemic contact than that afforded by narrative. At the same time, they also punish those who narrate them directly. In fact, much of the activity of fairies in stories is devoted to ensuring the epistemic and narrative indirectness of stories about fairies.[70] An early commentator on the Tommyknockers, Fisher Vane, stated this as well as anyone before or after:

> Of course you've heard of the tommyknocker. But have you ever *seen* one? Not on your life! Like their spirit kinfolk the gnomes, kobolds, pixies, imps and sprites, tommyknockers are invisible to adult mortal eyes. And in the nature of things, adult mortal eyes are, in the main, the only eyes that go underground. Wherefore, since members of this mischievous wing of the fairy race live nowhere else but undergound, and never venture into the light of day, only by their deeds and noises do we know them.[71]

As Vane notes, Knockers and Tommyknockers fall well within this set of behaviours, they are known mostly through their sounds, and they dislike direct visual contact with humans. The first story I want to relay is the most famous, the story of Tom and the Knackers.

TOM AND THE KNACKERS

The setting of the story of Tom and the knackers is an uncanny old mine, or *bal* as mines are called in Cornwall, associated with the 'old men' who worked it before Noah's flood, which is swarming with knackers and other kinds of fairies, including spriggans – who are associated with old men's works, abandoned ruins, old tools and treasure.[72] Tom is a skilled miner from another district, familiar with the natural end of mining, but unfamiliar with the supernatural end, for he does not know how to treat the spirits. His failure to engage in reciprocity with the mines' spirit leads him into financial failure until he fixes the situation through the supernatural mediation of a conjuror.

[Tom Trevorrow] went to Santust [St Just] to look for a job
and found work in Ballowal. Most people have heard of that
queer old bal [mine], that was worked before The Flood, they
say. There the old men's works, weth their deep open coffans
(pits) may still be seen, just as they left then, only wash'd
and run'd in a good deal one may suppose. That old bal,
everybody in Santust will tell 'e, have always been haunted
with knackers. And the burrows, in crofts and cleves around,
are swarman with them, and weth spriggans, wherever anything belongan to the old bal was buried. There these sprites
keep everlastan watch, though all the old men's tools or
treasures may be gone to rust, earth, and dust. One don't
often see them, 'tis true, but only break ground near them and
they'll show their ugly faces, as many have known to their
cost.[73]

Tom is a skilled miner, and not merely some unskilled refugee from the
declining agricultural sector fit only for menial tasks requiring more
strength than skill. More specifically, Tom is a tribute worker, working
a tribute contract places him at the apex of the labour hierarchy in the
Cornish mines. Working tribute contracts means that he contracts to
take a part of the mine, called a pitch, on a piecework system for a
given period of time. At the end of this period the tributer is paid in
terms of a fraction of the value of the ore he raises to the surface, or
'grass', expressed in a number of shillings to the pound of the value of
the ore. In effect, a tributer has an interest in the work lacking in other
wage contracts, and assumes part of the risk of the adventurer by
agreeing to calibrate his pay to the ore he produces. Pay becomes
uncertain, and work for such workers has some of the gratifying
properties of a game whose results and rewards are uncertain. This is
important to all the knacker stories, because knackers are spirits who
only appear to one class of miner, the elite, skilled miners who work on
tribute contracts.

Tom settles into his new job and his new life in Saint Just, and
it is not very long before he hears the knackers working the mine
when working alone. The knackers are presented as being engaged in
parallel work with the tinners, to the extent that, no longer 'old men'
with 'wooden picks and shovels', they have kept pace with all the latest
advances in mining technique, and have even learned the most recent
methods of blasting!

Tom had heard the knackers workan, away at a distance, all
the time he had been there, and took no notice of their noise,

but now that the boy stopped home, they came nearer and nearer every day, till he cud hardly hear the sound of his own tools with the din and clatter of theirs. As far as he could judge by the sound they were only two or three yards off, in the level close behind him, carryen on all sorts of underground work. Some appeared to be wheelan, some showlan, others boran; he could even hear them swab out their holes, put in the tampan, and shut (blast) like a pare (company) of regular tinners. Shuttan wasn't in vogue in their time, but they've learnt et.[74]

While Tom is a skilled tinner in the natural end of the trade, he does not know how to deal with the supernatural knackers, and he offends them:

One night . . . Tom got quite savage to hear their confoundan clatter, with their squeakan and tee-hee-an in a mockan way, if he made false strokes, or a clumsy blow; and being a devil-may-care sort of fellow, he, without thinkan of anything, threwed back a handful of small stones, towards the spot where they seemed to be workan, and called out at the same time without stopan or lookan up, 'Go to blazes, you cussed old Jews' sperrats; or I'll scat (knock) your brains out, ef you aren't gone from here.[75]

The knackers cause a small shower of stones in return, and when he begins to eat, they warn him in what sounds eerily like a children's rhyme that he can hardly make out because of their distant, squeakin voices:

'Tom Trevorrow! Tom Trevorrow!
Leave some of thy fuggan (food) for bucca (a sprite),
Or bad luck to thee, to-morrow!'[76]

Of course he does no such thing. He eventually falls asleep, when he wakes, he sees the knackers. Some of the features of knacker physiognamy is not only spriggan-like (size, for example), but also, possibly, stereotypical of Jewishness as well:

But when he waked up all was quiet. He rubbed his eyes, and lookan away in the end, where it was nearly dark, he seed scores of knackers restan on their tools. They were miserable, little, old, withered, dried-up creatures—the tallest of them no more than three foot six, or there away, with shanks like drum-sticks, and their arms as long or longer than their legs. They had big ugly heads, with grey or red locks, squintan eyes, hook noses, and mouths from ear to ear. The faces of many were very much like the grim visages on old cloman jugs, so Tom said, and more like those of brutes than Christians.[77]

This section of the mine is said by the other tinners to be the most haunted, called 'Buckshaft', so-called because 'a black buck goat, or a bucca in the shape of an, was seen to go down there, but never found below'.[78] From the moment Tom does not heed the reciprocity requested by the knackers, they are always working against Tom, causing a cave in that nearly kills him and also causes him to lose all the tin he had won on tribute, as well as his tools.[79] He has to go on 'subsist' (money advanced against future wages). Tom is further degraded from being a tributer to a tut-worker, that is, from someone whose wages are based on a percentage of the value of the ore to someone who works for a set amount per fathom driving shafts and clearing valueless 'country rock'. The knackers continue to torment him, and they drive him back to Lelant where he came from, no better off than when he left. Worse, his luck remains so bad that he is forced to take up agricultural work, a fate worse than death or the workhouse in the eyes of a skilled tinner. The narrator of the story comments that 'He had to work to the farmers for a long spell, and, as we all know, every tinner would just as soon go to the workhouse, or union; and for my part I'd rather be tied to a Bull's tail, and suffer the rest, than do either one.'[80] Tom's wife uses the money she makes from her knitting to hire a pellar (conjuror) with which to drive off Tom's bad luck, and Tom goes back to mining work and in general his fortunes change for the better.[81]

In the story of Tom Trevorrow, the knackers or mining spirits are assimilated to the world of fairies. The folklore collections of the late nineteenth century generally produce a neat typology of these creatures, which are divided into distinct groups, roughly corresponding to different occupational groupings they normally have dealings with or the types of places they haunt. According to these typologies, each class of fairy stands as a relevant other to a specific occupational grouping, each has a specific sort of locale or haunt, and each engages in a specific form of relation ranging from benevolent to malicious exchanges with humans.[82]

Each form of fairy creature represent an inversion of the occupational universe of nineteenth century Cornwall, for each form of occupation there is a fairy other: piskies and spriggans are associated with male agricultural and female domestic work, the unmarked category, mermaids with sailors and fishermen, and knackers with miners. Correspondingly, spatially there is a complementarity, so that spriggans haunt landscape features that are associated with ancient-ness, piskies with wildness and unenclosed or waste land (and have a loathing of the sea), mermaids with the sea. The knackers are associated with the state of being underground, which is the opposite of the normal state of being 'at grass', above ground. In this sense they are like the piskies, who inhabit the space beyond the enclosed fields of agriculture. But knackers particularly haunt those underground places that are associated with predecessors, 'mines worked before the Flood'. This makes them resemble spriggans, who are associated with ancient above ground ruins and rocks associated with giants as well as, occasionally, holes in the ground.

In this story, the relations of knackers with humans is one of refused reciprocity. The miner is working a tribute pitch, and the knackers demand a tribute themselves, a small one, which he refuses. Having refused this tribute, his own tribute pitches and luck fail. This association with tribute pitches is crucial, for the knackers, like spriggans, guard wealth, but they guard wealth of a very specific kind: wealth in its natural form, ore.

Knackers are 'hybrid race between ordinary ghosts and elves'.[83] They are liminal between two systems of alterity. On the one hand, they remain connected to the Jews of the earlier miners, on the other, like other fairies they are perceived to be connected to other forms of alterity, especially nature. This double alterity is expressed in their relationship to wealth. Knackers are insistently associated with pro-ductive lodes, therefore they are surefire guides to paying tribute pitches. A tribute pitch makes wealth a function both of the universe of exchange and the universe of production, culture and nature. If 'Jewish ghosts' are spirits of exchange, it might be said that fairies are nature spirits par excellence, and therefore spirits of production, human inter-action with nature. This hybrid of the nature spirit and figure of exchange expresses to some extent the way that wealth and risk for a miner working a tribute pitch is both a function of contract (exchange) and the position of lodes, natural wealth, in the rock (production).

As the story of Tom Trevorrow makes clear, the knackers are not simply underground spirits, they are occupational spirit others for miners, who bleed into other categories of fairies in the same way a human worker, like Tom, might move between different occupations. But knackers are not simply spirits of mining, they are spirits who are really relevant only to a certain class of miners, those working a tribute contract. That is, those whose wage contract makes their wages a function of risk, both natural and social. Just as the tribute wage contract itself is in part an expression of a contract between humans, the miner and the mine captain, the stories of knackers make the success of a tribute contract simultaneously the product of a similar contract with nature in the form of the knackers. In the story of Tom Trevorrow, it is simple use-values in the form of food that Tom should exchange for success in mining, but in the next story I want to discuss, the miners make a separate tribute contract with nature in the form of the knackers, who assume a passive role similar to mine adventurers. The moral of the story again is one in which greed and the desire for infinite gain leads to a refusal of reciprocity, breaking the contract with the spirits. The story begins:

> At Ransom Mine the 'Knockers' were always very active in their subterranean operations. In every part of the mine their 'knockings' were heard, but most especially were they busy in one particular end. There was a general impression that great wealth must exist at this part of the 'lode'. Yet, notwithstanding the inducements of very high 'tribute' were held out to the miners, no pair of men could be found brave enough to venture on the ground of the 'Bockles'. An old man and son, called Trenwith, who lived near Bosprenis, went out one midsummer eve, about midnight, and watched until they saw the 'Smae People' bringing up the shining ore. It is said they were possessed of some secret by which they could communicate with the fairy people. Be this as it may, they told the little miners that they would save them all the trouble of breaking down the ore, that they would bring 'to grass' for them, one-tenth of the 'richest stuff', and leave it properly dressed, if they would quietly give up this end. An agreement of some kind was come to. The old man and his son took the 'pitch', and in short time realized much wealth. The old man never failed to keep to his bargain, and leave a tenth of the ore for his friends. He died. The son was avaricious and selfish. He sought to cheat the Knockers, but he ruined himself by so doing. The 'lode' failed; nothing answered with him; disappointed, he took to drink, squandered all the money his father had made, and died a beggar.[84]

The knacker or knocker spirit is a hybrid other, a specifically capitalist spirit both having elements related to exchange and production, exchange value and use value, expressed in its dual identity as ghost of Jewish miner and underground nature spirit. But the function of these spirits as guardians of wealth is particularly to guard wealth in its natural form, the riches of the earth, ore and not money, their tappings are always a positive sign, not of danger but of wealth, of the mother lode or an impending lucky struck. And, as nature spirits, they express the element of risk involved in certain wage contract systems, the tribute contract where wages are functions both of natural and social variables. In these stories they are presented as a separate group with which a miner working a tribute pitch must make a separate tribute contract, a contract with the underground spirits of the rock that parallels the contract he made with the captain of the mine 'at grass'.

In the new world, tommyknockers lost *most* associations with elves and fairies as well as Jews, instead being associated with the ghosts of dead miners.[85] As they made this transition, they became less like mischievous, occasionally helpful spriggans and piskies guarding the wealth of the earth, and more like omens, hunches and ghosts, signs of danger and death.

TOMMYKNOCKERS

To finish this story, we must follow the knackers and the miners they haunted to the New World. The Cornish knackers were the only Old World mining spirits to get on board the boats to America. When they arrived, like many immigrants they changed their name, to 'tommy-knockers', and cast off their Jewish ethnicity and associations with fairies. Thus restyled, they were soon found in every mine, even those unpopulated by the people who brought them, the Cornish miners, themselves now known as 'Cousin Jacks'. Of the dozens of kinds of mining spirits in the Old World, all were stay-at-homes but the knackers, who proved as mobile as the Cousin Jacks themselves. In fact, the tommyknockers in the New World outlived their Old World predecessors, the knackers.[86]

The tommyknockers ruled the supernatural world of hard rock mining in much the same way that the Cousin Jacks ruled the natural world of mining. Just as the Cornish associated their ethnicity with skill in mining, monopolizing skilled positions in the hard rock mines of the New World and their techniques and terminology came to dominate the labour process of mining, so their spirits came to have authority over all the hard rock mines, no matter who worked them.[87] If, as a common Western American adage had it, 'a mine is a hole in the ground with a Cornishman at the bottom', then presumably any spirits in that hole would also be Cornish. Tommy knockers and knackers in both Cornwall and the New World even keep pace with the changes of technology of mining, like the Cousin Jacks themselves.[88] By contrast, the other European immigrants who entered the mines of the New

World were primarily unskilled in hard rock mining and from agricultural backgrounds.[89]

In this process, of course, both the Cornish and their spirits changed to adapt to new circumstances.[90] The nature of these mining sprites changed too, no longer indicating rich lodes of ore and 'lucky strikes', but rather the presence of danger. They also left behind their associations with Jews as well as fairies, and came to be associated with the ghosts of dead miners more generally.[91] A good representative of this change is Anthony Fitch's poem 'Tommy Knockers':

'Av you 'eard of the Tommy Knockers
In the deep dark mines of the West,
Which Cornish miners 'ear?
An' 'tis no laughin' jest.
For I am a Cornish miner,
An' I'll tell you of it today.
The knock-knock-knock of the tiny pick,
As we work in the rocks and clay.
. . .
Pick, pick, pick.
'As some one be'ind us knocked?
Pick, pick, pick—
No, 'tis the souls of dead miners locked,
For they're locked in the earthen wall,
Those that found death down there,
And 'tis the knock-knock-knock of their pick
W'ich makes on end stand our 'air.

An' we leave the 'aunted place,
For we won't work w'ere they be,
An' w'erever we 'ear them knockin'
We sure will always flee.
For it means w'oever hears it
Will be the next in line,
For the pick-pick-pick of the Tommy Knockers
Is the last an' awful sign.[92]

With a tributing system of wage contract, like that common in Cornwall and found for a time also in various New World mines, the risk assumed by the miner is a function of both natural and conventional factors. On the one hand, since the miner is paid a proportion expressed in shillings to the pound of the value of all ore he raises, natural features of the mine, such as the presence or absence of lodes and the unevenness of the distribution of ore in lodes add a significant element of chance to his wages. On the other hand, since the specific rate of tribute (in shillings to the pound of the value of the ore) itself is a negotiation, another kind of game, between worker and manager, the risk is partially constituted in cultural, conventional, terms. Risk then is related to wealth, fantasies of lucky strikes and mother lodes, and it is generated on the basis of variables both natural and conventional. The hybrid nature spirit (knacker) who is also a spirit of exchange (the ghost of a dead Jew) expresses the hybrid nature of the risk they superintend. However, with change to hourly wage contract systems, this game element is removed. If workers have any interest in the ore they are raising now, it is primarily in the form of 'high-grading' (stealing the richer ore to process at home).[93] Primarily the risk associated with mining is no longer a matter of wealth, it is purely a matter of personal safety. With this change, knockers lose all associations with guarding wealth and come to be assimilated to a different branch of mining superstition, omens or hunches.[94] At the same time, the knockers come to be precisely the ghosts of miners who have died as a result of cave-ins.

But these mining spirits had other functions before they died out, perhaps a victim of electrical lighting, perhaps a victim of changing modern notions of nature. The Cousin Jacks staked their claims to skill by identifying their ethnic essence with technical expertise underground, and the natural empire of Cousin Jack was identical to the supernatural empire of the Tommyknocker underground. But where the Cousin Jacks made their claim to authority over production on ethnic grounds by identifying ethnicity with technical authority, they had sharp competition from the Irish workers, who, it was said, controlled mines by their ethnic knack at politics above ground much as the Cousin Jacks ruled it below ground by their technical skill. Mines soon became divided between Cousin Jack mines and Irish mines, and conflicts that produced these divisions were sharp. Not all of the danger in mining, then, was natural. The last ghost story I want to tell, collected by Caroline Bancroft in Colorado in 1945, expresses these ethnic conflicts over the labour markets of mining.

> Up on Jones hill on the way to Nevadaville is the prize Seuderberg mine. Back in 1868 a man by the name of Connelly who was a great co-getter had a quarrel with a Cousin Jack by the name of Gleason over the end line. Gleason had a tribute pitch on the Prize and Connelly was leasing the Seuderberg . . . One night when Gleason was climbing the shaft after the day's work, Connelly leaned over

the collar and shot him. Connelly never paid for his crime as these mines were in the Irish end of town and all Connelly's compatriots refused to testify against him. Gleason's body fell to the bottom of the shaft, was shattered to bits and his spirit roams the Prize mine to this day demanding that justice be done. No Cousin Jack who understands the language will work there because they can't bear his beseeching them to do something about his case.[95]

In this final story, the mining ghosts have moved from being anonymous ethnic others, the ghosts of dead Jews, to named ghosts of the ethnic self, a murdered Cousin Jack named Gleason, both in very different ways expressing the relationship of ethnicity to production. Now the ghosts of named Cornish miners could become a sign of the ethnic processes by which the Cornish were *banished* from mines.

CONCLUSION

In the Old World, the Cornish had been involved in various occupations—mining, farming and fishing—but in the New World, the Cousin Jack was a hard rock miner. Those Cornish in the New World who were not hard rock miners in effect (it might be argued) ceased to 'be Cornish'. This reformulation of Cornish ethnicity, involving claims to a monopoly of technical mining skills, was especially addressed to the Irish, who were felt to have political powers outside of the point of production that gave them unfair advantages over the naturally more qualified Cousin Jacks.[96] In the same way, Cornish folklore had been populated with a complex otherworld that mirrored the features of this world, primarily consisting of fairies, each fairy type of which corresponded to some sector of the normal world, in particular occupational types. The knackers were merely one fairy among many in the Old World. But just as Cornish farmers and fisherman either became Cousin Jack miners or became lost 'in a sea of Britons' in the New World, so the knackers were the only fairies to get on the boat, and as they did, they left their fairy identity behind. Tommyknockers were, temporally as well as geographically, far-removed from their erstwhile 'Jewish' ancestors.

ACKNOWLEDGEMENTS

An earlier version of this article was presented to the Department of Anthropology at the University of Maynooth, and the faculty and students at Maynooth are gratefully acknowledged for the opportunity and impetus to finish this paper, as well as their helpful comments. I would also like to thank Steve Coleman, Anne Meneley, Devin Pendas,

Jamie Saris, Jane Schneider, Rupert Stasch, Lawrence Taylor, Donna Young, for encouragement and comments on various drafts. Ronald James deserves special thanks for both inspiring this paper with his own work as well as helping me with comments and generous provision of materials I did not otherwise have access to.

NOTES AND REFERENCES

1. Cited in Ronald M. James, 'Defining the Group: Nineteenth-Century Cornish on the North American Mining Frontier', in Philip Payton (ed.) *Cornish Studies: Two*, Exeter, 1994, pp. 40–1.

2. James, 1994, pp.40–1; Ronald D. James, 'Knockers, Knackers and Ghosts: Immigrant Folklore in the Western Mines', *Western Folklore,* 51: 2, 1992, 153–71; D. Mindenhall, 'Choosing the Group: Nineteenth-century Non-mining Cornish in British Columbia', in Philip Payton (ed.), *Cornish Studies: Eight*, Exeter, 2000, pp.40–53; Sharron Schwartz, 'Creating the Cult of "Cousin Jack": Cornish Miners in Latin America 1812–1848 and the Development of an International Mining Labour Market', 1999, available at: http://www.projects.ex.ac.uk/cornishlatin/ workingpapersandbibliography.htm; Philip Payton, *The Cornish Overseas: A History of Cornwall's Great Emigration*, Fowey, 2005.

3. This is clear both from the period sources as well as the secondary literature, for example George Henwood in his mid-nineteenth century portraits of Cornish miners discusses the mobility of the Cornish, attributing it primarily to temperance and resulting parsimony: 'Thousands, by abandoning the glass, have been able to secure the means of emigration, and after a few years in Australia or California return with a competence, or remain in the colonies as wealthy settlers; their mining experience being there turned to good account. Many mines in Cuba and South America are managed by Cornish agents and worked by Cornish miners' (George Henwood, *Cornwall's Mines and Miners*, edited by Roger Burt, Truro, 1972, p. 69). Henwood notes that the Cornish are found as managers and skilled labourers in mines 'in Cuba, Mexico, Lima, Coquimbo, Jamaica, Australia, Isle of Man, Ireland, Yorkshire, and Wales' (Henwood, 1972, p. 129), also pp. 165–6. The secondary literature on Cornish migrations in vast; I have found the above cited articles from the series *Cornish Studies* to be particularly useful, and references there, as well as the web page 'The Cornish in Latin America' (http://www.projects.ex.ac.uk/cornishlatin/index.php), and references there.

4. James, 1992, 1994; Schwartz, 1999.

5. By 'social ontology' I mean implicit or explicit cultural assumptions and presuppositions underlying explicitly articulated beliefs about what sorts of entities, things, forces and agents populate the social universe, such as, for example, the division of the universe into natural, preternatural and supernatural forces, the allocation of technical expertise and skill to the

natural world and the allocation of beliefs about spirits to the supernatural universe, and so on.

6. James, 1994; Schwartz, 1999, and references there.

7. On tributing see John Rule, '"The Perfect Wage System?" Tributing in the Cornish mines', in John Rule and Roger Wells, *Crimes, Protest and Popular Politics in Southern England, 1750–1850*, London, 1997, pp. 53–65; see also the essays in Roger Burt (ed.), *Cornish Mining: Essays in the Organization of Cornish Mines and the Cornish Mining Economy*, New York, 1969. On capital recruitment and contract systems in other British extractive industries see Paul Manning, 'Welsh Rocks and English Money: Ideologies of Divisions of Language and Divisions of Labor in Nineteenth Century Welsh Slate Quarries', *Comparative Studies in Society and History* 44:3, 2002, pp. 481–510; 'Owning and Belonging: a Semiotic Investigation of the Affective Categories of a Bourgeois Society', *Comparative Studies in Society and History* 46:2, 2004, pp. 300–25; 'The Streets of Bethesda: the Slate Quarrier and the Welsh Language in the Welsh Liberal Imagination', *Language and Society* 33:4, 2004, pp. 469–500. Schwartz, 1999, helpfully demonstrates the ways in which each of these elements encountered resistance to their attempted transplantation, and the ways in which the 'skill' of the 'Cousin Jack' was also a partially mythological creature.

8. For an anthropological discussion of the division, see Philippe Descola, 'Constructing Natures. Symbolic Ecology and Social Practice', in P. Descola and G. Pálson (eds), Nature and Society. Anthropological Perspectives, London, 1996, pp. 82–102; for the treatment of production as a natural category opposed to exchange under capitalism, see Moishe Postone, 'Anti-Semitism and National Socialism', in Anson Rabinbach and Jack Zipes (eds), *Germans and Jews Since the Holocaust*, New York, 1986, pp. 302–14; for the separation of natural and supernatural, an authoritative discussion is Katharine Park and Lorraine Daston, 'Unnatural Conceptions: the Study of Monsters in Sixteenth and Seventeenth-Century France and England', *Past and Present*, 92, 1981, pp. 20–54; Lorraine Daston and Katharine Park, *Wonders and the Order of Nature 1150–1750*, New York, 1998.

9. James, 1992, 1994; Schwartz, 1999, and references and discussion there. The origin of the ethnic term 'Cousin Jack' as applied to Cornish miners in the new world is often taken to be a joking reference to nepotistic hiring practices combined with creatively expansive reckoning of kinship so that all of Cornwall were reckoned cousins, see for example, Caroline Bancroft, 'Folklore of the Central City District, Colorado', *California Folklore Quarterly*, 4, 1945, p. 319; Wayland Hand, 'The Folklore, Customs and Traditions of the Butte Miner', *California Folklore Quarterly*, 7, 1946, pp. 174–5. According to Schwartz, 1999, p. 33 n1: 'There is no clear consensus on how the Cornish miners acquired this name, but evidence seems to point to the mines of Devonshire in the eighteenth century, where migrant Cornish miners sought work. The term "Cousin Jack" is also thought to have been used to express an

"otherness", the Cornish considering themselves a distinct people with specific mining skills that they jealously guarded.' See also Payton, 2005.

10. Burt 1969; Schwartz 1999.
11. James, 1992, 1994.
12. The analytic division of the process of production into a labour process and a valorization process is from Karl Marx, *Capital*, Volume 1, Translated by Ben Fowkes, London, 1990, pp. 283ff. The labour process can be thought of as the process of production of use-values, useful products, a process which varies according to the nature of the product to be produced, and the valorization process, which, very roughly, happens simultaneously under capitalism, but follows production under mercantilism, is the process of extracting surplus value ('exploitation'), which has consequences for the labour process.
13. For example, Hand, 1946, pp. 2–3; James 1992, p. 154.
14. Including bans on the presence of women, making the sign of the cross, and whistling, along with various hunches and omens. For details see Hunt, 1916, pp. 349–52; Wayland Hand, 'California miners folklore: Below ground,' *California Folklore Quarterly* 1, 1942, pp. 134–44; Bancroft, 1945, pp.322–36; Hand, 1946, pp. 11–25. However, we cannot immediately assume that such customs and beliefs are not also comparable to other ritual expressions of solidarity detailed from above ground streaming miners by Thomas Beare in 1586 (T. Beare, *Bailiff of Blackmoor 1586*, edited by J. A. Buckley, Camborne, 1994, pp. 60–4) and more generally in Western extractive industries by Nancy Quam-Wickham, 'Rereading Man's Conquest of Nature: Skill, Myths and the historical construction of Masculinity in Western Extractive industries', *Men and Masculinities* 2:2, 1999, pp. 135–51. For comparative purposes see for example the opposition between the Christian above ground and the underground world of the devil in Bolivian tin mines, interestingly, the sign of the cross is banned underground both in Cornish and Bolivian tin-mines, see June Nash, *We Eat the Mines and the Mines Eat Us*, New York, 1979, p. 7. Propitiatory clay figures of Tommyknockers in California mines (Hand 1942, p. 128; James 1992, p. 168) also resemble the propitiatory clay figures of the devil, or *Tio*, pictured as a 'gringo supervisor' in Bolivian tin mines, see June Nash, 'The devil in Bolivia's nationalized tin mines', *Science and Society* 36:2, 1972, pp. 224–5; Nash, 1979, pp. 4, 7, 190–4). Whether any of the historical 'gringo supervisors' in the Bolivian mines were members of the Cousin Jack diaspora is unclear from the existing historiography, although there were of course many Cornish in nineteenth-century Bolivia.
15. The material evidence of the wooden tools and ruined structures of the 'old men' are probably the single most insistent thread that connects these different strands of folklore together, being part of almost every old world account from 1586 to the nineteenth century. In addition to Beare (1586), Carew (1602), Kingsley (1853), Bottrell (1870–1880) cited below, natural historians like W. Pryce, *Mineralogia Cornubiensis: A Treatise on Minerals and Mining*, London, 1778, p. 68 and William Borlase, *The Natural History*

of Cornwall, Additions, Oxford, 1758, p. 20, make mention of wooden tools. In the mid Nineteenth century too, Henwood discusses the leavings of the 'old men' in various mines, including their wooden tools, Henwood, 1972, p. 109, 161–2, 178, 193–7. The works of the 'old men' are called by various names, including 'Attall Sarazen' (which Pryce glosses as 'Saxons or Jews offcast', Pryce, 1778, p. 316), 'coffin' ('workings all open like an intrenchment', Pryce, 1778, 318), 'learys' ('emptiness', Pryce, 1778, p. 324) and 'old men's workings' (Pryce, 1778, p. 325). The names given them in Beare's and Carew's day and later (Jew's houses'), being the most common name for an old ruined smelting house) associated the old men with Jews and Saracens (see below), while according to Henwood in the mid nineteenth century old men's workings are also called 'Piskies pits' (Henwood, 1972, pp. 195–6), associating the 'old men's workings' with a variety of fairy. The folklore texts regarding the old men in are not simply verbal, but exist in a close intertextual relationship with material artefacts, a relationship missing in the New World.

16. Schneider's discussion of fairy beliefs in the New World focuses on the way that these spirits embody an ethnic of reciprocity opposed to capitalist rationalization of exchange (the spirit of capitalism). See J. Schneider, 'Spirits and the Spirit of Capitalism', in E. Badone (ed.), *Religious Orthodoxy and Popular Faith in European Society*, Princeton, 1990, pp. 24–54 (Ronald James gives a similar account that locates fairy-like traits of knocker spirits in notions of reciprocity with nature and notions of a limited good (James, 1992, pp. 167–70)). The story she tells, which is slightly different from the one I am telling, the death of nature spirits is related to the rationalization of exchange, beliefs about nature, and the general disenchantment of the world associated with modernity (on which, see also Park and Daston, 1981; Daston and Park, 1998). We have here a case in which the spirits *are themselves* spirits of capitalism. The final fate of the spirits in this paper is documented in James Baker, 'Echoes of Tommy Knockers in Bohemia, Oregon, Mines', *Western Folklore*, 30, 1971, pp. 119–22.

17. James, 1992, pp. 168–72.

18. Natural and unnatural economy is used here in a broadly Aristotelian sense, where a natural economy is one founded on 'natural wealth', that is, use-values (and where use values are produced for consumption, and any exchange has as its final goal consumption) as opposed to a exchange based economy (where use-values are produced in order to be exchanged). On the various senses of 'natural' in Aristotle I have relied on the discussions in James Murphy, *The Moral Economy of Labor: Aristotelian Themes in Economic Theory*, New Haven, 1993; Scott Meikle, *Aristotle's Economic Thought*, Oxford, 1995. Aristotle's notions of wealth involve a sense of autarkic self-sufficiency of use-values which corresponds broadly to the peasant agriculturalist ideology I am reconstructing here.

19. Postone explains the naturalization of labour and production in productivism as follows: '[B]ecause labor . . . constitutes the relationship between humanity and nature, it serves as the standpoint from which

social relations among people can be judged: Relations that are in harmony with labor and reflect its fundamental significance are considered socially 'natural.' The social critique from the standpoint of 'labor' is, therefore, a critique from a quasi-natural point of view, that of a social ontology. It is a critique of what is artificial in the name of the 'true' nature of society.' Moishe Postone, *Time, Labor and Social Domination,* Cambridge, 1993, p. 65; for a discussion of productivism in relation to another British extractive industry see Manning, 2002, 2004.

20. On tributing see Rule 1997; Burt 1969. The natural historian W. Pryce gives one of the earliest detailed accounts of tributing (whether the working of whole mines on tribute or the working of parts of mines on tribute pitches, W. Pryce, *Mineralogia Cornubiensis: A Treatise on Minerals and Mining,* London, 1778, pp. 187–9. Pryce is also the first to explicitly note the game-like or gambling-like elements involved in this system of wage contract: 'It is an aphorism in mining, that "a Tinner has nothing to lose"; but upon tribute or searching for tin upon the mere strength of his labour, he puts himself in the way of fortune, to enrich himself by one lucky hit.' Pryce, 1778, p. 175; 'The spirit of adventure hath many times so prevailed among the lower people, that very large sums have been won and lost by this manner of gaming [tributing], much to the injury of the cashiers, who can have no recompense from poverty and rags.' Pryce, 1778, p. 192. For the element of risk and the interest and game-like qualities generated by piece-work systems in general see M. Burawoy, *Manufacturing Consent,* Chicago, 1979. On the linkage between the change in the wage system and change in beliefs, see James 1992, pp. 171–2.

21. James, 1992, pp. 167–74.
22. James, 1992.
23. James 1994; Schwartz 1999.
24. Mindenhall, 2000.
25. Baker, 1971, pp. 121–2; Lydia, Fish, 'The European Background of American Miners' Beliefs', in Kenneth Goldstein and Neil Rosenburg (eds), *Folklore Studies in Honour of Herbert Halpter,* Newfoundland, 1980, p. 157; James, 1992, p. 161.
26. Robert Hunt, *Popular Romances of the West of England,* New York, 1916, originally published in 1865, p. 341.
27. Beare, 1994, p. 1
28. Beare, 1994, p. 1.
29. Beare, 1994, p. 1.
30. Beare, 1994, p. 97. The story is recounted by natural historians like William Borlase, 1758, pp. 149 ff. In folklore of the nineteenth century, any ruins or dwellings built 'before Noah's flood' are persistently associated with the haunts of spirits (see below).
31. Richard Carew, *The Survey of Cornwall,* London, 1602, I.8. Original emphasis, but I have modernized the spelling.
32. For Greeks and Phoenicians, based on classical references, see Borlase, 1758, pp. 160, 189, for Jews see Borlase, 1758, p. 190.

33. Borlase, 1758, p. 163.
34. Borlase, 1758, p. 189.
35. Hunt 1916: 342.
36. Max Muller, 'Are there Jews in Cornwall? A riddle and its solution', *MacMillan's Magazine*, Volume 15, November 1867, Cambridge, pp. 484–94, p. 493.
37. Muller, 1867, p. 484.
38. Muller, 1867, p. 484.
39. Muller, 1867, p. 491.
40. Beare, 1994, pp. 6–8. Since the status of tinner carried with it a number of legal consequences, specifically whether one was under the jurisdiction of stannary courts. Lewis shows considerable flux in the definition of this term ranging from a narrow one limited to manual labourers to one comprising the entire trade, throughout the later middle ages, G. R. Lewis, *The Stannaries: A study of the English tin-miner*, Boston, 1908, pp. 96ff. The definition of 1588, immediately after Beare's writing, 'divided all tinners into two classes. In the first were manual labourers, "spaliers" and "pioneers;" these were not to sue or to be drawn into any foreign [i.e. non-stannary] jurisdiction for the trial of any case whatsoever, save matters concerning land, life, and limb. The other class comprised those gentlemen who had some share in tin works, or who received toll tin as lords or farmers, men who converted black tin into white, or who were necessary for the getting of tin, such as colliers, blowers, carpenters, smiths, tin merchants . . .' (Lewis, 1908, p. 99). Note that the second group is a mixed grouping of what we might now think of as 'productive' and 'non-productive' elements.
41. Beare, 1994, pp. 6–8, 58–60; Explicitly in Carew, 1602, p. 13, a dole is basically a measurement of labour obligation first and foremost: 'The worke thus found and bounded, looke how many men doe labour therein, so many *Doales* or shares they make thereof, and proportionately diuide the gaine and charges.'
42. Beare, 1994, pp. 6–8, 56–7; the spaliard according to Beare works by the day to save a working tinner from a fine for absence from work called a 'spale' (pp. 7, 58–60); the practice is mentioned in Henwood's account of the mid-nineteenth century as 'spoling', Henwood, 1972, p. 166.
43. Carew's account is the first place we find the term 'adventurer' applied to tinning. For Carew the term 'adventurer' (as opposed to tinner) is defined by delegating one's labour obligation on a dole by dole basis, *not* by ownership of shares or doles *per se* (since working tinners also have these): 'These partners consist either of such Tinners as worke to their own behoofe, or of such **aduenturers** as put in hired labourers. The hirelings stand at a certaine wages, either by the day, which may be about eight pence, or for the yeere, being between foure and six pound.' Carew, 1602, p. 10. By the time of later natural historians like Pryce or Borlase we have a clearer delineation between of a confrontation between capital and labour in the form of a collectivity of adventurers and a collectivity of workers, respectively, mediated by captains (Borlase, 1758, pp. 175ff;

Pryce, 1778, pp. 173ff). However, there are still important differences from the understanding prevailing under industrial capitalism. Even at this stage the wealth divided amongst the adventurers according to doles is expressed in terms of natural wealth (ore) and not money, as it would be under a truly capitalist form of organization (Borlase, 1758, p. 175). There arose around this time a distinction between in-adventurers, local adventurers who could contribute their quota of duties in materials or in labour, as opposed to out-adventurers, living at a distance, who contributed their quotas in money only and were not in daily attendance at the works (Pryce, 1778, pp. 174, 315). The latter more closely resemble the nineteenth century adventurer, though the distinction continues in some form in Cornish mining into the nineteenth century.

44. Beare, 1994, pp. 58–60.
45. Carew, 1602, p. 10.
46. Carew, 1602, p. 16–17.
47. I. Blanchard, 'The miner and the agricultural community in Late Medieval England', *Agricultural History Review*, 1972, p. 100. It is not until Carew's time that we begin to have evidence that a general neglect of agriculture by the mining population has begun to appear (Carew, 1602, p. 19).
48. For the customs of the tinners, most of which involve pranks and practical jokes, see Beare, 1994, pp. 60–4. The 'tinner's language' is an playful occupational language that expresses solidarity through tabooing certain words referring to animals (owls, foxes, hares, cats and rats) which must be referred to using kenning terms of the tinner's language (respectively 'broadface', 'long tayle', 'long yeer', 'rooker' and 'peeper'); the penalty for misuse is that the offender must buy a gallon of ale to be consumed convivially (Beare, 1994, p. 63–4). On anti-languages in general see M. A. K. Halliday, 'Anti-languages', *American Anthropologist* 78, pp. 570–84.
49. For comparison of other cosmologies that seem to oppose monetized to non-monetized domains of economy, the Bolivian tin-mining cosmologies explored by Nash, 1972, pp. 221–32; Nash, 1979. For an interpretation of this material see Michael Taussig, *The Devil and Commodity Fetishism in South America*, Chapel Hill, North Carolina, 1980; see also the papers in J. Parry and M. Bloch (eds), *Money and the Morality of Exchange*, Cambridge, 1989.
50. In Bottrell's account he is alleged to have mastered most trades and handicrafts. W. Bottrell, *Traditions and Hearthside Stories of West Cornwall*, Newcastle upon Tyne, 1970. Originally published in Penzance in 1870, p. 18.
51. Bottrell, 1970, p. 18.
52. Hunt, 1916, p. 63.
53. Bottrell, 1970, p. 19.
54. Hunt, 1916, pp. 66–7.
55. Hunt, 1916, p. 67. In Bottrell's version, Tom the Giant is much more insistently obtuse, refusing to account anything as wealth that is not immediately useful to the owner: 'I don't care for the tin and trash: all et's good for es to buy land, and havn't I got more acres, miles, of land already

than I can tell what to do weth; all stocked with the finest cattle. We shall never want for beef nor mutton, nor need we better clothing than our honest homespun.' (Bottrell, 1970, p. 22); 'But I tell thee, Jack, I don't care a cobbler's cuss about any more tin. As I have asked thee before, what need one wish for anything more than we have got?' (Bottrell, 1970, p. 27); 'Whatever could the ould giants do with such lumber' says Tom, 'I'd rather have one of my cows than all the glistening things in this hole,' (Bottrell, 1970, p. 28).

56. Hunt, 1916, pp. 68–9. In this respect Tom's notion of wealth is the same as Aristotle's, as opposed to a modern capitalist notion of wealth, see Meikle, 1995, pp. 43-67.

57. Hunt, 1916, p. 61. The tinkeard then repairs all the pots in the house, and shows how to string a bow thought unstringable but by strength using skill rather than raw strength (what appears again to be sleight of hand) (p. 62), brings the horticultural arts to Cornwall by planting the first garden (p. 64), and shows Tom how to use a knife to slaughter animals (instead of the rocks Tom had been using (p. 65)). Bottrell's longer version (1970, pp. 181–6) details these and far more examples of Jack's skills, and Tom's brutish stupidity.

58. On the opposition between 'farmers' and 'miners' in the Western industries see Hand, 1942, p. 147; Hand, 1946, p. 164; Quam-Wickham, 1999, pp. 135–151.

59. Not only did skilled miners insist not being confused with farmers, but also with unskilled labourers called Navvies, who engaged in tasks that superficially resembled their own. See Henwood, 1972, p. 66; Manning, 2004, pp. 533–5, 544 n.10, 545 n.14.

60. Quam-Wickham, 1999, p. 146.

61. Park and Daston, 1981; Daston and Park, 1998.

62. W. Bottrell, *Traditions and Hearthside Stories of West Cornwall*, Penzance, 1870–1880, Volume 2: p. 185, cited in James, 1992, pp. 165–6; on the hostility of Nonconformists (Wesleyans and Quakers) to these beliefs see also W. Bottrell, *Traditions and Hearthside Stories of West Cornwall, a Facsimile Selection*, Lampeter, 1989, p. 116; Henwood, 1972, pp. 125–30; 138–43.

63. From C. Kingsley, *Yeast: A Problem*, Chapter 13: A Village Revel, 2003, available at: (http://www.gutenberg.org/dirs/1/0/3/6/10364/10364.txt). Originally published in 1853.

64. W. Bottrell, *Stories and Folklore of West Cornwall*, Penzance, 1880, p. 165; Courtney 1973, p. 132. Interestingly, one place this song occurs is in a Cornish version of the Rumpelstiltskin story (Hunt, 1916, pp. 243, 245), a story of uncanny levels of *female* productivity in weaving achieved with supernatural aid, for an interpretation of which see, J. Schneider, 'Rumpelstiltskin's bargain: folklore and the merchant capitalist intensification of linen manufacture in early modern Europe', in A. Weiner and J. Schneider (eds), *Cloth and Human Experience*, Washington, DC, 1989, pp. 177–213.

65. Kingsley, 2003, *ibid.*

66. Schneider, 1990, on these two characteristics of being 'prior inhabitants' as well as contemporary nature spirits.

67. Bottrell, 1989, 152; goats, like fairies, are associated with 'moors, or among carns and in other out-of-the-way places', and fairies therefore sometimes take the guise of goats whose habitats they share (Bottrell, 1989, pp. 37–8). For the haunts of Cornish fairies, Bottrell, 1989, pp.32–4, 49.

68. Spriggans (and other fairies) are associated with ruins (Bottrell, 1970, p. 59), undergound places and holes (Bottrell, 1989, pp. 40, 99, 103, 151); Bukkas 'keep to old ruined castles' (Bottrell, 1880, p. 30). Haunted locations associated with Antediluvian architecture (Bottrell 1970: p. 52); 'They say that there are still to be seen about Trewe the remains of old bals which had been worked before the Flood.' (Bottrell, 1970, p. 72).

69. '"I wish we could but catch a spriggan, a piskey, or a knacker," says Capt. Mathy one night, "cf one can but lay hands on any of the smale people unawares before they vanish, or turn into muryans (ants), they may be made to tell where the goold es buried."' Bottrell, 1970, p. 74; also Bottrell, 1989, pp. 151–2.

70. Virtually all stories of fairy ointment revolve around this, Bottrell 1989, pp. 92–103; Bottrell 1970, pp. 207–14; Hunt, 1916, p. 84, pp. 109–13, 120–126; for stories of inquisitive humans being punished for spying on knockers, see Hunt, 1916, p. 88, Bottrell 1970, pp.76–8; for punishment for talking about fairies, see Hunt 1916, p. 97.

71. Fisher Vane, 'Spooks, Spectres and Superstitions in Mining', *The Mining Journal*, 30 May 1937, p. 5. I'd like to thank Ronald James for making this article available to me.

72. Bottrell, 1989, pp. 104ff; Bottell 1870–1880, Volume 2, pp. 186–93.

73. Bottrell, 1989, p. 104.

74. Bottrell, 1989, p. 105.

75. Bottrell, 1989, p. 105.

76. Bottrell, 1989, p. 105.

77. Bottrell, 1989, p. 106.

78. Bottrell, 1989, p. 107.

79. Bottrell, 1989, pp. 107–8.

80. Bottrell, 1989, p. 108.

81. Bottrell, 1989, pp. 108–9.

82. Some good examples of these typologies see Hunt, 1916, pp. 79–83, Bottrell, 1870, pp. 74–9; Bottrell, 1880, pp. 193–4; Bottrell, 1989, pp. 151–3; M. A. Courtney, *Cornish Feasts and Folklore*, New Jersey, 1973, originally published in 1890, pp. 120–9. Bottrell rather strongly denies that knockers are part of the fairy tribe, though he mentions them in this context, regarding them to be a 'hybrid race between ordinary ghosts and elves' (Bottrell, 1880, p. 193).

83. Bottrell, 1880, p. 193.

84. Hunt, 1916, pp. 90–91; Bottrell, 1870, pp. 76ff.

85. James, 1992, p. 168.

86. Fish, 1980, pp. 157–169; Baker, 1971; James, 1992, pp. 170–1.

87. Fish, 1980, p. 157; James, 1994, pp. 40–44.

88. Fish, 1980, p. 165.
89. Fish, 1980, p. 157.
90. James, 1992, pp. 154, 159.
91. Hand, 1946, pp. 3–7; James, 1992, p. 168.
92. Cited in Hand, 1946, pp. 4–5.
93. Interestingly, the last gasp of the tommyknockers is as a children's tale to cover the sound of high-graded ore being broken up in the basement at night. See Baker, 1971.
94. Bancroft, 1945, pp. 322–6, 329–33; Hand, 1942, pp. 129–30; Hand, 1946, pp. 4–7, 13–17; Fish, 1980, p. 160; James, 1992, p. 171.
95. Bancroft, 1945, p. 327. Cornish ethnicity was often expressed most palpably in linguistic terms, knowing how to speak 'Cornish' (in this case not the Celtic language, by then extinct, but presumably the dialect and perhaps the Western mining jargon to which the Cornish contributed disproportionately) as opposed to 'English' (presumably a more standard dialect) was often taken to be a guarantee vouchsafing possession of the skills of hard rock mining, Bancroft, 1945, pp. 318–22; Hand, 1942, p. 147; Hand, 1946, p. 175; Fish, 1980, p. 157; James, 1994, pp. 34–6. For a parallel mobilization of ethnic and linguistic difference as a sign of difference of technical competence in the same period, see Manning 2002, 2004; see also Quam-Wickham, 1999, pp. 143–4.
96. 'The Cornish may have been the experts underground, but the Irish could be proficient politicians on the surface . . . The Cornish could outcompete the Irish in the mines, but above ground Irish political organisation could defeat Cornish ambitions.' James, 1994, p. 41. This ideology of ethnic complementarity between the Cornish claim on *natural* technical skills *underground* as opposed to Irish *social* political power *above ground* again shows the process of naturalization of ethnicity with which I began.

MIGRATION NETWORKS AND THE TRANSNATIONALIZATION OF SOCIAL CAPITAL: CORNISH MIGRATION TO LATIN AMERICA, A CASE STUDY

Sharron P. Schwartz

INTRODUCTION

Impacting on communities at points of both origin and destination, migration has played, and continues to play, a central role in the creation of the modern world.[1] The cultural repercussions of this are felt on a global scale and migration and its consequences have now become major political issues. Yet, as Leslie Moch reminds us, migration is a 'normal and structural element of human societies', and has been an important feature of European history for centuries.[2] However, as Colin Pooley and Jean Turnbull point out, we still know relatively little in detail about migration in the past.[3]

Numerous demographers, economists and social scientists have grappled with how to overcome this problem. In 1960 Frank Thistlethwaite, speaking at the Eleventh International Congress of Social Historical Sciences at Stockholm, called for an analysis of the 'honeycomb of innumerable particular cells, districts, villages, towns, each with an individual reaction or lack of it to the pull of migration'.[4] Moreover, he stressed the need to treat migration as a dynamic, fluid, complex phenomenon involving onward, return and repeat migration, a message which was highly influential in Scandinavia and northern Europe, where comprehensive migration records exist.[5]

Yet in Britain there are no sources that were designed to collect direct information on population migration.[6] In the absence of such migration records, Dudley Baines used the Census Enumerator's books and devised a method of estimating the numbers of net emigrants from each county of all permanent emigrants in England and Wales from 1861 to 1900. He stressed the need for a revised focus of analysis of migration flows from Britain, as his work had uncovered uneven regional demographic patterns obscured by national figures.[7] Echoing Thistlethwaite, Baines considered that one of the key questions that needed to be addressed was the relative incidence of migration in the past: why did people migrate from some communities and not others? In considering European migration in general, Baines subsequently called for fine mesh local studies that would yield more insight about migrants' motivation than large-scale quantitative analyses.[8] Yet another important factor, highlighted by R. J. Johnston in 1971, was that not all people within past communities, even in similar circumstances, migrated. He argued that even in the modern world, noted for its high levels of mobility, only about 60–70 per cent of people move in any five-year period, suggesting that there are obviously varying levels of resistance to the idea of moving. There was therefore a need to examine the dichotomy of movers and stayers.[9]

Yet, almost two decades later, there are still relatively few investigations that examine the details of the migration process from England: who the migrants were, the type of communities they came from, and what kinship and recruitment networks supported their migration decisions (notable exceptions are Paul Hudson and Dennis Mills' study of mid-nineteenth-century migration from Melbourn in Cambridgeshire to Melbourne in Victoria, and Colin Pooley and Jean Turnbull's attempt to examine migration and mobility in Britain since the eighteenth century).[10] Observers of contemporary migration have also isolated the relative incidence of migration as one of the factors problematizing international migration analyses. Thomas Faist grappled with what he termed a baffling puzzle: 'Why are there so few migrants from so many places and so many from only a few places?'[11] It was possible, he noted, to speak paradoxically of mass immobility on the one hand and mass migration on the other, but was it possible to reconcile these two opposites?

The main deficiency in understanding international migration flows is attributable to the fact that most studies have not sufficiently explored the dynamics of the migration process. Micro-level studies focus on individual values and expectancies, including improving and securing survival, wealth, status, comfort, stimulation, autonomy affiliation and morality.[12] Macro-level analyses focus on structural opportunities and constraints in economics (income and employment differentials), politics (regulation of spatial mobility, repression and conflict), cultural setting (dominant norms and discourses)[13] and demography and ecology (population growth, level of technology, availability of natural resources). The meso-level approach focuses on social and symbolic ties and features collectives and social networks that include social ties within families, households and communities. It also covers symbolic ties present in kin, ethnic, national, religious, political and symbolic communities, and the content of ties, obligations, reciprocity and solidarity, as well as access to the resources of others.[14] Yet, the conundrum of mass mobility and mass immobility from various communities remains unsolved.

However, Faist claims that mass mobility and mass immobility in fact go hand in hand, as the resources inherent in ties between people bound together in networks, groups and communities, are often locally specific.[15] He stresses the need to move away from rigid micro vs. macro distinctions and notes the need to focus more on the form and content of migration flows. One of the main factors facilitating international migration according to him is social capital. Social capital can be thought of as the framework that supports the process of learning through interaction, and requires the formation of networking paths that are both horizontal (across agencies and sectors) and vertical (agencies to communities to individuals). Social capital refers to features of social organization such as networks, norms, and social trust, that facilitate coordination and cooperation for mutual benefit; it plays an important role in fostering the social networks and information exchanges needed to achieve collective action.[16]

Faist argues that social network analyses explain the direction of migration flows. They help to elaborate why migration stimulates more migration, but are deficient in explaining firstly, how migrant networks come into existence, and secondly, relative immobility.[17] Portes and others have begun to deploy concepts borrowed from economic sociology to aid in an understanding of how self-employed migrants' reciprocity and solidarity influence their successful integration in US society.[18] Faist stresses the need to build on this. Obligations, reciprocity, and solidarity are dimensions of social capital; the dimensions and benefits of social capital are, according to Faist, visible in kinship groups, neighbourhoods, formal organizations and specific migrant networks. Yet, he observes that social capital is location-specific and therefore is not easily transferred across borders and only do so under specific conditions. In order for this to occur, migrants need pioneer migrants and brokers who help to establish migrant networks and link up with institutions within such networks. Chain- and mass-migration can only begin once social capital ceases to be a wholly local asset but begins to function as a transnational transmission belt.[19]

He therefore stresses the need for an analysis of migration movements centred on the functions of migration networks. What is the specificity of migrant resources that enable the formation and sustenance of migration networks; how do these resources encourage or prevent migration; and importantly, how easily are these transferred overseas?[20] To this question we might add another obvious one, yet one that has been less well researched: how do migration networks break down? Work on emigration from northern Italy to Argentina has concluded that migration chains were not immutable and Monica Boyd has argued that greater attention should be given to the non-development and cessation of personal networks and the incorporation of personal networks in a broader migration systems approach.[21]

The problems facing British migration researchers are magnified for those studying Cornish migration, for the Cornish are invisible migrants, classed as English or British in official documentation. In order to examine migration flows from an area Baines highlighted as one of Europe's foremost emigration regions, and therefore worthy of further study,[22] Cornish migrants have to be disaggregated from English or British data, a process that is very time-consuming. A considerable literature concerning migration from Cornwall exists but, as Brettell and Hollifield have noted with respect to histories of other migrant groups, this is mainly a narrative of how the Cornish settled, shaped their communities and constructed their identity.[23] This has taken precedence over the analysis of the migration process, an omission noted by Wintle with respect to Zeeland more than a decade ago.[24] Rather surprisingly for one of Europe's significant migration regions, there have been few studies of Cornish recruitment networks compared to those of other northern European regions, and few quantitative analyses of overseas migration streams.[25] In 1999 I suggested that it was time to move away from a homogenous study of Cornish migration to focus on intra-county differences in the timing, occupational make-up, and communities of departure and settlement of migrants, and reiterated this in 2002 calling for 'quantitative evidence examining demographic flows at various spatial levels'.[26]

Although in no way comparable to the records available to Scandinavian and German researchers, this article rests on a close examination of 2,500 records of Cornish migrants to Latin America (South and Central America and the Spanish Caribbean) from 1811 to 1930.[27] It will identify some patterns of migration that will progress the fine-mesh local study of migration flows called for by Baines which are lacking in Cornish migration studies. It will tackle the issue of scale raised by Faist by looking at movements centred on the formation, sustenance and functions of Cornish migration networks to Latin

America, and their eventual demise. For the study of the history of past migrations helps us to contextualize the migrations of contemporary globalization, and can inform us more generally about the history of social life.

WHO WERE THE MIGRANTS AND WHERE DID THEY GO?

The parish of departure and country of destination in Latin America can be ascertained for just over half of the 2,500 records in the database. Proportional circles have been plotted on a map to reveal

Fig. 1.

what regions in Latin America received Cornish immigrant labour (Fig. 1). Here it is necessary to explain what countries fall within the seven categories devised for this study. The Pacific Littoral and the Andes includes Peru, Bolivia, Chile and Ecuador, and has by necessity been amalgamated to avoid confusion over border changes following the War of the Pacific (1879–1883) that saw parts of Peru and Bolivia, including the cities of Iquique and Tocopilla, ceded to Chile. Ecuador, which witnessed a very small Cornish labour migration, has been included due to its geographical proximity. Venezuela and the Colombia that once formed a part of Gran Colombia appear in the same category as British Guiana, Suriname and French Guiana, also included due to their geographical proximity. Central America includes those countries today known as Costa Rica, Panama, Nicaragua, Honduras, Belize, Guatemala and El Salvador. Argentina, Uruguay and Paraguay have been placed together for convenience; the remainder are countries in their own right.

The spatial distribution of migrants within each of these regions of Latin America was, in most cases, geographically quite specific and points to occupational specificity. For example, migration to Mexico, the most popular destination, was centred on the Pachuca-Real del Monte silver mining region in the state of Hidalgo. Far fewer worked in the silver mining centres of Fresnillo, Zacatecas and Guanajuato, the gold mines of Oaxaca, or copper mines of Chihuahua. In 1898 a Cornish Mine Captain noted that it was difficult to attract Cornish labour into the interior of Mexico even with the offer of good wages, as most headed straight for Pachuca which 'acted like a magnet to nearly every Cornishman who reached the country'.[28] It was likewise for migration to Brazil, where over 95 per cent of migrants went to the gold mining state of Minas Gerais where they settled in mining towns and villages such as Passegem, Morro Velho, Ouro Prêto, and Gongo Soco some 250 miles north of Rio de Janeiro. Meanwhile, migration to Cuba occurred mainly to the copper fields of Cobre near Santiago de Cuba in the south east of the island.

Migration to Chile, Bolivia, Peru and Ecuador was more complex, with Chile accounting for over seventy five per cent of the total, Bolivia and Peru just over 12 and 10 per cent respectively, and less than one and a half per cent migrating to Ecuador to work at the gold mines of Zaruma south of Guayaquil. The mining settlements of the Pacific Littoral were found mainly in the Norte Chico and Norte Grande of the country, the latter becoming Chilean territory after 1883–84. Primarily the Cornish settled in four main areas: in and around the copper, gold and silver fields of Coquimbo and the Copiapó Valley, the copper, silver and nitrate fields near Tocopilla, and the Iquique nitrate district. A few were resident in and around the capital Santiago and the coalfields near Conception in the south of the country. Regarding migration to the Andes, this occurred mainly to the tin and silver mining regions of Huanchaca, Potosí, and Oruro in Bolivia and to the silver mines of Cerro de Pasco and the poly-metallic mines of the Arequipa region in Peru.

With respect to Argentina, Paraguay and Uruguay, migration to Argentina makes up over 95 per cent of the migration to this region, with Buenos Aires being the most popular destination and the Famatina silver mining region near Chilecito also of significance. Paraguay is statistically invisible which is hardly surprising, as it possessed a very poor floor in metalliferous minerals, and Monte Video in Uruguay accounts largely for migration flows there. Migration to Colombia, Venezuela and British Guiana was dominated by migration to the former, making up over 70 per cent of the total, mainly to the silver and gold mining districts near Honda, Marmato, Antioquia, and Supía high in the Cordilleras. Venezuela accounted for just over 26 per cent, mainly to the Aroa copper mining district, with the gold and diamond fields of British Guiana contributing around 3 per cent. There were no recorded events in French Guiana or Suriname which were French and Dutch colonies respectively, and where alluvial gold mining did not require the hard rock skills possessed by the Cornish. The countries of Central America attracted nowhere near the numbers that migrated to other parts of Latin America, with Chontales and Rosario in Nicaragua, Choluteca in Honduras and Veraguas in Panama accounting for much of the migration.

Of those Cornish who migrated to Latin America and to whom an occupation could be ascribed, 62 per cent were industrial workers, three quarters of whom were connected to the mining industry.[29] This was also predominantly a male migration flow. The migration of females was small indeed accounting for thirteen and a half per cent of the total migration flow to Latin America with males just over four times more likely to migrate there than females. This is hardly surprising as demographic studies since Ravenstein have noted that women are less likely to migrate long distances within their country of origin or across international borders than men.[30]

ANALYSING MIGRATION FLOWS AT SUB-REGISTRATION DISTRICT LEVEL

It follows, therefore, that since a significant number of migrants to Latin America were involved in the mining industry, we should seek their communities of origin in the mining districts spread from St Just in the far west to the Tamar Valley on the Devon border (Fig. 2). The

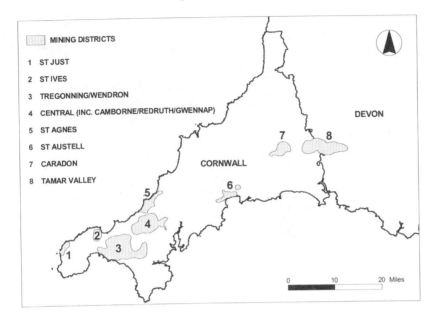

Fig. 2.

number of migrants with a known parish of departure in the database amounted to 1,235. This resulted in 95 per cent confidence intervals for point estimates that lay mainly within the range plus or minus 2 per cent. The resulting percentages, calculated against the total migrants from all Cornish sub-registration districts, were plotted on a map. The sub-registration district was used for this purpose, as figures for some parishes were far too small to be statistically meaningful (Fig. 3).

What immediately becomes apparent is that Cornish migration to Latin America was not at all uniform. There were in fact very few migrants from many mining areas and many from only a few, revealing how segmented the labour migration flows to Latin America were from this small region of Britain. The Central Mining District (Camborne, Redruth, and Gwennap), accounts for the majority of migration, followed by St Agnes, with St Austell, St Ives, and the Tregonning/ Wendron districts making a more limited impact, and those of St Just, Caradon, and the Tamar Valley even less. One might expect the more densely populated Central Mining District parishes to account for larger numbers of migrants than those less populated mining areas of Cornwall. Yet, the St Austell and St Just mining districts had urban centres comparable to those of Camborne and Redruth.

If migration figures to Latin America from each sub-registration

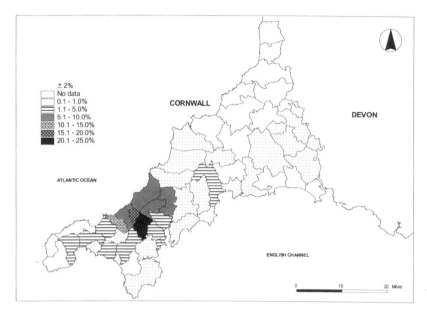

Fig. 3.

district are calculated against the total population of that sub-district in the year 1871, before population figures across Cornwall started to decline markedly, only Gwennap, Redruth, and Camborne, in that order of significance, are statistically visible. Population density was therefore not the only factor responsible for the presence of migration flows. Clearly, a large-scale analysis of migration flows to Latin America from Cornwall cannot expose the small-scale contrasts in this incidence, or the variations in the migration experience at the level of localities.

ANALYSING DIFFERENCES IN TIMING AND MIGRATION DESTINATION AT PAROCHIAL LEVEL

The top four Latin American receiving regions—Mexico, the Pacific Littoral (Chile, Bolivia, Peru, and Ecuador), Brazil and Cuba were selected and the migration flows to these regions compared with flows from the top three sub-registration districts in Cornwall (Fig. 4). Two of these, Camborne and Redruth, are parishes in their own right but Gwennap includes Stithians which represents a mere 4 per cent of migration from the sub-registration district of Gwennap. What immediately becomes apparent is that migration from these parishes to the four receiving regions was in no way homogenous.

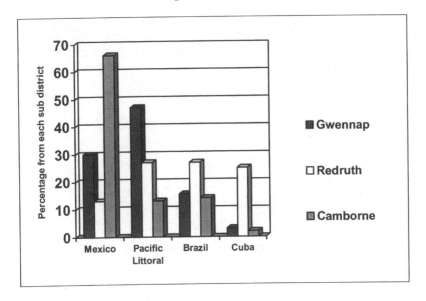

Fig. 4.

Gwennap and Stithians send 47 per cent of their migrants to the Pacific Littoral, almost double the number of migrants that migrated there from Camborne parish, but a mere 3 per cent of their migrants went to Cuba. Although neighbouring Redruth parish sends only half of Gwennap and Stithians' number of migrants to the Pacific Littoral, its figure for migration to Cuba is over eight times higher than that of Gwennap and Stithians. A similarly complex picture emerges for migration to Mexico. Mexico-bound migrants accounted for a staggering 66 per cent of migration from Camborne. But Gwennap and Stithians sent less than half this number, while Redruth sent around five times less. Indeed, Camborne was the parish from which the majority of Cornish migrants to Mexico originated, with Gwennap and Stithians next in order of significance. The migration flows from all parishes were extremely varied; this is surprising when we consider that the four parishes in question cover an area less than ten square miles.

We have established that there were marked differences in the direction of flows from the three sub-registration districts, but what of their timing? Decennial migration movements have been plotted for each sub-registration district and the migration from all Cornish sub-registration districts to Latin America has been provided for comparison (Fig. 5). Ewa Morawska has stressed that the character of the migrations between receiving and sending communities are not a constant but a variable affected by the economic, social, and political developments occurring in the country of departure and the country of arrival,[31] and this is illustrated in the migration flow from Cornwall to Latin America.

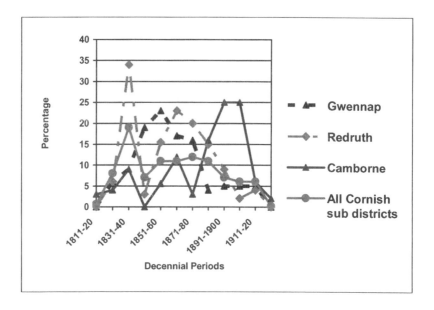

Fig. 5.

In the first half of the nineteenth century Cornwall was a dynamic industrial region in the vanguard of the British industrial revolution.[32] According to Pat Hudson the organization of work and work practice prevalent in successfully expanding industrial regions that begins to export its skill and labour often comes to influence the methods of an entire sector,[33] and this is noticeable in number of migrants leaving Cornwall for Latin America before the 1840s. The marked fall in numbers leaving Cornwall for Latin America in the 1840s and 1850s is noteworthy. Political turmoil swept Continental Europe in 1848 that drove down the market value of copper ore resulting in mine closures across Cornwall. This came at a time when the potato blight was causing widespread misery in many mining districts, while changing farming practises in the 1850s undermined collateral aids such as access to potato allotments.[34]

However, the fall in numbers of the 1840s is noteworthy for another reason; this was the first decade in which census records show a mass net out-migration. Many more people were leaving Cornwall, but not for Latin America. We may surmise that other, more attractive, migration destinations began to compete for and attract Cornish labour as the global mining economy and with it, the mining labour market, expanded. The collapse of several mining companies in Brazil, Chile, and Mexico coincided with the development of commercial mining in the English-speaking world of the western USA following the Californian gold rush of 1849. But it is more likely that the fall in figures for Latin America can be explained because people were making the most of free and assisted passages to the English-speaking British colonies particularly following the discovery of copper at Kapunda, South Australia in 1843, and the discovery of gold in neighbouring Victoria in the early 1850s, signalling the commencement of commercial mining in Australia.[35]

Migration figures to Latin America rallied again after the 1850s, a time when Cornish copper mining was at its zenith, accounting for over 80 per cent of Britain's copper and nearly a quarter of total recorded global copper ore output, although figures never returned to pre-1840s levels.[36] However, in 1866 the copper market crashed and by the mid 1870s the tin mining industry was in serious decline, resulting in the closure of many mines and widespread unemployment. The migration flow to Latin America remains fairly constant during the 1860s and 1870s before beginning to fall overall from the 1880s, and yet, as Baines' research has revealed, gross emigration ran at about 20 per cent of the male Cornish born population in each ten-year period from 1861 to 1900, and about 10 per cent of the female.[37] Overall migration flows from Cornwall were not ceasing but appear to have been changing direction once more as Latin America diminished in popularity as a migration destination in favour of elsewhere, probably South Africa where wages were initially much higher and transportation price reductions provided an added incentive to migration. The disastrous run to surface of the Morro Velho Mine in 1886, the under-capitalization of the Chilean copper mining industry and increased American control of the Mexican mining industry might well have been factors in this decline,[38] but equally the fluctuations point to the immutability of migration chains.

The overall flow for Cornish migration to Latin America supports Hudson's observation and casts doubt on the conventional gloom-laden crisis driven migration hypothesis.[39] Migration to Latin America before 1840 is symptomatic of success not failure, and represents the first significant overseas migration flow of skilled Cornish labour, setting the trend for what was to become a global phenomenon.[40] However, the overall pattern of migration to Latin

America obscures the considerable difference in the timing of decennial migration flows from sub-registration districts to Latin America. Redruth and Camborne are at opposite ends of the spectrum as regards timing, the former peaking relatively early, the latter much later, while Gwennap and Stithians fall somewhere between the two.

Noted by Hamilton Jenkin as the 'capital' of the largest and richest copper mining area of Cornwall in the early nineteenth century, Redruth, a dynamic, thrusting, industrial settlement was the undisputed commercial, residential and trading centre of a large (by Cornish standards) mining district.[41] The sharp drop in migration from Redruth to Latin America from the late 1830s is largely accounted for by the decline in migration to Cobre in Cuba where yellow fever was endemic that strongly dissuaded potential migrants. The decline thereafter parallels the fortunes of Redruth as an industrial centre, and the demise of copper mining.

Yet Camborne's migration pattern follows a somewhat different trajectory. First there are a series of fluctuations that highlight the inherent immutability of migration networks, as movement from Camborne to places such as the lead region of Wisconsin and Illinois gathered pace in the 1830s and 1840s.[42] Another fall occurred during the 1870s, the decade following the collapse of the copper mining industry. But the period after 1881 saw migration flows rise sharply to reach their acme in the two decades after 1891. Paradoxically this came at a time when, as the data for all sub-registration districts shows, migration figures from Cornwall to Latin America were falling and, according to Payton, migration attained its highest levels at the time that Cornish mining was in serious decline.[43] However, migration from Camborne to Latin America does not fit into the conventional picture of Cornish migration, for even in the crisis decade of the 1870s the movement of people to Latin America slowed down, confirming Wintle's observation that migration does not necessarily coincide with periods of the greatest economic stress.[44]

By the late nineteenth century Camborne had become Cornwall's premier tin mining and engineering centre, eclipsing Redruth. The latter town had reinvented itself in the 1880s as a largely post-industrial residential and commercial centre following the decline of copper mining.[45] In the early twentieth century the mining industry had all but contracted across Cornwall to a nucleus of activity centred on Camborne and district where the majority of Cornwall's remaining productive tin mines could be found. Additionally, Camborne could boast three engineering works, several other important foundries and two safety fuse manufactories, as well as the world famous Camborne School of Mines. Although Camborne had a rapidly growing population, it was simultaneously losing its population through out-migration, but this was not a result of crisis, rather of success. This highly populated industrial parish possessed a pool of skilled labour and was connected to dense transnational networks that had been in place since the early nineteenth century. Camborne and vicinity formed an ideal base for the continued recruitment and export of Cornish industrial labour.

Patterns from Gwennap and Stithians are more stable than those from Camborne and Redruth, showing a gradual rise throughout the early nineteenth century as the mining industry in Latin America expanded at the same as it was at its zenith in Gwennap, reaching a high point in the decade 1851–60. Thereafter numbers fall as the copper mining industry in the area was decimated. Apart from a brief reprieve in the period before World War One, migration to Latin America from Gwennap and Stithians fell from the mid nineteenth century and closely mirrored the conventional picture of Cornish migration as a response to mining decline. Yet gross out-migration figures from Gwennap show a continued demographic decline, the population of which shrank from 10,794 in 1841 to 5,662 in 1901. Clearly migration from this parish continued, but not to Latin America.

What the data does not depict is the regions in Latin América that attracted labour from the three sub-districts in each decennial period. Cuba attracted the majority of its migrants from Redruth in the 1830s while Camborne's migration pattern in the two decades after 1891 was largely accounted for by flows to Mexico. Gwennap and Stithians, the primary sending sub-district for migrants to the Pacific Littoral, saw migration flows peak in the decade 1851–60, and there-after decline.

The complexity of the patterns of migration at sub-registration district and parochial level clearly highlight the heterogeneity of flows to Latin America obscured by an overall Cornwall-wide analysis. The timing and direction of migration flows there are doubtless attributable to a number of mico- and macro-structural exogenous and endogenous political and economic factors, operating at local, national, and inter-national levels. But such factors cannot explain why so many people left Camborne for Mexico while far fewer migrated there from Redruth, a parish that lay only a few miles away.

SOCIAL NETWORK THEORY: SOME DRAWBACKS
Historians such as Burke have discussed Cornish migration from a macro-structural perspective: mass migration is made easier if the labour market for a specific highly specialized occupation is global, which in Cornwall's case, resulted in a global network of labour by the

mid-nineteenth century which shifted from one continent to another as the fortunes of the international mining economy waxed and waned.[46] Yet Cornwall, in common with many modern migration regions, was linked by migration 'chains'—personal or social networks that existed across time and space that bound migrants and non-migrants together in complex webs of social roles and interpersonal relationships—as the recent work of Roger Burt has highlighted with respect to the social networks of Cornish Freemasons.[47] As with modern migration, such networks represented conduits of information and social and financial assistance shaping migration outcomes, ranging from no migration, immigration, return migration or the continuation of migration flows.[48]

The data reveal that well over a quarter of migrants to Latin America returned to Cornwall at least once. Ewa Morawska, Charlotte Erickson, Rowland T. Berthoff and others have argued that return migration was an integral part of British labour migration.[49] The figure for Cornish return migration to Latin America is comparable to that observed by Nancy Foner who, analysing patterns of migration to and from the United States from Europe in the late nineteenth and early twentieth centuries, estimates that one quarter to one third of immigrants did not lose touch with their native communities and repatriated.[50] Migrants who return occasionally maintain ties with family, kin groups and organizations in their native communities, bringing with them invaluable social remittances, what Peggy Levitt describes as a local level migration-driven form of cultural diffusion.[51] Moreover, pioneer migrants in particular play an important role; viewed as more influential they get listened to more.

In recent years return migration has increasingly become the foci of academic scrutiny as the subject of citizenship has grown in importance; Ammassari and Black have noted the problems with categorizing the growing numbers of people who possess the nationality of a country through their parents or grandparents, yet have never lived there and at some point exercise their rights of residency.[52] How are these people to be classified—as return migrants? However, this type of movement is nothing new; eight per cent of the migrants in this study were born overseas to one or both Cornish-born parents and had later migrated to Cornwall. I did not categorize them as return migrants, but rather as 'overseas born'. The importance of highlighting the salience of this particular group is that this movement is indicative of strong transnational ties, for such people were born to families that were firmly connected to their ancestral homeland, betraying a continued commitment to sending-community life. Peggy Levitt observed this pattern when researching the modern communities of Miraflores in the Dominican Republic, and Jamaica Plain Boston, in the United States.[53]

In communities exposed to high levels of contact with people and places elsewhere, potential migrants see the advantages of moving, resulting in locally specific migration chains. Once set in motion, social networks assume a life of their own as generalized reciprocity and solidarity help to increase the scope for migrants by reducing the costs and risks of migration, driving up emigration in one place and immigration in another.[54] Levitt has argued that social networks increase the role that migrants can play in sending-country economies, heightening the intensity and durability of transnational communities within which migrants remain closely involved in the affairs of their communities of origin.[55] But in some instances, social networks can diminish as migrants become assimilated into their host society and engage in fewer cross-border activities.

However, in other cases connections between sending and receiving countries grow stronger as transmigrants and their society of origin forge a dense web of transnational relations that unites them in a continuous transterritorial social formation.[56] Thus emerges a 'transnational public sphere' or 'social field', where some members express their interests, conduct business, or raise families across borders.[57] This results in a culture of migration in those communities where there is a large reservoir of accumulated knowledge and experience of migration. Such communities form intimate ties focused on very specific localities elsewhere.[58]

Like many modern communities, a predisposition towards migration existed within Cornish mining communities that resulted in a reservoir of accumulated knowledge about migration that encouraged more migration. However, with respect to modern migration in general, Faist has alerted us to the fact that this does not explain how the networks came into being, were sustained thereafter, nor does it account for mass immobility. On all of these points scholars of Cornish migration have been silent. In order to understand the heterogeneity of migration flows from parishes only a few miles apart, the focus of analysis has to focus on the ties of individuals, how social action was facilitated and on the use of social capital that potential migrants drew upon to achieve goals.

This approach probes the interstices of individual and collective action found in intermediate groups such as communities, voluntary organizations, religious and fraternal groups, trade unions, and political parties, and allows the focus to shift to issues such as the exchange of information and goods, obligations, reciprocity, and solidarity among actors.[59] The migration networks to Latin America from Cornwall would not have existed had it not been for the human and social capital that of influential and entrepreneurial Cornish directors of British mining companies. This included their kinship and business networks that were forged within close-knit mining communities. This helped to foster and then sustain the first overseas migration networks in the wake of the migration of substantial British capital. Understanding how their considerable social capital ceased to be a wholly local asset and began to function as a transnational transmission belt holds the key to understanding how Cornish migration to Latin America was initiated and sustained.

THE TRANSNATIONALIZATION OF SOCIAL CAPITAL: CORNISH MIGRATION TO LATIN AMERICA

The data has revealed that there were hugely different patterns of migration from sending communities in Cornwall to Latin America. But what factors explain this patchwork quilt pattern of migration? It was undoubtedly the British capitalization of what was to become an integrated, international mining economy with its attendant labour market that provided the essential springboard for the migration of Cornish technological skill and expertise to the mines of Latin America. In the late eighteenth century Cornwall, one of Britain's earliest industrial regions, emerged as a centre of technological innovation in deep lode mining and steam engineering with a dynamic extra-regional export commodity: copper ore.[60] By the 1820s, with a powerful capitalized industry and hierarchically structured labour force, Cornwall was arguably the most advanced mining region in the world.[61] By contrast, Latin American mines that had long been the envy of the world lay flooded and in dereliction, ravaged by years of civil war. Latin American mine owners alarmed at the decline of their once mighty industry began to consider that the introduction of British technology might hold the answer to a revival in their fortunes.[62] People on both sides of the Atlantic were conversant with the successful Cornish system of mining. It was to Cornwall that new mining companies, financed by Britain, looked to provide technical expertise and labour creating the conditions for dynamic transnational linkages and migrant networks.[63]

Over one third of the British backed mining companies set up to operate in Latin America that were floated on the London Stock Exchange in 1824–5 had directors with Cornish connections.[64] These included nouveaux riche families such as the Foxes and Williams who controlled scores of Cornish mines, mineral ports and railways, as well as smelters and foundries in Cornwall and south Wales, and Norwich-born John Taylor, who held interests in mining concerns across

Cornwall and west Devon and who later founded the internationally known company, John Taylor and Sons. These men were intimately connected with many of the leading Cornish mine captains and engineers of their day who resided in occupationally homogenous communities of 'independent' mining families bound together by a faith in Methodism. These families lived within webs of deference woven by the old landed classes and the rising merchant bourgeoisie epitomized by the Williams and Foxes who had made their money through and because of mining, but whose dispersed interests obscured their role as a capitalist employing class.

Individuals known to men like John Taylor or the Williams through kinship and fraternal, religious, and business links in the mining industry, were offered jobs in Latin America, the genesis of the 'Cousin Jack network' (the worldwide nickname for a Cornish miner). Moreover, the Williams, and more particularly the Foxes, who had previously transferred some of their capital to invest in copper mines in the Quantocks, Somerset, and in foundries and copper smelting and mining in south Wales, had acquired the necessary social capital to expand the frontiers of their dynamic business interests across the Atlantic.[65]

Their task was aided in that Cornish miners and skilled artisans were already risk-averse to migration, a form of risk diversification very similar to that which has been observed in modern communities by Stark, Hoddinott, and Massey and Espinosa, and, as Justin Brooke's research demonstrates, had clearly been a feature of life in Cornish mining communities since the early eighteenth century.[66] In the first few decades of the 1800s Cornish miners, engaged in mining regions around the British Isles from Somerset and Shropshire to Wales and Ireland, had emerged as an 'aristocracy of labour'.[67]

Those Cornishmen selected for Latin American mines were recruited on a fixed contract for a specified annual wage, the transatlantic passage out and back was met by the company (sometimes redeemable from future wages), lodgings and healthcare were provided, and there was a system of home pay arranged for the maintenance of those families who remained in Cornwall. The risk to potential migrants under this type of contract was therefore minimal and by the 1840s most of the big mining companies of Latin America had their contingent of 'Cousin Jacks' who resided in distinct transnational communities.[68]

Migration to Latin America commenced as a result of selective recruitment within the mining industry by directors intimately involved with the Cornish mining industry. But they did not have the same level of investment, involvement or influence in all mining regions across

Cornwall that explains the relative immobility among potential migrant in mining districts such as Caradon, St Agnes, St Ives, St Just, and Tregonning/Wendron, all of which were witness to significant migration to other destinations in the nineteenth century. For example, the first manager of the Real del Monte Mining Company in Pachuca Mexico, John Rule, was a native of Camborne parish, where he spent his early years at the world-famous Dolcoath mine. He then worked as a mine captain in the parish of Gwennap some six miles to the east of Camborne where he met John Taylor in 1824 who was the manager of the Consolidated and United Mines and also a director of the Real del Monte Mining Company. Recruited by Taylor, Captain Rule was instructed to hand pick men for his Mexican company and became one of the pioneer Cornish migrants to Latin America.

It is no coincidence that Camborne sent the greatest number of migrants from Cornwall to Mexico followed by Gwennap. Once Rule began to recruit men he had worked with in mines in both parishes, migration chains began to form as migrants in turn provided information to family and friends back home about job opportunities, financial assistance and the offer of accommodation once in Real del Monte and Pachuca. By the late nineteenth century the name Rule was synonymous with this region of Mexico where Camborne-born millionaire-mining entrepreneur Francis Rule employed hundreds of men drawn from his native parish for his Santa Gertrudis, and Maravillas Anexas mining companies.[69] Migration networks arising initially through the recruitment of Cornish labour for British-financed mining companies, had assumed a life of their own, nurtured and sustained thereafter by kinship networks and the other informal links of expatriate Cornish mine managers and engineers, return migrants, Camborne School of Mines graduates, and members of fraternal and religious groups, all of which contributed to the complex phenomenon dubbed the 'Cousin Jack network'.

Moreover, the Rules were an old, well-established and respected Camborne family, with rites of life registers placing them in this parish since the early seventeenth century and were therefore likely to have had extensive kinship networks there. Charles Phythian-Adams has highlighted the central place of lineage when considering the role of families and communities: 'only at community cores—comprising the longest established local families—may "society" and "community" be said properly to meet at fixed points'.[70] Monica Boyd asserts that kinship ties are a major source of personal networks in migration and reveal the importance of social relations in migration behaviour.[71] As Barry Wellman and Charles Wetherell have discovered in their research, people form far-flung networks that contain a sizeable and varied number of ties with kith and kin that supply sociability, support, and information. These ties also provide indirect links to the people and resources of other social *milieux*.[72] Core families and their kinship connections undoubtedly had a role to play in the transnational transference of social capital.[73]

The data reveal that the parishes of Gwennap and Stithians feature strongly in migration to the Pacific Littoral, and this flow further exemplifies the salience of core families and their kinship networks. As with migration to Mexico, the discrete migration flows from this sub-registration district can be accounted for primarily due to the initial recruitment of men for British backed mining companies from the Gwennap mines in which mining entrepreneurs, the Williamses and Foxes had an interest. Once again, these networks were thereafter nurtured by informal links by pioneer migrants who maintained close links with their communities of origin.

The role of kinship in this process is exemplified by the families of Lean and Jose. The Gwennap parish registers confirm these families were resident in the parish from the late seventeenth and early eighteenth centuries respectively, and that a marriage occurred between Nicholas Jose and Elizabeth Lean in 1798.[74] This extended family of miners comprising brothers Joseph, John, William and Henry Jose and their cousin Samuel Lean, migrated to work in the early 1850s as contract labour for the British Copiapó Mining Company of Chile that was managed by a Mine Captain from nearby Scorrier, Sampson Waters. Lean was prospecting for the company in northern Chile and heard of mining opportunities to be had in Tocopilla that was at that time a part of the neighbouring Republic of Bolivia (it was later ceded to Chile following the War of the Pacific, 1879–83). He migrated there in 1853 and his Jose cousins soon followed. They established a highly successful copper mining and smelting company named Lean, Jose and Co., eventually bought out by John Taylor and Sons in 1881.[75]

These pioneer migrants looked primarily to their kin groups, friends and former work colleagues in Gwennap for labour. Friends were reunited, nephews joined uncles, sons joined fathers, cousins joined cousins and in laws were taken into the family business. These migrants in turn began to encourage and sponsor migration to Tocopilla among their own kin groups and friends. These two core Gwennap families therefore created a new locally specific migration network, one that was sustained by a constant flow of people, goods, remittances and news, that raised awareness of Tocopilla as a potential migration destination and reduced the costs and risks of migration, both financial and psychological. The data reveal that over 56 per cent of all Cornish migrants to Tocopilla came from a trio of Gwennap mining villages: Lanner, Carharrack, and St Day.

In these villages the once obscure Pacific Littoral port became a household name where people engaged in a transnational way of life for over a quarter of a century, raising their families across borders, benefiting from money sent home for chapel building, while remittances were spent in local shops.[76] Yet, in mining areas only a few miles away the links Gwennap enjoyed with Tocopilla would have been unusual unless there was a family connection or acquaintance with someone working with Gwennap expatriates in Tocopilla, or their kin groups back in Gwennap. This goes some way to explaining the relative immobility among potential migrants in other mining areas of Cornwall as regards this part of the Pacific Littoral.

Other localized migration networks are explained by the presence of mining company agents who interviewed and recruited migrant labour. Redruth is the most prominent sub-registration district for migration to Cuba and it is no accident that the recruitment agents for the Cobre Mining Company resided there in the early to mid-nineteenth century and where these migration brokers circulated advertisements for labour by hand bills in the town and nearby mining villages. In December 1836 the Cobre Mining Company's recruiting Agent, Alfred Jenkin, observed a handbill in Redruth stating that fifty miners were wanted for John Williams Junior and Brothers' mines at Cobre; in addition he wrote of an American gentleman in Redruth called Smith who was trying to engage fifty Cornish miners for the Cuba Mining Company.[77]

Yet again the presence of kinship is confirmed, for two of the mining captains of the Cobre Mining Company, William and James Reynolds, were brothers and their father was a brother in law to a man named Hocking who died at the mines.[78] Clearly strong transnational ties to Cobre were forged with Redruth and district, sustained by close community and familial relationships. The same picture emerges for Brazil. Gwennap and Redruth lay at the epicentre of the Williams of Scorrier's empire, whose mine captains and agents recruited heavily in both parishes, creating transnational migrant networks that were very locally specific, for example that of Gongo Soco and Gwennap, that thrived for three decades.

WHY DID MIGRATION NETWORKS TO LATIN AMERICA BREAK DOWN?

Yet, the research undertaken into migration networks to Latin America has revealed firstly, that chains were not immutable, and secondly, that they were extremely fragile. Their fragility is illustrated by the sudden decline in migration flows to Cuba from Redruth in the 1830s as news reached the town of the many deaths from yellow fever among extended families that dissuaded others from joining their kin at Cobre. Migration from the town to Cobre never attained the popularity it had enjoyed in the early 1830s as new networks had been forged elsewhere.

The immutability of migration networks is demonstrated by events such as wars or mine closures that led to chains switching direction. This occurred when the Imperial Brazilian Mining Company was wound up in 1856 and the Gwennap-dominated community of Gongo Soco was dispersed, causing the onward movement of Cornish labour to other parts of Brazil, particularly to the gold mine at Morro Velho in search of suitable mine work, or repatriation to Gwennap. The inception of the Mexican Revolution of 1910 and World War One, and the economic depression of the early 1920s, was compounded by the arrival of predatory American companies into the Mexican silver mining industry in the early 1900s. These companies were not necessarily predisposed towards Cornish labour considering Cornish mining to have had its day, and Francis Rule had sold many of his large mining concerns by 1914.[79] All these factors were responsible for the demise of migration networks between Camborne and Pachuca, as people repatriated or moved to mining fields in the USA or South Africa.

However, Phythian-Adams warns us that when kinship links are carried further afield on a permanent basis, they will then have to be regarded as essentially deactivated to a point that some spatial disjunction occurs.[80] We might therefore see this as contributing to the eventual demise of Cornish migration networks to Latin America. Inevitably there will be social networks that gradually diminish as migrants become assimilated into their host society and engage in fewer cross-border activities, losing touch with family and friends back home. Some Cornish immigrants were reunited abroad with their immediate family, others married into local families. When wars or mine closures led to the diminishing of, or cessation with, sending communities in Cornwall, it became more difficult to maintain trans-national relations.

Equally, the repatriation of pioneer or key individuals had a role to play. Migration from Gwennap to the Pacific Littoral began to fall in the late 1860s and this coincided with the repatriation of the Leans and Joses (and several other Gwennap migrants operating in the Pacific Littoral) who sold out some of their business interests, lessening the opportunity for employment in the Pacific Littoral by potential migrants from their native community. It also made it more difficult for those overseas dependent on pioneer migrants such as the Leans and Joses for work, as their labour skills were highly specialized and therefore largely non-transferable.

CONCLUSION: NEW DIRECTIONS IN CORNISH MIGRATION STUDIES

As a dynamic, early industrial region with a skilled labour force pre-disposed to migration and bound in webs of deference to an emerging new precocious merchant capitalist class holding interests in Latin American mines, the necessary conditions were in place for the transnational transferral of the considerable resources and social capital that existed within Cornish mining communities. And yet as this article has highlighted, while the overall migration flow to Latin America from Cornwall was closely governed by occupational specificity, the similarity ends there, for there were startling differences in the timing and direction of migration flows from mining parishes only a few miles apart.

This confirms Baines' insistence of the necessity of analysing very variegated migration streams at a very local level that even within a small territory such as Cornwall were startlingly heterogeneous. More-over, the timing of migration flows to Latin America from the three sub-registration districts analysed seems to confirm that migration is most pronounced when mining within them is at its zenith. This high-lights the danger of Cornwall-wide generalizations that argue that mass migration from Cornish mining communities coincided with economic decline; in fact it supports previous work by Wintle who called into question the observation that times of the greatest economic hardship witness the most migration.[81]

Why were there so few migrants to Latin America from so many areas in Cornwall and so many from only a few? To answer Faist's question with regard to Cornish migration to Latin America, it was, as he has suggested, due primarily to the mechanisms whereby social capital ceased to be a wholly local asset and began to function trans-nationally. A handful of mining entrepreneurs who were directors of British-backed mining companies with contacts and considerable resources in certain mining areas but not all, explain why those with similar skills and with the same predisposition to migration in some mining areas did not migrate to Latin America. In the Central Mining District the presence of such entrepreneurs positively encouraged migration in the 1820s and 1830s, but in St Just for example, their absence positively prevented it, hence the patchwork-quilt of migration patterns that depict mass immobility from some areas, mass migration from others.

This patchy recruitment pattern across Cornwall gave rise to locally specific networks that coalesced around kin groups that assumed a life of their own as the nineteenth century progressed. Close-knit and built upon localised mutuality, these vital conduits of information reduced uncertainty, limited overall transaction costs, fostered social capital by encouraging solidarity, promoted civic management and maximized efficient resource allocation in webs of affiliation that were truly transnational. However, they were exceedingly fragile, as the data have shown. The occupational specificity and resources that facilitated and sustained migration flows to Latin America in the early nineteenth century later had a negative impact, as mining skills were largely non-transferable. As quickly as they had emerged, these migration networks could break down, due to news of mortality from disease, decreasing British influence in the mining sector, local hostilities or the repatriation of key individuals, but primarily because of the limits enforced on the Cornish by their occupational specificity. What had been the *raison d'çtre* for their initial successful migration was to eventually prove their downfall.

However, this article rests on a close analysis of a small number of records and only to Latin America. Cornish migration studies, in common with historical migration studies in general, suffer from a problem highlighted by Lucassen and Lucassen and Brettell and Hollifield: the breakdown of migration studies into sub-specialisms, both within and between disciplines.[82] In addition to the problem of drawing together these sub-specialisms, researchers in the field meet another difficulty when seeking to conceptualise the process of migration in the past. For migration within the boundaries of the nation-state and emigration outside those boundaries have usually been treated separately. Indeed, Lucassen and Lucassen note how comparisons across international and internal migrations are rare.[83] Yet emigration and internal migration were likely to be subject to similar decisions whether made by individuals, families or communities. Baines proposes that detailed analysis of individual and family behaviour over the lifecycle in an area where internal and overseas migration overlap could help to answer questions about the existence and spread of migration networks.[84] And Cornwall was one such area.

Building on the type of work presented in this paper, a Leverhulme-funded research project entitled 'Contrasting Migrations: Migration and Community in 19th Century Cornwall,' has been set up at the Institute of Cornish Studies to address this gap in scholarship and to offer a new direction for Cornish migration studies.[85] It is engaging in a detailed comparison of migration from three occupationally contrasting communities, studying individual and family mobility over the life course, analysing how migrant selectivity operated across differing migration chains. Furthermore, it combines overseas emigration with migration within the UK, viewing these as parts of a single process of migration and thus dissolving sub-disciplinary boundaries.

Family reconstitution has been the preferred method for obtaining the detailed life-course data for such micro-studies of communities, as exemplified by the work of Pat Hudson, Steve King and Pamela Sharpe, although this practice has been in the main confined to the history of communities in the period before the mid-nineteenth century.[86] The 'Contrasting Migrations' project intends to adopt a more modest reconstitution aim, based on the nominal record linkage of age cohorts, a method applied by Robin to Colyton.[87] This longitudinal analysis, beginning with those aged 0-9 in the 1851 Census will attempt a partial, or focused, life-course reconstitution, linking in the first instance vital events to location, occupational and family data. To achieve this, large computerized databases kindly made available by the Cornwall Family History Society and the Institute's Cornish Global Migration Programme database will be used.

It is hoped that new light will be shed on a number of basic questions: what migration chains can be identified linking our selected communities to others? How were these maintained, were they interrupted in the second half of the 19th century and if so, how? Who moved, when, and from which sort of community? What were the family and community contexts of individual migration decisions? And crucially, it will address the problem of mass immobility raised by Faist and the dichotomy of movers/stayers noted by Johnston,[88] by looking at who stayed and why, making this project potentially one of the most important in British migration studies.

NOTES AND REFERENCES

1. See P. Levitt and R. de la Dehesa, 'Transnational migration and the redefinition of the state: variations and explanations', *Ethnic and Racial Studies* 26:4, 2003, pp. 587–611; T. Faist, *The Volume and Dynamics of International Migration and Transnational Social Spaces*, Oxford, 2000.
2. L. P. Moch, *Moving Europeans. Migration in Western Europe since 1650*, Indiana University Press: Bloomington, 1992.
3. C. G. Pooley and J. Turnbull, *Migration and mobility in Britain since the eighteenth century*, London, 1998, p. 1.
4. R. J. Vecoli, quoting F. Thistletwaite in R. J. Vecoli and S. M. Sinke (eds), *A Century of European Migrations, 1830–1930*, Urbana, 1991, p. 3.
5. Some examples of the resulting scholarship include R. Kero, *Migration from Finland to North America in the Years between the United States Civil*

War and the First World War, Vammala, 1974; F. Kraljic, 'Round Trip to Croatia, 1900–1914', in R. J. Vecoli, and S. M. Sinke, *A Century of European Migrations, 1830–1930*, Chicago, 1991, pp. 399–421; S. A. Wegge, 'Chain Migration and Information Networks: Evidence from Nineteenth-Century Hesse-Cassel', *The Journal of Economic History*, 58:4, 1998, pp. 957–86; S. A. Wegge, 'To Part or Not to Part: Emigration and Inheritance Institutions in Mid-19th Century Germany', *Explorations in Economic History*, 36:1: 1999, pp. 30–55; M. Dribe, 'Leaving home as a family strategy in times of economic and demographic stress: the case of rural Scania, Sweden 1829–1866', in F. Van Poppel, M. Oris, and J. Lee (eds), *The Road to Independence. Leaving Home in Western and Eastern Societies*, Bern, 2003; M. Dribe, 'Migration of rural families in 19th century southern Sweden. A longitudinal analysis of local migration patterns', *The History of the Family* 8, 2003, pp. 247–65; J. Langton, and G. Hoppe, 'Patterns of migration and regional identity: economic development, social change and the lifepaths of individuals in nineteenth-century western Ostergotland', in D. Postles (ed.), *Naming, society and regional identity. Papers presented at a symposium*, Oxford, 2002, pp. 229–67. P. Versteegh, '"The Ties That Bind": The Role of Family and Ethnic Networks in the Settlement of Polish Migrants in Pennsylvania, 1890–1940', *The History of the Family* 5, 2000, pp. 111–48.

6. Pooley and Turnbull, 1998, p. 23.

7. D. Baines, *Migration in a Mature Economy: Emigration and Internal Migration in England and Wales 1861–1900*, Cambridge, 1985, pp. 141–77.

8. D. Baines, 'European emigration, 1815–1930: looking at the emigration decision again', *Economic History Review* XLVII: 3, 1994, pp. 525–44; *Emigration from Europe 1815–1930*, Cambridge, 1995, p. 70.

9. R. J. Johnston, 'Resistance to Migration and the Mover/Stayer Dichotomy: Aspects of Kinship and Population Stability in an English Rural Area', *Geografiska Annaler, series B, Human Geography*, 53:1, 1971, pp. 16–27.

10. P. Hudson, and D. Mills, 'English Emigration, Kinship and the Recruitment Process: Migration from Melbourn in Cambridgeshire to Melbourne in Victoria in the Mid-nineteenth century', *Rural History* 10:1, 1999, pp. 55–74; Pooley and Turnbull, 1998.

11. Faist, 2000, p. 1.

12. See for example L. A. Sjaastad, 'The Costs and Returns of Human migration', *Journal of Political Economy* 70S, 1962, pp. 80–93; M. P. Todaro, 'A Model of Labor Migration and Urban Development in Less Developed Countries', *American Economic Review* 59,1969, pp. 138–49; M. P. Todaro, *Internal Migration in Developing Countries*, ILO: Geneva, 1976; J. R. Harris, and M. P. Todaro, 'Migration, Unemployment, and Development: A Two-Sector Analysis', *American Economic Review* 60, 1970, pp. 126–42; G. F. De Jong and R. W. Gardner, (eds), *Migration Decision Making: Multidisciplinary Approaches to Microlevel Studies in Developed and Developing Countries*, New York, 1981; A. Portes and R. Bach, *Latin Journey: Cuban and Mexican Immigrants in the United States*, Berkeley, 1985; T. Bauer, and K. F. Zimmermann, 'Occupational Mobility

of Ethnic Migrants', *IZA Discussion Papers* 58, Institute for the Study of Labor (IZA), 1999.

13. See for example, M. P. Todaro, and L. Maruszko, 'Illegal migration and U.S. immigration reform: a conceptual framework', *Population and Development Review* 13, 1987, pp. 101–14; S. Castles and M. Miller, *The Age of Migration*, London, 1993; C. W. Stahl, 'Theories of international labour migration: an overview', *Asian and Pacific Migration Journal* 4:2–3, 1995, pp. 211–32.

14. Some examples include G. Hugo, 'Village-Community Ties, Village Norms and Ethnic and Social Networks: A Review of Evidence from the Third World', in G. F. DeJong and R. W. Gardner, *Migration Decision Making: Multidisciplinary Approaches to Microlevel Studies in Developed and Developing Countries*, New York, 1981, pp. 186–224; M. Boyd, 'Family and Personal Networks in International Migration: Recent Developments and New Agendas', *International Migration Review* 23:3, 1989, pp. 638–70; D. S. Massey, R. Alarcón, J. Durand and H. González, *Return To Aztlan: The Social Process of International Migration from Western Mexico*, Berkeley, 1987; D. S. Massey, and F. Garcia-España, 'The social process of international migration', *Science* 237, 1987, pp. 733–8; D. S. Massey, L. P. Goldring and J. Durand, 'Continuities in transnational migration: an analysis of 19 Mexican communities', *American Journal of Sociology* 99, 1994, pp. 1492–1533; D. S. Massey, 'Social Structure, Household Strategies and the Cumulative Causation of Migration', *Population Index* 56:1, 1990, pp. 3–26; D. S. Massey and K. E. Espinosa, 'What's driving Mexico-U.S. migration? A theoretical, empirical, and policy analysis', *American Journal of Sociology* 102, 1997, pp. 939–99; O. Stark, *The Migration of Labor*, Oxford, 1991.

15. Faist, 2000, p. 33.

16. For differing definitions of social capital see P. Bourdieu, 'Forms of capital', in J. C. Richards (ed.), *Handbook of Theory and Research for the Sociology of Education*, New York, 1983, pp. 241–58; J. S. Coleman, *Foundations of Social Theory*, Cambridge, 1990; R. D. Putnam, *Making democracy work. Civic traditions in modern Italy*, Princeton, 1993.

17. See Hugo, 1981; Boyd, 1989; Massey, 1990; M. M. Kritz and H. Zlotnik, 'Global Interactions: Migration Systems, Processes and Policies', in. M. M. Kritz, L. L. Lim and H. Zlotnik (eds), *International Migration Systems. A Global Approach*, Oxford, 1992, pp. 1–16; Massey and Espinosa, 1997; Faist, 2002, p. 14.

18. A. Portes (ed.), *The Economic Sociology of Immigration: Essays on Networks, Ethnicity, and Entrepreneurship*, New York, 1995; A. Portes and J. Sensenbrenner, 'Embeddedness and Immigration: Notes of the Social Determinants of Economic Action', *American Journal of Sociology* 98:6, 1993, pp. 1320–50.

19. Faist, 2002, pp. 15–17.

20. Faist, 2002, p. 8.

21. M. Boyd, 'Family and Personal Networks in International Migration: Recent Developments and New Agendas', *International Migration Review*

23:3, 1989, pp. 638–70; S. L. Baily, 'The adjustment of Italian immigrants in Buenos Aires and New York, 1870–1914', *American Historical Review* 88:2, 1983, pp. 290–2; J. D. Gould, 'European inter-continental emigration. The role of "diffusion" and "feedback"', *Journal of European Economic History* 9, 1980, pp. 284, 304.

22. Baines, 1985, pp. 158–9.
23. C. Brettell and J. F. Hollifield (eds), *Migration Theory: Talking Across Disciplines*, London, 2000.
24. M. Wintle, 'Push-factors in Emigration: the Case of the Province of Zeeland in the Nineteenth Century', *Population Studies* 46, 1992, pp. 5230–37.
25. See S. Wegge, 1998 and 1999; Versteegh, 2000; Langton and Hoppe, 2002; M. Dribe, 'Migration and economic stress in nineteenth century Scania, Sweden', in J. Z. Lee, G. Songyi and D. Yizhuang (eds), *Marriage, Family Formation and Population Behavior in the Past: An East-West Comparison*, Beijing, 2000; Dribe, 2003. An exception of a quantitative analysis of Cornish migration is S. P. Schwartz, 'Cornish Migration to Latin America: A Global and Transnational Perspective', unpublished PhD thesis, University of Exeter, 2003, chapter 7.
26. S. P. Schwartz, 'Migration to the USA, 1815–1930: Preliminary Comparative Demographics for the Redruth and St Austell Registration Districts', *Cornish History Network Newsletter*, 1999; S. P. Schwartz, 'Cornish Migration Studies: An Epistemological and Paradigmatic Critique', in P. Payton (ed.), *Cornish Studies Ten*, Exeter, 2002, pp. 136–65.
27. This database was compiled for my PhD by tracing Cornish surnames from newspapers and journals, company work records, monumental inscriptions, censuses of population, genealogical information and shipping and banking records, which were nominally linked with Cornish census and parochial records to ensure accuracy.
28. *Cornishman*, 9 June 1898.
29. For the purposes of this survey the occupations of all migrants were categorized into the five groups as defined in the 1881 Census of Population for England and Wales: category one professional, two domestic, three commercial, four agricultural, five industrial and six indefinite and non-productive. The domestic category included all those adult female migrants (aged fifteen and over) with no specified occupation and those engaged generally in household duties or assisting in their husbands' businesses. It also included hotel or boarding house keepers, domestic servants and nurses. Category six comprised migrants whose occupations were indefinite or not stated, persons of rank or property not categorized under any occupation, and scholars and children below fifteen years of age. Students over fifteen were included under category one. As the stated occupations of female migrants in this study were so few as to be rendered almost statistically invisible, they have been included with the male figures.
30. D. B. Grigg, 'E.G. Ravenstein and the "Laws of Migration"', in M. Drake,

(ed.), *Time, Family and Community: Perspectives on Family and Community History*, Oxford, 1998, pp. 147–64.

31. E. Morawska, 'Return Migrations: Theoretical and Research Agendas', in R. J. Vecoli and S. M. Sinke (eds), *A Century of European Migrations, 1830–1930*, Chicago, 1991, p. 278; E. Morawska, "Immigrants, Transnationalism and Ethnicization: A Comparison of this Great Wave and the Last', in G. Gerstle and J. Mollenkopf (eds), *E Pluribus Unum? Contemporary and Historical Perspectives on Immigrant Political Incorporation*, New York, 2001, pp. 172–212.

32. B. Deacon, B., 'Proto-regionalisation: the case of Cornwall', *Journal of Local and Regional Studies*, 18:1, 1998, pp. 27–41.

33. P. Hudson (ed.), *Regions and Industries: A Perspective on the Industrial Revolution in Britain*, Cambridge, 1989, p. 23.

34. Bernard Deacon, 'Proto-industrialisation and Potatoes: A Revised Narrative for Nineteenth Century Cornwall', in P. Payton (ed.), *Cornish Studies Five*, Exeter, 1997, pp. 64–84.

35. For more on the Cornish and Australian mining, see P. Payton, *The Cornish Miner in Australia: Cousin Jack Down Under*, Redruth, 1984.

36. R. Burt, P. Waite and R. Burnley, *Cornish Mines: Metalliferous and Associated Minerals 1845–1913*, Exeter, 1987, p. xx.

37. Baines, 1985, pp. 158–9.

38. M. Eakin, *British Enterprise in Brazil: The St John d'el Rey Mining Company and the Morro Velho Gold Mine, 1830–1960*, London, 1989; J. Mayo, *British Merchants and Chilean Development, 1851–1886*, Boulder, 1986; M. D. Bernstein, *The Mexican Mining Industry 1890–1950: A Study of the Interaction of Politics, Economics, and Technology*, New York, 1964.

39. A. K. H. Jenkin, *The Cornish Miner*, Newton Abbot, 1927; P. Payton, *The Making of Modern Cornwall*, Redruth, 1992.

40. S. P. Schwartz, 'The Making of a Myth: Cornish Miners in the New World in the Early Nineteenth Century', in P. Payton (ed.), *Cornish Studies Nine*, Exeter, 2001, pp. 105–26; S. P. Schwartz, 'Exporting the Industrial Revolution: The Migration of Cornish Mining Technology to Latin America in the Early Nineteenth Century', in H. S. Macpherson and W. Kaufman (eds), *New Perspectives in Transatlantic Studies*, New York, 2002, pp.143–58; S. P. Schwartz, 'Creating the Cult of "Cousin Jack": Cornish Miners in Latin America and the Development of an International Mining Labour Market', in R. D. Aguirre and R. G. Forman, (eds), *Connecting Continents: Britain and Latin America 1780–1900*, Amsterdam, 2005.

41. A. K. H. Jenkin, *Mines and Miners of Cornwall: 3 Around Redruth*, Bracknell, 1979, p. 5.

42. Preliminary work is proving the existence of discrete migration networks from various parts of Cornwall to certain states in the USA. S. P. Schwartz and B. Deacon, 'Lives across a Liquid Landscape: Cornish Migration and the Transatlantic World', unpublished paper presented at the British World Conference, Auckland University, New Zealand, July 2005.

43. Payton, 1992, p.107–9.

44. Wintle, 1992, pp. 5230–7. He argues that people might not have had the necessary capital to fund overseas migration in periods of economic downturn. Deacon's work on Cornish migration streams to England and Wales appears to support this hypothesis: he argues that 'up-country' migration was more prevalent across Cornwall than overseas migration in the crisis decades of the 1860s and 1870s. See B. Deacon 'A forgotten migration stream: the Cornish movement to England and Wales in the nineteenth century', in Philip Payton (ed.), *Cornish Studies Six*, Exeter, 1998, pp. 96–117.

45. R. Perry and S. P. Schwartz, 'James Hicks: Architect of Regeneration in Victorian Redruth', *Journal of the Royal Institution of Cornwall*, 2001, pp. 66–71.

46. G. Burke, 'The Cornish Miner and the Cornish Mining Industry 1870–1921', unpublished PhD thesis, University of London, 1981.

47. R. Burt, 'Freemasonry and Business Networking During the Victorian Period' *Economic History Review* LVI, 4, 2003, pp.657–88. For more on migration chains see P. Levitt, 'Social remittances: migration driven local-level forms of cultural diffusion', *International Migration Review* 32:4, 1998, pp. 926–48 and E. Moretti, 'Social Networks and Migrations: Italy 1876–1913', *International Migration Review* 33:3, 1999, pp.640–57.

48. F. Gilliespie and H. Browning, 'The Effect of Emigration upon Socioeconomic Structure: The Case of Paraguay', *International Migration Review* 13:3, 1979, pp. 502–18 and L. L. Lim, 'IUSSP Committee on International Migration, Workshop on International Migration Systems and Workshops', *International Migration Review* 21:2, 1987, pp. 416–23.

49. S. Thernstrom and A. Orlov (eds), *Harvard Encyclopaedia of American Ethnic Groups*, Cambridge, 1980, pp. 1036–7; Morawska, 2001, pp. 172–212; C. Erickson, *American Industry and the European Immigrant*, Cambridge, 1957, pp. 49, 56; C. Erickson, *Invisible Immigrants. The Adaptation of English and Scottish Immigrants in Nineteenth Century America*, Coral Gables, 1972, pp. 61–2, 241; R. T. Berthoff, *British Immigrants in Industrial America 1790–1950*, Cambridge, Mass., 1953, pp. 80–4.

50. N. Foner, *From Ellis Island to JFK: New York's Two Great Waves of Immigration*, New Haven, 2000.

51. Levitt, 1998, pp. 926–48.

52. S. Ammassari, and R. Black, 'Harnessing the Potential of Migration and Return to Promote Development: Applying Concepts to West Africa', *Sussex Working Papers,* 2001, http://www.geog.sussex.ac.uk/transrede/TR01.pdf Downloaded from the Internet on 14 November 2001.

53. P. Levitt, *The Transnational Villagers*, Berkeley, 2001.

54. For a synopsis of diverse linkages between countries that stimulate, direct and maintain international flows of people, see J. T. Fawcett, 'Networks, Linkages, and Migration Systems', *International Migration Review* 23:3, 1989, pp. 671–80.

55. Levitt, 1998, pp. 926–48.

56. L. E. Guarnizo, 'The emergence of a transnational social formation and

the mirage of return migration among Dominican transmigrants', *Identities-Global Studies in Culture and Power* 4:2, 1997, pp. 281–322.

57. Y. Soysal, 'Changing parameters of citizenship and claims-making: organised Islam in European public spheres', *Theory and Society* 26, 1997, pp. 509–27; Levitt, 2001.

58. Massey and Garcia España, 1987, pp. 733–8.

59. Faist, 2000, p. 35.

60. S. Pollard, 'Industrialisation and the European Economy', *Economic History Review* XXVI. 4, 1973, pp. 636–48; Hudson, P., (ed.), *Regions and Industries: A Perspective on the Industrial Revolution in Britain*, Cambridge, 1989; E. Richards, 'The Margins of the Industrial Revolution' in P. O'Brien and R. Quinault, (eds), *The Industrial Revolution and British Society*, Cambridge, 1993, pp. 203–28.

61. R. Burt, 'The transformation of the non-ferrous metals industries in the seventeenth and eighteenth centuries', *Economic History Review* XLVII.1, 1995, pp. 23–45; J. Kanefsky and J. Robey, 'Steam engines in 18th Century Britain', *Technology and Culture* 2, 1980, pp. 176–7; Deacon, 1998, pp. 27–41.

62. S. Collier, T. E. Skidmore and H. Blakemore, (eds), *The Cambridge Encyclopaedia of Latin America and the Caribbean*, Cambridge, 1992, p. 223.

63. J. F. Rippy, 'Latin America and the British Investment "Boom" of the 1820's', *The Journal of Modern History*, 1947, pp. 122–9; R. W. Randall, *Real del Monte: A British Mining Venture in Mexico*, Austin, 1972, pp. 28–9; Eakin, 1986, p. 16.

64. Schwartz, 2001, p. 109.

65. For more on the involvement of the Foxes in Wales and Somerset see I. Ince, 'The Neath Abbey Ironworks', *Industrial Archaeology* 11:4 and 12:1, Spring 1977, pp. 21–37; J. Hamilton, and J. F. Lawrence, *Men and Mining on the Quantocks*, Bracknell, 1970.

66. See Stark, 1991; J. Hoddinott, 'A model of migration and remittances applied to Western Kenya', *Oxford Economic Papers – New Series* 46:3, 1994, pp. 459–76; Massey and Espinosa, 1997, pp. 939–99; J. Brooke, 'Henric Kalmeter's Account of Mining and Smelting in the South West in 1724–25', unpublished MPhil Thesis, University of Exeter, 1997, p. 239.

67. F. Thistlethwaite, 'Migration from Europe Overseas in the Nineteenth and Twentieth Centuries', in J. Vecoli and S. M. Sinke, (eds.) *A Century of European Migrations, 1830–1930*, Urbana, 1991, pp. 17–57.

68. Some miners took their wives/families with them, or sent for them later. For more on the growth and development of transnational Cornish communities in Latin America, see Schwartz, 2003, chapter 9.

69. Rule was born in the parish of Camborne in 1835 to John Rule and Anne Mayne.

70. C. Phythian-Adams, 'Introduction: an Agenda for English Local History', in C. Phythian-Adams, (ed.), *Societies, Cultures and Kinship, 1580–1850, Cultural Provinces and English Local History*, London, 1993, p. 19.

71. M. Boyd, 1989, pp. 638–70.

72. B. Wellman and C. Wetherell, 'Social Network Analysis of Historical Communities: Some Questions from the Present for the Past', *The History of the Family*, 1:1, 1996, pp. 97–121.
73. C. Phythian-Adams, 1993, p. 19.
74. The marriage took place at Gwennap Parish church on 12 March 1798.
75. See Schwartz, 2003, pp. 163–4.
76. For example, the Lanner Wesleyan Chapel acquired an imposing and expensive new granite façade and schoolroom in 1903 through the benevolence of return migrants, the Knuckeys and the Daveys of Tocopilla Chile, who gave in total about £500, a gift described as 'almost unique in Cornish village Methodism'. See the *Cornish Post and Mining News*, 19 February 1903.
77. See the Jenkin Letter Books H/J/1/17, Royal Institution of Cornwall.
78. Jenkin Letter Books, HJ/1/17.
79. The United States Smelting, Refining and Mining Company (USSR&M) purchased the Sociedad Aviadora de Minas del Mineral del Monte y Pachuca in 1906 which had been in Mexican possession since 1849. Besides renaming it the Real del Monte y Pachuca Mining Company, the USSR&M dismantled the Cornish pumps, hoists, and other equipment, installed a modern cyanide plant and electrified the entire enterprise. See Bernstein, 1964, p. 64.
80. C. Phythian-Adams, 1993, p. 19.
81. Wintle, 1992, pp. 5230–7.
82. J. Lucassen and L. Lucassen (eds), *Migration, Migration History, History: Old Paradigms and New Perspectives*, Bern, 1999; C. Brettell and J. F. Hollifield, 2000.
83. An exception is Baines, 1985.
84. Baines, 1994, pp. 525–44.
85. This one-year project is under the management of Bernard Deacon, with Sharron P. Schwartz as Research Fellow. The study areas are St Agnes (rural-industrial), Falmouth (urban-maritime) and a cluster of agricultural parishes east of Truro (Probus, Merther, Lamorran, Cornelly, St Michael Penkevil, Ruanlanihorne, Coby, Ladock, St Clement, St Erme and Tregony).
86. P. Hudson and S. King, 'Two textile townships, c.1660–1820: a comparative demographic analysis', *Economic History Review* LIII, 4, 2000, pp.706–41; P. Sharpe, 'The total reconstitution method: a tool for class-specific study', *Local Population Studies* 44, 1990, pp. 41–51; P. Sharpe, *Population and Society in an East Devon Parish: Reproducing Colyton 1540–1840*, Exeter, 2002.
87. Jean Robin, (1995), *From childhood to middle age: cohort analysis in Colyton, 1851–1891*, Cambridge Group for the History of Population and Social Structure Working paper Series No.1, Cambridge.
88. Faist, 2000; Johnston, 1971, pp. 16–27.

REMITTANCES REVISITED: A CASE STUDY OF SOUTH AFRICA AND THE CORNISH MIGRANT, c. 1870–1914[1]

Gary Magee and Andrew Thompson

INTRODUCTION

Historians of migration have written extensively on the diverse and trans-national nature of the emigrant experience. Publicity and recruitment for emigration schemes; migrant correspondence; settler ideologies and identities; return migration—all these have been the subject of recent attention.[2] Hence it is somewhat surprising to find that remittances—the transmission of funds by migrants to their family and friends back 'home'—have largely escaped their attention. Indeed, only in the case of the Cornish 'diaspora' has there been any real attempt to explore the motivation for, size of, and consequences flowing from so-called 'migrapounds'. This essay builds on scholarship by Gillian Burke, Richard Dawe, Philip Payton, Ronald Perry and Sharron Schwartz to look further into the movement of capital between Britain and South Africa during the later nineteenth and early twentieth centuries.[3] Specifically, it provides an account of the main mechanisms by which remittances were transferred (with a particular focus on the money and postal order systems set up and run by the British Post Office); a series of new estimates of the actual volume of remittances sent between Britain and South Africa; a comparison of South African remittances with those flowing to and from the other 'neo-Britains' (Australia, New Zealand, Canada) and the USA; and an analysis of different types of factor motivating the typical South African remitter. The importance of the Cornish migrant in the story of South African remittances is emphasized throughout.

THE RISE OF REMITTANCES

What is known about remittances can be fairly briefly stated. Although their payment was common throughout the nineteenth century, it is not until the 1870s that their total volume began to rise rapidly, a product of the growing wealth of emigrants and the increasing ease with which funds could be transferred internationally.[4] Several factors appear to have motivated remitters. Most obviously, there was the sense of obligation to fund the next round of emigration *via* the one-off payments and pre-paid tickets that financed the voyages of other family members. (This sense of obligation may not have been as strong in the case of South Africa; after the discovery of diamonds [1867] and gold [1886], emigration to the Northern Cape and the Transvaal tended to be temporary—young, single males who were apt to return rather than to bring out their families to join them). Significant for South African migrants—especially those from Cornwall—was the desire to provide more regular material support to the relatives and friends whom they had left behind.[5] Finally, remittances were also sent for the relief of distress: for example, relatively large sums of money were transferred *via* settler and ethnic societies and other related organizations, in particular by the Cornish Associations that proliferated in and around Johannesburg.[6]

Migrants wanted to transfer their funds safely, reliably and—crucially—cheaply. By the second half of the nineteenth century, there were three mechanisms open to them. The simplest was to rely on existing means of communication or one's own personal contacts. Thus 'migrapounds' could be sent through the mail, either in cash or kind, or carried personally by the migrant or one of his or her associates on trips back 'home'. Although seemingly widely practised, these types of 'pocket' and 'envelope' transfers were largely invisible to official eyes, so no record of their magnitude exists. Anecdotal evidence, however, suggests that the amounts involved were probably not trivial.[7] A much securer way of conveying remittances was through the intermediacy of a financial institution such as a bank or merchant house.[8] Financial institutions were particularly suitable to those wishing to remit large sums of money; for the bulk of remitters who sent smaller amounts, they were less popular.[9] The third mechanism available were the money order systems operated by the British and colonial postal offices.[10] These systems were ideal for remitters, for they were specifically designed for sending small amounts of cash through the mail.

In the UK, a Money Order Office was formed in 1838, a separate and specialized department of the Royal Mail that had its origins in an officially sanctioned private business carried on from the late eighteenth century.[11] The office grew rapidly, and a limited overseas service was introduced in 1856 as a result of the Crimean War. At the end of the decade, orders were for the first time exchanged between Britain and Canada; they then spread to many other parts of the Empire. By 1873, a reliable international money order service was in full operation between the United Kingdom and the majority of its colonies,[12] as well as with a number of other countries, not least the USA.[13]

From its inception, this modern money order system proved very popular, bringing large volumes of funds into the UK. Within the Empire, the major sources of remittances by this mechanism were Canada (27.7 per cent), South Africa (23.8 per cent), Australia (14.7 per cent), India (11.2 per cent) and New Zealand (5.9 per cent). Overall, though, the United States was by far the biggest sender of money orders.[14] Between 1880 and 1913, some £47 million worth of money orders arrived from America, an amount equivalent to around a third of all money orders received.

Figure 1 plots the growth of funds transmitted to the UK *via* the money order system from the USA, Canada, Australia and South Africa, the four most important sources. Together these countries accounted for around two-thirds of all money orders sent to the UK over the period in question. It demonstrates that while there were certainly parallels between these series, specifically in their general upward drift, they nonetheless differ in terms not only of the level of

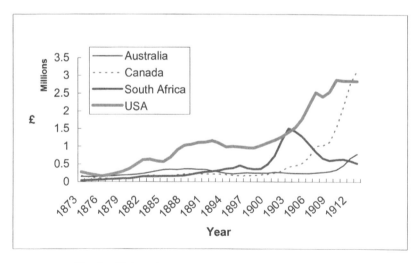

Fig. 1. Value of money orders to the UK, 1873–1913

Table 1. South African Remittance flows to the UK, 1875–1913 (in £)

Year	Gross (current prices) Est. 1	Gross (current prices) Est. 2	Net (current prices) Est. 1	Net (current prices) Est. 2	Real Gross (1913 prices) Est. 1	Real Gross (1913 prices) Est. 2	Real Net (1913 prices) Est. 1	Real Net (1913 prices) Est. 2
1875	28437	36354	23252	30864	26089	33352	21332	28316
1876	38825	50204	33229	44279	35949	46485	30768	40999
1877	51728	67766	45454	61123	47896	62746	42087	56595
1878	56889	74230	49853	66780	55774	72775	48875	65471
1879	64228	83653	56333	75293	64877	84498	56902	76054
1880	70245	92041	61489	82770	68199	89360	59698	80359
1881	90790	118779	79661	106995	89891	117603	78872	105936
1882	128492	169968	115140	155830	128492	169968	115140	155830
1883	104683	135953	88149	118445	104683	135953	88149	118445
1884	98449	127525	80685	108716	103631	134237	84932	114438
1885	103447	133458	85778	114750	116233	149953	96380	128933
1886	102523	132243	83682	112293	117843	152003	96186	129072
1887	112557	146314	94450	127142	130880	170133	109826	147840
1888	118818	154453	98972	133439	138160	179597	115084	155162
1889	147056	191160	123648	166375	169030	219724	142124	191236
1890	172484	224213	144640	194732	198257	257716	166253	223830
1891	188711	245308	156685	211398	216909	281963	180098	242986
1892	203008	263893	164933	223577	230691	299878	187424	254065
1893	223132	290052	177606	241847	256474	333393	204145	277985
1894	251982	327554	200716	273273	303593	394643	241827	329245
1895	266962	347027	213030	289922	329583	428428	263000	357928
1896	317997	413368	260026	351986	392589	510331	321020	434551
1897	263739	342837	208751	284614	317758	413057	251507	342908
1898	244790	318206	185552	255483	284640	370007	215758	297073
1899	264020	343203	184595	256930	314310	408575	219756	305869
1900	361765	470262	269196	368878	406478	528384	302467	414470
1901	532707	692472	438985	588140	605349	786900	498847	668341
1902	847616	1101824	702232	939559	963200	1252073	797991	1067681
1903	1110214	1443179	925469	1236360	1247431	1621549	1039853	1389169
1904	1049841	1364700	865497	1158627	1166490	1516333	961663	1287363
1905	979535	1273307	853224	1139567	1088372	1414786	948027	1266186
1906	861074	1119319	739129	990201	946235	1230021	812230	1088133
1907	750652	975780	637874	856369	807153	1049226	685886	920827
1908	673229	875137	568229	763961	739812	961689	624427	839518
1909	642192	834792	545525	732439	698035	907383	592962	796129
1910	677171	880262	584394	782027	720395	936449	621696	831944
1911	669918	870834	578529	774069	705177	916667	608978	814809
1912	608274	790702	512996	689820	620688	806839	523465	703898
1913	557349	724504	463183	624799	557349	724504	463183	624799

monies being remitted, but in the directions and timings of their movements. For example, money order remittances from South Africa grew extremely rapidly throughout the nineteenth century, reaching a peak during the Boer War (1899–1902), when thousands of British servicemen are known to have remitted part of their pay back to their families.

Table 1 provides new information on *total* gross and net remittance flows to Britain from South Africa from 1875 to 1913[15]—the distinction here being between the absolute amount of money remitted to Britain from South Africa (gross flows), and that amount remitted after flows out of Britain to South Africa have been subtracted (net flows). The four columns for 'real' remittances express these flows in terms of constant 1913 prices, and therefore capture the purchasing power of remittances across time. Table 1 also gives both lower (Estimate 1) and upper (Estimate 2) series for remittances. The idea here is to reflect the sensitivity of the data to certain key assumptions —in other words, these lower- and upper-bound estimates fix the likely parameters of remittance flows.

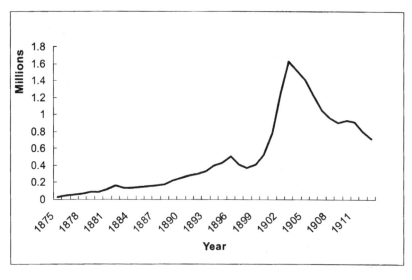

Fig. 2. Real Remittances to UK from South Africa (£ 1913)

Looking at the series presented in Table 1 (of which Estimate 2 for real remittances is graphed in Figure 2), it can be seen that between 1875 and 1913 South Africa remitted in real terms between £15.5 and £20.2 million back to the UK, an amount that made it the single largest source of remittences from the empire.[16] When allowance is made for the corresponding flow of funds out of Britain (see below), the net gain to the UK from South Africa was around £12.9 to £17.4 million— equivalent to between 53.8 and 72.5 per cent of all British exports to the colony or between 0.57 and 0.78 per cent of UK GDP in 1913. These new data also show that South African real remittances in- creased regularly and rapidly across this period. Between 1875 and 1900, they grew on average at 11.7 per cent per annum, an annual rate of growth that jumped to 45.3 per cent during the Boer War. Not surprisingly, following the war, the volume of remittances declined, though in 1913 they still stood 37.1 per cent higher than in 1900.

Did the South African migrant tend to send more money home than British migrants elsewhere? Figure 3 addresses this question by providing estimates of real remittance to the UK per remitter from different parts of the English-speaking world. A number of things immediately stand out. First, in all cases, the usual remitter in 1910–13 sent significantly more funds back to the UK than did his or her counterparts in 1875–79. Within the Empire, South Africans and New Zealanders were typically the most generous remitters. In fact, up until the second half of the 1890s they matched, if not exceeded, Americans in the sums of monies they were willing to remit. One of the other striking features of Figure 3 is the scale and almost continuous growth of remittances received from the average American remitter. Starting

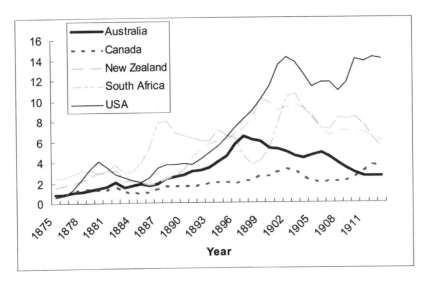

Fig. 3.   Real Remittances Per Remitter, 1875–1913 (£ 1913)

from a situation of parity in 1875–79 (at around £1 per year), the average Briton residing in the United States by the outbreak of the First World War was remitting more than three times as much per annum as their compatriots in the settler societies of the Empire (roughly £14 compared to £4).[17] Even in those parts of the British world where individuals were most keen to remit back to Britain—New Zealand and South Africa—the amounts each remitter transferred in 1910–13 (between £6 and £7 per annum) were the equivalent to no more than half of the corresponding American figure.[18]

INVESTING FOR BRITAIN

Thus far attention has focused on the extent to which individuals outside Britain chose to remit funds there. But Britain was not a passive beneficiary of the process. Viewed from the perspective of the recipient country, remittance flows may be seen as a return to countries that exported their labour, a return made possible by the existence of wage and income differentials between the migrant's source and destination countries.[19] Understood in this way, the migration of a worker from a distressed region of the UK to South Africa can be regarded as a sound investment for Britain. Not only might his or her departure reduce social tensions, it would in time engender a regular inflow of otherwise unobtainable funds once gainful employment had been acquired. Figure 4, which presents net real remittances per person leaving the UK, gives an idea of the extent of the returns associated

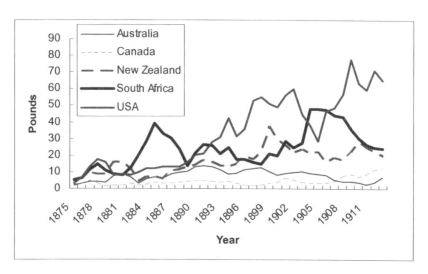

Fig. 4. Net Real Remittances per UK emigrant, 1875–1913 (£ 1913)

with exporting labour to various destinations. While it is clear that in every period the return per emigrant to Britain was significantly higher for those who went to the United States than for those who chose the neo-Britains or other parts of the Empire, it is also evident that those bound for South Africa and New Zealand typically brought better returns than those who had made their way to Australia and Canada.[20] In the case of South Africa this is probably explained both by the characteristics of British migration there (temporary skilled workers, many of whom left Cornwall with the intention of returning), and by the relatively high wages earned by Cornish miners on the Rand (which made it possible to save considerable sums of money and to then remit some of that money 'home').[21]

SOUTH AFRICA: A LIFELINE FOR CORNWALL
Of crucial importance in the South African context were the Cornish miner migrants.[22] Several scholars have shown how migration was deeply woven into the fabric of Cornish life.[23] From the 1880s, the Cornish provided a highly mobile and skilled workforce that made a significant contribution to the gold-mining industry around Johannesburg—they formed about a quarter of the white mine work-force by the beginning of the twentieth century, some 10,000 miners all-in-all.[24] Though some were permanent settlers who took their loved ones with them, most went alone. Separated from their home community in Cornwall, the families who they left behind anxiously awaited the arrival of a regular remittance in the South African mail.[25]

According to contemporary estimates, in the mid-1890s in Redruth alone a weekly sum of £1,000 to £1,300 was received, and by the early 1900s it was thought that every mail was bringing £20,000 to £30,000 for 'the wives and families and the old folks at home'.[26] What this means is that many families were reliant on the money that came to Cornwall from South Africa. Hence when the Cape mail arrived, people would flock into the towns from the surrounding villages to collect their money, and the business in local shops would boom.[27] Conversely, when the 'home pay' did not arrive, Cornwall's Boards of Guardians were left to pick up the pieces—though they themselves were helped by the charitable work of several Cornish Associations on the Rand, organizations which also played a key role in raising relief funds for the widows and orphans of miners killed by accidents or by lung disease. Other beneficiaries of remittances (whether from organizations or individuals) included Cornish schools, places of worship and com-munity projects that used these 'migrapounds' to finance equipment and interior refurbishment, and to clear their debts. In this way, Cornish miners were able to strengthen and reaffirm ties to their former communities.[28] Moreover, it has recently been argued that the inflow of 'migrapounds' need not necessarily be viewed pessimistically (in terms propping up an ailing Cornish economy), but that they played a more constructive role by 'lessening constraints upon production and investment' in several areas of Cornwall.[29] What is clear is that, whether remittances are viewed negatively or positively, South Africa's constant flow of money orders back to the UK provided a lifeline for Cornwall until at least the 1920s.

FURTHER ISSUES

There is not the space here to open up a detailed discussion of remittance flows from the UK to other English-speaking societies, or the importance of these transfers for recipients in destination countries. The scale and pattern of such flows to South Africa over this period (in total about £2.7 million) are given in Figure 5. In overall terms, Australia and Canada received transfers from Britain worth 56 and 42 per cent respectively of their remittances to the UK; America 12 per cent; and South Africa 17 per cent. Three issues thus spring to mind. First, why were there substantial subsidies flowing from the UK to the colonies (this stands in contrast to current cases of large-scale migration from developing to more developed countries)? Second, what explains the differential nature of migration and remittance flows across different English-speaking societies (the sums to the US and South Africa, while not insubstantial, are clearly different in magnitude

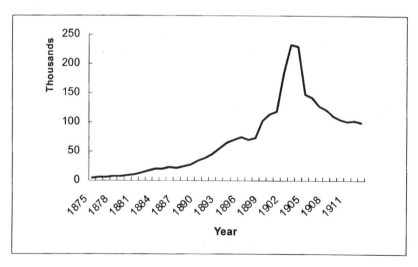

Fig. 5. Real Remittances from the UK to South Africa, 1875–1913 (£ 1913)

to those to Australia and Canada)? Third, why does the average amount of individual remittance appear to have increased from the UK to the colonies after the Boer War, while that from the colonies to the UK remained approximately constant?[30] The flow of remittances *from the UK* merits a paper of its own.

It is possible to probe further the motivation for remittance flows from South Africa to Britain.[31] Existing research suggests that they were used for two primary purposes: first, to help family and community members back home during periods of financial hardship ('distress' remittances); second, as part of a family's strategy to diversify against income uncertainty at home ('required' remittances).

Examples of distress remittances range from emergency relief in times of disaster, acute economic distress or illness to the funding of special events such as weddings and funerals.[32] Cornish Associations played a key role in raising 'distress' remittances, raising relief funds for the widows and orphans of Cornish miners killed in South Africa in mine accidents or by the miners' lung disease phthisis, and making donations to local communities in Cornwall following industrial accidents or mine closures resulting in large-scale injuries and unemployment.[33] 'Required' remittances,[34] meanwhile, relate to the migrant's sense of obligation to those left behind. The basic idea is that 'there exists some benchmark, or minimum remittance level, that all migrants are expected to provide'.[35] Thus they were more like an insurance premium than emergency relief, and consequently their payment continued over longer periods. Required remittances are said to have their roots in two sources. The first source is altruistic: the desire to support dependent friends and relatives notwithstanding the costs to oneself. This type of behaviour is tied to a family's economic and social needs.[36] Alternatively, advocates of the 'new economics' of labour migration have argued that 'required' remittances may be driven by an implicit contract between the migrant and the household that he or she has left behind. In their view, the decision to migrate, and any resulting remittances, are best seen as part of a familial or household strategy to maximise income and well-being. *Ex hypothesi*, remittances are paid to compensate other family members for their assistance in enabling the migrant to establish him or herself in more economically rewarding circumstances.[37]

Econometric analysis reveals that 'required' remittances from South Africa were the highest of all English-speaking countries: £3.73 per remitter, whereas for Australia the figure was £2.04 and the US £0.75. Why was this so? The reason may well be the high percentage of Cornish miners among British emigrants to South Africa. As we know, many (perhaps the majority) of these miner migrants were not intent on making a permanent move; so much is attested to by the outbreak of the Boer war, when, rather than sign up for military service, sizeable numbers of Cornish miners appear to have packed their bags and returned home.[38] The key point here is that many of these miners continued to support the families they had left behind in Cornwall with their South African wages. Thus, the migration of Cornish miners is known to have had particularly important consequences both for the 'family economy' and for the life of many Cornish women. Early marriage, coupled with migration, resulted in wives and mothers staying behind in Cornwall with full responsibility for maintaining the family home, while their husbands spent several years in South Africa in order to boost the family income. The well-being of many Cornish families was effectively determined by the prosperity of the Johannesburg gold mines.

Another interesting feature of remittances from South Africa is that when, for whatever reason, a typical remitter was forced temporarily to suspend sending funds home, there was a tendency for him to compensate for the money 'lost' to his family by remitting additional sums in future years. (On average, approximately 65 per cent of the 'lost' money that would otherwise have been sent home to the UK in one year tended to be compensated for in the following).[39] This finding implies that for many Cornish remitters the commitment to remit was an earnest one. At least with respect to family responsibilities, bygones were not simply regarded as bygones.

Finally, it is clear from our econometric analysis of South African remittance flows that regional distress was a significant factor in influencing the volume of monies transferred. Take the experience of the Cornish copper industry, an integral part of Cornwall's traditional economy. Its profound decline had severe consequences for entire communities. Particularly sharp downturns, where the industry's output in a short space of time fell alarmingly, occurred not only in the disastrous 1860s but thereafter in the periods 1886–87, 1893–95, 1902–03, and in 1913.[40] Given the Cornish economy's former heavy dependence on this industry, such occurrences had grave economic and social consequences for entire towns, promoting precisely the types of crises for the region that would have elicited emergency relief for overseas. The level of remittances from South Africa in these years indicates that this is indeed what happened. For each year a severe and sudden downturn in the copper trade was experienced, an additional £95,000 of money orders tended to be remitted from South Africa to the UK.

CONCLUSION

This article follows recent scholarship in the field of Cornish Studies in emphasizing the importance of emigration as a factor in the socio-economic history of Cornwall during the 'long' nineteenth century. Specifically, it sets the likely parameters of remittance flows between Cornwall and South Africa from 1870 to 1914, and provides a new quantitative dimension to what other scholars have observed largely by way of example and case study. This quantitative dimension shows that the injection of 'migrapounds' into the Cornish economy was substantial and likely to have far-reaching repercussions—no wonder South Africa was referred to as 'Greater Cornwall' and Johannesburg as but a suburb of the Duchy.[41] Moreover, the article has probed the motivations for remittance activity, and offered a new framework of interpretation based on concepts of 'distress' and 'required' remittances—the two single most significant reasons for sending monies 'home' in the Cornish case. Finally, the article has raised fresh questions regarding the outflow of money from the UK (which was relatively low to South Africa compared to the other colonies), and flagged this as an area for future research.

Throughout the article, we have tried to show how remittance flows, while interesting in themselves, are part of a bigger story concerning the forging of what social theorists have recently called the 'trans-national public sphere'. Clearly, remittances alone did not and could not nurture trans-national social networks; other aspects of the migration process were equally if not more important here: return migration; migrant correspondence; settler societies; religious organizations; and various forms of migrant publicity. Nonetheless, the willingness of Cornish migrants to remit ever larger amounts of their incomes is testimony to their determination to bridge the gap between their 'host' and 'home' societies, and to the increasing interdependence between Cornwall and South Africa at this time. For many Cornish migrants, their departure from Britain was not so much a case of 'cut and run' as of run, remit and (eventually) return.

APPENDIX

A note on methodology and the construction of estimates
Figure 1 is based on money order data extracted from the Postmaster
General's *Annual Reports* in the Post Office Archives, Farringdon
Road, London (Post 27). However, although money orders were the
main, they were not the only, mechanism for transferring funds back to
Britain. In terms of the Post Office, postal orders were also of growing
importance. Beyond the post office one needs to take account of a
range of other mechanisms—especially emigrant and other banks and
the Reuters news agency remittance service. As already noted, pocket
and envelope transfers were widely used. The volume of remittances
through banks and financial institutions can be gauged from Board
of Trade data found in H. G. Calcraft, *Statistical tables relating to
emigration and immigration, from and into the United Kingdom in the
year 1887, and report to the Board of Trade thereon*, H.C. London 1888
(2), cvii. Figures 2 to 5 and Table 1 capture all types of remittance flows
and not just money order transfers. The stock of remitters used in the
estimates were derived from data on the number of British migrants
travelling to different locations and come from I. Ferenczi and W. F.
Wilcox, *International migration, volume 1: statistics*, New York, 1929,
and US Department of Commerce, *Historical statistics of the United
States, colonial times to 1957*, Washington, 1961, series C90 and C91,
pp. 56–7. Average income is calculated by dividing GNP by population.
GNP data for the six countries come from N. G. Butlin, *Australian
domestic product, investment and foreign borrowing, 1861–1938/39*,
Cambridge, 1962, p. 6; M. C. Urquhart, *Gross national product,
Canada, 1870–1926: the derivation of estimates*, Kingston, 1993, pp.
24–5; K. Rankin, 'New Zealand's gross national product: 1859–1939',
Review of Income and Wealth, 38, 1992, pp. 60–1; B. R. Mitchell,
International historical statistics: Africa, Asia and Oceania, 1750–1988
New York, 1995, p. 987; and N. S. Balke and R. J. Gordon, 'The
estimation of prewar gross national product: methodology and new
evidence', *Journal of Political Economy* 97 (1989), p. 84. Population
data for all countries are taken from A. Maddison, *Monitoring the
world economy, 1820–1992*, Paris, 1995, appendix A. Further details on
the construction of our estimates can be found in G. B. Magee and A.
S. Thompson, 'Lines of credit, debts of obligation: migrant remittances
to Britain, c.1875–1913', *Economic History Review* (forthcoming). That
paper also provides both lower- and upper-bound estimates for
remittances (though frequently only the latter are given in this article).
Full details of the econometrics and evidence lying behind the
conclusions made here about required and distress remittances can be

found in G. B. Magee and A. S. Thompson, 'The global and local: explaining migrant remittance flows in the Anglo-World, 1880–1914' (forthcoming).

NOTES AND REFERENCES

1. Versions of this article were presented at the 4th British World Conference at the University of Melbourne in June 2004 and at seminars at the University of Oxford and the National University of Singapore. We are grateful in particular to Stephen Constantine, Kent Fedorowich, Philip Payton, Eric Richards and Graeme Snooks for their comments on earlier versions of this article.
2. For a selection of the recent historiography, see J. Belich, 'The rise and fall of the AngloWorld: settlement in North America and Australasia, 1784–1918', paper given to the 3rd British World Conference, University of Calgary, July 2003; M. Harper, *Adventurers and Exiles: The Great Scottish Exodus*, London, 2004, and 'Enticing the emigrant: Professional Agents and the Promotion of emigration from the British Isles', paper given to the 2nd British World Conference, University of Cape Town, January 2002; E. Richards, *Britannia's Children: Emigration from England, Scotland, Wales and Ireland since 1600*, London, 2004, and idem, 'The British Diaspora: In Wide Angle', paper given to the 4th British World Conference, University of Melbourne, July 2004.
3. G. Burke, 'The Cornish Miner and the Cornish Mining Industry, 1870–1921', unpublished University of London PhD, 1981, pp. 413–15, 440–51; R. Dawe, *Cornish Pioneers in South Africa. 'Gold and Diamonds, Copper and Blood'*, St Austell, 1998, pp. 118–20, 122, 123, 129, 172, 227, 228, 273; G. B. Dickason, *Cornish Immigrants to South Africa. The Cousin Jack's Contribution to the Development of Mining and Commerce, 1820–1920*, Cape Town, 1978, p. 71; P. Payton, *The Cornish Overseas*, Fowey, 1999, pp. 245, 346, 367; S. Schwartz, 'Cornish Migration Studies: An Epistemological and Paradigmatic Critique', in P. Payton (ed.), *Cornish Studies: Ten*, Exeter, 2002, esp. pp. 149–52.
4. A. H. Imlah, *Economic Elements in the Pax Britannica: Studies in British Foreign Trade in the Nineteenth Century*, New York, 1958, p. 57; D. C. North, 'The United States Balance of Payments, 1790–1860', in National Bureau of Economic Research, *Trends in the American Economy in the Nineteenth Century: Studies in Income and Wealth*, Princeton, 1960, p. 616.
5. D. Baines, *Migration in a Mature Economy: Emigration and Internal Migration in England and Wales, 1861–1900*, Cambridge, 1985, p. 17; C. Erickson, *Invisible Immigrants: The Adaptation of English and Scottish Immigrants in Nineteenth-Century America*, 1972, pp. 38, 238, 242; P. O'Farrell, *The Irish in Australia*, Kensington, NSW, 1986, pp. 69, 86; A. Schrier, *Ireland and the American Emigration, 1850–1900*, Minneapolis, 1958, pp. 16–17 and 103; North, 1960, p. 616; A. C. Todd, *The Search for Silver: Cornish Miners in Mexico, 1824–1947*, Padstow, 1977, p. 171. For further discussion of the range of possible motivations driving remittances

more generally, see N. P. Glytsos, 'Determinants and Effects of Migrant Remittances: A Survey', in S. Djajic, (ed.), *International Migration: Trends, Policies and Economic Impact*, 2001, pp. 250–68.

6. A. S. Thompson, 'The Languages of Loyalism in Southern Africa, c.1870–1939', *English Historical Review*, Vol. CXVIII, 2003, pp. 629–30, and see below for further details.

7. Feinstein attributed, for example, £200 to each Briton returning to the UK in the 1920s and 1930s. It is unclear from his discussion how much of this money was actually remittance and how much was merely the capital that travellers brought with themselves for personal use in the UK. See C. H. Feinstein, *National Income, Expenditure and Output of the United Kingdom, 1855–1965*, Cambridge, 1972, p. 125.

8. Banks dedicated to meeting the needs of certain types of migrants in particular were an important channel of funds. See, for example, C. O'Grada and E. N. White, 'The panics of 1854 and 1857: A View from the Emigrant Industrial Savings Bank', *Journal of Economic History*, 63, 2003, pp. 213–40.

9. However, towards the end of the nineteenth century, an alternative way of making modest financial transfers, cheaper than the banks, was provided by the Reuters news agency. Indeed, running private remittances services (and telegrams) proved very profitable for Reuters in the pre-war period. Two-thirds of its business came from Australia, the land boom of the early 1890s having drawn the general public into its offices, and given an initial boost to the practice of transferring earnings home in this way. See D. Read, *The Power of News: The History of Reuters*, Oxford, 1999, pp. 64 and 80.

10. In addition to money orders, British post offices offered other services that could be used for remittances. The most important of these was the postal note or order, introduced in the UK in 1881. With the creation of Imperial Postal Order Service in 1904, the system was officially extended to parts of the empire. Australia and Canada, however, opted not to participate, and postal orders were not exchanged between Britain and foreign countries. L. Stephen, *Life of Henry Fawcett*, London, 1885, pp. 427–9; 'Imperial Postal Order Service. Heads of Arrangement, 11/7/1904' and 'Report on the Imperial Postal Order Scheme Two Years After Its Commencement', Post Office archives, Post 27 (131). In the decade prior to the First World War, the telegraph also began to be used for transferring funds. However, the sums involved in telegraph money orders were relatively small: they totalled only 169,301 in number and £1,470,795 in value for the years 1900–10. Business did not even commence with Canada and the United States until 1910, and proposals for extending the service to India, Ceylon, South Africa, Australia and New Zealand were still under consideration in 1913–14. Postmaster General (hereafter PMG), *Annual Report, 1913–14*, p. 8.

11. The standard text is H. Robinson, *The British Post Office. A History*, Princeton, 1948, pp. 149–50; but see also M. J. Daunton, *Royal Mail: The*

Post Office since 1840, 1985, p. 84 and C. R. Perry, *The Victorian Post Office: The Growth of a Bureaucracy*, Woodbridge, 1992, p. 16.

12. PMG, *Annual report, 1873*, p. 11. The main exceptions were British Central Africa and Southern Rhodesia, both of which joined the money order system only in 1901. Many colonies, such as Australia and Canada, even adopted their own money order services. These were in effect, largely extensions of the existing British money order system. See Commonwealth Bureau of Census and Statistics, *Official year book of the Commonwealth of Australia, Containing Authoritative Statistics for the Period 1901–1907*, Melbourne, 1908, pp. 616–17; J. Viner, *Canada's Balance of International Indebtedness, 1900–1913*, Cambridge MA, 1924, p. 60; H. Smith, *Official Year Book of New South Wales, 1919*, Sydney, 1920, pp. 151–2; E. P. Ramsay, *The History of the Post Office in South Australia since the Foundation of the Colony*, Adelaide, 1934, pp. 18 and 36; and H. Robinson, *A History of the Post Office in New Zealand*, Wellington, 1964.

13. In 1868, the UK's first money order agreement was signed with a foreign country (Switzerland). Other agreements quickly followed, a convention with the USA, for example, being entered into in 1871. Schrier, *American emigration*, p. 107.

14. PMG, *Annual Report, 1872*, p. 15.

15. For an explanation of the methods employed to calculate remittance flows, see the appendix.

16. By comparison, Australia remitted between £8.6 and £11.1 million, Canada £14.6 and £18.9, and New Zealand £4 and £5.2. Only the much larger USA remitted more to the UK, somewhere between £86.1 and £117.9.

17. If the size of the average US remittance presented in this article seems high, it is worth remembering that (a) the nature of the US labour market and the cheapness and ease of getting there made it more favourable to early returnees who brought back capital to buy assets in the UK; and (b) it was far from unusual for migrants to exceed average savings rates as many left Britain on their own, but determined to either bring their families out later or themselves to return—contemporary remittance behaviour underlines this point.

18. Nonetheless, this still represented a relatively high proportion of average South African income, approximately between 10 and 12 per cent in 1913. Seen from this perspective, the gap between the typical South African and US remitter (who sent home between 13 and 18 per cent of their income) becomes less stark.

19. T. P. Lianos, 'Factors Determining Migrant Remittances: The Case of Greece', *International Migration Review*, 31, 1997, p. 72; T. Rod and J. Murphy, *Immigrant Transfers and Remittances*, Canberra, 1997, p. 30; Glytsos, 'Determinant's, p. 259.

20. For example, in the period 1910–13 for each migrant who travelled to South Africa, £26 on average was returned to the UK; for the neo-Britains as a whole the corresponding figures was only around £11.

21. Dawe, 1998, pp. 123, 144; Payton, 1999, p. 353.

22. Our reason for selecting Cornwall to illustrate the importance of remittances for local communities is simple: there is a rich historiography on the Cornish 'diaspora', much of which has been published under the aegis of the Institute of Cornish Studies at the University of Exeter. However, the social and economic impacts of remittance transfers can also be explored for other regions in the UK, if perhaps not so effectively or extensively. Here the reader's attention is directed towards M. Harper's seminal studies of Scottish emigration, helpfully summarised in her recent *Adventurers and Exiles: The Great Scottish Exodus*, London, paperback edition 2004, which, *inter alia*, highlights the function of remittances in chain migration; the close relationship between remittances and migrant correspondence; the different patterns of remittance behaviour between farmers and artizans; and the hardship caused by a breakdown in the transmission of earnings to dependants at home (see esp. pp. 93, 111, 188, 279 and 306). Meanwhile, C. Erickson's *Emigration from Europe, 1815–1914. Select Documents*, London, 1976, pp. 139 and 231–2 and Richards, 2004, pp. 144 and 166–8, lay emphasis on the importance of remittances in providing the pre-paid tickets which brought the friends and relatives of migrant labourers and artizans to the US. Richards, in particular, suggests that this classic chain of plebeian emigration may well have been significant in terms of its impact upon the population structure of the areas from which migrants were drawn. For migrants who remitted money in anticipation of their return, or who returned with their savings (for example, Aberdeen stonemasons in New England; English bricklayers in New York, Welsh colliers in Pennsylvania, and Sheffield steelworkers in Pittsburgh) see J. Bodnar, *The Transplanted: A History of Immigrants in Urban America*, Bloomington, 1985, pp. 60–1; K. S. Inglis, 'Going Home: Australians in England, 1870–1900', in D. Fitzpatrick, (ed.), *Home or Away? Immigrants in Colonial Australia,* Canberra, 1992, pp. 112–13; W. D. Jones, *Wales in America: Scranton and the Welsh, 1860–1920*, Cardiff, 1993, pp. 11, 16, 178–86, 195–201; M. Harper, 'Transient Tradesmen: Aberdeen Emigrants and the Development of the American Granite Industry', *Northern Scotland*, 9, 1989, pp. 56–7; A. Murdoch, *British Emigration, 1603–1914*, Basingstoke, 2004, pp. 111 and 118; S. Thernstrom (ed.), *Harvard Encyclopedia of American Ethnic Groups* (Cambridge, MA, 1980), pp. 326 and 330. Some, but by no means all, of these skilled workers were seasonal, and moved freely and frequently within the 'Atlantic economy' to work for higher wages. They tended to save as much money as they could with a view to setting up businesses or acquiring land in the UK, or alternatively providing for their old age on their return. They were a source of investment in local economies, therefore. Other migrants became much wealthier as a result of their travels, and returned to the UK to acquire substantial properties and estates. In the case of Irish migrants, relatively more money may have been remitted because of the greater number of relatives working on farms and marginal land who were in need of financial support: see Baines, 1985, p. 85. There is some evidence from official colonial records to suggest that English and Scottish

clerks and artizans did accept a degree of responsibility for their aged parents and dependent relatives back home: see A. Ross McCormack, 'Networks among British Immigrants and Accommodation to Canadian Society, 1900–1914', in H. Tinker (ed.), *The Diaspora of the British*, Collected Seminar Papers, No. 31, Institute of Commonwealth Studies, University of London, London, 1982, p. 58, which deals with the Canadian case, citing evidence from the Winnipeg Board of Trade, and M. Harper, *Emigration from North-East Scotland, Vol. 1: Willing Exiles*, Aberdeen, 1988, pp. 207–8, which shows how settlers in Canada voiced concern for the financial circumstances of the family's they had left behind, and even sent funds home for their education. At least some of the above evidence points to an ongoing psychological commitment on the part of the British emigrant to support family and kinship networks in the British homeland. Some of it also shows how many migrants continued to remain interested and participate in their 'home' societies well after their point of departure. But further study of the social significance of remittances for 'domestic' British history (beyond Cornwall) is certainly required.

23. See, for example, Burke, 1981, pp. 413–15.
24. Dawe, 1998, pp. xv and 123.
25. S. Schwatrz and R. Parker, *Tin Mines and Miners of Lanner: The Heart of Cornish Tin*, 2001, pp. 157–8.
26. C. Lewis Hind, *Days in Cornwall* (2nd edn, 1907), p. 352, quoted in Payton, 1999, p. 347.
27. Payton, 1999, p. 245.
28. S. Schwartz, 'Cornish Migration to Latin America: A Global and Trans-national Perspective', unpublished Ph.D. dissertation, University of Exeter, 2003, vol. 2, pp. 240–2.
29. Schwartz, 2002, pp. 149–52 [quotation from p. 151].
30. Calculated from money order data, available only for the colonies and not the US.
31. For full details of this analysis, see the appendix and G. B. Magee and A. S. Thompson, 'The Global and Local: Explaining Migrant Remittance Flows in the Anglo-World, 1880–1914' (forthcoming).
32. Dawe, 1998, pp. xv and 123.
33. Payton, 1999, p. 367; Dawe, 1998, pp. 118, 129, and 272.
34. N. P. Glytsos, 'Remittances in Temporary Migration: A Theoretical Model and its Testing with the Greek-German Experience', *Weltwirtschaftliches Archiv*, 124, 1988, pp. 524–49.
35. J. Hoddinott, 'A Model of Migration and Remittances Applied to Western Kenya', *Oxford Economic Papers*, 46, 1994, p. 461.
36. K. Osaki, 'Migrant Remittances in Thailand: Economic Necessity or Social Norm?', *Journal of Population Research*, 20, 2003, pp. 203 and 212.
37. R. E. B. Lucas and O. Stark, 'Motivations to Remit: Evidence from Botswana', *Journal of Political Economy*, 93, 1985, pp. 901–18; Glytsos, 1988.
38. See Thompson, 2003, pp. 625–8 for an assessment of the Transvaal's

English-speaking population, and the place of the Cornish community within it.

39. In other words if, for example, the average South African remitter normally sent £100 of remittances via money orders to relatives in the UK per annum, but failed to do so in one year, then in the next year he or she would, *ceteris paribus*, send £165: the usual £100 plus 65 per cent of the expected funds withheld in the previous year.

40. The crisis periods represent both the years in which there was an actual crash in output plus the year that immediately followed. The latter is included to allow for the lagged effects of the downturn. The copper series used comes from B. R. Mitchell, *British Historical Statistics*, Cambridge, 1988, p. 310.

41. Burke, 1981, pp. 440–51; Payton, 1999, p. 347.

REVIEW ARTICLE

RETHINKING HENRY JENNER

Amy Hale

Derek R. Williams, editor. *Henry and Katherine Jenner: A Celebration of Cornwall's Culture, Language and Identity.* London: Francis Boutle Press, 2004, 267pp., illustrations, ISBN 1 903427 193.

For many Cornish cultural and language activists today, Henry Jenner is the undisputed 'Father of the Cornish Revival'. Often pictured in his Gorseth robes with his flowing white beard, he certainly looks the part of an archetypal and venerable 'Druid', a fitting Celtic Revivalist figurehead. His achievements are certainly heralded in the histories of the Cornish Revival: Jenner wrote the first usable text for the Cornish revival, *Handbook of the Cornish Language*, in 1904. He has been credited with securing the place of Cornwall in the Celtic Congress of 1904. He was the first Grand Bard of the Cornish Gorseth, first president of the Old Cornwall Societies. There is no doubt that his work was absolutely central to the development of the early Cornish Revival. As such, his life and work has received renewed interest in the past couple of years. 2004 marked the centenary anniversary of Jenner's *Handbook* which provided the impetus for a new collection on his life and work, *Henry and Katherine Jenner: A Celebration of Cornwall's Culture, Language and Identity,* edited by Derek K. Williams.

In many respects this volume is very welcome. It combines historical essays on aspects of the Jenners' lives and work with reprints of some of Henry Jenner's more important documents and Kitty Lee

Jenner's poetry. There are eight research-based essays by respected writers on the Cornish Movement, among them, Tim Saunders, Donald Rawe, Alan M. Kent, and Brian Coombes, covering Henry Jenner's involvement with institutions of the Cornish movement (his work on the Cornish language being perhaps the most crucial) and also detailing his connections with the Gorseth, his poetry, his interest in Anglo-Catholicism, and his 'local patriotism'. Derek Williams own thorough research and editorship gives good organizational structure to the book, providing an introduction and chronology of Henry and Katherine's lives, as well as providing a select bibliography of both their works at the end.

One very useful aspect to the volume as a whole are the essays which focus on Henry Jenner's life and relationship with his wife, the writer and poet Katherine Lee Rawlings, perhaps better known as Kitty Lee. Alan M. Kent's valuable contribution, which uncovers much of their personal romantic correspondence, helps elucidate more of Henry Jenner's own life and the development of his academic focus over time. It also rightfully emphasizes Kitty Lee's contribution to the Cornish Movement, which has been overshadowed by her more colourful and enigmatic husband. Likewise, the short reprinted essay by Emma Harvey James recollecting her visit as a young girl to the Jenners' home 'Bospowes' provides a sense of colour and context of the Jenners' home life. These glimpses into Henry Jenner's personal life and surroundings help to make a more human figure out of a man who is often portrayed as a rather larger-than-life persona, and suggest more than a few clearly restrained eccentricities.

It is especially nice to have all in one collection a number of Jenner's essays on 'Celtic' Cornwall, including the landmark 'Cornwall: A Celtic Nation', which was read at the Celtic Congress of 1904 and is considered to have been the speech which apparently was so moving that it convinced the delegates of the Congress to accept Cornwall as a Celtic peer. In fact, the wealth of primary documents in this volume, essays, quotes, photographs and poems is probably what makes this collection so unique and valuable. Although the historical information within is very useful, Jenner remains a curious figure and perhaps the best way to understand him is through his own words. The photos and illustrations are also quite useful, as they are a reminder of the importance of pageantry and display during the earliest stages of the Celtic Revival, providing an often lost or misunderstood visual context for the time period.

Yet, when reading this collection there remains the sense that Jenner's rank within the Cornish Revival is still too monolithic to be really approached critically. Sometimes the praise heaped on Jenner in the text reads a little too extravagantly, which detracts from the overall objectivity of the historical essays. It is certainly valid to argue that a volume designed as a celebration of a couple's life and work need not take an overly revisionist or analytical stance. However, there is still the sense that we do not yet understand the full story of this truly fascinating couple. For instance, despite the wealth of historical data about the Jenners that this volume presents, there is little broad historical or comparative context for the Jenners' rather exceptional views. While this volume gives a lot of the 'who', 'what' and 'when', it does not provide much of the 'why'. With the exception of the essays by Saunders and Kent we get very little analysis of Jenner's position or motives, or even a sense of a coherent vision for Cornwall. In fact, what emerges from this text is the suggestion that Jenner's vision for Cornwall was quite fragmented and at odds with not only most of Cornwall's political and cultural trajectory of the time, but also with the more dominant of the emerging trends in wider Celtic ethnonationalist politics of the period. Yet his actual role within the Cornish Revival is never satisfactorily assessed. In fact, although his vision and beliefs shared some features with Celtic nationalist platforms in other nations, particularly his love of Catholicism, a number of his beliefs and interests were never embraced by other members of the Cornish Revival, particularly his form of Royalism, which was Jacobite and did not focus on the Duchy as a Royalist institution of Cornish accommodation. His right-wing political stance and sympathy for Fascist leaders like Mussolini are not elaborated on in this volume.

Additionally, although Jenner is given credit for 'spearheading' a number of Cornish revivalist institutions as first president of the Old Cornwall Societies and the first Grand Bard of the Gorseth, it could be argued that Jenner was more of a figurehead for the emerging movement, not one of its primary strategists. The correspondence between Jenner and Robert Morton Nance makes it quite clear that Jenner was selected for these roles because his knowledge lent gravitas to the wider project. After the first meeting of the Old Cornwall Society in St Ives in 1920, Nance wrote to Jenner and asked him to be the Society's president, praising his reputation and the public enthusiasm for his scholarship. He assured Jenner that he would not have to attend meetings, even if he agreed to the post.[1] That was a strategic move by Nance who knew what would be required for his movement to have public success. Likewise, it was really Nance who secured the Cornish Gorseth and suggested Jenner as its head. Jenner was probably similarly deployed earlier on in his career by W. S. Lach-Szyrma and L. C. Duncombe Jewell, both of whom needed the support and talents of the top scholar of the Cornish language to complete their own revivalist research and agendas. Indeed, it could be argued that *The Handbook* itself was produced primarily at the request of Duncombe-Jewell as part of his Cowethas Kelto-Kernuak project, and its publication was not quite the burning issue for Jenner.

Jenner had the one thing on which the foundation of the Celtic Cornish Revival rested: enough expert knowledge of the Cornish language to be central in its resurrection as a spoken and written tongue. This was a key political element in securing Cornwall's position in the emerging Pan Celtic movement, and it caught the attention, although not initially the practical interest, of people in Cornwall as well. For this reason, if no other (and there were other reasons), the work of Henry Jenner built the Cornish Revival. Jenner's great enthusiasm and tremendous capacity for research was perhaps better applied by 'cultural engineers' working to shape a movement, which they could not have done without Jenner's knowledge. Tim Saunders pulls no punches about the importance of this knowledge for the Cornish Revival at this time and his essay on Jenner's actual view of Cornish reflects Jenner's ambivalence at the actual revival of the language well. Interestingly, Jenner did not fetishize Cornish as a marker of Cornish ethnicity or difference in the way that others who drew on his talents did. Indeed, Jenner placed the origin of the nation not as much in essentialized constructs of shared culture, language or religion, but in national consciousness determined by historical events. This may be more a more complex and progressive viewpoint than other right-wing views of his would suggest.

Saunders raises very interesting questions here in his discussions of Jenner's view of Cornish as a racial signifier, yet not a distinguishing feature which suggested any concomitant political autonomy. Saunders tells us that Jenner's ideal position for Cornwall was some sort of 'modified Unionism' which was clearly Catholic, with a reinstated Stuart monarchy (p. 41). Clearly this was not going to be a viable Revivalist agenda for Cornwall, and Jenner more than likely was aware of this which is why he was satisfied being a figurehead and not a strategist. Nevertheless, as Sharon Lowenna points out, although Jenner's interests may have been idiosyncratic, they were not formed in isolation and without analogues in other spheres, even within Cornwall, which had Jacobite sympathisers as well.[2] Comparative data from other Jacobite and Legitimist movements in Europe during this time period may be useful in helping us theorize about lesser researched trends in the Celtic revivalism of the day which inspired Jenner and were ultimately rejected by Celtic ethnonationalists. Donald Rawe in his chapter on Jenner's poetry gives us a tantalizing hint of this trend in comparing Jenner's poetry with that of Hawker, who also had Jacobite sympathies.

Jenner's Catholicism is another area which deserves a more critical and comparative look. The suggestion that the early goals of the Revival were Catholic, anti-Modernist and Medievalist in nature is a point that some contemporary Revivalists take a great deal of issue with, despite the overwhelming evidence to support this assertion. Even Brian Coombes in his chapter on the establishment of the Gorseth serves as a Jenner apologist, suggesting that Jenner's vision for the Revival was deeply inclusive of the modern Cornish character (p. 175). This was most likely not Jenner's initial agenda as he was first of all an antiquarian and language scholar, not a Cornish activist, although in his later years when the Revival called for more practical considerations he did become much more populist in his sensibilities. In the early days of Pan Celtic nationalism, and even now in some quarters, Catholicism is a marker of Celtic identity, and when it was important to establish an essentialist ethnic discourse, as it was in the late nineteenth and early twentieth centuries, the envisioning of a pure, Catholic Cornwall made some sort of sense. Catholicism was used not only to establish 'difference' from the English who ultimately had chosen the 'Reformed Faith,' but also to allow comment on the religious and spiritual nature of the Celtic peoples who—it was thought —would by their very nature have needs for a more expressive, ritualistic religion than most forms of Protestantism would offer.

Taking some of Jenner's pet interests into a wider religious and historical context of the late nineteenth and early twentieth century, what would at first appear to be a focus on Cornish particularities provides a suggestion of his deep and wider commitment to the role of Catholicism in promoting a uniquely British spiritual identity. Although King Arthur has been a central figure to the Cornish for possibly fifteen hundred years, during Jenner's life Arthur and the Grail legend enjoyed renewed interest amongst Anglo-Catholic activists who interpreted them as evidence and symbolic of a native British Catholic tradition. Regardless of Jenner's commitment to making Cornwall the undisputed home of Arthur, the wider depth of meaning apparent in the Arthurian tradition would not have been lost on him. Similarly, the Archangel Michael, from whom Jenner took his bardic name, was not only the patron saint of Cornwall, he was also a symbol of a renewed, uniquely British spirituality. Esoteric beliefs concerning Michael from the late nineteenth century onward interpreted him as the central figure in a renewed Christian Europe with Britain at the helm. He was also related to the figure of King Arthur, who was believed to be doing the work of Archangel Michael in Britain.[3] As Cornwall was Michael's land, this made the territory the holiest of the holy. While Jenner may not have espoused these beliefs personally, he most certainly would have been aware of them. As a result, Jenner's work as a Cornish antiquarian and later as an activist of sorts involves symbols and themes which are not only central to Cornish identity but also are richly layered and have a wider British significance.

Henry and Katherine Jenner certainly reaffirms Jenner's place at the head of the canon of Cornish Revivalist luminaries. However, part of what makes Jenner truly so fascinating is that while the scope of his work was in some ways intensely localized to Cornwall, his range of influences and interests was in fact international. From his interests in Church reform and Catholicism to restoring 'legitimate' monarchs to the thrones of Europe, there is no doubt that Henry Jenner was interested in bigger fish than Cornwall, regardless of his interests in actually guiding the processes which would progress the causes he supported. There is a strong sense that comparative research on these other tangential movements and some of their other supporters might provide a more complete picture of Jenner and his place in modern Cornish history. Nevertheless, Williams' volume is a very important start in helping to understand a figure who only becomes more interesting with time, and to reveal the importance of a woman whose contributions to Cornwall need to be much more widely recognized.

NOTES AND REFERENCES

1. Robert Morton Nance to Henry Jenner, 14 February 1920.
2. S. Lowenna '"*Noscitur A Sociis*" Jenner, Dunbombe-Jewell and their milieu' in Philip Payton (ed) *Cornish Studies: Twelve*, Exeter, 2004, pp. 61–87.
3. For a discussion of the role of Michael and Cornwall in early twentieth-century Britain see A. Hale, 'The Land Near the Dark Cornish Sea: The Development of Tintagel as a Celtic Pilgrimage Site', in *The Journal of the Academic Study of Magic*, Vol. 2, pp. 211–14, 2004.

NOTES ON CONTRIBUTORS

Michael Bender is a consultant clinical psychologist, now working part-time in Cornwall. He recently completed an MA in English Studies at the University of Exeter, where he is embarking on doctoral research on changing concepts of masculinity as illustrated in boating narratives from the 1850s onwards. A keen yachtsman, he has sailed past Godrevy many times and was aware of the discrepancy in the location of *To the Lighthouse*.

Amy Hale teaches Humanities and Anthropology for St Petersburg College, Florida, United States of America. She has been researching contemporary Cornish culture for over a decade, and is particularly interested in cultural regeneration and policy issues. Recent publications include articles in *Ethnohistory* and the *Journal for the Academic Study of Magic*.

Alan M. Kent is Lecturer in Literature at the Open University and was recently Visiting Lecturer in Literature at the University of Coruna in Galicia, Spain. He has written and published widely on the literary and cultural history of Cornwall. His most recent works include an English-language poetic translation of the *Ordinalia* (2005), a volume of poetry, *Assassin of Grammar* (2005) and a novel, *Proper Job, Charlie Curnow!* (2005).

Cynthia Lane completed her first degree at Edith Cowan University in Perth, Western Australia, and is shortly to embark upon doctoral research. In addition to her interests in nineteenth-century Cornwall, she has also written on aspects of Western Australian local history.

Gary Magee is Associate Professor of Economics in the Faculty of Economics and Commerce at the University of Melbourne, Australia. His research specialism is nineteenth- and twentieth-century British, Australian and American economic history. His most recent book is *Knowledge Generation, Technological Change and Economic Growth in Colonial Australia* (2000). He has also written a series of essays on migrant remittances with Andrew Thompson.

Paul Manning is Assistant Professor of Anthropology at Trent University, Ontario, Canada. He obtained his PhD in Linguistics from the University of Chicago, writing on Welsh and Cornish historical syntax. His research interests include print culture and nineteenth-century workers (Welsh quarriers and Cornish miners) and the contemporary ethnography of the Republic of Georgia. Recent publications include articles in *Comparative Studies in Society and History, Russian Review, Semiotica, Language and Communication* and *Language in Society.*

Philip Payton is Professor of Cornish Studies and Director of the Institute of Cornish Studies at the University of Exeter in Cornwall. Recent publications include *Cornwall: A History* (new edn., 2004), *The Cornish Overseas: A History of Cornwall's Emigration* (new edn., 2005), *A. L. Rowse and Cornwall: A Paradoxical Patriot* (2005) and an Introduction to a new edition of A. L. Rowse's *Tudor Cornwall* (2005).

Sharron P. Schwartz is Research Fellow in Migration Studies at the Institute of Cornish Studies, University of Exeter in Cornwall. She recently (2003) completed her doctoral thesis at the University of Exeter, which examined Cornish migration to Latin America from a global and transnational perspective. She is the author of numerous articles on mining and migration and co-authored parts of *The Cornish Family* (2004) with Bernard Deacon.

Matthew Spriggs is Professor of Archaeology and Director of the Centre for Archaeological Research at the Australian National University in Canberra. Descended from the Cornish Spriggs, who are now sadly extinct in Cornwall, he has long had an interest in the social history of the Cornish language, as well as in Southeast Asian and Pacific archaeology.

Andrew C. Symons is a freelance writer and lecturer who lives and works in Penzance. He has published extensively on Cornish literary matters, and has a particular interest in the Cornish poet and novelist Jack Clemo. He is co-editor with Alan M. Kent and John Hurst of *Jack Clemo: The Awakening, Poetry Newly Found* (2003).

Andrew Thompson is Professor of Commonwealth and Imperial History, and Pro-Dean for Learning and Teaching, in the Faculty of Arts at the University of Leeds. His most recent publication is *The Empire Strikes Back? The Impact of Imperialism on Britain from the Mid-Nineteenth Century* (2005).

Malcolm Williams is Professor of Social Research Methodology at the University of Plymouth. He is the author of five books on social research method and methodology. His research in Cornwall has focused mainly on the relationship between migration and economy and on migration and housing.